Here Comes The Guide™ *To*

Party Places©

The Most Outstanding Locations for
**Parties, Special Events
and Business Functions**
in the Bay Area and Beyond

LYNN BROADWELL

with

Jan Brenner

Here Comes The Guide™ *To*
Party Places©

Copyright © 1990 by Lynn Broadwell

The author and publisher have tried to ensure accuracy and completeness, however, we assume no responsibility for errors, inaccuracies, omissions or any other inconsistency herein.

Illustrations have been reproduced from authors' photos, facilities' brochures or literature with permission of the establishments.

This is the second in a series of *Here Comes The Guide* ™ resource books and products.

Library of Congress Cataloging-in-Publication Data

Broadwell, Lynn 1951—
Here Comes The Guide™ *To*
Party Places©
First Edition
Includes Index

Library of Congress Catalog Card Number Pending
ISBN 0-9625155-1-5

Cover Illustration: Sarah Waldron
Inside Illustration: Michael Tse, Lynn Broadwell
Printed in the U.S.A. by R.R. Donnelley & Sons Company

For information, write:
HOPSCOTCH PRESS
1563 Solano Ave., Suite 135
Berkeley, CA 94707

Contents

Memorable Moments from from California Notables

Cartoons by John Grimes

Acknowledgements

I dedicate this book to my husband, Doug,
whose patience, support and understanding
are responsible for making *Party Places* a reality.
He deserves a lot of credit for being able to juggle a
full time job, classes at night and the care of
our two-year-old when I'm glued
to the computer or phone.

Doug's been the major support for the
consulting practice and the entire
Here Comes The Guide series,
for which I am more than grateful.
Thank you, thank you, DB.

I'd also like to offer thanks to PA Thurmon
for her unwavering support and assistance,
and to Karen Merrill, for her steadfast
persistence in getting quotes from
Northern California notables.

Preface

Searching for a place to have an event is not easy and usually not much fun. The amount of time consumed in calling up places, asking questions and compiling information can be mind-boggling. And who has that kind of time nowadays? Certainly not people who work full time, have kids or run households. *Party Places*, the second book in the *Here Comes The Guide* series, is intended to cut your search time by ninety percent!

The first book in the series, *Here Comes The Guide*, grew out of my own frustration in trying to find a place to get married. I was absolutely amazed that *nobody* had a comprehensive list with the kind of detailed information I needed! *Here Comes The Guide* was designed specifically to help couples searching for wedding and reception sites in the Greater Bay Area.

The response to the first edition of the wedding location guide has been overwhelming, and a second edition is in the works. I've received hundreds of 'thank you' calls and letters not only from brides and grooms-to-be, but from others who have used *Here Comes The Guide* to find non-wedding locations! On talk shows, I always field questions from audiences interested in special sites: places for birthdays, anniversaries, business meetings and retreats, and locations for awards ceremonies, fund raising events and celebrations. Clearly, there is a genuine need for a comprehensive guide that includes not only places for parties, but special events and business functions, too.

So here it is—the essential resource for anybody planning an event in Northern California, with extraordinary sites for everybody and every pocketbook. *Party Places* offers practical tips and step-by-step guidance for reviewing, selecting and evaluating both event sites *and* services. This book will save you an enormous amount of time and aggravation, and since detailed information about fees, deposits and in-house catering costs have been included, you can comparison shop and save money, too.

I can't publish the names of all the sites I've discovered, so I keep a database that includes exclusive locations that want to be known strictly by word-of-mouth. Given the number of places I've personally inspected, screened and reviewed, I'm sought after as a location scout, conducting searches for corporate and individual clients who are seeking particularly hard-to-find spots. Even with over 300 places in this book and over 500 in the database, I'm still finding out about more sites because people like you call in with new leads. And I'm always impressed by the countless variations in ambiance, price and services available to those willing to explore a bit further.

It takes a lot of work to create a memorable party. Don't pick a place that's just so-so when you can select one that is extraordinary. Have your birthday bash aboard a vintage 1940s airplane or your business conference on a lighthouse island! Or imagine a New Year's Eve celebration on a restored Pullman train car or next to an aquarium kelp forest! Whatever your tastes, whether you're a newcomer or native to Northern California, I know you'll find this book to be an entertaining, comprehensive and indispensable guide.

Introduction

This is a unique guidebook.

Party Places is loaded with invaluable information that has been selectively compiled with your needs in mind. We've tried to anticipate the questions you'd ask and collect data that is important for decision-making. If you find that the most popular spots are already booked (especially around the holidays), you'll still have a long list of wonderful locations from which to choose. You'll discover delightful places that you might not have found on your own and party ideas that you might never have considered. This book is intended to open your eyes to a variety of new possibilities. We give you tips to help you quickly select and evaluate dozens of sites and their services—and no matter what kind of place you finally select, *Party Places* is designed to make all your planning efforts *a lot* easier.

Note that this is *not* advertising for these facilities. We have personally inspected and featured *only* those we consider outstanding or exceptional in some way. Since we take *no money* from the locations listed in this publication, we're able to include a wide range of sites, even those that never advertise and those that are considered exclusive.

One of the greatest benefits of using *Party Places* is the enormous amount of time you'll save. And, you can save even more time using the find-it-fast feature. Because of the sheer number of facilities included in this book, we've designed a helpful matrix, placed conveniently in front of the main body of *Party Places*. It enables you to breeze through all of the entries by city, capacity and other important criteria, and preselect those sites you wish to read about in more depth.

This book includes only exceptional event sites. But for those who'd like to know how we personally rate the locations in *Party Places*, we've used ★★ to indicate those facilities that we think are extraordinary. This is, of course, our subjective rating based on our observations of the physical layout *and* the intangible qualities of each site. One ★ denotes a site that we think is terrific and two ★★ indicate one that we consider absolutely the best!

Take advantage of the fact that Northern California is home to some of the most outstanding facilities in the United States. There are so many locations that offer exceptional environments, top notch cuisine and professional event services, you're sure to find a special place that suits your needs. So grab this guide and explore! When you discover the perfect spot for your event, you'll feel confident that you made the right choice because you did your homework using *Party Places*.

This book is published by Hopscotch Press. It's the publication 'arm' of Lynn Broadwell & Associates, a marketing consulting group specializing in services for the event industry. Our publications help both the novice and professional event planner alike However, it is the marketing organization that offers distinct services to facility managers and event professionals.

Lynn Broadwell & Associates
A Consulting Group for Event Professionals

Hopscotch Press is one part of Lynn Broadwell & Associates, a firm that provides marketing consulting to two types of clients: managers/owners of facilities that accommodate parties, special events and business functions *and* event service professionals such as caterers, musicians, florists, event planners and others. Our publications are an extension of the services we provide our clients.

Our mission is twofold:

1. To provide the event industry with professional services & quality products *and*
2. Link up people who need event facilities and services with those that can provide them.

Our firm helps both facilities and service providers:

- improve and expand their businesses
- identify and analyze profitable markets
- develop strategic marketing plans for long-term growth
- improve the success rate of existing marketing methods and materials
- develop professional marketing graphics and copywriting
- develop a rationale and framework for advertising

A Clearinghouse for Information

Lynn Broadwell & Associates is also an information clearinghouse. As part of our consulting service, we maintain a database of up-to-date information regarding many aspects of the party and event industry in Northern California. This is especially helpful to clients who want to know what their competitors are doing in terms of pricing, extent of services provided and policy making.

The readers of our guidebooks tell us that they want information about equally terrific services: caterers, cake makers, performers, musicians, florists, event planners, party rentals and props, costumes and supplies. There is a big difference between bad and mediocre services and the best. For those who want to know about outstanding party services and products, our newsletter *Only The Best!* highlights our discoveries. Because we've screened and selected *only* those in the event industry that are a cut above, both the novice and the professional party planner benefit.

Services Designed for the Public and Event Professional

Our firm also offers a professional referral service for those seeking great party products and services, a location scouting service and vehicles for targeted advertising and promotion.

The referral service *can be used by anyone*, but is especially designed for the event professional or facility manager who needs *good* information fast. Our reputation is based on the quality of our referral list, composed of suppliers and vendors that have been thoroughly screened so *only* those that are exceptional are included. Close follow-up is maintained to confirm that the quality of services and products is consistently high. If it falls below our standards, the product or service is deleted from our database.

We offer a location scouting service for corporations, associations or individuals who need personal assistance in locating hard-to-find sites. Our database includes hundreds of locations, many of which want to remain just word-of-mouth.

Lynn Broadwell & Associates offers 'no-waste' advertising vehicles for event professionals and facilities. We publish guidebooks, a newsletter, event newspapers and mailing lists that target the party and event industry.

How To Use This Guidebook

A Few Thoughts On Picking a Geographical Location

Your first *big* decision is the selection of a geographical location that will make sense to you and the majority of your guests or business associates. If you have an event planned close to home or the office, there's little to consider. But if you pick a spot out of town, you need to think about the logistics of getting everyone to your site.

If there are few financial or other constraints, then it really doesn't matter how far from your home base you go. If, however, you live or work in Oakland and want to have a function in Carmel, it's worth considering the total driving time to and from your destination. When the distance is over 2 hours driving time, an overnight stay may be in order. A distant event location may limit you to a Saturday night function since guests may have to spend many hours traveling. And if you have guests arriving by plane, it's certainly helpful if there's an airport nearby. If you'll be serving alcohol, and you know your friends enjoy drinking, try to house them close to the party site. Check out the average temperatures where you plan to hold your event—it may be sunny in Marin in June but foggy and cold in Monterey.

There's no reason why you can't contemplate a party in Napa Valley or in the wilds of Big Sur. Just remember that the further out you go, the more time it will take—and you may end up having to delegate the details of event planning to someone else.

Selecting a Party Location

Identify What Kind of Party You Want and Establish Selection Criteria Early

Before you jump into the facility descriptions in *Party Places*, take stock of all your needs and wants. Here are some basics:

Your Budget

This is a big one. You'd think that it's an obvious consideration, but you'd be surprised how many people are unrealistic about what they can afford. Throwing a party or organizing an event can be *very* expensive. Part of the problem is that most novice planners aren't experienced with event budgeting and don't know how to estimate, in advance, what products and services will finally cost. Who is paying for the event? Can your pocketbook cover the price of a seated dinner, or should you opt for hors d'oeuvres and cocktails only? Is this a fundraiser, and do you anticipate that your guests will pay a percentage of the total event tab? If so, are you prepared to financially back an event where the proceeds are not guaranteed up front? Whoever foots the bill, be advised that doing the homework here really counts. Pin down your costs early on in the planning stage and get all estimates in writing.

Style

Do you know what kind of function and ambiance you want? Will it be a formal or informal event, a traditional affair or a creative, innovative party? Will the function be held at night or during the day, indoors or outdoors? Know what you want *before* you look for a location or the sheer number of options will be overwhelming.

Guest Count

How many people are anticipated? Many facilities want a guaranteed guest count 60 to 90 days in advance of your function—and they will want a deposit based on the figure you give them. It's important to know what the numbers are, early on.

Seasonal Differences

The time of year and hours of the day may be a major factor in site selection, so be clear about the seasonal temperatures where your function is planned. There's a good reason why most places are booked spring through fall. If you're arranging an outdoor winter party, make sure you have a backup plan that includes an inside space.

Special Requirements

Sometimes, places have strict rules and regulations. If most of your guests or business associates smoke, then pick a location that does not restrict smoking. If alcohol is going to be consumed or sold on site, make sure it's allowed. If dancing or a big band are critical, then limit yourself to those locations that can accommodate it and the accompanying decibels. Do you have children, seniors or disabled guests on your list? If so, you need to plan for them, too. It's essential that you identify the special factors that are important for your event *before* you sign a contract.

Age Group

What age group will constitute the majority of the guests? If it's a prom night, with most guests under 20 years of age, be aware that many facilities will charge an extra fee to cover anticipated damage and cleanup. If guests are over 60 years, make sure that the site and restrooms have adequate access.

Parking

Where to put your car is usually not a critical factor if your event occurs outside an urban area. However, if you're planning a party in downtown Sacramento, San Francisco, Monterey or Carmel, make sure you understand what arrangements need to be made to facilitate parking.

Professional Help

If you are a busy person, and have limited time to plan and execute a party, then pick a facility that offers complete services, from catering and flowers to decorations and bar service. Or better yet, hire a professional event consultant. Either way, you'll make your life considerably easier by having someone else handle the details.

Selecting a Location for Business Functions

Some of the party considerations above are appropriate for business functions. Here are some business factors that may apply:

Ambiance

If you are setting up a retreat for small groups to discuss vital issues, consider a quiet spot conducive to contemplation, renewal or creative thinking. If you've got a large conference, note that *Party Places* highlights many unusual facilities that can accommodate big groups—you are not locked into making arrangements in a hotel. There's a major difference between a hotel room and a small, personalized bed and breakfast inn or retreat. You *can* set the ambiance or tone of the workshop, seminar or meeting by selecting the right location.

Services Needed

Many conferences require full service capability, including private phone lines, fax, audio-visual equipment and all-day coffee/food service. Make sure you know precisely what's necessary for the function to flow smoothly and submit an itemized list to the facility. Request conference materials and equipment well in advance so you don't end up competing with the group down the hall for a projector or screen. One of the most common mistakes is to bring in AV equipment, only to find that there are no meeting rooms which can be darkened enough for presentations. It's helpful to organize breaks and something for participants to do during relief periods. Pick a place that can provide other non-meeting amenities such as a spa, a beach or bicycles. If the business event is several days long, supplemental activities are important to revitalize meeting-weary participants.

Food Quality

For parties and events, food is a big deal. Everybody is concerned about the type, quantity and quality of meals and countless hours are spent pouring over menu details. Food should also be an important consideration for business meetings, conferences and seminars—but often it's not. We suggest you pay critical attention to the food services offered prior to confirming reservations. What does Continental Breakfast really mean— Sanka and a jelly donut or freshly brewed coffee and a flaky croissant? These details make a difference and might not cost much more.

Hidden Costs

This may come as a surprise, but business services and equipment are not always covered in the rental fee. Get it in writing! The cost of paper, pencils, pens, audio-visual equipment, coffee service and all extraneous elements can really add up. Save yourself some aggravation by understanding exactly what's included *before* you sign the contract.

The important point we're trying to make here is that if you know what kind of event you want, and are clear about the essentials, your search will be made faster and easier. If you try to pick a location before you've made basic decisions, selection will be a struggle and it will take longer to find a spot that will make you happy.

Understanding the Information in *Party Places*

Each location entry in *Party Places* follows the same format. To help you understand *our* thinking, what follows below is an explanation of the selection criteria, in the same order as it appears.

Reserve In Advance

What we've indicated here is only a *suggested* time frame for making reservations in advance. Naturally, if a popular spot books 12 months in advance and you want to have an event there next week, your choice may prove unrealistic. If the *reserve in advance* information is in conflict with your plans, don't despair! Find out if your particular date is available. Who knows? There are always cancellations and occasionally a popular date is not booked. If there's a location that seems just perfect for you, take a chance and call, even if it seems an unlikely possibility.

Description

Once you've selected a geographical area and you're clear about your needs, then thoroughly review all of the sites listed in your area of preference. If you're pressed for time, you can read through the *find-it-fast matrix* first to preview facilities for location, capacity and other critical factors. Then, you can forge ahead to the main body of *Party*

Places and read the descriptions of *only* those sites that seem to be a good fit, based on your preliminary preview. If the facility still appeals to you after reading the description *and* it fulfills your location requirements, mark it with a ✔ and then move on to capacity.

Capacity

By now you should have a rough idea of how many people will be attending. If not, you may be in trouble since many facilities want a deposit based on an estimated head-count. Look at the capacity figures for each event location. *Seated* or *sit-down* capacity refers to guests seated at tables. *Reception* or *standing* capacity refers to a function where the majority of guests are not seated, such as a cocktail party. *Theater-style* refers to auditorium row seating, with chairs arranged closely together, and *classroom-style* refers to an orga-nized table and chair arrangement, usually in rows. Put a ✔ next to those facilities that fit your guest or business requirements. If you're planning well in advance and don't have your guest list whittled down yet, then you'll just have to estimate and refine the count as the date draws near. There is a big difference in cost and planning effort between an intimate party of 60 and a large function with over 500 guests. Pin down your numbers as soon as you can.

Meeting Rooms

We've highlighted those rooms which can accommodate meetings and have listed the number of participants each room can hold.

Fees and Deposits

Look at the data regarding fees and deposits and remember that these figures change regularly and *usually in one direction.* If you're planning far in advance, anticipate increases by the time your function occurs. Once you are definite about your location, it's a good idea to lock in your fees in a contract, protecting yourself from possible rate increases later. Make sure you ask about every service provided and are clear about all of the extras that can really add up. Don't be surprised to see taxes and gratuities in set amounts applied to the total bill if restaurant or catering services are provided by the facility.

Sometimes deposits are nonrefundable. If the deposit is a large percentage of the total bill, make sure you know whether it's refundable or not. If refundable, then read the cancellation policy thoroughly. Also make sure you understand the policies which will ensure you get your cleaning and security deposit returned in full.

Food costs vary considerably. Carefully plan your menu with the caterer, event consultant or chef. Depending on the style of service and the type of food being served, your total food bill will vary dramatically even if provided by the same caterer. Expect a multi-course seated meal to be the most expensive part of your party.

Alcohol is expensive, too. Look closely at the alcohol restrictions. Can you bring your own wine or champagne? Does the facility charge a corkage fee? Some restaurants discourage you from bringing your own (BYO) by charging exorbitant fees for removing the cork (corkage) and pouring services. Other facilities have permits which do not allow them to serve alcohol or restrict them from serving certain kinds; some will let you sell alcohol on site, others won't. Make sure you know what's allowed. Decide what your budget is for alcohol and determine what types you're willing to provide. And keep in mind that the catering fees you are quoted *rarely* include the cost of alcohol. A comment about trends in alcohol consumption is warrented. People are drinking less wine and hard alcohol than ever before and consumption of mineral water is on the rise. If you provide the alcohol, make sure you keep your purchase receipts so you can return any unopened bottles.

How much money can you afford to spend? Facility deposits are usually not large, but sometimes the rental fees plus food and beverage services can add up to $30,000 and more depending on the location and number of guests. Be sure you have a sensible handle on your budget and read all the fine print before you sign any contract.

Availability

Some facilities have unlimited hours available for social and business functions, others offer very limited "windows". If you'd like to save some money, consider a week-day or weeknight event. Even the most sought-after places have openings midweek, and at reduced costs. *Facilities want your business* and are more likely to negotiate terms and prices if they have nothing else scheduled. Again, read all the fine print carefully, and ✔ those facilities that have time slots that meet your needs.

Services/Amenities

Most facilities provide something in the way of services. We've attempted to give you a brief description of what each individual location has to offer. Because of space limitations, we have shortened words and have developed a key to help you decipher our abbreviated notations. Please refer to the *Services/Amenities and Restrictions Key* for clarification and explanation. When you become familiar with our notation style, go back to *Services/Amenities* and put a ✔ where your requirements are met by the facility. You'll be able to quickly see what essentials on your list are covered and which ones are not.

Previewing a Facility

Once you've tallied up all your ✔ marks, you should have a handful of sites that require a personal preview. If you plan to visit a lot of locations, here are some handy tips.

Appointments

Should you attempt to drive by first or schedule an appointment? If you reviewed the description and liked what you read, then we recommend you make an appointment to see each location. Sometimes, the exterior of a great building looks worse than the beautiful and secluded garden it hides from the street. And sometimes, vice versa—a stunning facade will attract you and upon entry you discover an interior that doesn't appeal to your taste.

When you call for appointments, try to cluster your visits so that you can easily drive from one place to another without backtracking. Get a good, detailed street map of the area, and before you go to the sites, locate each one on the map in red or another contrasting color. Schedule at least 30 minutes per facility and arrange for ample driving time in between each stop. The key here is efficiency. Don't over-schedule yourself, however. It's best to view places when you're fresh. If you've reached your saturation point after five visits and you still have several more to go, those last places might get "bad reviews" simply because you're looking at them through bleary eyes and can't absorb any more information. While you want to accomplish as much as you can in as brief a time as possible, you will ultimately do yourself a disservice if your judgment is clouded by fatigue.

Make sure when you're previewing a facility to check out the meeting rooms, restrooms, dance floor and kitchen facilities. Sometimes it's easy to get carried away by a great view or an extraordinary gold ceiling so that you forget a major item—like a place for the band.

Be Organized

Whether you're visiting a handful of facilities or canvassing an entire region, be organized. After you've decided on your event requirements, selected the facilities you want to see and arranged a workable visiting schedule, there are still things you can do to make this process easy on yourself.

Bring a camera. Take pictures of whatever you want to recall about a place—the front exterior, meeting rooms, etc. A polaroid is wonderful for this because it gives you instant "memories". Make sure to write the name of the facility on the photo. You'd be surprised how easy it is to confuse various sites when you've got a dozen of them competing for space in your mind and you can't remember which garden or dining room corresponds to which place.

Bring a tape recorder. During or after each visit, record your immediate impressions. Your likes, dislikes and any other observations can be quickly recorded. You can write up your notes when you have more time. If you don't have a recorder, jot down your comments in *Party Places* itself or in a notebook. No matter how you do it, thorough note-taking is crucial if you are going to be able to adequately evaluate everything you have seen and heard.

File everything. Many facilities will provide you with pamphlets, menus, rates charts and other materials. One good way to handle the deluge is to put each facility's paperwork in a 9" x 12" manila envelope with its name on it. A binder with plastic pocket inserts is also handy. The idea is to avoid having to sort through a pile of things later. You want to keep your notes, photos and handouts clearly identified and easily accessible.

Bring snacks. Driving from place to place can make you hungry. If you take a little something to eat you can munch en route and keep your energy level up.

Working with a Facility

Confirm All the Details

When visiting sites you have chosen from *Party Places*, the first thing to do is confirm that the information presented is still valid. Show the site's representative the page in the book that refers to his/her facility, and have them inform you of any changes. If there have been significant increases in fees or new restrictions that you can't live with, cross it off your list and move on. If the facility is still a contender, request a tour. Once you have determined that the physical elements of the place suit you, it's time to discuss details. Ask about services and amenities or fees that may not be listed in the book and make a note of them. Outline your plans to the representative and make sure that the facility can accommodate your particular needs. If you don't want to handle all the details yourself, find out what the facility is willing and able to do, and if there will be additional fees for their assistance. Facilities often provide planning services for little or no extra charge.

The Importance of Rapport

Another factor to consider is your rapport with the person(s) you are working with. Are you comfortable? Do they listen well and respond to your questions directly? Do they inspire trust and confidence? If you have doubts, you need to resolve them before embarking on a working relationship with these folks—no matter how wonderful the facility itself is. Discuss your feelings with them, and if you're still not completely satisfied, get references and call them. If at the end of this process you still have lingering concerns, you may want to eliminate the facility from your list even though it seems perfect in every other way.

Working with a Caterer

Get References

If you are selecting your own caterer, don't just pick one at random out of the yellow pages. Get references from friends and acquaintances or call local facilities listed in *Party Places* for suggestions. Some caterers offer only preset menus while others will help you create your own. Prices and menus vary enormously, so know what you want and what you are willing to spend. After you have talked to several caterers, and have decided which ones you want to seriously consider, get references for each one and call them. Ask not only about the quality of the food, but about the ease of working with a given caterer. You'll want to know if the caterer is professional: fully prepared and equipped, punctual and organized.

Facility Requirements

Often the facility you have chosen will have specific requirements regarding caterers. Whether they have to be licensed and bonded, out by 11pm or fastidiously clean—make sure that before you hire a caterer, he or she is compatible with your site. In fact, even if the facility does not require it, it's a good idea to have your caterer visit the place *in advance* to become familiar with any special circumstances or problems that might come up. You'll notice throughout *Party Places* the words "provided" or "preferred" after the word *Catering*. Sites that have an exclusive caterer or only permit you to select from a preferred list do so because each wants to eliminate most of the risks involved in having a caterer on the premises who is not accustomed to working in that environment. Exclusive or preferred caterers have achieved this exalted status because they provide consistently excellent services. If your facility has confidence in them, generally you can, too. Whether you are working with one of your facility's choices or your own, make sure that your contract includes everything you have agreed on before you sign it.

Working with an Event Planner or Consultant

Consultants Handle Details

Opting to hire a professional may be a wise choice. If you can afford it, engaging someone to "manage" your event can be a godsend. A good consultant will ask all the right questions, determine exactly what you want, and put together your entire affair. Your role will largely be to select from the options presented and write checks. A consultant is also valuable if you have difficulty coping with the often overwhelming number of details and decisions involved. He or she can provide whatever guidance, support and decision making you need to implement your party. So if the planning process is just too much for you to handle, and you don't mind the expense, definitely consider hiring a professional. Most of the principles used in selecting a caterer apply to hiring an event planner. Try to get suggestions from friends or facilities, follow up on references the consultants give you, compare and contrast service fees and make sure you and the consultant are compatible. The range of professionalism and experience varies greatly, so it really is to your advantage to investigate consultants' track records. Again, once you have found someone who can accommodate you, get everything in writing so that there won't be any misunderstandings down the road.

Insurance Considerations

You may want to consider getting extra insurance coverage for your event. Since this is now a major consideration for many facilities (and service providers), you may not have an option. More and more facilities are requiring either proof of insurance or a certificate guaranteeing additional coverage.

Deep Pockets

These days, if someone gets injured at a party or something is damaged at or near the event site, it's likely that somebody will be sued. Unfortunately, that's the way it is. Event sites and service providers are very aware of their potential liability and all have coverage of one kind or another.

In the past, usually the facility was sued. Nowadays, everybody gets sued, and that may mean you. Whoever has the most insurance is said to have the 'deepest pockets' and will be pursued to pay the bulk of the claim. To protect themselves, facilities have begun to require additional insurance from service providers *and* their clients. The goal is to spread the risk among all parties involved. Don't panic. Although *event insurance,* per se, is impossible to obtain, *extra* insurance for a specified period of time is easy to get and relatively inexpensive.

Obtaining Extra Insurance

Facilities often require between $500,000 and $1,000,000 worth of extra coverage. If you are a home owner, just ask your insurance agent to tack on a rider to your home owner's policy to cover the event date and time period. The company will issue you a certificate of insurance specifically for your function in the amount selected. To finalize your rental agreement, you will have to present this certificate to the facility owner or representative as proof of insurance.

Many facilities are able to offer additional insurance through their own policies. You will pay an extra charge, but it's usually nominal.

It Can't Happen To Me

Don't be lulled into the notion that it can't happen to you. Naturally, there is more likelihood of risk with a wild New Year's eve party or a high school prom night. But we could tell you stories of upscale functions where something *did* happen and a lawsuit resulted. Many event sites have plenty of coverage and are willing to assume the *'deep pocket'* risk. Others don't and won't. Take into account the type of event and the factors that may affect liability. Even if extra insurance is *not* required, you may want to consider additional coverage anyway, especially if alcohol is being served.

Do Your Part: Recycle

You wonder why we're including a brief item about recycling in a book like *Party Places*? Because most of the time, parties, special events and even business functions generate recyclable materials *and* excess food. Many caterers often have leftover food since the host or hostess doesn't want to take it home. Nowadays, you and the caterer can feel good about doing your part by donating the excess. You also can recycle glass, metal, paper and plastic bottles. An added benefit is that food donations are tax deductible for either you or the caterer. And, if you recycle, the cost for extra garbage containers (bins) can be eliminated or reduced.

Food donations are distributed to teenage drop-in centers, youth shelters, alcoholic treatment centers, aids hospices, senior centers and refugee centers throughout the region. You should also know that a 1989 state law has been passed that protects the donor from liability.

How do you make a donation? Call the following organizations to make arrangements for pickup. Your packaged food can be picked up the day of the event or brought back to the caterer's kitchen to be picked up later on. Place food in clean plastic bags, plastic containers or boxes. Food must be edible. For example, if dressing has been poured over a salad, most likely it won't be worth eating the next day.

Other recyclable materials must be separated. Call your local recycling center to arrange a pickup.

San Francisco: Food Runners	415/929-1866
Berkeley: Daily Bread Project	415/848-3522
Oakland: Oakland Pot Luck	415/272-0414
San Mateo and Santa Clara counties:	415/578-0796

In other areas, contact your local Food Bank. The number is in most phone books.

Services/Amenities & Restrictions Key

SERVICES/AMENITIES

Restaurant Services

yes: the facility has a restaurant on site which is available for catering your event or is accessible to your guests

Catering

provided: the facility provides catering • *provided, no BYO:* the facility arranges catering; you cannot arrange your own • *preferred list:* you must select your caterer from the facility's approved list • *provided, can BYO; provided, BYO ok:* the facility will arrange catering or you can select an outside caterer of your own • *BYO, must be licensed:* arrange for your own licensed caterer

Kitchen Facilities

ample: large and well-equipped • *moderate:* medium-sized and utilitarian • *minimal:* small with limited equipment, may not have all basic appliances • *n/a:* not applicable when facility provides catering • *fully equipped:* major appliances and space

Tables & Chairs

some provided or *provided:* facility provides some or all of the tables and chairs • *BYO:* make arrangements to bring your own

Linens, Silver, etc.

same as above

Restrooms

wca: wheelchair accessible • *no wca:* not wheelchair accessible

Dance Floor

yes: an area for dancing (hardwood floor, cement terrace, patio) is available • *CBA, extra charge:* you can arrange for a dance floor to be brought in for a fee

Parking

descriptions are self explanatory; *CBA:* can be arranged

Overnight Accommodations

if overnight accommodations are available on site, the number of guestrooms is listed

Telephone

restricted: calls made on the house phone must be local, collect or charged to a credit card • *guest phones:* private phones in guestrooms • *house phone:* central phone used by all guests

Outdoor Night Lighting

yes: indicates that there is adequate light to conduct your event outdoors after dark • *no* or *limited:* lighting is sufficient for access only

Outdoor Cooking Facilities

BBQ: the facility has a barbecue on the premises • *BBQ, CBA:* a barbecue can be arranged through the facility • *BYO BBQ:* make arrangements for your own barbecue

Cleanup

provided: facility takes care of cleanup • *caterer:* your caterer is responsible • *caterer, renter:* both you and your caterer are responsible for cleanup

Other, Special

description of any service or amenity not included in above list

RESTRICTIONS

Alcohol

provided, no BYO: the facility provides alcoholic beverages (for a fee) and does not permit you to bring your own • *BYO:* you can arrange for your own alcohol • *BYO corkage, $/ bottle:* if you bring your own alcohol, the facility charges a fee per bottle to remove the cork and pour • *WCB only (or any combination of these three letters):* only wine, champagne and/ or beer are permitted

Smoking

allowed: smoking is permitted throughout the facility • *outside only:* smoking is not permitted inside the facility • *not allowed:* smoking is not permitted anywhere on the premises

Music

Every facility allows acoustical music unless stated otherwise. Restrictions refer to amplified music • *amplified ok:* amplified music is acceptable without restriction • *amplified outside only:* no amplified music allowed inside • *inside only:* no amplified music permitted outside • *amplified with limits or restrictions:* amplified music allowed but there are limits on volume, hours of play, number of instruments, etc.

Wheelchair Access

Accessibility is based on whether a facility is wheelchair accessible or not • *yes:* the facility is accessible • *limited:* the facility is accessible but with difficulty • *no:* the facility is not accessible

Insurance

Many facilities require that you purchase and show proof of some insurance coverage. The type and amount of insurance varies with the facility, and some facilities offer insurance for minimal charge. *required, certificate required or proof of insurance required:* additional insurance is required • *not required:* no additional insurance is required

Other

decorations restricted: the facility limits the use of tape, nails, tacks, confetti, and other decorations

Find-It-Fast

We know your time is valuable.

If you've got to find an event site *fast* and you don't have enough time to leisurely read through all the location descriptions, use this convenient chart. It lists each facility by *region* and *city* in alphabetical order and highlights essential information for each one. This makes it easy to quickly identify the event locations that are most appropriate for you.

Once you've identified a handful of places that seem to meet your needs, read each *Party Places* entry for more complete information.

Target your area of geographical preference first.

Pick the cities that are best for your function and/or guests, keeping in mind the location selection advice in the "How To Use This Guidebook" section.

Identify the facilities that fit your needs.

Read through the columns, from left to right noting which features are essential to your function. If a site seems to offer what you need, put a light check mark next to it or better yet, *xerox the pages and use color highlighters.* Keeping these pages free of permanent markings will prevent confusion the next time you refer to the find-it-fast section for another type of event. Go to the index in the back of the book, find the page numbers of the locations you've checked and read the full descriptions for each entry. If you still need more information, call the facility.

Remember, the find-it-fast section is not perfect.

The purpose of this matrix is to reduce your searching time. However, because the information presented is abbreviated, it won't be perfect. A • in the *Amplified Music Restricted* column, for example, may mean that amplified music is not allowed, or it may only mean that you can't have it outside. To find out how the restriction affects your function, *you have to read the full description.* The following is a brief explanation of the matrix headings.

Matrix Headings

Maximum Capacity

Most of the numbers shown are for standing receptions. However, some might be for theater or classroom-style seating. If the capacity looks *about* right, it's important that you read the corresponding *Party Places* entry to confirm. The numbers marked with asterisks * indicate that the figure may be very inexact. For instance, we may have been given the maximum capacity for *only* the largest room in a multi-room facility. Consequently, the maximum capacity if all the rooms are combined is unknown. A facility with a large total capacity may also be able to comfortably accommodate a small event in one of its rooms. If a location seems perfect but the numbers are not quite right, we suggest you read the entry and then call to make sure.

Indoor and Outdoor Facilities

These columns are self explanatory.

Meeting Space Available

There is space for meetings. However, read the facility description and call to confirm that the facility can accommodate your particular meeting needs. Also, if a facility seems right for you but does not have a • in this column, call anyway. The facility may have expanded its services and can now provide meeting space.

In-house Catering and BYO Catering

In-house means that the facility can cater your event or arrange to have it catered. BYO indicates that you can make arrangements for your own caterer.

Alcohol Provided or Alcohol BYO

If you see a • in the *Alcohol Provided* column and a • in the *Alcohol BYO*, that means the facility can provide alcohol *and* they will also let you bring your own. Note that many facilities charge a corkage fee if you BYO. If there's a • in the *Alcohol Provided* column, but not in the *Alcohol BYO* column, you cannot bring your own alcohol. If there isn't a • in either column it means that alcohol is not allowed.

Restaurant On Site and Guestrooms Available

These columns are self explanatory.

Event Coordination

Many facilities provide event planning and coordination, everything from catering to theme parties or custom party favors. This service may be free or there may be an additional charge. Be sure to ask.

Wheelchair Access Restricted

Indicates access problems ranging from a single step into a building to total inaccessibility. It doesn't mean you *can't* get into a site—it just denotes that there may be some degree of difficulty.

Smoking Restricted

Means no smoking or smoking in designated areas only.

Insurance Required

Proof of insurance or a certificate of insurance may be required.

Amplified Music Restricted

Means amplified music is not allowed or is permitted with inside/outside constraints and/or volume limits.

SAN FRANCISCO

FACILITY	MAXIMUM CAPACITY	Indoor Facilities	Outdoor Facilities	Meeting Space Available	In-house Catering	BYO Catering	Alcohol Provided	Alcohol BYO	Restaurant On Site	Guestrooms Available	Event Coordination	Wheelchair Restricted	Smoking Restricted	Insurance Required	Amplified Music Restricted
Alamo Square Inn	200	•		•	•		•	•		•	•	•	•	•	
Archbishop's Mansion	100	•		•	•	•	•	•		•	•	•	•		•
Blue & Gold Fleet	300	•		•	•		•	•			•	•			
Cable Car Barn & Museum	800	•			•		•						•		
Cable Car Exclusive	45	•			•		•					•			
Cafe Majestic	125	•			•		•	•	•	•			•		•
California Academy of Sciences	3000	•		•	•	•	•				•			•	
California Culinary Academy	500 *	•		•	•		•	•	•		•				
California Palace of the Legion of Honor	600	•			•		•						•	•	•
California Spirit, The	149	•			•		•	•			•		•		
Campton Place	26 *	•		•	•		•	•	•	•	•		•		•
Carnelian Room	500	•		•			•				•				
Cartoon Art Museum	125	•			•		•						•	•	•
Casa de la Vista	225	•	•	•	•		•				•				
Casa San Gregorio	100	•	•	•	•	•	•			•		•		•	
Chateau Tivoli	125	•		•	•	•	•			•		•	•		•
Circle Gallery	350	•			•		•				•				
City Club, The	500	•		•	•		•		•		•				
Coit Tower	250	•	•				•						•	•	•
Conservatory of Flowers, The	200	•					•						•	•	•
Contract Design Center	500	•	•	•			•				•			•	
De Young Memorial Museum	800	•					•						•	•	•
Fairmont Penthouse Suite	50	•			•		•		•	•	•				•
Fashion Center	5000	•		•			•	•			•			•	
Flood Mansion, The	450	•					•						•	•	
Forest Hill Club House	200	•	•				•					•			
Fort Mason Conference Center	300	•		•			•						•		
Fort Mason Cowell Theater	439	•		•	•	•	•						•		
Fort Mason Firehouse	150	•		•			•						•		
Galleria Design Center	2500	•		•	•	•	•				•			•	
Gift Center Pavillion	2500	•		•	•	•	•	•			•			•	
Golden Gate Park	25000		•				•								•
Golden Sunset	100	•		•	•		•	•			•	•	•		
Grand Hyatt San Francisco	1000	•		•	•		•	•	•	•	•		•		
Green Room, The	500	•		•		•	•						•	•	•
Greens	250	•			•			•							
Haas-Lilienthal House	225	•		•		•	•						•		•
Hamlin Mansion	350	•			•		•				•	•			

FACILITY	MAXIMUM CAPACITY	Indoor Facilities	Outdoor Facilities	Meeting Space Available	In-house Catering	BYO Catering	Alcohol Provided	Alcohol BYO	Restaurant On Site	Guestrooms Available	Event Coordination	Wheelchair Restricted	Smoking Restricted	Insurance Required	Amplified Music Restricted
Herbst & Festival Pavilions	5000	•				•		•					•	•	
Hornblower Dining Yachts	750 *	•		•	•		•	•		•	•	•			
Julius' Castle	150	•			•		•		•			•			•
Lascaux	35 *	•			•		•	•	•				•		•
Mansions Hotel, The	225	•	•	•	•		•	•	•	•	•	•	•		
Mark Hopkins, The	1000 *	•		•	•		•	•	•	•	•				
Nimitz Conference Center	500 *	•	•	•	•		•				•				
Pacific Spirit, The	97	•			•		•	•			•	•	•		
Page-Brown Mansion, The	250	•		•	•	•	•	•			•	•	•	•	•
Palace of Fine Arts, The	300		•			•		•					•		•
Red & White Fleet	500 *	•		•		•	•	•			•		•		
Regina Del Mare I & II	400 *	•		•	•		•	•			•	•			
Rendezvous Charters	150 *	•			•	•	•	•			•	•	•		
Rincon Hill Spectrum	700	•		•		•	•	•					•		
Rock & Bowl	300	•				•	•								
Rotunda, The	350	•			•		•	•	•						
Sailing Ship Dolf Rempp	800	•	•		•	•	•		•		•				
San Francisco Commercial Club	800	•		•	•	•	•	•			•		•		
San Francisco Maritime Museum	450	•			•		•						•		
San Francisco Mart	800	•			•	•	•	•					•		
San Francisco Spirit, The	700	•		•	•		•				•		•		
San Francisco Zoo	500	•	•		•	•	•					•	•	•	•
Sherman House, The	80	•	•		•		•		•	•	•		•		•
Showplace Design Center	500	•		•	•	•	•				•	•		•	
SS Jeremiah O'Brien	300	•			•			•			•	•	•		
Stanford Court	800 *	•		•	•		•		•	•	•		•	•	
St. Francis Hotel, The	1000 *	•		•	•		•	•	•	•	•				
Trocadero, The	400 *	•	•	•		•		•							
Tuba Garden	120	•	•		•		•				•		•		•
Wattis Room, The	200	•			•	•	•	•							
White Swan Inn	70	•		•	•		•	•				•			•
Whittier Mansion	300	•		•		•		•				•			

HALF MOON BAY

FACILITY	MAXIMUM CAPACITY	Indoor Facilities	Outdoor Facilities	Meeting Space Available	In-house Catering	BYO Catering	Alcohol Provided	Alcohol BYO	Restaurant On Site	Guestrooms Available	Event Coordination	Wheelchair Restricted	Smoking Restricted	Insurance Required	Amplified Music Restricted
Douglas Beach House	150	•		•		•		•				•			
Mill Rose Inn	60 *	•	•	•	•	•		•		•	•		•		
Strawberry Ranch	50	•		•	•		•	•			•	•	•	•	•

FACILITY	MAXIMUM CAPACITY	Indoor Facilities	Outdoor Facilities	Meeting Space Available	In-house Catering	BYO Catering	Alcohol Provided	Alcohol BYO	Restaurant On Site	Guestrooms Available	Event Coordination	Wheelchair Restricted	Smoking Restricted	Insurance Required	Amplified Music Restricted
NORTH BAY															
Belvedere															
China Cabin	65	•				•		•				•	•	•	
S.F. Yacht Club	300	•	•		•		•		•						
Fairfax															
Deer Park Villa	300 *	•	•	•	•		•	•	•						•
Greenbrae															
Joe LoCoco's Restaurante	250	•	•		•		•								
Larkspur															
Lark Creek Inn, The	150 *	•	•		•		•	•	•				•		
Mill Valley															
Mill Valley Outdoor Art Club, The	200	•	•	•		•		•							
Mountain Home Inn	110	•			•		•	•	•	•					
Muir Beach															
Pelican Inn	45	•	•	•			•	•	•	•					•
Nicasio															
Shadows, The	120	•	•	•	•	•		•		•			•	•	
Ross															
Caroline Livermore Room	500	•	•	•		•		•						•	•
Ross Garden Restaurant	150	•	•		•		•	•	•						•
San Rafael															
Dominican College	500	•	•	•	•			•				•		•	
Falkirk Mansion	125	•	•		•			•					•	•	•
San Rafael Improvement Club	160	•	•		•			•					•	•	
Sausalito															
Alta Mira, The	200 *	•	•	•	•		•	•	•	•	•	•		•	•
Casa Madrona	140 *	•	•	•	•		•	•	•	•	•	•	•		
Sausalito Woman's Club	275 *	•	•	•		•	•					•	•	•	
Tiburon															
Corinthian Yacht Club	250	•			•		•	•	•			•			•

FACILITY	MAXIMUM CAPACITY	Indoor Facilities	Outdoor Facilities	Meeting Space Available	In-house Catering	BYO Catering	Alcohol Provided	Alcohol BYO	Restaurant On Site	Guestrooms Available	Event Coordination	Wheelchair Restricted	Smoking Restricted	Insurance Required	Amplified Music Restricted
NORTH COAST															
Bodega															
School House Inn	100	•		•		•			•		•	•	•	•	
Bodega Bay															
Bay Hill Mansion	50	•		•	•	•			•		•	•	•		•
Terra Nova Institute	50	•	•	•		•					•	•	•		•
Cazadero															
Timberhill Ranch	26	•	•	•	•		•	•	•	•	•	•	•		•
Fort Bragg															
Mendocino Coast Botanical Gardens	50		•			•		•					•		•
Gualala															
St. Orres	100	•	•	•	•		•		•	•		•	•		
Jenner															
Murphy's Jenner Inn	60	•		•	•	•	•	•	•	•		•	•		
Little River															
Glendeven	50	•		•		•		•			•	•	•		•
Inn at School House Creek	50 *	•	•	•	•	•		•		•	•	•	•		
Rachel's Inn	125	•	•	•	•		•	•			•	•			
Stevens Wood	250	•	•	•	•		•	•			•		•		
Marshall															
Marconi Conference Center	175	•		•	•				•	•	•	•	•		•
Mendocino															
Ames Lodge	30	•	•	•		•			•		•	•	•		•
Hill House	100	•		•	•		•	•		•	•		•		•
Mendocino Hotel	110	•		•	•		•		•	•	•	•	•		•
Winning Images	varies	•	•	•		•		•		•	•	•	•	•	•
Monte Rio															
Huckleberry Springs	50	•	•	•	•	•	•			•		•	•	•	
Occidental															
Heart's Desire Inn	150	•	•	•	•	•		•		•			•		•

FACILITY	MAXIMUM CAPACITY	Indoor Facilities	Outdoor Facilities	Meeting Space Available	In-house Catering	BYO Catering	Alcohol Provided	Alcohol BYO	Restaurant On Site	Guestrooms Available	Event Coordination	Wheelchair Restricted	Smoking Restricted	Insurance Required	Amplified Music Restricted
PENINSULA															
Atherton															
Holbrook Palmer Park	500 *	•	•	•		•		•					•	•	•
Belmont															
Ralston Hall	250	•		•		•		•				•	•	•	
Burlingame															
Kohl Mansion	600 *	•	•	•		•		•					•	•	
Hillsborough															
Crocker Mansion, The	300	•	•			•							•	•	
Menlo Park															
Latham Hopkins Gatehouse	100	•	•			•		•					•	•	•
Portola Valley															
Fogarty Winery & Vineyards	225 *	•	•	•		•	•					•	•	•	•
Ladera Oaks	350	•	•	•		•		•							•
EAST BAY															
Alameda															
Garratt Mansion	75	•	•	•	•	•				•	•	•	•		
Albany															
The Turf Club	1500	•		•	•		•	•							
Benicia															
Camel Barn Museum	200	•				•		•					•		
Captain Dillingham's Inn	225	•	•			•		•		•	•	•			•
Clock Tower	700	•				•		•						•	
Berkeley															
Berkeley City Club	325 *	•		•	•		•		•	•	•		•	•	
Berkeley Conference Center	350 *	•		•	•		•	•		•	•		•		
Brazilian Room	250	•	•	•	•			•					•	•	•
Crystal Room	150	•			•		•		•	•			•		
Gramma's Inn	200 *	•	•	•	•		•			•	•		•		
Hillside Club	150	•		•		•		•				•	•		
Crockett															
Crockett Community Center	400	•	•	•		•		•							

Facility	Maximum Capacity	Indoor Facilities	Outdoor Facilities	Meeting Space Available	In-house Catering	BYO Catering	Alcohol Provided	Alcohol BYO	Restaurant On Site	Guestrooms Available	Event Coordination	Wheelchair Restricted	Smoking Restricted	Insurance Required	Amplified Music Restricted
Danville															
Behring Museum	600 *	•			•	•	•	•			•		•	•	
Emeryville															
Chalkers Billiard Club	225	•			•	•	•	•					•		
Fremont															
Ardenwood Historic Preserve	1200		•		•		•				•				
Palmdale Estate, The	1000	•	•	•			•				•		•	•	
Livermore															
Ravenswood	150	•	•	•			•		•				•	•	•
Wente Bros. Estate Winery	600	•	•		•		•						•		
Wente Bros. Sparkling Wine Cellars	700	•	•	•	•		•		•				•		
Moraga															
Hacienda De Las Flores	200 *	•	•	•			•						•	•	•
Oakland															
Camron-Stanford House	250	•	•	•			•		•			•	•	•	•
Claremont, The	500 *	•	•	•	•		•		•	•	•				
Dunsmuir House	3000	•	•		•	•	•	•					•	•	
Jack London's Pavilion	2000	•	•		•		•	•			•		•	•	
Lake Merritt Hotel, The	300	•			•		•					•			•
Mills College Conference Facilities	500 *	•	•	•		•	•				•	•	•	•	
Oakland Museum	1000 *	•	•		•	•	•	•	•				•	•	
Otis Spunkmeyer Air	18	•			•		•					•			
Paramount Theatre	500 *	•		•	•		•						•		
Sailboat House	225	•				•		•				•	•		
Scott's Seafood Grill & Bar	280	•	•	•	•		•	•	•			•			
Sequoia Lodge	150	•				•							•		
Piedmont															
Piedmont Community Center	300 *	•	•	•		•	•						•	•	
Pleasanton															
Century House	125	•	•	•		•	•						•	•	•
Pleasanton Hotel, The	200	•	•		•		•	•	•		•				
Point Richmond															
East Brother Light Station	200	•	•	•	•	•	•	•		•			•	•	

FACILITY	MAXIMUM CAPACITY	Indoor Facilities	Outdoor Facilities	Meeting Space Available	In-house Catering	BYO Catering	Alcohol Provided	Alcohol BYO	Restaurant On Site	Guestrooms Available	Event Coordination	Wheelchair Restricted	Smoking Restricted	Insurance Required	Amplified Music Restricted
Linsley Hall	160	•	•	•		•		•				•	•		•
San Leandro															
Best House	150		•			•		•		•		•	•		
San Pablo															
Rockefeller Lodge	500	•	•	•	•						•				•
Sunol															
Elliston Vineyards	200	•	•		•		•	•			•		•		
Vallejo															
California Maritime Academy	500	•	•	•	•	•		•	•	•			•		
Foley Cultural Center	600	•	•	•	•	•							•		
Herbert House, The	85	•	•	•		•							•	•	
Walnut Creek															
Houston, The	12	•			•		•				•	•	•		
Mansion at Lakewood, The	20	•	•	•	•						•	•	•	•	•
SOUTH BAY															
Campbell															
Campbell House Restaurant	16	•			•		•		•			•	•		•
Martha's Vineyard	175	•		•	•		•	•	•						
Pruneyard Inn	120	•		•	•		•	•		•	•		•		•
Sebastian's & Club Jenine's	170	•			•		•	•			•		•		
Cupertino															
De Oro Club	150	•		•	•		•					•	•		
Sunrise Winery	200	•	•		•		•								
Gilroy															
Fortino Winery	250	•	•				•	•							
Gilroy Historical Museum	75	•			•		•					•	•		•
Hecker Pass	5000	•	•		•	•					•			•	
Los Gatos															
Village House & Garden Restaurant	130	•	•	•	•		•	•	•						
Morgan Hill															
Flying Lady, The	500 *	•		•	•		•	•	•				•		
Golden Oak Restaurant, The	400 *	•	•	•	•		•	•			•		•		

FACILITY	MAXIMUM CAPACITY	Indoor Facilities	Outdoor Facilities	Meeting Space Available	In-house Catering	BYO Catering	Alcohol Provided	Alcohol BYO	Restaurant On Site	Guestrooms Available	Event Coordination	Wheelchair Restricted	Smoking Restricted	Insurance Required	Amplified Music Restricted
Emilio Guglielmo Winery	80	•	•		•	•	•						•		
San Jose															
Abigail's Pub & Flowers	75	•		•	•	•	•	•	•				•		
Briar Rose, The	150	•	•	•	•	•	•	•		•	•	•	•	•	•
Children's Discovery Museum	1200	•	•				•		•				•	•	
Eulipia Restaurant & Bar	200	•		•	•		•	•	•		•	•			•
Event Center	6500 *	•					•	•	•				•	•	
d.p. Fong Galleries	175	•					•		•				•	•	•
Hensley House	150	•	•	•	•		•	•		•	•	•	•	•	•
Hochburg Von Germania	250	•			•	•	•	•	•		•				
Katia Lacoste Gallery	200	•					•		•					•	•
Le Petit Trianon	650	•	•	•			•				•		•	•	
Mirassou	120	•	•	•	•		•						•		
San Jose Athletic Club	400	•		•	•	•	•		•		•				
San Jose Historical Museum	1000 *	•	•	•			•		•		•		•	•	•
Victorian Garden Restaurant	200	•	•		•		•	•	•		•		•		
Winchester Mystery House	450 *	•	•		•	•	•	•				•	•		
Santa Clara															
Decathlon Club	700 *	•	•	•	•		•		•		•				
Madison Street Inn	75	•	•	•	•		•			•	•	•			•
Triton Museum of Art	1500	•	•	•			•						•	•	
Saratoga															
Cinnabar Vineyards	100	•	•	•	•	•	•					•	•	•	•
Congress Springs Winery	250	•	•	•			•	•			•		•		
Hakone Gardens	250	•	•	•			•	•				•	•	•	•
Mountain Winery, The	350	•	•	•			•	•			•	•	•	•	
Saratoga Foothill Club	185	•	•	•			•		•			•	•		•
Villa Montalvo	150	•	•				•		•				•		•
WINE COUNTRY															
Alexander Valley															
Chateau Souverain	100	•			•		•	•	•				•	•	
Calistoga															
Calistoga Inn	250	•	•	•	•		•	•	•	•	•		•		
Clos Pegas	400	•	•	•		•	•						•		
Once In A Lifetime Balloon Co.	8		•									•	•		•
Sterling Vineyards	350	•	•				•	•					•		•

FACILITY	MAXIMUM CAPACITY	Indoor Facilities	Outdoor Facilities	Meeting Space Available	In-house Catering	BYO Catering	Alcohol Provided	Alcohol BYO	Restaurant On Site	Guestrooms Available	Event Coordination	Wheelchair Restricted	Smoking Restricted	Insurance Required	Amplified Music Restricted
Geyeserville															
Isis Oasis Retreat Center	100 *	•	•	•	•	•	•	•		•	•	•	•	•	
Guerneville															
Estate, The	20	•	•	•	•		•	•		•	•		•		•
Healdsburg															
Alderbrook Winery	200	•	•	•		•	•						•	•	
Madrona Manor	135	•	•	•	•		•		•	•	•				•
Kenwood															
Kenwood Depot	125	•		•	•	•	•							•	
Oreste's Golden Bear	200	•	•		•		•	•	•						
Napa															
Chimney Rock Winery	150	•	•			•	•	•					•		
Churchill Manor	215	•	•	•	•		•			•		•	•		•
Embassy Suites Hotel	250	•		•	•		•		•	•	•				
Napa River Boat	100	•		•	•	•	•		•		•	•	•		
Napa Valley Country Club	150	•			•		•	•	•			•			
Napa Valley Wine Train	240	•			•		•	•	•			•	•		•
Silverado Country Club & Resort	1000 *	•	•	•	•		•		•	•					
Petaluma															
Garden Valley Ranch	200		•			•	•								
Rutherford															
Auberge du Soleil	120 *	•	•	•	•		•		•	•	•				•
Rancho Caymus Inn	60	•	•		•		•		•	•	•	•			
Santa Rosa															
Chateau Debaun Winery	800	•	•	•		•	•						•	•	
Sonoma															
Buena Vista Winery	400	•	•			•	•						•		•
Depot Hotel 1870	125	•	•		•		•	•	•						
Sonoma Hotel	50 *	•	•		•		•	•	•	•			•		•
Sonoma Mission Inn & Spa	275 *	•	•	•	•		•	•	•	•	•		•		

FACILITY	MAXIMUM CAPACITY	Indoor Facilities	Outdoor Facilities	Meeting Space Available	In-house Catering	BYO Catering	Alcohol Provided	Alcohol BYO	Restaurant On Site	Guestrooms Available	Event Coordination	Wheelchair Restricted	Smoking Restricted	Insurance Required	Amplified Music Restricted
St. Helena															
Cain Cellars	80	•	•	•	•		•						•		
Meadowood Resort Hotel	250 *	•	•	•	•		•		•	•	•				•
Merryvale Vineyards	160	•	•		•	•	•						•		
Robert Keenan Winery	150	•	•	•	•		•				•		•		•
Spring Mountain Vineyards	80		•		•		•							•	•
V. Sattui Winery	800	•	•	•	•		•							•	•
White Sulphur Springs	250	•	•	•	•	•			•		•	•	•	•	
Yountville															
Drums Restaurant	400	•	•		•		•	•	•					•	
MONTEREY PENINSULA															
Big Sur															
Nepenthe	200	•	•		•				•						•
Carmel															
Carmel Beach House, The	40	•			•				•		•	•	•	•	
La Playa Hotel	200 *	•	•	•	•		•		•	•	•				
Mission Ranch	200 *	•	•		•		•		•	•	•				•
Highlands Inn	150 *	•	•	•	•		•		•	•	•				•
Carmel Valley															
Carmel Valley Ranch Resort	300	•	•	•	•		•		•	•	•				
Ridge Restaurant, The	250	•	•	•	•		•		•	•	•				
Stonepine	250	•	•	•	•		•		•	•	•	•			
Monterey															
La Mirada	350	•	•	•	•	•			•		•		•		•
Monterey Bay Aquarium	2000	•		•	•		•	•	•				•	•	
Monterey Plaza	600	•	•	•	•		•		•	•	•				
Old Monterey Inn	20	•	•	•	•		•	•		•		•	•		•
Old Whaling Station	150	•	•			•	•					•	•		•
Victorian Carriage House & Garden	250	•	•				•		•						
Pacific Grove															
Asilomar Conference Center	1200	•	•	•	•		•		•	•		•	•		
Green Gables Inn, The	30	•		•	•	•	•				•	•	•		
Martine Inn	120 *	•	•	•	•		•				•	•		•	•

FACILITY	MAXIMUM CAPACITY	Indoor Facilities	Outdoor Facilities	Meeting Space Available	In-house Catering	BYO Catering	Alcohol Provided	Alcohol BYO	Restaurant On Site	Guestrooms Available	Event Coordination	Wheelchair Restricted	Smoking Restricted	Insurance Required	Amplified Music Restricted
Pebble Beach															
Beach & Tennis Club	250 *	•	•		•		•		•		•				
Inn at Spanish Bay, The	300 *	•	•	•	•		•		•	•	•				
Lodge at Pebble Beach, The	330 *	•	•	•	•		•	•	•	•	•				
SANTA CRUZ AREA															
Aptos															
Mangels House	25	•	•	•		•		•		•			•	•	•
Veranda, The	175	•	•		•		•		•	•			•		
Ben Lomond															
Highlands House & Park	200	•	•	•		•		•					•		•
Capitola															
Inn at Depot Hill, The	60	•	•		•	•	•		•		•		•		
Shadowbrook	200 *	•			•		•		•						•
Felton															
Hallcrest Vineyards	100		•			•	•						•	•	•
Roaring Camp	2000		•		•			•			•	•			•
Santa Cruz															
Chaminade	400	•	•	•	•		•		•	•	•				•
Cocoanut Grove	600 *	•		•	•		•	•	•		•			•	
Darling House	75	•	•	•	•	•		•		•	•	•	•		•
Hollins House	250	•	•	•	•		•		•		•				
GOLD COUNTRY															
Amador City															
Imperial Hotel	60	•		•	•		•		•	•				•	•
Auburn															
Auburn Valley Country Club	400	•	•	•	•		•	•	•						
Powers Mansion Inn	75	•	•	•	•					•			•	•	
Victorian Hill House	300	•	•	•	•	•				•			•	•	
Columbia															
Angelo's Hall	200	•		•	•	•		•				•	•	•	•
Avery Ranch	250	•	•	•	•	•	•	•		•	•	•	•	•	
City Hotel	100	•		•	•		•	•	•	•			•		•
Fallon House Theatre	275	•	•	•	•	•	•	•			•		•	•	

FACILITY	MAXIMUM CAPACITY	Indoor Facilities	Outdoor Facilities	Meeting Space Available	In-house Catering	BYO Catering	Alcohol Provided	Alcohol BYO	Restaurant On Site	Guestrooms Available	Event Coordination	Wheelchair Restricted	Smoking Restricted	Insurance Required	Amplified Music Restricted
Ione															
Heirloom, The	150	•	•	•		•	•			•	•	•	•		
Jackson															
Windrose Inn	150	•	•	•	•	•	•			•	•		•	•	
Jamestown															
Jamestown Hotel	140	•			•		•	•	•	•	•	•			
National Hotel, The	120	•	•		•		•	•	•	•		•			
Railtown 1897	450	•	•		•	•	•				•		•	•	•
Sutter Creek															
Gold Quartz Inn	80	•		•	•		•	•		•	•		•		•
Tuolumne															
Oak Hill Ranch	100	•	•			•		•		•	•	•	•		•
YOSEMITE AREA															
Groveland															
Iron Door Saloon, The	150	•			•		•		•		•			•	
Yosemite															
Yosemite Facilities	250 *	•	•	•	•		•		•	•	•		•		•
SACRAMENTO VALLEY															
Marysville															
Marysville Art Club	248	•	•	•		•		•				•	•	•	•
Oroville															
Jean Pratt's Riverside Bed & Breakfast	34 *	•	•	•		•		•		•		•	•		•
Rocklin															
Finnish Temperance Hall	300	•		•		•		•							
Sunset Whitney Country Club	300	•	•	•	•		•		•						
Roseville															
Haman House Restaurant	300	•	•	•	•		•	•	•		•		•	•	
Maidu Community Center	450	•	•	•		•	•						•	•	
Roseville Opera House	400	•		•		•	•				•	•		•	

FACILITY	MAXIMUM CAPACITY	Indoor Facilities	Outdoor Facilities	Meeting Space Available	In-house Catering	BYO Catering	Alcohol Provided	Alcohol BYO	Restaurant On Site	Guestrooms Available	Event Coordination	Wheelchair Restricted	Smoking Restricted	Insurance Required	Amplified Music Restricted
Sacramento															
Amber House	50	•		•			•			•	•	•	•		•
Aunt Abigail's Bed & Breakfast	35	•	•	•			•			•			•	•	•
Bear Flag Inn	10	•		•			•			•			•	•	•
Blue Diamond Visitors Center	230	•		•			•						•	•	•
California State Railroad Museum	600	•					•						•	•	
Capitol Plaza Halls	500	•		•	•	•	•	•				•			
Driver Mansion Inn	100	•	•	•	•		•			•		•	•		•
Fairytale Town	3500		•			•	•								
Hyatt Regency Sacramento	1500 *	•	•	•	•		•		•	•	•			•	
Masonic Temple	500	•		•		•	•						•	•	
Penthouse, The	245	•		•	•	•	•	•					•	•	
Rancho Arroyo	6000 *	•		•	•	•	•				•		•	•	
River Boat Delta King	150 *	•	•	•	•		•		•			•			•
River Rose Inn	200	•	•	•	•		•		•	•	•		•		
Sacramento History Center	700	•		•		•	•						•	•	
Sterling Hotel	200	•		•	•		•	•	•				•		•
Towe Ford Museum	500	•				•	•						•	•	
Traveler Centre, The	300	•				•	•							•	
Yuba City															
Harkey House	160	•	•	•		•		•			•		•	•	
Refuge, The	400	•		•	•		•	•	•					•	
Wicks, The	75	•		•	•		•	•		•		•	•		•
THE DELTA															
Ryde															
Grand Island Inn	700	•	•	•	•		•	•	•	•					
Walnut Grove															
Grand Island Mansion	1000	•	•	•	•		•	•				•	•		
SAN JOAQUIN VALLEY															
Lodi															
Japanese Pavilion & Gardens	175	•	•	•	•	•							•		
Wine & Roses Country Inn	200	•	•	•	•	•	•			•	•		•	•	•
Stockton															
Boat House	50	•	•		•	•		•					•		

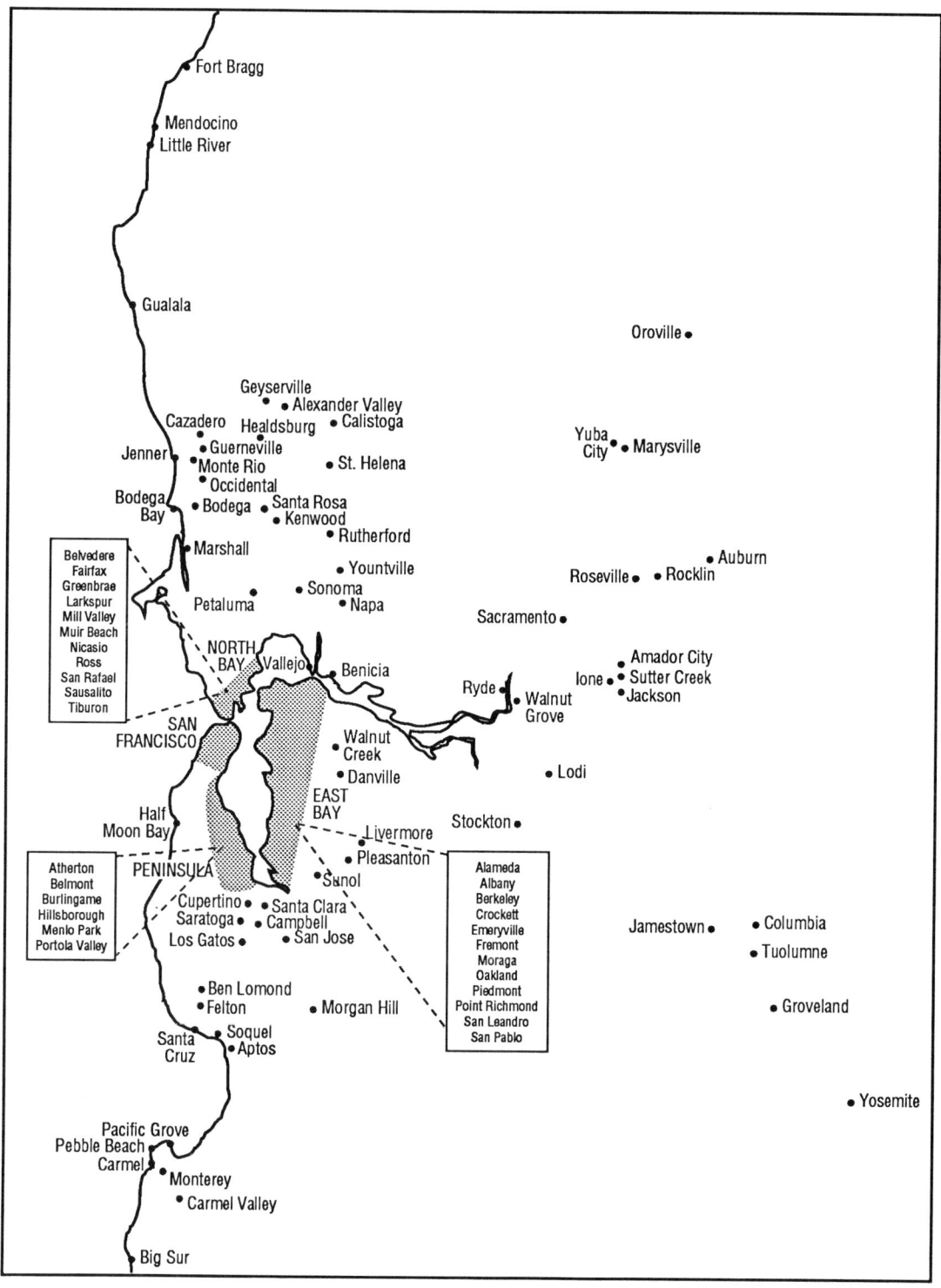

Fort Bragg

Mendocino
Little River

Gualala

Oroville •

Geyserville
Cazadero • Alexander Valley
Healdsburg • Calistoga
Jenner • Guerneville
Monte Rio
Occidental
Bodega • Bodega • Santa Rosa
Bay • Kenwood
Marshall • Rutherford

St. Helena

Yuba
City • Marysville

Roseville • • Rocklin

• Auburn

Belvedere
Fairfax
Greenbrae
Larkspur
Mill Valley
Muir Beach
Nicasio
Ross
San Rafael
Sausalito
Tiburon

• Yountville
Petaluma • Sonoma
• Napa

Sacramento •

NORTH
BAY • Vallejo • Benicia

Ryde • Amador City
Ione • • Sutter Creek
Walnut • Jackson
Grove

SAN
FRANCISCO

Walnut
Creek
• Danville

• Lodi

Half
Moon Bay

EAST
BAY

Stockton •

Livermore
PENINSULA • Pleasanton

Atherton
Belmont
Burlingame
Hillsborough
Menlo Park
Portola Valley

Cupertino • Santa Clara
Saratoga • • Campbell
Los Gatos • • San Jose

• Sunol

Alameda
Albany
Berkeley
Crockett
Emeryville
Fremont
Moraga
Oakland
Piedmont
Point Richmond
San Leandro
San Pablo

Jamestown • • Columbia

• Tuolumne

Ben Lomond
Felton • Morgan Hill

• Groveland

Soquel
Santa • Aptos
Cruz

Pacific Grove
Pebble Beach
Carmel • Monterey
• Carmel Valley

• Yosemite

Big Sur

Party Places

LOCATION LISTINGS

Our Subjective Rating Symbols

★   This symbol denotes a facility we think is terrific!

★★   This symbol denotes a facility we think is absolutely the best!

San Francisco

ALAMO SQUARE INN

719 Scott Street at Fulton
San Francisco, CA 94117
(415) 922-2055 Wayne Corn
Reserve: 1–6 months in advance

Located along the perimeter of the much photographed Alamo Square, made famous by the row of restored, colorful Victorians, the Alamo Square Inn is a special place for business conferences, corporate retreats, special events and holiday parties. Built in 1895, the mansion combines both Queen Anne and Neoclassical Revival styles, with rich woodwork and oak floors, high ceilings, chandeliers and a stately staircase illuminated by a stained glass skylight. The Inn is actually a bed and breakfast complex of 2 houses adjoined in back by a garden and solarium/atrium. All of the downstairs rooms in both houses are available for events and meetings. Of special note are the triple bay windows in the drawing room and the formal parlor which has a vista overlooking Hilltop Park.

CAPACITY: The Inn can accommodate 200 people for a stand-up reception and 125 for a sit-down affair.

FEES & DEPOSITS: For special events, $1000 is required to secure your event date; $500 of this is a refundable security deposit. For business conferences, the fee is $50/person per day and includes breakfast, coffee service, lunch and mid-afternoon treats. Tax and a 15% gratuity are additional. For events, the facility costs $250/hour with a 3-hour minimum rental required. Event staff run $15/hour/person (5 hour min.). Catering is provided. Mid-afternoon buffets start at $25/person and sit-down functions start at $35/person. Gratuity is 15%, sales tax 7.25%. The remaining balance, based on an estimated head count, is due in full at the beginning of the event week.

AVAILABILITY: Any time. Events must end by 10:30pm with guests out by 11pm.

SERVICES/AMENITIES:

Restaurant Services: no
Catering: provided, no BYO
Kitchen Facilities: n/a
Tables & Chairs: provided
Linens, Silver, etc.: provided
Restrooms: no wca
Dance Floor: yes

Parking: off street lot, on street, valet CBA
Overnight Accommodations: 15 guestrooms
Telephone: guest phone
Outdoor Night Lighting: yes
Outdoor Cooking Facilities: no
Cleanup: provided
Other: audio-visual equipment

RESTRICTIONS:

Alcohol: provided, BYO corkage $3/bottle,
red wine seated meals only
Smoking: smoking porch only

Music: amplified within reason
Wheelchair Access: no
Insurance: events binder required

ARCHBISHOP'S MANSION

1000 Fulton Street at Steiner
San Francisco, CA 94117
(415) 563-7872   Kathleen Austin
Reserve: 2 months in advance

Built in 1904 as the residence for the archbishop of San Francisco, this elegant historic landmark with handpainted ceilings, fine woodwork and distinguished period furnishings, has been restored to its original splendor. The first floor dining room, main hallway and parlor are available for meetings and receptions. Facing Alamo Park, the mansion is a regal bed and breakfast inn with 15 guest rooms that can be made available to party guests.

CAPACITY: For a stand-up reception, 100 people, and for a sit-down meal, approximately 50 can be accommodated.

MEETING ROOMS: Several rooms are available for 5–50 people. The Mansion can cater for small business groups.

FEES & DEPOSITS: A deposit of 50% of the estimated fee is needed in order to secure your event date. A $375 refundable security deposit is also required. This facility is rented at $150/hour, measured from the arrival of the caterers to their departure. A 4-hour minimum rental is required. The balance and security deposit are due 1 week prior to the event. The smaller meeting rooms run $250/day.

AVAILABILITY: Sun–Thurs, all day up to 11pm; Fri & Sat up to 5pm only.

SERVICES/AMENITIES:
Restaurant Services: no
Catering: CBA or BYO, must be licensed
Kitchen Facilities: ample
Tables & Chairs: some provided
Linens, Silver, etc.: caterer
Restrooms: no wca
Dance Floor: no dancing

Parking: on street, valet CBA
Overnight Accommodations: 15 guestrooms
Telephone: house phone
Outdoor Night Lighting: no
Outdoor Cooking Facilities: no
Cleanup: caterer
Other: baby grand piano

RESTRICTIONS:
Alcohol: provided, corkage fee if BYO
Smoking: outside only
Music: no amplified

Wheelchair Access: no
Insurance: not required
Other: decorations restricted

BLUE AND GOLD FLEET

Pier 39
San Francisco, CA 94133
(415) 781-7890
Reserve: 2–3 months in advance

Ready to accommodate big and small parties alike, the Blue and Gold Fleet proudly offers three vessels with two classes available for private charter. The Golden Bear, Old Blue and Oski make it possible to have a scenic and entertaining event while cruising San Francisco Bay. Note that there are alternate docking sites available for your party for a minimal extra charge. The B&G staff are extremely helpful with DJ selection, live entertainment, flowers and decoration, plus theme party planning.

CAPACITY: These boats usually carry over 100 people. Each vessel can accommodate 200 for a buffet dinner dance and 300 for standing receptions.

FEES & DEPOSITS: A $500 deposit is required 10 working days after arranging a tentative date. The fees vary depending on season and day of the week:

	Friday	*Saturday*	*Sunday*	*Mon–Thurs*
April-October	—	$2700	$3000	$2500–$2300
November-March	$2400	$2700	$2300	$2100

The above rental fees are for a 4-hour minimum cruise. Fees are increased for major holidays. Catering is provided. Blue and Gold catering costs range from $7/person to over $20/person depending on menu arrangements. Gratuity 15%, sales tax 7.25%.

CANCELLATION POLICY: Your deposit is returned if a cancellation is made 45 days prior to the event.

AVAILABILITY: June–Sept 5, no charters are available before 6pm. Sept 5–May 30, one boat is available during the day, with a 4-hour minimum rental required. Evenings are generally available for private functions.

SERVICES/AMENITIES:

Restaurant Services: no
Catering: provided, no BYO
Kitchen Facilities: no
Tables & Chairs: provided
Linens, Silver, etc.: provided
Restrooms: no wca
Dance Floor: yes

Parking: Pier 39 garage
Overnight Accommodations: no
Telephone: emergency only
Outdoor Night Lighting: yes
Outdoor Cooking Facilities: BBQ
Cleanup: provided

RESTRICTIONS:

Alcohol: provided, BYO corkage $3/bottle
Smoking: allowed
Music: amplified ok

Wheelchair Access: yes, on main deck only
Insurance: not required

CABLE CAR BARN AND MUSEUM

1201 Mason St. at Washington
San Francisco, CA 94108
(415) 923-6202   Jim Tomes
Reserve: 3–24 months in advance

The Barn and Museum are two really unusual sites to hold an event. The cavernous Barn is a working "corporation yard" for the cable cars. The Museum houses historical displays and has a sensational view down into the drive wheels that run the cable car system. Cable cars are usually lined up in the Barn to section off actual working areas from the party space. For a really dramatic entry, you and your group can even arrive riding on one! Note that neighborhood parking is impossible; guests may arrive by cable car or other forms of public transit. A Muni-approved parking plan must be in place before they'll allow the rental to occur.

CAPACITY: Barn and Museum, combined, can hold 800 people for a standing reception and 400 for a sit-down function.

FEES & DEPOSITS: $1000 plus a $500 refundable cleaning deposit are required to secure a date. The deposit is payable 2 weeks from making a tentative booking. The refundable portion is usually returned within a week after the event. $1850 is required for Barn and Museum combined. Any remaining unpaid balance plus use permit and insurance paperwork are due 2 weeks prior to the event.

CANCELLATION POLICY: During the holiday season or peak use periods, you must cancel at least 2 months in advance to receive a full refund.

AVAILABILITY: 7 days a week. The Barn is available 5pm–10:30pm. The Museum, during the summer 6pm–11pm, during the winter 5pm–11pm. Guests must be out by 11pm. No events are scheduled on Christmas, Thanksgiving, New Year's or Easter holidays.

SERVICES/AMENITIES:

Restaurant Services: no

Catering: BYO

Kitchen Facilities: no

Tables & Chairs: BYO

Linens, Silver, etc.: BYO

Restrooms: wca

Dance Floor: no

Parking: no

Overnight Accommodations: no

Telephone: office phone

Outdoor Night Lighting: no

Outdoor Cooking Facilities: no

Cleanup: caterer

Other: cable car arrivals CBA

RESTRICTIONS:

Alcohol: BYO

Smoking: allowed

Music: amplified up to 10pm

Wheelchair Access: yes

Insurance: event liability required

Other: permit required

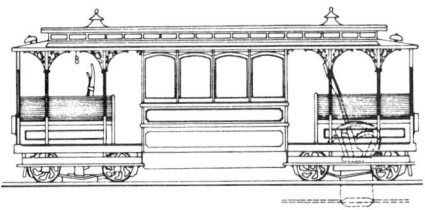

CABLE CAR EXCLUSIVE

San Francisco, CA
(415) 923-6202   Jim Tomes
Reserve: by special arrangement

Yes, you can lease a bona fide cable car, complete with gripman and conductor for your celebration! So hop on and have your party on the streets of San Francisco with your select group of friends, family or business associates. Bring your own food, photographer, and entertainment aboard. For 4 hours, the cable car is dedicated exclusively to your event. Because cable cars are historic vehicles, you may decorate, but no tacks, tape or staples allowed. The City of San Francisco requests that you treat them with respect during your party.

CAPACITY: 40–45 guests maximum, mostly standing if you bring a big group along.

FEES & DEPOSITS: A $300 refundable cleaning deposit is required. The fee is $800 for 4 hours minimum rental.

AVAILABILITY: Each event must be arranged individually. Summer months may be difficult to reserve.

SERVICES/AMENITIES:
Catering: BYO
Tables & Chairs: seats provided
Linens, Silver, etc.: BYO

Restrooms: none
Parking: any City parking garage
Cleanup: whoever caters event

RESTRICTIONS:
Alcohol: BYO
Smoking: allowed
Music: allowed

Wheelchair Access: no
Insurance: liquor liability required if alcohol served

CAFE MAJESTIC

1500 Sutter Street
San Francisco, CA 94109
(415) 776-6400   Chris Stellman
Reserve: 6 weeks in advance

Cafe Majestic is an appetizing restaurant in both cuisine and decor. We were surprised to learn that many of the menu selections are derived from old San Francisco cookbooks. The owner, Thomas Marshall, has a penchant for 'vintage' recipes, and is enthusiastic about offering a dining environment reminiscent of the City's genteel past. The refreshing interior has peach walls, a high ceiling, and tall windows along the street side of the room. The warm wall color contrasts nicely with light teal wainscotting, shutters and trim. Small

Kentia palms provide the perfect green accent next to the crisp white table settings. In addition to a charming ambiance and superb food, overnight accommodations are available in the adjacent Hotel Majestic.

CAPACITY: The Main Dining Room can hold 20–125 seated guests, the Board Room 10–20.

FEES & DEPOSITS: A refundable deposit of $10/person is required when the date is confirmed. To rent the entire restaurant (80 guests minimum to waive rental fee), a nonrefundable $1000 deposit is required. With food, there's usually no rental fee. Meal service per person rates: for breakfasts $3–9, luncheon entrees $10–14.50, dinner entrees $15–24, first courses $4.50–8, hors d'oeuvres start at $12. The balance is due the day of the event. Tax of 7.25% is additional.

CANCELLATION POLICY: With 1 week's notice, your deposit will be refunded.

AVAILABILITY: Year-round, every day from 7am–midnight. Closed Memorial Day, July 4th, Labor Day, December 26th and January 2nd. You can reserve the entire restaurant every night except for Saturday.

SERVICES/AMENITIES:

Restaurant Services: yes

Catering: provided, no BYO

Kitchen Facilities: n/a

Tables & Chairs: provided

Linens, Silver, etc.: provided

Restrooms: wca

Dance Floor: yes

Parking: valet

Overnight Accommodations: 60 guestrooms

Telephone: pay phone

Outdoor Night Lighting: no

Outdoor Cooking Facilities: no

Cleanup: provided

Other: nightly pianist, grand piano

RESTRICTIONS:

Alcohol: provided, BYO corkage $12/bottle

Smoking: designated areas

Music: amplified restricted

Wheelchair Access: yes

Insurance: not required

CALIFORNIA ACADEMY ★★ OF SCIENCES

Golden Gate Park
San Francisco, CA 94118
(415) 750-7221   Deidre Kernan
Reserve: 3 months in advance

Although first and foremost a public museum, the California Academy of Sciences offers an incredibly wide range of sensational spaces for private parties. Located in Golden Gate Park, the museum is one of the largest natural history museums in the world and the oldest in the Western U.S. Use the dynamic and dramatically lit exhibits as backdrops for events, and reserve well in advance for parties scheduled between September and Christmas.

African Hall: Authentic sights and sounds of a busy savannah watering hole, featuring majestic dioramas filled with exotic birds and animals.

Earth and Space Hall: Features celestial bodies, a neon solar system and earthquake simulation. Note that laser shows at night have public access.

Far Side Gallery: For you fans of Gary Larson's hilarious cartoon creations, a small gallery lined with original Far Side cartoons is available for rental.

Hall of Human Cultures: Otherwise known as Wattis Hall, this large room holds dioramas depicting man's adaptation to his natural environment.

Temporary Exhibit Space: Special exhibits, like the most recent dinosaur show, are changed often. Call to find out what's current.

Life Through Time: Dinosaur fossils and moving models demonstrate the evidence for evolution. Available for cocktail receptions only.

Wild California and Mineral Halls: Wild California is remarkable for its lifelike exhibits. The battling sea lions and coastal dioramas are terrific. Mineral Hall is for cocktails only.

Aquarium: Sensational exhibits of reptiles and amphibians, exotic fish, penguins, dolphins and seals. The fish roundabout is a spiral ascending ramp with tanks along the outer wall. The top platform, a circlular space surrounded by blue-green lit tanks, with large fish swimming in one direction, is one of the most extraordinary party spaces we've seen. Also, check out the swamp with crocodiles—it's a favorite spot for unique celebrations.

Museum Store: Can be opened on request. Guests must be notified in advance so they can remember to bring funds and credit cards for purchases.

CAPACITY, FEES & DEPOSITS: A nonrefundable deposit of 30% of the estimated fee is due within 21 days of contract receipt. The remaining 70% and a $500 refundable security deposit are due three weeks prior to the event. For holiday rentals (December 1–24) the remaining fees are due 90 days prior to the event. The security deposit is returned after your function, pending the facility's condition. If cleanup assistance is necessary, $150/hour will be billed.

	Fees	Standing Capacity	Seated Capacity	Standing & Seated
African Hall	$3500	400	300	150
African Annex	500	100	80	—
Hohfeld I & II	1500	capacity varies	—	—
Lovell White	1500	capacity varies	—	—
Space Hall	1500	150	100	60
Wattis Hall	3500	400	150	100
Aquarium, Swamp, Roundabout Combo	3500	400	200	—
Roundabout Only	1500	125	70	60
Wild Calif. & Mineral	3500	300	150	150
Life Thru Time/Oceans	3500	capacity varies	—	—
Auditorium	1000	—	400	—
Planetarium	1200	—	300	—
Entire Academy	8,000–12,000	to 3000		

Combinations of different halls can be arranged for any sized gathering. The above fees include an Academy representative and security guards.

AVAILABILITY: The Academy is available September 1st–July 3 from 6pm–12:30am; July 4–September 1 from 8pm–12:30am; and the first Wednesday of every month from 10pm–12:30am. With prior notice, you can extend your party for an extra $150/hour.

SERVICES/AMENITIES:

Restaurant Services: no
Catering: provided, or BYO from approved list
Kitchen Facilities: no
Tables & Chairs: BYO
Linens, Silver, etc.: BYO
Restrooms: wca
Dance Floor: CBA

Parking: museum lot
Overnight Accommodations: no
Telephone: pay phone
Outdoor Night Lighting: no
Outdoor Cooking Facilities: no
Cleanup: caterer & museum janitorial

RESTRICTIONS:

Alcohol: BYO, license required
Smoking: allowed
Music: amplified ok except for aquarium

Wheelchair Access: yes
Insurance: indemnification clause required
Other: decorations need approval, catering restrictions

CALIFORNIA CULINARY ACADEMY

625 Polk Street
San Francisco, CA 94102
(415) 771-3500
Reserve: 1–3 months in advance

Located in the lovely and architecturally significant California Hall, a 1912 historic landmark, the California Culinary Academy makes available a number of interesting and varied spaces for parties and events. The main dining room, Careme, is like a formal theater. It's ornate, large and formal with an awesome ceiling extending up three floors. When dining here, you can observe hundreds of young, aspiring chefs cooking for you. Circling above the main floor is a balcony called Cyril's, a dining area with fabulous views of the lower dining room and ceiling. The main bar is lovely, warm and intimate with dark wood, mirrors and an old bar. The Private Dining Room is small and intimate without ornamentation. The Academy Grill is a more informal space. Winetasting, cooking demonstrations and Grand Buffet are offered in addition to sensational chocolate and Viennese desserts. Note that the food service here is really exceptional; the Academy is one of the world's foremost culinary schools.

CAPACITY, FEES & DEPOSITS: To secure your date, a refundable $1000 deposit is required at the time you reserve a space.

	Standing Capacity	*Seated Capacity*	*Fees*
Main Dining Room	500	280	$1000
Main Bar	150	60	350
Private Dining Room	60	30	150
Cyril's	150-175	80	500
Academy Grill	200	200	—

The Academy office will determine when 50% of the estimated fee total is due prior to the event. Also note that for private parties, a combination of rooms with special rates can be arranged. Food service is provided. Hors d'oeuvres start at $5.50/person, luncheons at $15.50/person and dinners at $25.95/person. A 7.25% sales tax and 15% gratuity will be applied to the final bill.

CANCELLATION POLICY: Your deposit will be refunded up to 30 days prior to your event.

AVAILABILITY: Weekends, all day. You need a minimum of 150 people to open the Culinary Academy on a weekend for which there is an additional $750 charge. There's no minimum rental block, but there's a 5-hour maximum. On weekdays, since the Academy operates a school, guests must arrive between 11:30am–12:30pm for lunch and 6pm–7:30pm for dinner.

SERVICES/AMENITIES:

Restaurant Services: yes
Catering: provided, no BYO
Kitchen Facilities: ample
Tables & Chairs: provided
Linens, Silver, etc.: provided
Restrooms: wca
Dance Floor: $350 setup charge

Parking: garage nearby
Overnight Accommodations: no
Telephone: pay phone
Outdoor Night Lighting: no
Outdoor Cooking Facilities: no
Cleanup: provided
Other: ice sculpture

RESTRICTIONS:

Alcohol: provided, BYO corkage $5/bottle
Smoking: allowed
Music: amplified after 7:30pm

Wheelchair Access: yes
Insurance: not required

BOB SARLATTE
Radio and TV Personality

My wife and I used to throw some of the greatest New Year's Eve parties in town. We would invite 50-100 people to come over to bring in the New Year. My wife is a gourmet cook, and she would prepare huge platters of food. There would be plenty of dancing and this was B.K. (before kids), however, so we'd get pretty rowdy. It was the one time of year we really blew it out. On one such occasion a friend's wife even broke her arm. The mornings after used to be like a scene from the movie 'The Sting', with a big community ice cube. We stopped having these parties because we decided it was getting a little too much when we started not to recognize some of our guests the next morning. We held these parties for about five years and the kids came along shortly afterward. Those New Year's parties were some great times with great friends.

CALIFORNIA PALACE OF ★ THE LEGION OF HONOR

34th and Clement, Lincoln Park
San Francisco, CA 94121
(415) 750-3683 Kate Schlafly
Reserve: 1–12 months in advance

The Palace of the Legion of Honor is located in Lincoln Park, on the edge of the Pacific, set against spectacular views of the Golden Gate Bridge and the City. It's a dramatic and impressive looking museum, its design adapted from the neoclassical Hotel de Salm in Paris, where Napoleon headquartered his famous order of the Legion d'Honneur. Arriving guests are greeted by Rodin's famous 'Thinker,' while inside, one of the world's finest collections of Rodin sculpture is exhibited along with eight centuries of European art. After hours, the Rodin Galleries are available for corporate receptions and dinners only. Impress your guests—the Palace is both classic and elegant, offering a stylish environment for any type of business event. And, if your guests are interested in expanding their libraries, the museum book shop can be opened for any function.

CAPACITY: The Rodin Galleries can accommodate 160 seated guests, 600 for a reception.

FEES & DEPOSITS: A refundable deposit of 30% of the rental fee, which is applied toward the rental, is required to confirm reservations and the balance is due 2 weeks prior to the function. An event plan must be submitted at least 1 month prior to the event. The rental fee for 2 hours is $5000, for 4 hours $7500.

AVAILABILITY: Year-round, Monday and Tuesday from 8am, Wednesday–Sunday from 6:30pm.

SERVICES/AMENITIES:

Restaurant Services: no
Catering: BYO w/approval
Kitchen Facilities: no
Tables & Chairs: BYO
Linens, Silver, etc.: BYO
Restrooms: wca
Dance Floor: no dancing

Parking: large lot
Overnight Accommodations: no
Telephone: pay phone
Outdoor Night Lighting: no
Outdoor Cooking Facilities: BYO
Cleanup: caterer & custodian

RESTRICTIONS:

Alcohol: BYO w/approval
Smoking: outside only
Music: amplified restricted

Wheelchair Access: yes
Insurance: certificate required
Other: no open flames

THE CALIFORNIA SPIRIT

Pacific Marine Yacht Charters
Berthed at San Francisco Yacht Harbor, Gate 11
San Francisco, CA
(415) 388-3400
Reserve: 1–6 months in advance

The California Spirit is Pacific Marine's newest, most spacious and opulent yacht. Decorated in muted shades of mauve and cream, this 100-foot luxurious, custom-designed vessel boasts an impressive grand salon complete with dance floor, several bars, an intimate observation salon, plush upper salon and sunlit outside deck. You can cruise around the Bay in a superbly appointed yacht whose services can be specifically tailored for your party or business function. The California Spirit is usually berthed in front of the St. Francis Yacht Club at Gate 11, but other boarding locations can be arranged for an additional fee. What an exciting place for a floating party.

CAPACITY: The California Spirit can accommodate up to 149 guests plus 15 crew.

FEES & DEPOSITS: A $1000 deposit is required. If you arrange for your own entertainment, a refundable security deposit of $350–500 is also required. Both deposits are payable when you reserve your event date. Rental fees are $625/hour weekdays (before 5pm) and $750/hour (after 5pm), $825/hour weekends and holidays. A 3-hour weekday minimum rental is required, 4 hours on Saturdays and holidays. Some 2-hour rentals can be arranged in advance. A guaranteed guest count is required 7 days prior to departure. The remaining balance is due 5 days prior to your charter date.

Special packages are offered, including yacht rental, food (all freshly prepared on board) and beverage service plus entertainment. A 75–100 passenger minimum is required for package cruises on this vessel.

CANCELLATION POLICY: If you cancel 60 or more days prior to your event, 90% of the deposit will be refunded. If less than 60, you will forfeit the deposit and be refunded the $350–500 security deposit.

AVAILABILITY: Any time, no limits.

SERVICES/AMENITIES:

Restaurant Services: no
Catering: provided, no BYO
Kitchen Facilities: ample
Tables & Chairs: provided
Linens, Silver, etc.: provided
Restrooms: wca
Dance Floor: yes

Parking: Marina lot
Overnight Accommodations: no
Telephone: cellular phone & radio
Outdoor Night Lighting: yes
Outdoor Cooking Facilities: no
Cleanup: provided
Other: full event coordination

RESTRICTIONS:

Alcohol: provided, BYO corkage fee $7/bottle
Smoking: outside only
Music: amplified ok

Wheelchair Access: yes, CBA
Insurance: not required

CAMPTON PLACE

340 Stockton Street
San Francisco, CA 94108
(415) 781-5555   Catering Coordinator
Reserve: 2 weeks in advance

Campton Place is a small hotel with an understated elegance that becomes apparent the moment you enter the lobby. The beige marble floor, stunning floral centerpiece and warm background colors invite you to linger a while. Upstairs, the Conference Room and Board Room accommodate small business functions in comfort and style. Both have beautiful custom-made mahogany tables and upholstered chairs. For a more informal atmosphere, two suites include a bedroom, sitting room and many of the comforts of home. Done in off-white, pastels and beige, the suites are perfect spots for small intimate gatherings. Campton Place pays attention to small details. Colors throughout are soothing, there are flowers in every room, and dining here can be a sublime experience.

CAPACITY: The Conference Room seats 10, the Board Room 16, the Penthouse Suites can accommodate up to 26 for a reception.

FEES & DEPOSITS: No deposits are required. Prior to the event, credit and payment are established. The Conference and Board Rooms rent for $225 (8 hours) and $125 (4 hours) and the Penthouse Suites $350 (3 hours). For functions with banquet service, the room rental fees for the Conference and Board Room may be waived. Food service per person rates: continental breakfasts $13, luncheons $20–40, dinners $45–55 and hors d'oeuvres start at $24. Tax of 7.25% and a 15% gratuity are additional. The balance is due the day of the event.

CANCELLATION POLICY: 24 hours' notice is requested for cancellation. A small fee will be charged.

AVAILABILITY: Year-round, any day, any time.

SERVICES/AMENITIES:

Restaurant Services: yes
Catering: provided, no BYO
Kitchen Facilities: n/a
Tables & Chairs: provided
Linens, Silver, etc.: provided
Restrooms: wca
Dance Floor: no
Parking: valet $19/day

Overnight Accommodations: 126 guestrooms
Telephone: pay phone
Outdoor Night Lighting: no
Outdoor Cooking Facilities: no
Cleanup: provided
Other: event coordination, business equipment extra charge

RESTRICTIONS:

Alcohol: provided, BYO corkage fee $15/bottle
Smoking: designated areas
Music: no amplified

Wheelchair Access: yes
Insurance: not required

CARNELIAN ROOM

555 California Street
San Francisco, CA 94104
(415) 433-7500   Marco or Phil
Reserve: 2 weeks–6 months in advance

The Carnelian Room is truly a "room with a view." Occupying an enviable location on the top floor of the Bank of America building, it overlooks the Bay, both bridges, the Embarcadero and the East Bay hills. Long and spacious with white beamed ceiling, warm wood paneling, and oxblood leather chairs, the restaurant has a decidedly masculine feel. A climatized, glass-encased wine cellar is built into one wall, displaying the Carnelian Room's extensive wine collection. A wide variety of menus is available, or consult with the catering director and create your own. Experienced staff are also on hand to coordinate any details of your special event.

CAPACITY: The Main Dining Room is available for 150–500 guests; a minimum food and beverage total is required to close the room for a private party. There are also 12 private suites, the largest of which can hold up to 150 for a sit-down event.

FEES & DEPOSITS: A refundable deposit of $150 is required when reservations are confirmed. Small suites rent for $50/event and the large suites, $150/event. Pre-selected menus are developed in advance of any event. Dinners start at $34/person and substantial hors d'oeuvres start at $16/person. 80% of the estimated event total is payable 10 days prior to the function. The balance is due the day of the event. Tax of 7.25% and gratuity at 15% will be applied to the final bill.

CANCELLATION POLICY: With 48 hours notice, the deposit will be refunded.

AVAILABILITY: Year-round, Monday–Friday from 3pm, Saturday from 4pm and Sunday from 10am. Closed most major holidays.

SERVICES/AMENITIES:
Restaurant Services: yes
Catering: provided, no BYO
Kitchen Facilities: n/a
Tables & Chairs: provided
Linens, Silver, etc.: provided
Restrooms: wca
Dance Floor: CBA

Parking: garage $5/car
Overnight Accommodations: no
Telephone: pay phone
Outdoor Night Lighting: no
Outdoor Cooking Facilities: no
Cleanup: provided
Other: full event coordination

RESTRICTIONS:
Alcohol: provided, BYO corkage fee $10/bottle
Smoking: allowed
Music: amplified ok

Wheelchair Access: yes
Insurance: not required

CARTOON ART MUSEUM

665 3rd Street at Townsend
San Francisco, CA 94107
(415) 546-3922 Mary Bisbee
Reserve: 2 months in advance

The museum, located in an upstairs office of the old Hills Bros. Coffee Corporate Offices in the heart of the factory outlet area, is a unique facility for a fun event. Although small (1000 sq ft), its ceilings are high and the walls are brick. These walls and room dividers are covered with original cartoons and comic book art along with other displays and informational exhibits. A recent exhibit featured original Batman comic art, however, exhibits change quarterly, so call for current information. If you're interested in a Christmas party, reserve early.

CAPACITY: The room can accommodate 125 guests for a stand-up reception and 50 for a sit-down affair.

FEES & DEPOSITS: A nonrefundable deposit of $100 is needed to secure your event date and is due when the booking is made. A refundable cleaning deposit of $100 is also required. The rental is $300 for 2 hours at $150/hour. An hourly rate of $100 will be charged for any time over 2 hours. All fees are due by the day of the event.

CANCELLATION POLICY: To obtain a refund, cancellation must be made 15 days prior to your party.

AVAILABILITY: Every day, 7pm–midnight and 9am–5pm during Museum off-hours or by special arrangement. The Museum can be rented for a maximum of 8 hours, but not past midnight.

SERVICES/AMENITIES:

Restaurant Services: no
Catering: BYO
Kitchen Facilities: minimal
Tables & Chairs: BYO
Linens, Silver, etc.: BYO
Restrooms: wca
Dance Floor: no

Parking: on street
Overnight Accommodations: no
Telephone: emergency only
Outdoor Night Lighting: no
Outdoor Cooking Facilities: no
Cleanup: caterer

RESTRICTIONS:

Alcohol: BYO
Smoking: not allowed
Music: acoustical until midnight

Wheelchair Access: yes
Insurance: indemnification clause required

CASA DE LA VISTA

Building 271, Avenue of the Palms
Treasure Island
San Francisco, CA 94130
(415) 395-5151
Reserve: 1–8 months in advance

If Treasure Island actually possesses any treasures, Casa de la Vista could very well be one of them. Situated on the edge of the island, it has unobstructed views of the entire San Francisco skyline, both bridges, Alcatraz, and Marin. The facility itself is quite pleasant. It's light and airy with a long wall of floor-to-ceiling glass that overlooks the Bay. Painted in a soft mauve overall, the vaulted ceiling is accented by light blue beams and pink pillars provide colorful support. A modern fireplace with brass chimney and a convenient bar are located near one end, leaving the majority of the room open for flexible arrangements. In back, olive trees shade a large brick patio which can also be set up for your event. Only recently made available to the public, Casa de la Vista is a terrific spot for parties or conferences because it's very private *and* has knockout views. Additionally, there's the benefit of having a central location, great for guests coming from either San Francisco or the East Bay.

CAPACITY: This facility can hold 225 for a reception or 170 guests for a seated affair.

FEES & DEPOSITS: A nonrefundable $200 deposit is required when the rental agreement is submitted. The rental fee is $200 for meetings (8 hours max) or dinners/receptions (5 hours max) with the balance payable 3 days before the event. A final guest count is due 4 days in advance. With meal service, the rental fee may be waived. Any extra hours over 5 are available for an additional charge. Per person rates: dinners/buffets $10.50–19, luncheons $7.50–14, hors d'oeuvres 100 pieces $45-200. Any menu can be customized, no tax is required, gratuity is 15%. Bartenders are available for $50/bartender. A business breakfast can be arranged along with coffee service for meetings.

AVAILABILITY: Year-round, every day. Saturday & Sunday 7am-1am, Monday-Friday until 1am. Closed most holidays but will open for parties with a guaranteed 150 guests.

SERVICES/AMENITIES:
Restaurant Services: no
Catering: provided, no BYO
Kitchen Facilities: n/a
Tables & Chairs: provided
Linens, Silver, etc.: provided
Restrooms: wca
Dance Floor: yes

Parking: large lot
Overnight Accommodations: no
Telephone: pay phone
Outdoor Night Lighting: yes
Outdoor Cooking Facilities: CBA
Cleanup: provided
Other: event coordination, piano

RESTRICTIONS:
Alcohol: provided, no BYO
Smoking: allowed
Music: amplified ok

Wheelchair Access: yes
Insurance: not required
Other: votive candles only

CASA SAN GREGORIO

398 Pennsylvania Avenue
San Francisco, CA 94107
(415) 641-1902
Reserve: 3–6 months in advance

Located in the sunny Potrero Hill District, this bed and breakfast inn offers a unique location as well as distinctive party spaces. The inn's modern design features an indoor pool, a well-appointed second level dining area plus a remarkable deck on top of the building which offers incredible, 360-degree views of Downtown and the Bay. There's also an enclosed patio area perfect for barbecues or small receptions. For a small business or private party, this is an unusual event site.

CAPACITY: The Inn can hold 50–100 for a stand-up reception or 30–50 guests for a seated affair.

FEES & DEPOSITS: $1000 is required to secure your date, $500 of which is a refundable security deposit. Rental fees are $175/hour with a 3-hour minimum rental required. Event staff run $15/hour per person (5-hour min).

CANCELLATION POLICY: With less than 2 weeks' notice, $300 of the deposit will be forfeited.

AVAILABILITY: Year-round, every day. The event must end by midnight, with guests out by 11:30pm.

SERVICES/AMENITIES:

Restaurant Services: no
Catering: provided or BYO
Kitchen Facilities: ample
Tables & Chairs: provided
Linens, Silver, etc.: CBA or BYO
Restrooms: no wca
Dance Floor: no

Parking: on street
Overnight Accommodations: 3 suites
Telephone: guest phone
Outdoor Night Lighting: yes
Outdoor Cooking Facilities: BBQ
Cleanup: provided

RESTRICTIONS:

Alcohol: provided, BYO $3/bottle corkage,
red wine at seated meals only
Smoking: allowed

Music: amplified within reason
Wheelchair Access: no
Insurance: required

CHATEAU TIVOLI
JACKSON/KRELING HOUSE

1057 Steiner at Golden Gate
San Francisco, CA 94115
(800) 228-1647 or (415) 776-5462
Reserve: 1–2 months in advance

Built by the Oregon lumber baron Daniel Jackson in 1892, this ornate and colorful Victorian has been restored with incredible attention to detail. The roof alone has undergone an extensive restoration that involved installing a three-tone roof of composite slate material in stripes and diamond patterns. Even the metal detailing along the roof peaks has been custom crafted to match the Victorian style of 1892. The grand downstairs rooms all have oriental carpets, fine period furnishings and detailed woodwork. Upstairs are 5-plus suites, with marble baths and sumptuous bedrooms. Both downstairs and upstairs rooms are available for events.

CAPACITY: The Chateau can accommodate 125 guests for a standing reception and 50-60 for seated meals.

MEETING ROOMS: 2 suites, 15–35 participants.

FEES & DEPOSITS: A nonrefundable $250 deposit plus half of the rental cost are required to secure your event date. A $250 security deposit is also required, refundable within 30 days after event.

The rental fee for special events is $750–1200 for a 4-hour minimum rental, depending on the number of guests attending and the number of floors reserved. A $200/hour fee will be applied for any time over 4 hours. The antique piano can be rented for $50/event. If you wish to relocate major furniture pieces, a moving fee can be negotiated. For meetings, the fee is $250–1200, depending on the number of rooms and people attending.

CANCELLATION POLICY: If canceled 30 days in advance, the deposit will be refunded.

AVAILABILITY: 9am–11pm every day. Guests must be out by 11pm, caterer by midnight.

SERVICES/AMENITIES:

Restaurant Services: no
Catering: provided or BYO
Kitchen Facilities: moderate
Tables & Chairs: BYO
Linens, Silver, etc.: BYO
Restrooms: no wca
Dance Floor: yes

Parking: valet CBA, pkg lot CBA
Overnight Accommodations: 5 suites
Telephone: house phone
Outdoor Night Lighting: no
Outdoor Cooking Facilities: no
Cleanup: whoever caters event
Other: antique piano, $50

RESTRICTIONS:

Alcohol: BYO, no red wine
Smoking: outside only
Music: no amplified

Wheelchair Access: no
Insurance: not required

CIRCLE GALLERY

140 Maiden Lane
San Francisco, CA 94108
(415) 989-2100   Karen Anderson
Reserve: 1–2 months in advance

Located in the only Frank Lloyd Wright designed building in San Francisco, the Circle Gallery is found on a small, trendy street off Union Square. It's a superb address for corporate or nonprofit organization cocktail parties. Developed as a prototype for the Guggenheim Museum in New York City, the Circle Gallery offers a distinguished environment for people who appreciate contemporary art, with rotating exhibits that profile different artists. Wright's design creates perfect spaces for both large and small receptions, with two levels connected by a spiral ramp. Popular for holiday parties, reserve this gallery well in advance. No private parties are permitted.

CAPACITY: The Gallery can hold up to 350 guests for a reception. No seated functions.

FEES & DEPOSITS: A letter of intent is required to reserve your date. A deposit of 50% of the rental fee is required 1 week prior to your function and the balance is due at the beginning of the event. The rental fee is usually $1600 for a 5-hour block which includes insurance, staff and security along with the gallery space. The fee may vary depending on the guest count and the time of day.

CANCELLATION POLICY: With advance notice, the deposit will be refunded.

AVAILABILITY: Year-round, every day for group events (depending on group size) from 5pm–9pm. Closed major holidays.

SERVICES/AMENITIES:

Restaurant Services: no
Catering: preferred list or BYO with approval
Kitchen Facilities: no
Tables & Chairs: BYO
Linens, Silver, etc.: BYO
Restrooms: no wca
Dance Floor: no dancing

Parking: Union Square or Stockton Sutter garage
Overnight Accommodations: no
Telephone: office phone
Outdoor Night Lighting: no
Outdoor Cooking Facilities: no
Cleanup: caterer

RESTRICTIONS:

Alcohol: BYO, no red wine
Smoking: outside only

Music: amplified within limits
Wheelchair Access: yes

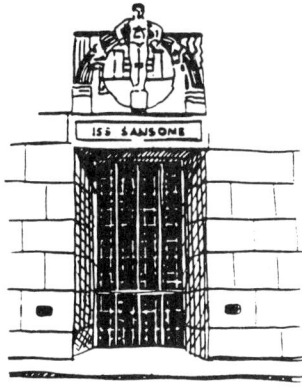

THE CITY CLUB ★★

155 Sansome Street
San Francisco, CA 94104
(415) 362-2480   Ellen Cafri
Reserve: 3–6 months in advance

Just walking into the lobby of the Stock Exchange Tower, situated in the heart of the financial district, gives you an inkling of what's to follow. The entry has highly polished black and green marble floors and black and white marble walls, gold ceiling and finely detailed metal elevators that whisk you up to the 10th floor. Here you enter the former watering hole for the Pacific Stock Exchange which has been painstakingly restored to its original integrity. The Club is located on the 10th and 11th floors and features one of the most striking and exquisite Art Deco interiors we've seen. Although the City Club is now a private club, you can arrange your event here if you're sponsored by a Club member or associate. This may not be too difficult a requirement if you have lots of friends who live or work in the City. The Club's 10th floor entry is through bronze-framed elevator doors decorated in silver, bronze and brass appliqué. A remarkable interior staircase complete with an original 30-foot high Diego Rivera fresco leads to the 11th floor. Furnishings are original Art Deco pieces and appointments are generously clad in black marble, silver and brass. The ceiling is stunning, covered with burnished gold leaf squares. The white baby grand piano is indicative of this facility's elegance and attention to detail. Make every attempt to find a sponsor—this is a truly exceptional place to hold a party, reception or business event.

CAPACITY: For private parties, the entire club (10th and 11th floors) must be reserved. The total capacity is 500 for a standing affair or 200 for a seated function.

MEETING ROOMS: 6 rooms, maximum 60 people.

FEES & DEPOSITS: A deposit is required, the amount dependent on several variables. Make sure you get specific information over the phone. For Saturday and Sunday parties, the minimum rental fee is $1000 for a 5-hour block. Should you desire more time, additional fees will apply. On weeknights, Monday through Friday, the fee for the Main Dining Room is $300 and for both floors, $600.

Food services are provided. On weekdays, there is a seated food and beverage service minimum of $3000, or a cocktail/hors d'oeuvres minimum of $2000. The weekend food and beverage service minimum is $4000. These fees do not include a 7.25% sales tax or 20% gratuity which are applied to the final bill.

CANCELLATION POLICY: If you cancel over 120 days in advance of your event, you will receive a full refund.

AVAILABILITY: The Club's Main Dining Room is available Monday–Friday after 4pm. The City Club is available on weekends.

SERVICES/AMENITIES:
Restaurant Services: yes
Catering: provided, no BYO
Kitchen Facilities: ample
Tables & Chairs: provided

Linens, Silver, etc.: provided
Restrooms: wca
Dance Floor: yes
Parking: CBA

Overnight Accommodations: no
Telephone: pay phone
Outdoor Night Lighting: no

RESTRICTIONS:
Alcohol: provided, no BYO
Smoking: allowed
Music: amplified ok

Outdoor Cooking Facilities: no
Cleanup: provided
Other: white baby grand piano

Wheelchair Access: yes
Insurance: not required

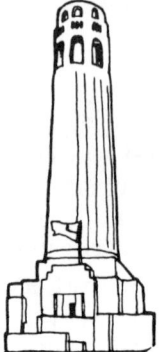

COIT TOWER

Telegraph Hill
San Francisco, CA
(415) 666-7024
Reserve: 2–12 months in advance

Before the Transamerica Pyramid, this was *the* symbol of San Francisco. Rising 180 feet above Telegraph Hill, this memorial to San Francisco's volunteer firemen is famous for its views of the City and the Bay. Upon her death, Lilly Coit left a sizable donation from which Coit Tower was developed in 1933. At the age of 15, she was the official mascot of knickerbocker Engine Co. #5 Volunteer Fire Department, and was best known for her life-long passion for firefighting. Lilly rarely missed a blaze. The historic murals inside were the first WPA-commissioned art project. Because of the fragility of these recently renovated frescoes, the caterer must set up outdoors or in tented areas around the Plaza. Bar setups are permitted in the upper level of the Tower.

CAPACITY: The Tower and Plaza can accommodate up to 250 guests.

FEES & DEPOSITS: Currently, a nonrefundable deposit of 10% of the total rental cost is due when the reservation is made. The rental fee ranges from $150–2500 depending on setup and tent arrangements. The fee balance plus any security and/or cleaning deposits are required 10 business days prior to the event. Fees are undergoing change; call for exact figures.

CANCELLATION POLICY: For cancellations made more than 10 (working) days prior to the event, a full refund will be given minus a $25 administration fee and/or the deposit.

AVAILABILITY: Year-round, after 5pm.

SERVICES/AMENITIES:
Restaurant Services: no
Catering: BYO
Kitchen Facilities: no
Tables & Chairs: BYO
Linens, Silver, etc.: BYO
Restrooms: wca
Dance Floor: no

Parking: shuttle buses or valet recommended
Overnight Accommodations: no
Telephone: pay phone
Outdoor Night Lighting: no
Outdoor Cooking Facilities: no
Cleanup: whoever caters event

RESTRICTIONS:
Alcohol: BYO
Smoking: outside only
Music: no amplified

Wheelchair Access: yes
Insurance: certificate required
Other: security guard required, decorations restricted

THE CONSERVATORY OF FLOWERS

Golden Gate Park
San Francisco, CA 94117
(415) 641-7978
Reserve: 6–9 months in advance

This large, graceful, ornate and mostly glass structure is the oldest existing building in Golden Gate Park and probably the best example of Victorian Greenhouse Architecture in the United States. Built in 1879, it's a national historic landmark, visited by over 250,000 people a year. (Be careful that you don't confuse this structure with the Hall of Flowers building.) The entire Conservatory is available for parties and special events. The West Wing is particularly well suited for dinners. It features a brick interior patio and displays of seven seasonal flower types. The East Wing features two ponds, waterfalls, rare aquatic plants and flowers. Palms and orchids abound in exotic profusion. The Conservatory is such a sensational and historically unique facility, your guests will never forget your event!

CAPACITY: The Conservatory accommodates 200 standing guests and 70 seated.

FEES & DEPOSITS: A nonrefundable $150 deposit is due when the contract is signed. The rental fee is $1200 for the evening and a refundable $300 damage deposit is also required. These fees are payable 2 weeks prior to your party and include the services of a security and staff person. The damage deposit will be returned within 6 weeks following your party.

CANCELLATION POLICY: If you cancel, your $150 deposit is forfeited.

AVAILABILITY: There are no day-time rentals. From April 1st to October 30th, 6:30pm–midnight, daily and holidays. From October 30th to April 1st, 5:30pm–midnight. Everyone, including the caterer, must vacate the premises by midnight.

SERVICES/AMENITIES:
Restaurant Services: no
Catering: BYO, licensed
Kitchen Facilities: minimal
Tables & Chairs: BYO
Linens, Silver, etc.: BYO
Restrooms: wca
Dance Floor: CBA, extra charge

Parking: large lot
Overnight Accommodations: no
Telephone: office phone
Outdoor Night Lighting: no
Outdoor Cooking Facilities: BYO BBQ
Cleanup: caterer

RESTRICTIONS:
Alcohol: BYO

Smoking: outside only

Music: no amplified
Wheelchair Access: yes

Insurance: liability required

CONTRACT DESIGN CENTER

600 Townsend Street
San Francisco, CA 94103
(415) 864-1500 Donna or David
Reserve: 3–6 months in advance

An atrium on a smaller scale, the Contract Design Center has a crisp, cool, clean style. White terrazzo flooring leads to a wall of uniquely constructed glass and a white vaulted ceiling gives the center height and interest. Adjacent to the atrium is a fully equipped conference room, ideal for business functions. And behind the atrium, visible through the glass wall, is a very versatile courtyard. Tented or left open to the sun, the spacious white aggregate patio lends itself to a variety of outdoor events.

CAPACITY, FEES & DEPOSITS:

Area	*Seated*	*Reception*	*Rental Fees*
Atrium	225	500	$2500/day
The Courtyard	250	500	—
Atrium & Courtyard	—	—	$3000/day
Conference Center	—	—	$500/day

A nonrefundable deposit of 50% of the rental fee is required when the contract is submitted. The balance is due 30 days prior to the event. Fees include a house technician.

MEETING ROOMS: The Conference Center holds up to 200 seated; the room can be divided into smaller sections.

CANCELLATION POLICY: The fees and deposits can be applied toward another event within a 90-day period.

AVAILABILITY: Year-round, Monday–Friday after 3pm, Saturday and Sunday from 8am. The Conference Center Monday–Friday from 8am.

SERVICES/AMENITIES:

Restaurant Services: no
Catering: preferred list or BYO w/approval
Kitchen Facilities: minimal
Tables & Chairs: provided
Linens, Silver, etc.: BYO
Restrooms: wca
Dance Floor: terrazzo floor

Parking: street, garage
Overnight Accommodations: no
Telephone: pay phones
Outdoor Night Lighting: yes
Outdoor Cooking Facilities: yes
Cleanup: provided
Other: event coordination, technician provided

RESTRICTIONS:

Alcohol: provided, no BYO
Smoking: allowed
Music: amplified ok

Wheelchair Access: yes
Insurance: certificate required

M. H. DE YOUNG
MEMORIAL MUSEUM

Golden Gate Park
San Francisco, CA 94118
(415) 750-3683   Kate Schlafly
Reserve: 1–12 months in advance

We think this is a very special site. Others agree—President Reagan hosted a State dinner for Queen Elizabeth II in the de Young's grand Hearst Court, a large, airy and regal space, with Spanish tile, arched ceiling and skylights. You can have your event here, too, if you're a corporation or a business association. The Museum sits in the heart of Golden Gate Park, next to the Japanese Tea Gardens. Here you can be treated to private tours of one of our country's finest collections of American art, featuring the works of Copley, Paul Revere, Remington, Winslow Homer, Grant Wood and Mary Cassatt. For corporate breakfasts, luncheons, cocktail receptions or formal dinners, the de Young offers impressive spaces for private entertaining. And, if your guests are interested in expanding their libraries, the museum book shop can be opened for any function.

CAPACITY: The Museum can hold up to 340 seated guests, 800 for a reception.

FEES & DEPOSITS: A refundable deposit of 30% of the rental fee is required to confirm reservations and the balance is due 2 weeks prior to the function. An event plan must be submitted at least 1 month prior to the event. The rental fee for 4 hours is $8500, for 2 hours, $6000. Fees include security, technician, custodial service, docents, coat check and event staff.

AVAILABILITY: Year-round, Monday and Tuesday from 8am, Wednesday–Sunday from 6:30pm.

SERVICES/AMENITIES:
Restaurant Services: no
Catering: BYO w/approval
Kitchen Facilities: no
Tables & Chairs: BYO
Linens, Silver, etc.: BYO
Restrooms: wca
Dance Floor: Hearst Court
Parking: large lot in front of building

Overnight Accommodations: no
Telephone: pay phone
Outdoor Night Lighting: no
Outdoor Cooking Facilities: BYO
Cleanup: caterer & custodian
Other: docent tours, coat check, security, engineer, event staff

RESTRICTIONS:
Alcohol: BYO
Smoking: outside only
Music: amplified restricted

Wheelchair Access: yes
Insurance: certificate required
Other: no open flames

FAIRMONT PENTHOUSE SUITE

Atop Nob Hill
San Francisco, CA 94106
(415) 772-5000 Sharon Arnold
Reserve: 3–12 months in advance

Atop posh Nob Hill, occupying an entire floor of the Fairmont Hotel, is a very exclusive and opulent penthouse suite. With black and white marble entry, a 40'x60' wood paneled drawing room, elaborate billiard room hand-tiled to resemble a Persian courtyard, 3 bedrooms with accompanying marble bathrooms (and gold plated knobs), two-story circular library with the celestial bodies painted in gold on the domed ceiling, four fireplaces inlaid with lapis, marble and wood, secret passageway and burglar-proof vault, this has to rank as one of the plushest places around for a private party. Surprise your friends. You can be assured they'll never forget your event if you have it here!

CAPACITY: Although size could permit more, the Fairmont restricts attendance to 50 people.

FEES & DEPOSITS: The entire $6000 fee for one evening is due when the reservation is made. The rental is $6000/night. Of course, an around-the-clock maid and butler come with the penthouse as do round-trip airport limousine service and a complementary bottle of champagne and glasses. Catering is provided by the Hotel's catering staff who are willing to customize any menu of your choice. Food, gratuity and taxes are not included in the room rate. Your final bill is payable on vacating the hotel premises.

AVAILABILITY: Any day, any time.

SPECIAL PACKAGE: For a mere $20,000 a night, your party of 20 guests can be wined and dined for the evening in luxurious style. Included are three Rolls Royces, accommodations for 6 in the penthouse, suites for 14 friends in the adjoining Fairmont Tower (so guests can stay overnight) followed by breakfast-in-bed for all and use of the Hotel's health club. Such a deal!

SERVICES/AMENITIES:

Restaurant Services: yes
Catering: provided, no BYO
Kitchen Facilities: ample
Tables & Chairs: provided
Linens, Silver, etc.: provided
Restrooms: wca
Dance Floor: yes

Parking: valet, extra charge
Overnight Accommodations: 600 rooms
Telephone: house phone
Outdoor Night Lighting: yes
Outdoor Cooking Facilities: no
Cleanup: provided
Other: stocked bar, maid & butler

RESTRICTIONS:

Alcohol: provided
Smoking: allowed
Music: no amplified

Wheelchair Access: yes
Insurance: not required

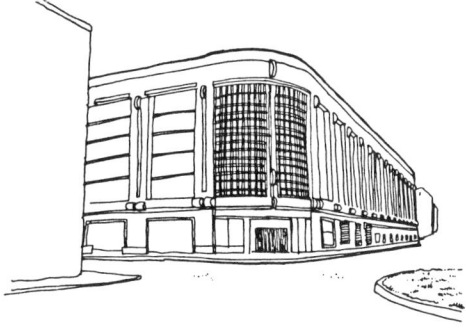

FASHION CENTER

699 8th Street
San Francisco, CA 94103
(415) 864-1500 Donna or David
Reserve: 3–6 months in advance

Brand new and monumental, the Fashion Center hosts events on a grand scale. Even the Lobby, a totally modern pre-function area, is almost 200 feet long! The Grand Atrium Theatre is the centerpiece of the building. Reminiscent of the Hyatt Regency downtown (they share the same architect) it is an immense atrium with an equally expansive skylight that fans out over a large seating area. Four floors, defined by white metal railings, offer a terrific view of the stage. The entire interior is painted white, providing a clean, neutral backdrop for all types of events. Downstairs, the Exhibition Hall is even more vast. Completely unadorned, this sea of space can easily seat 5,000. You provide the decor.

CAPACITY, FEES & DEPOSITS:

Area	Seated	Reception	Rental Fees
Exhibition Hall	4000	5000	$7500–10,000
Lobby	—	1000	negotiable
Atrium	1500	3000	$6500–7500
Meeting Rooms	see below	—	$350/day

A nonrefundable deposit of 50% of the rental fee is required when the contract is submitted. The balance is due 30 days prior to the event. Fees include a house technician.

MEETING ROOMS: 2 meeting rooms for 175–225 seated participants. A conference room is also available on the third floor for 225, theater-style.

CANCELLATION POLICY: The fees and deposits can be applied toward another event within a 90-day period.

AVAILABILITY: Year-round, every day Monday–Friday from 3pm, Saturday and Sunday from 8am. Closed for private functions during seasonal market periods.

SERVICES/AMENITIES:

Restaurant Services: no
Catering: preferred list, BYO w/approval
Kitchen Facilities: minimal
Tables & Chairs: provided
Linens, Silver, etc.: BYO
Restrooms: wca
Dance Floor: yes

Parking: street, roof garage
Overnight Accommodations: no
Telephone: pay phones
Outdoor Night Lighting: no
Outdoor Cooking Facilities: no
Cleanup: provided
Other: event & fashion show coordination

RESTRICTIONS:

Alcohol: provided, no BYO
Smoking: allowed
Music: amplified ok

Wheelchair Access: yes
Insurance: certificate required

THE FLOOD MANSION ★

2222 Broadway
San Francisco, CA 94115
(415) 563-2900   Mrs. Hackman
Reserve: 3–12 months in advance

The Flood Mansion is a symphony of classical styles—Italian Renaissance, Rococo, Tudor and Georgian. This elegant marble building, constructed in 1915, has remained well preserved since Mrs. Flood donated her home to the Religious of the Sacred Heart in 1939. Although the building is now used as a private school, it is available for special events after school hours. The Mansion is impressive. Its Grand Hall is 140 feet long with marble floors and great views of the Bay. The Adam Room, near the entry, is quite lovely with high, ornate ceilings, specially designed wood tables and chairs plus a marble fireplace. The beautiful Reception Room, at the end of the Grand Hall, boasts magnificent coffered ceiling, painted murals in golds, blues and greens, and hardwood parquet floors. This room is architecturally complex and detailed. A pretty, enclosed courtyard off of the Grand Hall is available for outdoor gatherings, weather permitting. The Mansion is definitely the place for a stately and elegant party.

CAPACITY: The entire main floor has a standing capacity for 450 people, and a seated capacity of approximately 300. Individual seated capacities: the Grand Hall, 200; the Adam Room, 60; and the Reception Room, 80–100 people. In addition, there is a theater area downstairs.

FEES & DEPOSITS: 50% of the total rental fee is the deposit required to secure your event date. Also required is a $1000 custodial and security fee, some of which may be reimbursable. The rental fee is $5000 for the facility. The final balance is due 2 weeks prior to the event.

CANCELLATION POLICY: Should you cancel, the rental deposit is not refundable. The $1000 custodial and security deposit is refundable.

AVAILABILITY: Fridays after 3pm, Saturday and Sunday all day. All events must end by midnight. No hourly minimum rental block is required.

SERVICES/AMENITIES:

Restaurant Services: no
Catering: select from list
Kitchen Facilities: ample
Tables & Chairs: BYO
Linens, Silver, etc.: BYO
Restrooms: wca
Dance Floor: yes

Parking: valet CBA, extra charge
Overnight Accommodations: no
Telephone: pay phone
Outdoor Night Lighting: no
Outdoor Cooking Facilities: no
Cleanup: caterer
Other: 2 baby grand pianos

RESTRICTIONS:

Alcohol: BYO
Smoking: outside only
Music: amplified until 11:30pm

Wheelchair Access: yes
Insurance: extra liability required

FOREST HILL CLUB HOUSE

381 Magellan Ave.
San Francisco, CA 94116
(415) 664-0542 Will Connolly
Reserve: 3–6 months in advance

The Club House, an architectural gem designed by Bernard Maybeck, is tucked away in a very nice neighborhood of private residences. Completed in 1919, the building's exterior and interior are decorative yet rustic, representing the final phase of the turn-of-the-century American Arts and Crafts movement. The interior features a large, long room with hardwood floors and a sizable fireplace. The furniture in several rooms may have been designed by Bernard Maybeck. The adjacent brick patio and garden completed in 1966 is a great spot for outdoor parties in warm, sunny weather. For weekday meetings, the Club House is available with little advance notice. This is a small but charming facility.

CAPACITY: The Club House can accommodate 200 standing guests and approximately 100 seated guests. The dance floor is large enough for 50 dancers.

FEES & DEPOSITS: 50% of the total rental fee is required when you reserve your date. A $250 refundable security/cleaning deposit is due 6 weeks prior to the event and is usually returned within 30 days after the event. On Friday, Saturday and Sunday, the fee is $950–1000. Weekdays, it is $500. Overtime is permissible at $50/hour. The remaining 50% balance is due when the contract is signed, about 6 weeks before the event.

CANCELLATION POLICY: 50% of the rental fee is retained if the date can not be rebooked. If rebooked, the entire rental deposit will be refunded.

AVAILABILITY: Any time, up to midnight. An 8-hour block is the required minimum.

SERVICES/AMENITIES:

Restaurant Services: no
Catering: BYO
Kitchen Facilities: moderate
Tables & Chairs: some provided
Linens, Silver, etc.: BYO
Restrooms: wca limited

Dance Floor: yes
Parking: on street
Overnight Accommodations: no
Telephone: pay phone
Outdoor Night Lighting: yes
Outdoor Cooking Facilities: BYO BBQ
Cleanup: caterer & renter

RESTRICTIONS:

Alcohol: BYO
Smoking: allowed
Music: amplified ok

Wheelchair Access: limited
Insurance: not required

FORT MASON
CONFERENCE CENTER

Fort Mason Center
San Francisco, CA 94123
(415) 441-5706 Conference Center Director
Reserve: 6 months in advance

Located at the south end of Landmark Building A at Fort Mason, the Conference Center is well situated to provide an extraordinary environment for functions: meetings, seminars, art exhibits, trade shows and fund raisers. Three different sized rooms, with track lighting, carpets, high ceilings and hanging banners offer varied meeting and party opportunities. The view of the Golden Gate Bridge is outstanding, as is the view of the nearby yacht harbor, especially when lit up at night.

CAPACITY: The Conference Center includes 1 large room, seated capacity 300; a mid-size room for up to 80; and 2 breakout rooms, each with a seated capacity of 20.

FEES & DEPOSITS: A $50–350 security deposit is required, depending on the size and type of event, and is returned after the function. Payment of the deposit secures your event date. Rental rates vary depending on the type of event, day and number of rooms rented. For the largest room, the fee is $300–600; $150–175 for the medium-sized room; and $100 for the smaller room. The deposit is due when reservations are made; the rental fee is due 1 month prior to the event date.

CANCELLATION POLICY: If you cancel more than 30 days prior to your function, a full refund minus a $25 processing fee will apply. If under 30 days, Fort Mason will normally refund the security deposit, minus the $25 fee, only if they can rebook the space.

AVAILABILITY: From 7:30am Monday–Friday; from 8am on weekends. Guests and caterer must vacate the premises by midnight; 1am by request.

SERVICES/AMENITIES:

Restaurant Services: no
Catering: BYO
Kitchen Facilities: no
Tables & Chairs: provided
Linens, Silver, etc.: BYO, can be rented
Restrooms: wca
Dance Floor: can be rented

Parking: large lot
Overnight Accommodations: no
Telephone: pay phone
Outdoor Night Lighting: no
Outdoor Cooking Facilities: CBA
Cleanup: caterer & Fort Mason

RESTRICTIONS:

Alcohol: BYO
Smoking: outside only
Music: amplified ok

Wheelchair Access: yes
Insurance: not required

FORT MASON
COWELL THEATER

Fort Mason Center
San Francisco, CA 94123
(415) 441-5706   General Manager
Reserve: 3 months–2 years in advance

Fort Mason's Cowell Theater, located on the north end of historic Pier 2 has spectacular views of the Golden Gate Bridge, the Bay and the hills of Marin. San Francisco's newest performance facility is a fully equipped, state-of-the-art 440-seat theater. As a part of the Fort Mason Center, Cowell Theater is dedicated to serving the needs of performing artists, as well as to accommodating a wide diversity of community events, benefits, conferences, seminars and corporate meetings.

CAPACITY: The Theater has 439 permanent seats and 10 spaces for wheelchairs. The spacious lobby can hold 125 people for receptions and other gatherings.

FEES & DEPOSITS: A $250–500 refundable security deposit reserves your date. The rental fee ranges from $500–1000/day. For a lobby reception the additional fee is $75. The balance of the rental fee and security deposit are due 30 days prior to the event.

CANCELLATION POLICY: If you cancel, the deposit is forfeited; with less than 3 months' notice, the rental fees may be forfeited.

AVAILABILITY: Any day from 8am–midnight.

SERVICES/AMENITIES:
Restaurant Services: no
Catering: provided for public performances, BYO for private events
Kitchen Facilities: CBA
Tables & Chairs: limited
Linens, Silver, etc.: BYO
Restrooms: wca
Dance Floor: no

Parking: large lot
Overnight Accommodations: no
Telephone: pay phone
Outdoor Night Lighting: no
Outdoor Cooking Facilities: no
Cleanup: caterer & Fort Mason

RESTRICTIONS:
Alcohol: BYO
Smoking: outside only
Music: amplified ok

Wheelchair Access: yes
Insurance: not required

FORT MASON FIREHOUSE

Fort Mason Center
San Francisco, CA 94123
(415) 441-5706   Conference Center Director
Reserve: 2 weeks–3 months in advance

The Firehouse is a separate warehouse-looking building within Fort Mason Center, located right on the water's edge and next to the docked Liberty Ship, SS Jeremiah O'Brien. This is really an old firehouse which has been renovated to accommodate events. The 27ft x 47ft foot central room is airy and pleasant, with Casablanca fans and colorful pastel banners flying from the tall ceiling. Three adjacent breakout rooms make the Firehouse well suited for meetings and other business functions. The view of Alcatraz and the Bay is sensational.

CAPACITY: The Firehouse can accommodate 150 standing guests and 132 with theater-style seating.

FEES & DEPOSITS: A $100–300 security deposit, depending on the size and type of event, is required and is returned after the function. Payment of the deposit secures your event date. The $200–450 rental fee varies depending on type of event and day of the week. The deposit is due when reservations are made; the fee is due 1 month prior to the event.

CANCELLATION POLICY: If you cancel more than 30 days prior to your function, a full refund minus a $25 processing fee will apply. If under 30 days, Fort Mason will normally refund the security deposit, minus the $25 fee, only if they can rebook the space.

AVAILABILITY: From 7:30am Monday–Friday; from 8am on weekends. Guests and caterer must vacate premises by midnight; 1am by request.

SERVICES/AMENITIES:

Restaurant Services: no
Catering: BYO
Kitchen Facilities: no
Tables & Chairs: provided
Linens, Silver, etc.: BYO, can be rented
Restrooms: no wca
Dance Floor: can be rented

Parking: large lot
Overnight Accommodations: no
Telephone: pay phone
Outdoor Night Lighting: no
Outdoor Cooking Facilities: BYO BBQ
Cleanup: caterer & Fort Mason

RESTRICTIONS:

Alcohol: BYO
Smoking: outside only
Music: amplified ok

Wheelchair Access: yes
Insurance: not required

GALLERIA DESIGN CENTER ★

101 Kansas Street
San Francisco, CA 94103
(415) 864-1500 Donna or David
Reserve: 3–6 months in advance

The Galleria Design Center is renowned around the Bay Area as *the* place to celebrate. A spectacular four-story atrium, it soars 60 feet to a retractable skylight. Sun pours in when the weather's fine, and at night you really can see the stars. Hundreds of glittering lights enhance the exposed infrastructure and tall plants provide the only other decoration. A large, theatrical stage is ready-made for corporate events, fashion shows, and superb parties. Tiered levels provide dining or meeting space with excellent views of the stage. Vast and inviting, the Galleria is a distinctive event spot.

CAPACITY, FEES & DEPOSITS:

Area	Seated	Reception	Rental Fees
Atrium	1200 (4 floors)	2500	$5500/day

A nonrefundable deposit of 50% of the rental fee is required when the contract is submitted. The balance is due 30 days prior to the event. Fees include a house technician.

CANCELLATION POLICY: The fees and deposits can be applied toward another event within a 90-day period.

AVAILABILITY: Year-round, Monday–Friday after 3pm, Saturday and Sunday from 8am except for seasonal market periods.

SERVICES/AMENITIES:

Restaurant Services: no
Catering: in-house caterer or BYO w/approval, extra fee
Kitchen Facilities: minimal
Tables & Chairs: some provided
Linens, Silver, etc.: BYO
Restrooms: wca
Dance Floor: terrazzo floor

Parking: street, garage
Overnight Accommodations: no
Telephone: pay phones
Outdoor Night Lighting: no
Outdoor Cooking Facilities: yes
Cleanup: provided
Other: event coordination, stage, equipment & technician provided

RESTRICTIONS:

Alcohol: provided, no BYO
Smoking: allowed
Music: amplified ok

Wheelchair Access: yes
Insurance: certificate required

GIFT CENTER PAVILION ★

888 Brannan Street
San Francisco, CA 94103
(415) 861-7733 Evelyn Marks
Reserve: 1–12 months in advance

The Gift Center Pavilion is an extremely appealing event space. Four stories high, it is painted light dusky pink and teal, and is capped by a skylight that covers most of the ceiling and opens to sun or stars. The center of the room is sunken, making a natural area for dancing or presentations. Seating is often arranged above on the surrounding tiers and second and third floors, giving guests a great view of the activities below. The Gift Center also has a large stage, and a quarter of a million dollars worth of sound and lighting equipment. And if all this were not enough, they are noted for innovative decorations with streamers, banners and neon lights that will make your event a visual treat.

CAPACITY: The Pavilion can hold 150–2500 for a cocktail reception, 1100 seated guests or 1800 for a reception with food service.

FEES & DEPOSITS: A nonrefundable deposit of 50% of the total rental package is due when the contract is submitted. The total balance is due 10 days prior to the event. Rental fees range from $3500–6000 depending on the day of the week, level(s) rented and guest count. The fee includes setup, janitorial services, 2 security guards plus lighting and sound services. For technical personnel, there will be additional charges.

AVAILABILITY: Year-round, every day from 6am–2am, except during gift shows.

SERVICES/AMENITIES:
Restaurant Services: no
Catering: inside caterer, BYO w/approval
Kitchen Facilities: fully equipped
Tables & Chairs: provided or BYO
Linens, Silver, etc.: provided or BYO
Restrooms: wca
Dance Floor: yes

Parking: large lots, street
Overnight Accommodations: no
Telephone: pay phone
Outdoor Night Lighting: no
Outdoor Cooking Facilities: no
Cleanup: provided

RESTRICTIONS:
Alcohol: caterer, BYO corkage $5-7/bottle
Smoking: allowed
Music: amplified ok

Wheelchair Access: yes
Insurance: certificate required
Other: guests must be over 21 years of age

GOLDEN GATE PARK ★

Golden Gate Park
San Francisco, CA 94117
(415) 666-7024   Marketing Section
Reserve: 1–12 months in advance

In Golden Gate Park, the variety of locations for parties and corporate outdoor functions are almost unlimited. The City's Recreation and Parks Department even offers deluxe 'Play Packages' which can include activities such as paddleboating, mountain biking, tennis, flycasting and golf, to name a few. Whether it's exclusive use of the Carrousel, the Conservatory of Flowers or tours through the Strybing Arboretum and Japanese Tea Garden, it can be arranged. There's even an equestrian arena in the park to accommodate a private rodeo. Specific locations include but are not limited to the following:

The Shakespeare Garden	Japanese Tea Garden	Carrousel
Queen Wilhelmina Tulip Garden	Equestrian Arena	Strybing Arboretum
The Rose Garden	Conservatory of Flowers	Pioneer Log Cabin Area
Marx Meadow	Lindley Meadow	Children's Playground
Sharon Arts Building	County Fair Building	

CAPACITY: Varies greatly, from 100-25,000 people. Call for specifics about each area.

FEES & DEPOSITS: Fees and deposits vary depending on the space(s) desired and the number of people attending. Corporate picnics average $500/day; private parties $100/day.

CANCELLATION POLICY: If you cancel 30 days prior to the event, 90% of the deposit is refunded; if less than 5 working days prior to your event, no refund.

AVAILABILITY: Park areas are usually available from 9am to dusk every day. Special arrangements must be made for evening use.

SERVICES/AMENITIES:

Restaurant Services: no

Catering: BYO

Kitchen Facilities: no

Tables & Chairs: BYO

Linens, Silver, etc.: BYO

Restrooms: location and wca varies

Dance Floor: no

Parking: on street

Overnight Accommodations: no

Telephone: pay phones

Outdoor Night Lighting: no

Outdoor Cooking Facilities: designated areas

Cleanup: whoever caters event

RESTRICTIONS:

Alcohol: BYO

Smoking: allowed

Music: no amplified

Wheelchair Access: yes

Insurance: not required

Other: you must provide your own security

GOLDEN SUNSET

Blue and Gold Fleet, Pier 37
San Francisco, CA 94133
(415) 781-7890
Reserve: 1–6 months in advance

The Golden Sunset is a new, sleek yacht available for private party and corporate entertaining charters on San Francisco Bay. The vessel is comprised of 3 decks housing a master stateroom with a queen bed, VCR and private marble bath with jacuzzi. Entertainment can be brought aboard or supplied through an elaborate state-of-the-art sound system complete with compact disc and cassette capabilities. Since there's no structured route, feel free to plan your individual charter around the Bay with the captain, or arrange (for an additional charge) for another pick up or drop-off point other than Pier 39. For a memorable board meeting or sales and promotion event, this is a unique choice.

CAPACITY: The Golden Sunset can accommodate 44–100 guests on board, depending on the function. The vessel can hold standing receptions for 80–100 people, seated meals for approximately 44.

FEES & DEPOSITS: To secure your date, a $500 refundable deposit is required 10 working days after making a reservation. Yacht rental is $700/hour, 2-hour minimum rental during the day (provided that the vessel returns by 6pm), 3-hour minimum rental is required after 6pm. Some holidays carry a 4-hour minimum yacht charge. Catering is provided. Hors d'oeuvres start at $14.50/person and seated meals from $22.50/person. Hosted bars require a deposit of $500. Gratuity is 18% with a minimum service charge of $250, sales tax 7.25%. The final balance is due 10 working days prior to your event.

CANCELLATION POLICY: Your deposit is returned if you cancel 30 days prior to the party.

AVAILABILITY: Any time. Bookings are tight June through September.

SERVICES/AMENITIES:

Restaurant Services: no
Catering: provided, no BYO
Kitchen Facilities: n/a
Tables & Chairs: provided
Linens, Silver, etc.: provided
Restrooms: no wca
Dance Floor: CBA

Parking: Pier 39 garage
Overnight Accommodations: no
Telephone: emergency only
Outdoor Night Lighting: yes
Outdoor Cooking Facilities: no
Cleanup: provided
Other: VHS capability

RESTRICTIONS:

Alcohol: provided, BYO corkage $10/bottle
Smoking: outside only
Music: amplified ok

Wheelchair Access: no
Insurance: not required

GRAND HYATT ★
SAN FRANCISCO
At Union Square

345 Stockton Street
San Francisco, CA 94108
(415) 398-1234
Reserve: 1 week–12 months in advance

On December 4, 1989, The Hyatt on Union Square closed for renovations. Two months later, completely refurbished at a cost of $20 million, it reopened as the Grand Hyatt San Francisco. Located in the heart of The City, just minutes from the financial district and convention center, the new Hyatt offers exceptional facilities for business events. Featuring 22,000 square feet of meeting space and a 7,000 square foot ballroom, the hotel is the perfect choice for meetings and conferences. The Hyatt's Conference Theater is a fabulous room for presentations. In addition to the functional elements of stage, screen and AV equipment, it was carefully designed with plush leather upholstered seating and individual curved table areas with lighting in front of each seat. The Executive Business Center is another feature businesses will appreciate: word processing, secretarial, notary public, language translation, fax, and airline ticketing services are all available. The Grand Hyatt is not just a business person's paradise, however. Many areas easily accommodate all types of events. The Bayview and Union Square rooms on the 36th floor are perfect for parties or receptions. Designed with an abundance of glass and subtle decor, they offer a spacious and inviting environment with extraordinary views of the city and bay below. The Grand Hyatt is a cosmopolitan hotel with the staff, facilities and services to satisfy the needs of every guest.

CAPACITY:	*Area*	*Classroom-style*	*Banquet*	*Theater-style*	*Reception*
	Plaza Ballroom	640	720	1000	1000
	Conference Theater	70	—	—	—
	Union Square/				
	Bayview Rooms	150	250	—	300

MEETING ROOMS: 19 rooms that can accommodate 5–1000 guests.

FEES & DEPOSITS: A deposit is required to secure your date and is due when the contract is submitted. The amount is negotiable depending on the guest count, date and room(s) reserved. Room rental charges vary from $150–$10,000 and normally apply only when there is no food or other service required; these may be waived depending on the total amount of services provided. Usually, the estimated food and beverage total plus the final guest count are required 72 hours prior to the event. The final balance is due 7 working days prior to the event unless credit has been established. Average rates, per person: hors d'oeuvres $15, continental breakfasts $10, seated breakfasts $16, brunch $30, luncheons $24 and dinners $33. Tax of 7.25% and a 15% gratuity are additional.

CANCELLATION POLICY: If the space(s) can be rebooked, the deposit is refunded.

AVAILABILITY: Year-round, every day, any time.

SERVICES/AMENITIES:

Restaurant Services: yes
Catering: provided, no BYO
Kitchen Facilities: n/a
Tables & Chairs: provided
Linens, Silver, etc.: provided
Restrooms: wca
Dance Floor: yes
Parking: valet

Overnight Accommodations: 693 guestrooms
Telephone: pay phones
Outdoor Night Lighting: yes
Outdoor Cooking Facilities: CBA
Cleanup: provided
Other: event coordination, conference & convention planning

RESTRICTIONS:

Alcohol: provided, BYO corkage $15/bottle
Smoking: designated areas
Music: amplified ok

Wheelchair Access: yes
Insurance: not required

THE GREEN ROOM ★

Veterans Building, Second Floor
San Francisco, CA 94102
(415) 621-6600 Elizabeth or Alberta
Reserve: 9–12 months in advance

The Green Room is actually green. But don't let that stop you from taking a healthy interest in this fabulous party facility. It's an outstanding and elegant place for a meeting, reception or performance. The Room has an incredibly high ivory and gold leaf ceiling, hardwood parquet floor, large pillars, mirrors and five stunning chandeliers adorning its interior. The Green Room opens onto a terra cotta-tiled loggia (balcony) which overlooks the enormous rotunda of City Hall. At night, from the loggia's vantage point, the view of the lighted City Hall is truly breathtaking.

CAPACITY: The room can accommodate 500 standing and 300 seated guests if there's no dancing. Dancing will reduce guest capacity.

FEES & DEPOSITS: To secure your date, a nonrefundable $100 deposit is required plus a $200 refundable cleaning deposit. The rental fee is $500 plus the event manager's cost at $21.24/hour. Holidays are an additional $50. Fees include pre-custodial service. Any other assistance is additional, such as setup/ breakdown attendant, security or custodial services.

AVAILABILITY: Any time. If you rent this facility before 8am or after midnight, you will be charged for staff at time and a half.

SERVICES/AMENITIES:

Restaurant Services: no
Catering: BYO
Kitchen Facilities: minimal

Tables & Chairs: provided, extra charge
Linens, Silver, etc.: BYO
Restrooms: wca

Dance Floor: yes
Parking: nearby garage
Overnight Accommodations: no
Telephone: pay phone, lines CBA at extra cost

RESTRICTIONS:
Alcohol: BYO
Smoking: outside only
Music: amplified ok with restrictions

Outdoor Night Lighting: on loggia
Outdoor Cooking Facilities: no
Cleanup: whoever caters event

Wheelchair Access: yes
Insurance: extra liability & damage required
Other: decorating restrictions

GREENS

Fort Mason, Building A
San Francisco, CA 94123
(415) 771-7955 Rick Jones
Reserve: 1–6 months in advance

Greens is a special restaurant, not just because it's located at Fort Mason, or because it's owned by a Zen Buddhist organization, or because it only serves gourmet vegetarian fare with flair. This place is special because the space makes you feel so good. Greens has enormous multi-paned windows extending the entire length of the restaurant. These windows have superb views of the Golden Gate Bridge and of the boat harbor which lies directly beyond the building. At sunset, the waning light reflected off the bridge and boats is a stunning sight to see. The interior of Greens is also exceptional, with really good original art work, unusual carved wood seating and tables, plus a high vaulted ceiling. The overall impression is light, airy and comfortable.

CAPACITY: Greens can accommodate 140 for a sit-down meal, and 250 for a cocktail reception.

FEES & DEPOSITS: A $250 nonrefundable damage deposit is required to secure your event date. It is due when the event date is booked, and is credited to the final billing. Full meal service is provided. Rates vary according to group size: $45–55/person for a 50-person dinner; $25–35/person for 100 guests. These figures include space rental for 4 hours, labor, linens, flowers and candles. Gratuity and tax will be added to the final billing. Beyond 4 hours, there is a $200/hour fee.

AVAILABILITY: Restricted to Sundays from 5pm onwards and Mondays from 10am-10pm.

SERVICES/AMENITIES:
Restaurant Services: yes
Catering: no BYO
Kitchen Facilities: n/a
Tables & Chairs: provided
Linens, Silver, etc.: provided
Restrooms: wca
Dance Floor: CBA, extra cost

Parking: large lot
Overnight Accommodations: no
Telephone: pay phone
Outdoor Night Lighting: no
Outdoor Cooking Facilities: no
Cleanup: provided

RESTRICTIONS:
Alcohol: provided, WBC only
Smoking: allowed
Music: amplified ok

Wheelchair Access: ramp
Insurance: not required

HAAS-LILIENTHAL HOUSE

2007 Franklin Street at Washington
San Francisco, CA 94109
(415) 441-3011 Events Coordinator
Reserve: 6 months in advance

The Haas-Lilienthal House is a stately gray Victorian located in Pacific Heights. It is one of the few houses that remains largely as it was when occupied by the Haas and Lilienthal families from 1886–1972. The house provides a unique and intimate environment for an event or meeting (the ballroom is great for business presentations). The main floor has 13-foot ceilings, two large parlors and formal dining room, foyer and hall. The interior is very attractive, with subtle colors, oriental carpets, rich woodwork and turn-of-the-century furnishings. This architectural treasure is very comfortable and warm inside.

CAPACITY: The house can accommodate 225 guests for a standing reception; 80 seated in the ballroom and 50 seated on the main floor. The ballroom can seat 100 auditorium-style.

FEES & DEPOSITS: A $500 refundable deposit is required and is usually returned 30 days after the event. Fees range from $750–2000 depending on the number of guests.

CANCELLATION POLICY: You must cancel 90 days prior to your party to receive a refund.

AVAILABILITY: Monday, Tuesday and Thursday until 10pm; Friday and Saturday until 11pm; Wednesday and Sunday 5pm–10pm.

SERVICES/AMENITIES:

Restaurant Services: no
Catering: BYO, select from list
Kitchen Facilities: yes
Tables & Chairs: most provided
Linens, Silver, etc.: BYO
Restrooms: no wca
Dance Floor: yes

Parking: on street, valet CBA
Overnight Accommodations: no
Telephone: emergency only
Outdoor Night Lighting: no
Outdoor Cooking Facilities: BYO BBQ
Cleanup: caterer

RESTRICTIONS:

Alcohol: BYO, no red wine at stand-up events
Smoking: outside only
Music: amplified with restrictions

Wheelchair Access: no
Insurance: not required

HAMLIN MANSION

2120 Broadway
San Francisco, CA 94115
(415) 331-0544
Reserve: 6–12 months in advance

The Hamlin Mansion is an impressive structure, both inside and out. The interior features the elegant and spacious Foyer and the two-story Great Hall, complete with ornate oak columns, herringbone hardwood floors and crowned by a richly detailed leaded glass skylight. The magnificent staircase, backed on the landing by a huge leaded glass window, is perfect for dramatic entries. The Main Dining Room has a striking black marble and gold fireplace and great views of the Bay. With Italian hand-laid mosaic tile on its floor and walls plus lovely leaded Tiffany-style skylights, the Solarium is a jewel of old-fashioned craftsmanship. Upstairs are several rooms with sensational ornate plaster ceilings, painted detailing and fireplaces. Use the downstairs rooms or setup bar and tables on the upstairs balcony. With classic lines and plenty of rich detailing, the Mansion makes a wonderful place for an upscale party or business function.

CAPACITY: The Mansion can hold up to 200 seated guests; or 350 for a standing reception.

FEES & DEPOSITS: A $500 security deposit is required when the contract is signed. The rental fee for a 7-hour block is $3500, payable 2 months prior to the event. Valet service runs $400–1000 and a security guard is $140/event.

CANCELLATION POLICY: $150 is refundable with notice of 90 days or more.

AVAILABILITY: Sunday–Thursday to 10pm, Friday–Saturday to 11:30pm.

SERVICES/AMENITIES:

Restaurant Services: no
Catering: provided, no BYO
Kitchen Facilities: n/a
Tables & Chairs: provided
Linens, Silver, etc.: caterer
Restrooms: wca
Dance Floor: yes

Parking: valet
Overnight Accommodations: no
Telephone: pay phone
Outdoor Night Lighting: no
Outdoor Cooking Facilities: no
Cleanup: caterer
Other: baby grand piano

RESTRICTIONS:

Alcohol: BYO
Smoking: allowed
Music: amplified with volume limit

Wheelchair Access: limited, elevator
Insurance: recommended
Other: decorations restricted

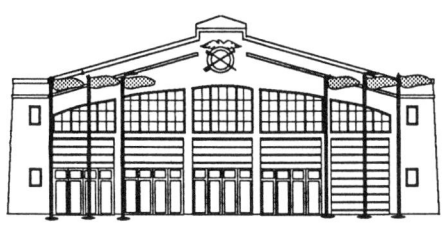

HERBST AND FESTIVAL PAVILIONS

Fort Mason Center
San Francisco, CA 94123
(415) 441-5706 Director of Sales
Reserve: 3 months–2 years in advance

Theme parties, festivals, trade shows, exhibits and conventions all come alive in these historic waterfront spaces. The Festival Pavilion (Pier 3) has an extraordinary 50,000 sq. ft. of clear-span space, which includes a mezzanine cafe/bar with great views of the Bay and Golden Gate Bridge. The Herbst Pavilion (Pier 2) has 30,000 sq. ft. of open space and offers the same flexible and highly unique surroundings. Both piers have recently undergone extensive renovations and have white interiors, stunning glass entries, stainless steel food preparation areas and tiled restrooms. If you've got a large crowd, the Pavilions can handle it.

CAPACITY: Festival Pavilion up to 5,000; Herbst Pavilion up to 3,000 people.

FEES & DEPOSITS: A $100–3000 portion of the rental fee reserves your date along with a $2000–3000 refundable security deposit. The rental fee is $1500–3250/day depending on the type of event and Pavilion selected. The balance of the rental fee and security deposit are due 30 days prior to the event. If food is served on site, there is a catering fee $.50–1.00/person.

CANCELLATION POLICY: If you cancel, the deposit is forfeited; with less than 3 months' notice, the rental fees may be forfeited.

AVAILABILITY: Year-round, every day 8am–midnight.

SERVICES/AMENITIES:

Restaurant Services: no
Catering: BYO
Kitchen Facilities: large food prep
Tables & Chairs: limited numbers
Linens, Silver, etc.: BYO
Restrooms: wca
Dance Floor: can be rented

Parking: large lots
Overnight Accommodations: no
Telephone: pay phone, client phone lines
Outdoor Night Lighting: no
Outdoor Cooking Facilities: BYO BBQ
Cleanup: client provides

RESTRICTIONS:

Alcohol: BYO
Smoking: outside only
Music: amplified ok

Wheelchair Access: yes
Insurance: required

HORNBLOWER DINING YACHTS

Various Locations
(415) 394-8900 ext 6
Reserve: see each vessel below

Hornblower Dining Yachts offers a wide range of vessels for hire, from sleek yachts to a replica of a turn-of-the-century coastal steamer, and an assortment of services from customized banners and buoys to balloons and flowers. With so many facilities available, you're sure to find something that will fit your needs and budget. Packages for a minimum of 30 people are available and include boat rental, food, beverage, entertainment, gratuity and tax. Also note that remote pickups and dropoffs can be arranged at many locations for an additional charge. Some good news is that Hornblower offers a 'good weather' guarantee that applies to rentals made between November 1st and March 31st.

CAPTAIN HORNBLOWER & ADMIRAL HORNBLOWER

These two vessels are similar in design, including full galley, 2 decks, parquet floors, bar and sound systems. **Reserve:** 1–3 months in advance.

CAPACITY: Each boat has standing room for 75 people, and for a seated function, room for 60.

FEES & DEPOSITS: A $1000 deposit is required and is due 7–10 days after setting a tentative date. Rental rates run $175–325/hour (weekends are more) for a 3-hour minimum rental. Catering is provided and approximate food service costs are $30/person for a cocktail reception, $50/person for a seated meal, and bar setup $150. Gratuity 15%, tax 7.25% are not included in these rates. Any remaining balance is due 3 days prior to your function.

CANCELLATION POLICY: You must cancel 2 months in advance of the event or forfeit the deposit. If the date can be rebooked, it will be refunded.

AVAILABILITY: Any time, 8am–2am.

LORD HORNBLOWER

This is a brand new copy of a turn-of-the-century coastal steamer with 2 large dining salons, 2 bars, full galley, parquet dance floor, sound system and sun deck. **Reserve:** 1–3 months in advance. (Available late 1990.)

CAPACITY: This vessel can accommodate 450 for cocktails/buffet and 300 for seated meals.

FEES & DEPOSITS: A $200–3000 deposit is required 7 days after booking. Fees vary:

Days	Hours	Fee	Min. Rental
Monday–Friday	before 6pm	$1000/hr	3 hours
Sunday–Thursday	after 6pm	$1500/hr	3 hours
Weekends	6pm Fri–	$1800/hr	4 hours Sat
	6pm Sun		3 hours Sun

Catering is provided and approximate food service costs are $30/person for a cocktail reception, $50/person for a seated meal, and bar setup $150. Gratuity 15%, tax 7.25% are not included in these rates. A package for a minimum of 150 people is available which includes boat rental, food, beverage, entertainment, gratuity and tax. Any remaining balance is due 3 days prior to your function.

CANCELLATION POLICY: You must cancel 120 days in advance of the event or forfeit the deposit. If the date can be rebooked, it will be refunded.

AVAILABILITY: Monday through Sunday, any time

COMMODORE HORNBLOWER

A gracious, custom built motor yacht which offers 2 decks, all wood interiors, parquet dance floor, 2 bars, full galley and sound system. **Reserve:** 3–6 months in advance.

CAPACITY: This vessel can hold up to 150 for a standing reception, and 130 for a sit-down affair.

FEES & DEPOSITS: A $2000 deposit is due after setting a tentative date.

Days	*Hours*	*Fee*	*Min. Rental*
Monday–Friday	before 6pm	$400/hr	3 hours
Sunday–Thursday	after 6pm	$650/hr	3 hours
Weekends	6pm Fri–	$800/hr	4 hours Sat
	6pm Sun		3 hours Sun

Catering is provided and approximate food service costs are: $30/person for a cocktail reception, $50/person for a seated meal, and bar setup $150. Gratuity 15%, tax 7.25% are not included in these rates. A package for a minimum of 80 people is available which includes boat rental, food, beverage, entertainment, gratuity and tax. Any remaining balance is due 3 days prior to your function.

CANCELLATION POLICY: You must cancel 90 days in advance of the event or forfeit the deposit. If the date can be rebooked, it will be refunded.

AVAILABILITY: No limits. Summer, spring, early fall and December are booked early.

EMPRESS HORNBLOWER

This 95-foot vessel offers 2 large indoor decks, 1 large outdoor deck, parquet dance floor, 3 bars, full galley and sound system. **Reserve:** 1–3 months in advance

CAPACITY: 400 for a standing reception and 280 for seated meals. You can also charter 1 deck.

FEES & DEPOSITS: A $2000–3000 deposit is required 7 days after booking.

Days	*Hours*	*Fee*	*Min. Rental*
Monday–Friday	before 6pm	$1000/hr	3 hours
Sunday–Thursday	after 6pm	$1500/hr	3 hours
Weekends	6pm Fri–	$1800/hr	4 hours Sat
	6pm Sun		3 hours Sun

Catering is provided and approximate food service costs are: $30/person for a cocktail reception, $50/person for a sit-down meal, and bar setup $150. Gratuity 15%, tax 7.25% are not included in these rates. A package for a minimum of 150 people is available which includes boat rental, food, beverage, entertainment, gratuity and tax. Any remaining balance is due 3 days prior to your function.

CANCELLATION POLICY: You must cancel 120 days prior to the event to obtain a full refund. If the date can be rebooked, your deposit will be refunded.

AVAILABILITY: Monday through Sunday, any time.

CITY OF SAN FRANCISCO

Patterned after a classic steamer of the early 1900s, this large vessel has 3 decks, 2 dining salons, 2 parquet dance floors, 4 bars, full galley, 2 lounges, sound system and expansive sun deck. **Reserve:** 1–3 months in advance.

CAPACITY: The City can accommodate 750 for cocktails/buffet and 480 for seated meals. You can also rent 1/2 of the City. The capacity would then be 375 and 240, respectively.

FEES & DEPOSITS: A $3000–5000 deposit is required 7 days after booking.

Days	Hours	Fee	Min. Rental
Monday–Friday	before 6pm	$1500/hr	3 hours
Sunday–Thursday	after 6pm	$2500/hr	3 hours
Weekends	6pm Fri–	$3000/hr	4 hours Sat
	6pm Sun		3 hours Sun

Catering is provided and approximate food service costs are: $30/person for a cocktail reception, $50/person for a sit-down meal, and bar setup $150. Gratuity 15%, tax 7.25% are not included in these rates. A package for a minimum of 300 people is available which includes boat rental, food, beverage, entertainment, gratuity and tax. Any remaining balance is due 3 days prior to your function.

CANCELLATION POLICY: Cancel 120 days prior to the event to obtain a full refund.

AVAILABILITY: Monday through Sunday, any time.

FERRY BOAT SANTA ROSA

This elegantly restored ferryboat is the only vessel in the Hornblower fleet that is permanently dockside. It's perfect for events when guests need arrival and departure flexibility. There's 1 large dining salon, 2 bars and a full galley. **Reserve:** 1–3 months in advance.

CAPACITY: The Santa Rosa can accommodate up to 600 guests.

FEES & DEPOSITS: A $2000 deposit is required 7 days after booking.

Days	Hours	Fee	Min. Rental
Monday–Friday	before 6pm	$350/hr	3 hours
Sunday–Thursday	after 6pm	$550/hr	3 hours
Weekends	6pm Fri–	$750/hr	4 hours Sat
	6pm Sun		3 hours Sun

Catering is provided and Hornblower food service costs are: $30/person for a cocktail reception, $50/person for a sit-down meal, and bar setup $150. Gratuity 15%, tax 7.25% are not included in these rates. You may use your own caterer for functions on this vessel.

CANCELLATION POLICY: Cancel 120 days prior to the event to obtain a full refund. If the date can be rebooked, it will be refunded.

AVAILABILITY: Monday through Sunday, any time.

PAPAGALLO II

This is a sleek yacht, featuring 2 decks, 2 salons, bar, full galley and master suite with spa. Papagallo II is available for private parties by special arrangement. **Reserve:** 1–3 months in advance.

CAPACITY: The boat can hold up to 50 guests for a standing reception, 24 people for seated meals.

FEES & DEPOSITS: $1000 is required 7 days after booking.

Days	Hours	Fee	Min. Rental
Monday–Friday	before 6pm	$350/hr	3 hours
Sunday–Thursday	after 6pm	$400/hr	3 hours
Weekends	6pm Fri–	$450/hr	4 hours Sat
	6pm Sun		3 hours Sun

CANCELLATION POLICY: You must cancel 60 days in advance for a full refund.

AVAILABILITY: Any time. This boat is available for overnight and extended cruises.

SERVICES/AMENITIES FOR ALL VESSELS:

Restaurant Services: no
Catering: provided
Kitchen Facilities: minimal-moderate
Tables & Chairs: provided
Linens, Silver, etc.: provided
Restrooms: varies, no wca
Dance Floor: varies per vessel

Parking: Mariott's lot Berkeley
or Pier 33 lot San Francisco
Overnight Accommodations: Papagallo II
Telephone: boat phone, credit card phones
Outdoor Night Lighting: varies
Outdoor Cooking Facilities: no
Cleanup: provided

RESTRICTIONS:

Alcohol: provided, BYO corkage $5/bottle
Smoking: allowed
Music: amplified ok

Wheelchair Access: limited
Insurance: not required

JULIUS' CASTLE

1541 Montgomery Street
San Francisco, CA 94133
(415) 362-3042
Reserve: 2 months in advance

Located in the heart of Northbeach, situated high atop Telegraph Hill, is Julius' Castle, an unusual place to hold an event. It was built in 1922 by Julius Roz who used materials and craftsmen from the 1915 Panama-Pacific Exposition to design a restaurant to look like a 'medieval castle'. The restaurant's main attraction, besides the cuisine, is its unparalleled panoramic views of the Bay from interior windows and outdoor deck on the upper floor. This deck opens off of the second floor Penthouse Dining Room and is an exceptional spot for cocktails before dinner. You may rent the second floor or the entire restaurant with enough advance notice.

CAPACITY: The Penthouse Dining Room has seating capacity for 60 people; the Main Dining Room up to 90.

FEES & DEPOSITS: Approximately $1000, depending on the size of your party. No rental fee is required. Food service costs range from hors d'oeuvres, $4–$21/person to full meals from $35–$75/person. Gratuity and taxes are not included in the above prices.

AVAILABILITY: From noon to 1am, every day.

SERVICES/AMENITIES:

Restaurant: yes

Catering: no BYO

Kitchen Facilities: ample

Tables & Chairs: provided

Linens, Silver, etc.: provided

Restrooms: no wca

Dance Floor: limited

Parking: valet only

Overnight Accommodations: no

Telephone: pay phone

Outdoor Night Lighting: no

Outdoor Cooking Facilities: no

Cleanup: provided

RESTRICTIONS:

Alcohol: provided

Smoking: allowed

Music: no amplified

Wheelchair Access: no

Insurance: not required

LASCAUX

248 Sutter Street

San Francisco, CA 94108

(415) 391-1555 Manager

Reserve: 30 days in advance

A descent into this subterranean restaurant evokes the beauty and mystery of the Lascaux caves in France. Subdued lighting casts a soft, warm blush throughout. Wall surfaces suggest a cave's interior—uneven, tactile, earthy. A large stone fireplace provides a glowing focal point. Another contibutor to the restaurant's unique ambiance is a rotisserie for meat specialties. Adjacent to the dining area, it is completely visible to all patrons, actively including them in the cooking process. It's not surprising that Lascaux has won San Francisco Focus Magazines's "Best Restaurant Design Award" two years in a row. For small business and private affairs, Lascaux is a real gem.

CAPACITY: Lascaux can accommodate a group of 30–35 guests. The entire facility can be reserved for a private party by prior arrangement; food and beverage minimums apply.

FEES & DEPOSITS: A refundable deposit of 20% of the estimated food and beverage total is required when reservations are confirmed. The balance is payable upon completion of the event. Luncheons range from $22–25/person, dinners $35–40/person; buffets can be arranged. Tax of 7.25% and a 15% gratuity are additional.

CANCELLATION POLICY: 72-hour advance notice is required for a refund.

AVAILABILITY: Year-round, every day from 11:30am–11pm, except for major holidays.

SERVICES/AMENITIES:

Restaurant Services: yes

Catering: no BYO

Kitchen Facilities: n/a

Tables & Chairs: provided

Restrooms: wca

Dance Floor: no

Parking: valet $5/car, adjacent garage
Overnight Accommodations: no
Telephone: pay phone
Linens, Silver, etc.: provided

RESTRICTIONS:
Alcohol: provided, BYO corkage $10/bottle
Smoking: designated areas
Music: no amplified

Outdoor Night Lighting: no
Outdoor Cooking Facilities: no
Cleanup: provided

Wheelchair Access: yes, elevator
Insurance: not required

THE MANSIONS HOTEL

2220 Sacramento Street
San Francisco, CA 94115
(415) 929-9444 Tracy or Robin
Reserve: 2–6 months in advance

Two adjoining historic homes combine to form The Mansions Hotel. Each features a different ambiance but both have fine art, fanciful sculpture and eclectic furniture. There are meeting rooms, billiard room, cabaret with stage and theatrical lighting, courtyard sculpture gardens and several dining rooms. Featuring treasured antiques, stained glass walls and panoramic murals, the Mansions Hotel is a fun and different spot for a great celebration or office party.

CAPACITY: The Mansions can hold up to 225 for a standing reception and 140 for seated meals.

FEES & DEPOSITS: A nonrefundable $525 deposit is required when a tentative date is set. 50% of estimated total food and beverage cost is due 10 working days prior to the event. The fee is $525 for a 3 to 4-hour minimum rental depending on day of the week. A $50/hour fee will be applied to any time over the agreed rental period. Catering is provided and food service rates start at $18/person for hors d'oeuvres, $35/person for seated meals. Saturday night a minimum of $4500 in food, alcohol and room rental is required. Gratuity 15% and tax of 7.25% are not included in the above fees. The remaining balance is due on the event day.

AVAILABILITY: Parties and receptions are usually held between 11am and 5pm on Saturdays, noon to 10pm on Sundays. Saturday night bookings are negotiable.

SERVICES/AMENITIES:
Restaurant Services: yes
Catering: no BYO
Kitchen Facilities: ample
Tables & Chairs: provided
Linens, Silver, etc.: provided
Restrooms: no wca
Dance Floor: CBA

Parking: Webster/Clay garage
Overnight Accommodations: 29 guestrooms
Telephone: pay phone
Outdoor Night Lighting: yes
Outdoor Cooking Facilities: yes
Cleanup: provided
Other: 2 pianos, billiard room

RESTRICTIONS:

Alcohol: provided, corkage $7.50-10/bottle
Smoking: allowed
Music: amplified until 10:30pm

Wheelchair Access: no
Insurance: not required

THE MARK HOPKINS

1 Nob Hill
San Francisco, CA 94108
(415) 392-3434 Catering Department
Reserve: 1 week–12 months in advance

The Mark Hopkins is a hotel with a history. Gold Rush merchant Mark Hopkins built the original mansion on this site to satisfy the social aspirations of his wife. Never enamored with the idea, he referred sarcastically to his construction project as the "Hotel de Hopkins" and never spent a night in it, dying before its completion. The mansion burned down during the 1906 quake, and it wasn't until 1926 that the real Mark Hopkins Hotel opened its doors. Situated high on Nob Hill, the hotel has been a mecca for royalty, statesmen, and celebrities from all over the world. It is probably most famous, however, for the "Top of the Mark" a popular lounge on the top floor of the hotel. The Mark, as it is called by locals, is a great spot for evening functions. Entirely surrounded by glass, it has a spectacular 360-degree view of the city and glittering Bay below. More traditional business functions and events are accommodated on the main floors of the hotel. The Peacock Court, which accommodates large events, has a 20-foot ceiling, a view of downtown, and a huge gold peacock that has presided over the room since the hotel was built. Smaller rooms are available for a wide variety of functions, and some retain old fashioned features such as arched windows that actually open to the outside! The Mark Hopkins has gone through numerous changes over the last sixty years, but it still remains a San Francisco landmark.

CAPACITY:

Room	Classroom-Style	Banquet	Reception	Theater
Room of the Dons	160	220	300	250
Peacock Court	350	450	800	600
Dons & Peacock	510	600	1100	850
Six Continents Room	70	90	120	130
Top of the Mark	—	250	300	—

MEETING ROOMS: The Mark Hopkins has 15 meeting rooms, 5–1100 participants.

FEES & DEPOSITS: A refundable deposit, applied toward the cost of the event, is payable when the contract is submitted. 80% of the estimated total food and beverage cost is required 5 working days prior to the event. The balance is due the day of the event. With food service, room rental fees are sometimes applied. Per person rates: breakfasts starts at $9, luncheons at $18.50, dinners at $32.50, buffets, hors d'oeuvres and coffee service for meetings can be arranged. For business functions without food, room rental starts at $250. Coffee service for meetings starts at $10/person.

CANCELLATION POLICY: With 45 days' notice, the deposit is refunded.

AVAILABILITY: Year-round, every day, any time.

SERVICES/AMENITIES:

Restaurant Services: yes
Catering: provided, no BYO
Kitchen Facilities: n/a
Dance Floor: yes
Parking: Hotel garage
Overnight Accommodations: 394 guestrooms
Telephone: pay phone

Tables & Chairs: provided
Linens, Silver, etc.: provided
Restrooms: wca
Outdoor Night Lighting: no
Outdoor Cooking Facilities: no
Cleanup: provided

RESTRICTIONS:

Alcohol: provided, BYO corkage $10.50/bottle
Smoking: allowed
Music: amplified ok

Wheelchair Access: yes
Insurance: not required

NIMITZ CONFERENCE CENTER

Building 140, California Ave.
Treasure Island
San Francisco, CA 94130
(415) 395-5151
Reserve: 1–8 months in advance

The Conference Center, one of the oldest buildings on Treasure Island, offers a variety of meeting and event spaces. The Patio Room is like part of an old ranch style house. Painted light gray, it is a simple uncluttered space with a pleasant view of lawn and trees. The adjacent room has a tile floor, cafe tables, and a wall of glass overlooking the landscaped yard. Doors open out onto the terrace, a lovely event spot when the weather cooperates. This is an ideal area for small receptions and dinners. While this part of the Center feels homey and intimate, the majority of the event spaces are much more modern and accommodate larger functions. The Ballroom has a permanent dance floor, vaulted ceiling with skylight, and contemporary art on the walls. The L-Bar and Garden Rooms are popular for meetings and receptions. Whatever area you choose, the Conference Center will set it up any way you like.

CAPACITY:	*Room*	*Seated*	*Reception*	*Classroom*
	Ballroom	300	500	200
	Garden Room	225	350	150
	L-Bar Room	60	100	50

MEETING ROOMS: 5 rooms that can accommodate 5–500 participants.

FEES & DEPOSITS: A nonrefundable $200 deposit is required for the Ballroom and Garden Room, smaller rooms $50, due when the rental agreement is submitted. The rental fee is $200 for meetings (8 hours max) or dinners/receptions (5 hours max) with the balance payable 3 days before the event. A final guest count is due 4 days in advance. With meal service, the rental fee may be waived. Any extra hours over 5 are available for an additional charge. Per person rates: dinners/buffets $10.50–19, luncheons $7.50–14, hors d'oeuvres (100 pieces) $45–200. Any menu can be customized, no tax is required, gratuity is 15%. Bartenders are available for $50/bartender. A business breakfast can be arranged along with coffee service for meetings.

AVAILABILITY: Year-round, every day. Saturday & Sunday 7am–1am, Monday–Friday until 1am. Closed most holidays but will open for parties with a guaranteed 150 guests.

SERVICES/AMENITIES:

Restaurant Services: no
Catering: provided, no BYO
Kitchen Facilities: n/a
Tables & Chairs: provided
Linens, Silver, etc.: provided
Restrooms: wca
Dance Floor: yes

Parking: large lot
Overnight Accommodations: no
Telephone: pay phone
Outdoor Night Lighting: yes
Outdoor Cooking Facilities: CBA
Cleanup: provided
Other: event coordination

RESTRICTIONS:

Alcohol: provided, no BYO
Smoking: allowed
Music: amplified ok

Wheelchair Access: yes
Insurance: not required
Other: votive candles only

THE PACIFIC SPIRIT

Pacific Marine Yacht Charters
Berthed at Schoonmaker Point Marina
Sausalito, CA
(415) 388-3400
Reserve: 1–6 months in advance

The Pacific Spirit is an 83-foot white luxury Broward Yacht with sleek styling and open top deck. You can cruise around the Bay in this superbly appointed vessel with services specifically tailored for your business or personal event. Pacific Marine provides almost unlimited event services. Let your guests enjoy the comforts of being treated in style while touring San Francisco Bay. The Pacific Spirit is berthed in Sausalito, but other boarding locations can be arranged for an additional cost.

CAPACITY: The Pacific Spirit can hold up to 97 guests plus crew.

FEES & DEPOSITS: An $800 deposit is required. If you arrange for your own entertainment, a refundable security deposit of $350–500 is also required. Both deposits are payable when you reserve your event date. Rental fees are $375/hour weekdays (before 5pm), $400/hour weekdays (after 5pm) and $475/hour weekends and holidays. A 3-hour minimum rental is required, 4 hours on Saturdays and holidays. Some 2-hour rentals can be arranged in advance. For groups of less than 20, the rental rates are: weekdays $325/hour and weekends $375/hour (except holidays).

Package cruises for party or business groups are available which include yacht rental, beverages, food and entertainment. Package rates range from $32/person–$124/person depending on menus and day of the week selected.

CANCELLATION POLICY: If you cancel, 90% of the deposit will be refunded with 60 or more days notice prior to your event. If less than 60, you will forfeit the deposit and be refunded the $350–500 security deposit.

AVAILABILITY: Any time, no limits.

SERVICES/AMENITIES:

Restaurant Services: no

Catering: provided, no BYO

Kitchen Facilities: ample

Tables & Chairs: provided

Linens, Silver, etc.: provided

Restrooms: no wca

Dance Floor: in aft salon

Parking: Marina lot

Overnight Accommodations: no

Telephone: cellular and radio

Night Lighting: yes

Outdoor Cooking Facilities: no

Cleanup: provided

Other: full event coordination

RESTRICTIONS:

Alcohol: provided, BYO corkage $7/bottle

Smoking: aft enclosed salon

Music: amplified ok

Wheelchair Access: no

Insurance: not required

THE PAGE BROWN MANSION
The Pacific Heights
Conference Center

2212 Sacramento Street
San Francisco, CA 94115
(415) 928-5131 W. Ray Smith
Reserve: 3–6 months in advance

This stately and historic turn-of-the-century mansion is an architectural jewel that remains in its original magnificent condition. Built in 1893, it was a private residence until January of 1990. The main stairway is illuminated by an extraordinary stained glass window which gives the reception hall a warm, rose-colored glow. Woodwork is varied and unusual, from bird's eye maple to quarter sawn oak paneling and polished burl redwood. Floors are inlaid hardwood and house fixtures are original. The main floor's grand entryway, French parlor, paneled dining room, music room and study are available for all types of events.

CAPACITY: The facility can accommodate 250 guests for a reception, and 175 for a seated function.

FEES & DEPOSITS: The $1500 rental fee serves as the deposit and is required to secure an event date. The entire Mansion rents for $1500 for a 5-hour period. Each additional hour is $100. Rental of separate rooms begins at $375/day. Catering is provided and food service ranges from reception cocktails at $20/person and seated buffets at $28/person to seated dinners starting at $35/person. There is a $1500 minimum for catering services. A 15% gratuity and tax of 7.25% are added to the final bill.

CANCELLATION POLICY: The deposit is fully refundable with a 90-day written notice.

AVAILABILITY: Noon to 10:30pm every day.

SERVICES/AMENITIES:

Restaurant Services: no
Catering: provided or BYO by arrangement
Kitchen Facilities: moderate
Tables & Chairs: provided
Linens, Silver, etc.: provided
Restrooms: no wca
Dance Floor: yes

Parking: Webster/Clay garage
Overnight Accommodations: no
Telephone: pay phone
Outdoor Night Lighting: yes
Outdoor Cooking Facilities: BBQ
Cleanup: provided
Other: grand piano

RESTRICTIONS:

Alcohol: provided, BYO corkage $7.50/bottle
Smoking: restricted
Music: amplified ok, approval needed

Wheelchair Access: no
Insurance: sometimes required

THE PALACE OF FINE ARTS ★★

Lyon at Marina Boulevard
San Francisco, CA
(415) 666-7035 Recreation & Parks
Reserve: 3–12 months in advance

Designed by architect Bernard Maybeck for the Panama-Pacific Exposition of 1915, the Palace of Fine Arts is a magnificent San Francisco landmark and one of the most glorious spots you can imagine for an outdoor party. Located in the Marina District, the picturesque shaded lagoon, ducks and swans, landscaped island and spraying fountain offer an exceptional setting for a celebration. Seated functions are possible under the grand and impressive classic Roman rotunda. Your guests can roam anywhere around the lagoon's perimeter; the entire setting is idyllic and highly romantic. Although this is a public park space, you are allowed to rope off an area for your party or hire security personnel. Given the low fees for use of this spectacular park, we'd say this is a real find.

CAPACITY: The rotunda and park can accommodate 200–300 guests.

FEES & DEPOSITS: A 10% nonrefundable deposit of the total fee is required and is due 5 days from the time you make your reservation. The rental fee for 2 hours is $200 (corporate fee is $500), and for each hour over that, the fee is $35/hour. Any remaining fees are required 30 days prior to your event.

AVAILABILITY: Any weekend, from 9am to dusk.

SERVICES/AMENITIES:

Restaurant Services: no
Catering: BYO
Kitchen Facilities: no
Tables & Chairs: BYO

Linens, Silver, etc.: BYO
Restrooms: by Exploratorium
Dance Floor: no
Parking: on street

Overnight Accommodations: no
Telephone: pay phone
Outdoor Night Lighting: no

RESTRICTIONS:
Alcohol: BYO
Smoking: allowed
Music: no amplified

Outdoor Cooking Facilities: no
Cleanup: caterer

Wheelchair Access: yes
Insurance: sometimes required

RED AND WHITE FLEET

Pier 41, Fisherman's Wharf
San Francisco, CA 94133
(415) 546-BOAT,
(800) BAY-CRUISE ext. 2655 or 2845
Reserve: 3 months in advance

The Fleet consists of ten ferry boats, all of which are available for private parties in addition to their regular tours during the day. The sheer number of boats, vessel size and docking sites from which to choose, offer remarkable versatility to the party or corporate events planner with a large guest list. A nice feature is that BBQs are available, upon request, for outdoor cooking on the Bay.

CAPACITY: The capacity varies from 50 to 500 people per boat depending on boat size.

FEES & DEPOSITS: The refundable deposit ranges from $800–$1400, depending on boat size. The deposit is required within 10 working days of making a reservation. Fees vary:

Winter weekday/weekend	$1625–$6550
Summer midweek	$1875–$6600
Summer weekend	$2200–$7350

Your rental fee will depend on the size of vessel selected. A bar setup fee of $200 is required for a no-host bar and is returned if a service minimum is reached. The final balance is due 10 working days in advance of the event.

CANCELLATION POLICY: You must notify the Fleet 45 days prior to your event to receive a full refund.

AVAILABILITY: Evenings after 7pm the boats are available for a 4-hour minimum rental until 2am. Midday, there is a 3-hour minimum for the charter.

SERVICES/AMENITIES:
Restaurant Services: no
Catering: BYO or preferred caterer
Kitchen Facilities: no
Tables & Chairs: varies/vessel
Linens, Silver, etc.: caterer
Restrooms: wca varies per vessel
Dance Floor: varies per vessel

Parking: CBA
Overnight Accommodations: no
Telephone: radio
Outdoor Night Lighting: yes
Outdoor Cooking Facilities: BBQs
Cleanup: provided
Other: many departure points

RESTRICTIONS:

Alcohol: provided, BYO corkage $5/bottle
Smoking: allowed on outside decks
Music: amplified ok

Wheelchair Access: yes
Insurance: not required

REGINA DEL MARE I & II DINING YACHTS

Pier 28 and Pier 40
San Francisco, CA 94105
(415) 541-7710
Reserve: 1–6 months in advance

These yachts bring the exhilaration of sun, salt air and sea breezes to your event. Regina Del Mare I is an elegantly decorated, four-level facility that can comfortably accommodate most special events or business functions. Every table in the Main Dining Salon has a window seat, white table cloth and cushioned banquettes. Dining can also be arranged outside on some of the decks, and if you'd like a little less sun or wind, a canopy or wind screen is provided. The Yacht also has a full bar, comfortable Lounge and dance floor. On the business side, Regina Del Mare I can handle presentations simultaneously. Audio-visual equipment can be provided and the interior can be darkened as needed. This is the only luxury yacht on the Bay to have computerized stabilizers, assuring a smooth ride. Regina Del Mare II is a new vessel, a two-hull catamaran with several decks, perfect for more intimate parties. Enjoy a bird's eye view of the sea and skyline during your social or corporate event. Regina Del Mare I and II are truly a notable departure from the ordinary.

REGINA DEL MARE I

CAPACITY:

Area	Level	Seated	Reception
Private Conference Room	First	15	—
Main Salon	Second	100	—
Aft Deck & Clearstory	Third	50–80	—
Observation Deck	Fourth	30	—
Entire Vessel	All	200	400

FEES & DEPOSITS:

Guests	Fees/Hour	Guests	Fees/Hour
0–149	$800	250–299	$1300
150–199	1000	300–349	1400
200–299	1200	350–400	1500

REGINA DEL MARE II

CAPACITY:

Area	Level	Seated	Reception
Entire Vessel	First & Second	49	49

FEES & DEPOSITS: The charter rate is $275/hour, any day.

A minimum $2500 refundable deposit is required for Regina del Mare I, $1000 for del Mare II, when reservations are confirmed. The balance and final guest count are due 7 days prior to departure. Charter packages include mid-week M–F luncheons (100-guest min. for vessel I, 30-guest min. for vessel II) for 2 hours at $28.50/person; a 3-hour luncheon charter any time for $39.00/person and a dinner buffet/dance cruise for 3 hours starting at $55/person. Separate menus include luncheon and dinner entrees (per person rates) starting at $12, dinner buffets at $15.50, brunch buffets at $16 and hors d'oeuvres at $12. Tax of 7.25% and gratuity 15–18% are additional.

CANCELLATION POLICY: With 90 days' notice, the deposit will be refunded minus a 10% cancellation charge. With less than 90 days, refunds only if the space can be rebooked.

AVAILABILITY: Year-round, every day, any time.

SERVICES/AMENITIES:

Restaurant Services: no
Catering: provided, no BYO
Kitchen Facilities: n/a
Tables & Chairs: provided
Linens, Silver, etc.: provided
Restrooms: wca varies per vessel
Dance Floor: yes

Parking: Pier 40 on the Embarcadero
Overnight Accommodations: no
Telephone: marine radio
Outdoor Night Lighting: yes
Outdoor Cooking Facilities: some BBQs
Cleanup: provided
Other: entertainment, theme parties, event coordination

RESTRICTIONS:

Alcohol: provided, BYO corkage $7/bottle
Smoking: outside decks
Music: amplified ok

Wheelchair Access: varies per vessel
Insurance: not required

RENDEZVOUS CHARTERS

Pier 40, South Beach Harbor
San Francisco, CA 94107
(415) 543-7333
Reserve: 2 weeks–12 months in advance

THE BRIGANTINE RENDEZVOUS

The Rendezvous is the largest Coast Guard-certified sailing vessel in San Francisco Bay. Built in 1933 as a family pleasure boat, this 78-foot square rigger is known in sailing circles as a 'Brigantine'. The interior is comprised of mahogany, pecan and rosewoods with brass fixtures and plush appointments. It offers guests a rare and invigorating experience, perfect for casual corporate events, private parties or intimate gatherings. Fully restored in 1986, the Rendezvous helps you step back in time as the sails unfurl and the boat heels as it gains speed. So don your Levis, deck shoes and sweaters and hang on to your wine glass—this is a bona fide sailing experience.

CAPACITY: 49 passengers, 7 crew

FEES & DEPOSITS: 50% of the total charter cost is due when the contract is submitted. The midweek fee for 2 hours minimum is $275/hour. Weekend excursions are $950 for the first 3 hours, each hour thereafter, $300. Weekend rates start at Friday 5pm and end Sunday at midnight. Meals are served buffet style, approximately $10–25/person; 7.25% tax and gratuity at 15% are additional. Menus can be customized. The balance is required 7 days prior to departure. On this vessel, you can bring your own caterer for an extra fee of $150.

THE RENAISSANCE

Scheduled to be launched in November, 1990, the Renaissance is a brand new turn-of-the-century fantail replica. This 65-foot motor yacht will be shiny and untarnished, yet will have the appearance of an old, classic vessel. The interior is designed with mahogany detailing, plush carpeting and cushions plus brass accessories. As a dining boat, The Renaissance will be unparalled with its fully equipped galley and stable ride. Stately and refined in appearance, this yacht will offer guests both luxury and fun for on-the-water parties and business events.

CAPACITY: The vessel can hold 150 passengers for a reception, 130 for seated meals.

FEES & DEPOSITS: 50% of the total charter cost is due when the contract is submitted. The charter fee Monday–Friday is $400/hour before 6pm. Sunday–Thursday after 6pm it's $650/hour. From Friday 6pm–Sunday 6pm, the charter is $800/hour. Charter packages for seated meals and receptions are available. Per person rates: hors d'oeuvres start at $7.50, lunch buffets $24 and diner buffets $30. Seated meals from the menu: luncheons start at $35/person, dinners at $56/person; 7.25% tax and 15% gratuity are additional. The balance is required 7 days prior to departure. For this vessel, no outside caterers allowed.

CANCELLATION POLICY: For both vessels, with 30 days' notice, the deposit is refunded.

AVAILABILITY: Both vessels, year-round, any day, any time.

SERVICES/AMENITIES:

Restaurant Services: no

Catering: provided or BYO, see above description

Kitchen Facilities: varies per vessel

Tables & Chairs: n/a or provided

Linens, Silver, etc.: n/a or provided

Restrooms: no wca

Dance Floor: varies per vessel

Parking: Pier 40 on the Embarcadero

Overnight Accommodations: no

Telephone: marine radio & cellular phone

Outdoor Night Lighting: yes

Outdoor Cooking Facilities: varies per vessel

Cleanup: whoever caters event

Other: decorations, theme parties

RESTRICTIONS:

Alcohol: provided, no BYO

Smoking: outside decks

Music: amplified ok

Wheelchair Access: limited

Insurance: sometimes required

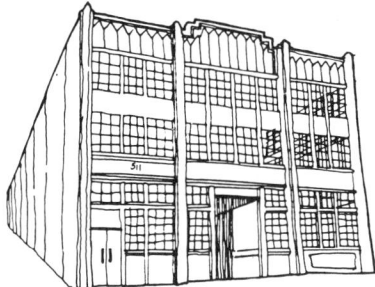

RINCON HILL SPECTRUM

511 Harrison Street
San Francisco, CA 94105
(415) 495-1111 Thomas Roedoc
Reserve: 2 weeks in advance

The Rincon Hill Spectrum is a new fine art gallery specially designed as the ideal site for all kinds of business and social events. Adaptable and adjustable, this newly renovated concrete and glass facility offers just about every amenity you could want: state-of-the-art lighting, first rate sound and PA system, huge restrooms, electrical outlets everywhere, and much more. It is spacious and dramatic, with 16-22 foot ceilings and a wall of glass overlooking downtown San Francisco. Flexibility is key here—you can create your own environment by rearranging the sculptures, using special draperies and placing the stage and dance floor where you wish. Groups as small as 100 or as large as 700 can feel equally comfortable here. The Spectrum was designed to satisfy every client's needs, and does so in a fresh, high tech and aesthetic way.

CAPACITY: This facility can hold 100–400 seated guests, 12—500 for dance parties and 150–700 for receptions; up to 125 classroom-style and 250 theater-style.

FEES & DEPOSITS: A nonrefundable deposit of 50% of the rental fee is due when reservations are confirmed. Evening rental rates are $2200–3000, daytime rates $1100–1500. A refundable $1000 cleaning and damage deposit is payable 30 days prior to your function along with the rental balance. In-house bar service can be provided for an extra charge.

CANCELLATION POLICY: The cleaning/damage deposit is refundable.

AVAILABILITY: Year-round, every day from 8am–2am.

SERVICES/AMENITIES:

Restaurant Services: no
Catering: BYO licensed and insured
Kitchen Facilities: moderate
Tables & Chairs: BYO
Linens, Silver, etc.: BYO
Restrooms: wca
Dance Floor: yes
Parking: valet, street, adjacent lots

Overnight Accommodations: no
Telephone: pay phones
Outdoor Night Lighting: no
Outdoor Cooking Facilities: no
Cleanup: caterer and Spectrum
Other: business equipment, stage
Special: theatrical lighting and sound, projection screen

RESTRICTIONS:

Alcohol: provided, BYO extra fee
Smoking: allowed
Music: amplified ok

Wheelchair Access: yes
Insurance: required

ROCK & BOWL

1855 Haight Street
San Francisco, CA 94117
(415) 826-BOWL
Reserve: 1 week–9 months in advance

This is one of those places you just have to experience. By day, it's a mild-mannered bowling alley. By night (Friday and Saturday, that is) it becomes the infamous, raucous and outrageous Rock & Bowl. TV monitors over each lane run nonstop rock videos long into the night. Music blasts from overhead speakers, making every cell in your body vibrate with heretofore unknown energy. And—people actually bowl! Parties here are nothing if not unique. Reserve a bunch of lanes, bring in some swell food and knock down those pins! Dancing is ok, talking loud is ok (and often required), and looking cool is de rigeur. This writer and her friends spent an evening at the alley, never bowled better in our lives and never had a better time doing it.

CAPACITY: This facility can hold 300 guests (4 is the minimum for a group reservation). With over 60 guests, you can reserve the entire facility.

FEES & DEPOSITS: The deposit for 3 lanes or more is $2/person. To reserve the entire facility, the deposit is 33% of the rental fee which is $1000–2500, depending on the day, time and league bowling schedules. Deposits are refundable and due when the reservation is confirmed. Fees include bowling lanes, shoes, balls and use of pool tables.

CANCELLATION POLICY: If lanes can be rebooked, the deposit is refunded.

AVAILABILITY: Year-round, every day from 10am–2am except Christmas day.

SERVICES/AMENITIES:

Restaurant Services: snack bar
Catering: BYO
Kitchen Facilities: CBA
Tables & Chairs: some provided
Linens, Silver, etc.: BYO
Restrooms: no wca
Dance Floor: bowling areas

Parking: street, Keizar Stadium lot
Overnight Accommodations: no
Telephone: pay phones
Outdoor Night Lighting: no
Outdoor Cooking Facilities: BYO
Cleanup: renter or provided, extra charge

RESTRICTIONS:

Alcohol: provided, no BYO
Smoking: allowed
Music: amplified ok

Wheelchair Access: yes
Insurance: not required

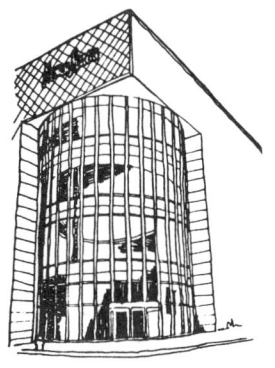

THE ROTUNDA
At Neiman Marcus

150 Stockton Street
San Francisco, CA 94108
(415) 362-4777   Diana Parker
Reserve: 2 weeks–12 months

The Rotunda at Neiman Marcus is famous for good reason. Located on the top floor, it has seating in the round beneath an extraordinary stained glass dome. The skylight is really a painting in glass—a sea theme with Neptune presiding. Constructed of 2600 pieces of clear, rust, and variegated green glass, the "ceiling" bathes diners in a warm glow. Every table here has a view of Union Square through a curved wall of glass descending four stories down to street level. Decorated in muted colors, much of the seating is arranged in tiered, private banquettes. Also well known for its San Francisco 'taste tour,' the restaurant creates numerous buffet tables decorated in themes of famous San Francisco spots such as Chinatown, Fisherman's Wharf, the Mission, North Beach and Japantown. Each table, of course, serves a theme-related food. During the holiday season, with Neiman Marcus' renowned Christmas tree rising up through the center of the restaurant and Union Square ablaze with lights, the Rotunda is breathtaking.

CAPACITY: The entire Rotunda can hold 350 for a reception and 200 seated guests.

MEETING ROOMS: 1 room that can accommodate 25 seated.

FEES & DEPOSITS: A refundable deposit of 50% of the total estimated food and beverage cost is due when the contract is submitted. There is no rental fee with food service. The balance is due the day of the event. Per person rates: continental breakfasts $6.75, full breakfasts $13.75, hors d'oeuvres $2–5, dinners start at $40, buffets at $18. Tax of 7.25% and gratuity of 18% are additional. For you Neiman Marcus cardholders, note that you can make payment using your NM card to gain *Incircle* points.

CANCELLATION POLICY: With 2 weeks' notice, the deposit is refunded.

AVAILABILITY: Year-round, every day from 8:30am–10:30 and 6pm–midnight.

SERVICES/AMENITIES:
Restaurant Services: yes
Catering: provided, no BYO
Kitchen Facilities: n/a
Tables & Chairs: provided
Linens, Silver, etc.: provided
Restrooms: wca
Dance Floor: yes

Parking: Union Square garage
Overnight Accommodations: no
Telephone: pay phone
Outdoor Night Lighting: no
Outdoor Cooking Facilities: no
Cleanup: provided

RESTRICTIONS:
Alcohol: provided, BYO corkage $6/bottle
Smoking: allowed
Music: amplified ok

Wheelchair Access: yes
Insurance: not required

SAILING SHIP DOLF REMPP

Pier 42-44 on the Embarcadero, South of
Market St.
San Francisco, CA 94107
(415) 777-5771 or 543-4024   Camille Barnes
Reserve: 1 week–2 months in advance

This impressive, 3-masted schooner is now permanently landbound. It rests in a specially devised concrete cradle at the southwest end of the Embarcadero. The Sailing Ship Dolph Rempp was built in 1884 as a trading vessel in the Baltic Sea, and has had an illustrious career as a rum-runner, pleasure craft and a World War I supply carrier (used for espionage!). You and your guests will feel like stars in your own movie production when you board the Sailing Ship since it was, in fact, a location set for more than 100 Hollywood films. It now combines its rich history with elegant dining and fabulous views of the City, Bay Bridge and the colorful new South Beach Harbor Marina.

CAPACITY: 800 people can be accommodated for a stand-up reception, up to 150 for a sit-down meal and 400 for a buffet dinner or luncheon. Outdoor tents on the front deck and canopies on the back deck can be erected for an additional 200 guests.

FEES & DEPOSITS: A negotiable fee is due 1 month before your event to secure the date and cover the security deposit. A rental fee/person is required, based on the guest count. Food service is provided. Cocktail hors d'oeuvres run $7–14.50/person, luncheons or dinners are $12–50/person. A sales tax of 7.25% and an 18% gratuity are applied to the final bill.

CANCELLATION POLICY: Normally 1 month's notice is allowed unless you have booked during the holiday season, in which case, 2 months' notice is required.

AVAILABILITY: 7 days a week, including major holidays.

SERVICES/AMENITIES:

Restaurant Services: yes

Catering: if BYO, extra charge

Kitchen Facilities: n/a

Tables & Chairs: provided

Linens, Silver, etc.: provided

Restrooms: no wca

Dance Floor: yes

Parking: on street, valet recommended

Overnight Accommodations: no

Telephone: pay phone

Outdoor Night Lighting: yes

Outdoor Cooking Facilities: BBQ CBA

Cleanup: provided

RESTRICTIONS:

Alcohol: provided

Smoking: allowed

Music: amplified ok

Wheelchair Access: yes

Insurance: not required

SAN FRANCISCO COMMERCIAL CLUB

465 California Street
San Francisco, CA 94101
(415) 982-2929
Reserve: 1 week–6 months in advance

The moment you step out of the elevator on the fifteenth floor of the Merchant's Exchange Building, you feel you have entered another era, rich in the opulant heritage of early San Francisco. Cloaked in mahogany paneling and dark wood, the Game Room is subdued. With its wonderful masonry fireplace, curving wooden bar and specially molded panels, it has the flavor an English country manor. In contrast, the Dining Room is a very large space with a high ceiling and 8-foot windows all along the street side. On the opposite side, arched glass panels reflect light back into the room. The focal point is a 15-foot masonry fireplace which, bordered by dark wood walls and patterned carpet, maintains the masculine tone of the club.

CAPACITY: The Main Dining Room can accommodate 325 seated guests, 800 for a reception. There are 5 private rooms that can hold up to 60 seated guests.

FEES & DEPOSITS: A refundable deposit is due when the date is confirmed. The fee for the Main Dining Room is $350–$700 depending on the type of event and guest count. For the private meeting rooms, the fee is $100/half day functions. The balance is payable the day of the event. For some functions an additional security deposit may be required.

CANCELLATION POLICY: With 30 days' notice, the deposit will be refunded.

AVAILABILITY: Year-round, every day Monday–Friday after 3pm, weekends and holidays any time.

SERVICES/AMENITIES:
Restaurant Services: no
Catering: provided or BYO, extra fee
Kitchen Facilities: fully equipped
Tables & Chairs: provided
Linens, Silver, etc.: provided or BYO
Restrooms: wca
Dance Floor: CBA

Parking: adjacent garages
Overnight Accommodations: no
Telephone: pay phone
Outdoor Night Lighting: no
Outdoor Cooking Facilities: no
Cleanup: whoever caters event
Other: event coordination

RESTRICTIONS:
Alcohol: provided, BYO corkage $7/bottle
Smoking: allowed
Music: amplified ok

Wheelchair Access: yes
Insurance: certificate required

SAN FRANCISCO ★ MARITIME MUSEUM

900 Beach Street at the foot of Polk
(415) 556-2904 Michael Delano
Reserve: 1–2 months in advance

Located across from Ghirardelli Square, in the heart of Aquatic Park, stands the Maritime Museum. It houses hundreds of artifacts, photographs and documents of West Coast seafaring history. The building was cleverly designed to resemble a cruise ship, even down to the nautical looking air vents. The Museum is superb for an event because it is a marvel of Art Deco style, with classic tile work, terrazzo floors, murals and chrome detailing. Loaded with marine artifacts and historical memorabilia, the main exhibit room is terrific, and other rooms are pretty interesting, too. Many guests opt for a celebration on the long 'deck' overlooking the Aquatic Park Fishing Pier. From here the views towards the harbor and Alcatraz are unobstructed, and the water so close you can hear the waves lapping against the sand. Do yourself a favor and ask for a tour. This is a real find.

CAPACITY: For a stand-up reception, the building can accommodate 450 guests. For a seated function, approximately 150 guests.

FEES & DEPOSITS: A $1500 security deposit is required. The deposit is usually returned 2 weeks after the event. A minimum of $500 is needed to rent the Museum. The total fee is based on the length of your event and the number of guests. Work out the fee details with the Park Service. The fee includes a National Park Ranger on duty during your event.

CANCELLATION POLICY: All deposits are fully refundable.

AVAILABILITY: Year-round, 5pm–midnight.

SERVICES/AMENITIES:

Restaurant Services: no
Catering: BYO
Kitchen Facilities: minimal
Tables & Chairs: BYO
Linens, Silver, etc.: BYO
Restrooms: wca
Dance Floor: no

Parking: on street, nearby garage
Overnight Accommodations: no
Telephone: pay phone
Outdoor Night Lighting: no
Outdoor Cooking Facilities: no
Cleanup: caterer

RESTRICTIONS:

Alcohol: BYO
Smoking: outside only
Music: amplified until 11pm

Wheelchair Access: yes
Insurance: not required

SAN FRANCISCO MART ★

1355 Market Street
San Francisco, CA 94103
(415) 552-2311 Public Relations Department
Reserve: 2 weeks–12 months in advance

A walk into the newly restored San Francisco Mart is a walk into an Art Deco wonderland. Dramatic and glitzy, the central Rotunda sparkles with unexpected colors, textures and lighting. Nine structural columns clad in polished stainless steel overlaid with an intricate bronze pattern support a ceiling ringed by concenric circles of incandescent and neon lights. A trip up the escalator to the mezzanine gives you an overview of the space below and a fuller appreciation of the terrazzo floors, laid out in a complex star pattern. Two large rectangular areas on either side of the rotunda accommodate dining, presentations, and other event activities. One of these areas serves as an exhibition space which may be incorporated into your event. No matter how you choose to use it, The San Francisco Mart will leave an indelible impression.

CAPACITY, FEES & DEPOSITS:

Room	Theater	Seated	Reception	Fee
Mart Exchange	500	250	—	$1500 (24 hours)
Lobby/Rotunda	—	500	800	$3500 (24 hours)

A refundable deposit of 50% of the rental fee is due when reservations are confirmed. A refundable $1000 security and cleaning deposit, certificate of insurance plus the balance of the rental fees are payable 10 days prior to the function. Extra security is occasionally required.

CANCELLATION POLICY: With 90 days' notice, you'll receive a full refund; with 60 days', a 50% refund. In December, no deposits are refunded. The security and cleaning deposit is usually refunded.

AVAILABILITY: Year-round; any day, any time.

SERVICES/AMENITIES:

Restaurant Services: no
Catering: preferred caterer or BYO extra charge
Kitchen Facilities: setup only
Tables & Chairs: BYO
Linens, Silver, etc.: BYO
Restrooms: wca
Dance Floor: terrazzo floor

Parking: garage ex. charge, behind building free
Overnight Accommodations: no
Telephone: pay phones
Outdoor Night Lighting: no
Outdoor Cooking Facilities: no
Cleanup: caterer and Mart

RESTRICTIONS:

Alcohol: provided or BYO extra charge
Smoking: allowed
Music: amplified

Wheelchair Access: yes
Insurance: certificate required
Other: no open flames

THE SAN FRANCISCO SPIRIT

Berthed at the Embarcadero Waterfront
San Francisco, CA 94132
(415) 366-3400
Reserve: 2–9 months in advance

In June 1991, Pacific Marine Yacht Charters will christen the San Francisco Spirit, their new 150-foot motor yacht. Custom designed as a larger version of Pacific Marine's California Spirit, this vessel can accommodate groups of up to 700 guests on three beautifully appointed decks. Her layout provides a sense of intimacy for smaller groups, utilizing two levels with plush furnishings, outside deck area and formal dining setup in the Main Salon. Half of the San Francisco Spirit can be chartered for groups of 300 or less. Two dance floors, three bars, a central sound system, grand staircase, and attractive appointments make this a wonderful yacht for entertaining large parties on the Bay.

CAPACITY: The San Francisco Spirit can hold up to 700 guests for receptions. Formal dinner seating for 300 in the Main Salon, 174 on the Upper Salon, and 26 in the VIP Lounge Bridge Deck.

FEES & DEPOSITS: A $2,000 deposit is required when you reserve your event date. If you arrange for your own entertainment, a refundable $500 security deposit due 45 days prior to your event is also required. Rental fees are $1800/hour weekdays, $2000/hour weekdays after 5pm, $2,500/hour weekends and holidays. A 3-hour minimum rental is required, 4 hours on Saturday evenings and on holidays. Catering costs: hors d'oeuvres start at $15/person and seated meals at $25/person. 50% of the total charter cost is due 45 days prior to the event. A guaranteed guest count is required 7 days prior to departure, the remaining balance is due 5 days prior to your event.

CANCELLATION POLICY: If you cancel 60 or more days prior to your event, 80% of the deposit will be refunded. If less than 60, the deposit will be forfeited.

AVAILABILITY: Any time, no limits.

SERVICES/AMENITIES:
Restaurant Services: no
Catering: provided, no BYO
Kitchen Facilities: n/a
Tables & Chairs: provided
Linens, Silver, etc.: provided
Restrooms: wca
Dance Floor: yes

Parking: commercial lots
Overnight Accommodations: no
Telephone: cellular phone & radio
Outdoor Night Lighting: yes
Outdoor Cooking Facilities: no
Cleanup: provided
Other: full event coordination

RESTRICTIONS:
Alcohol: provided, BYO corkage fee $7/bottle
Smoking: outside only
Music: amplified ok

Wheelchair Access: yes
Insurance: not required

SAN FRANCISCO ZOO

Sloat Boulevard at 45th Avenue
San Francisco, CA 94132
(415) 666-7024 Marketing Section
Reserve: 2 weeks–6 months in advance

The San Francisco Zoo? Oh yes, you can rent this place, too! The Aviary, Children's Zoo, Insect Zoo, Lion's House, Terrace Cafe, Wildlife Theater and Carrousel plus areas that can be tented are all available for private functions. With Zebra Train Tours, Theme Parties and 'Behind the Scene' tours, your business associates, friends and family will have a wonderful time.

In addition, the Zoo hosts children's birthday parties, providing all eating utensils, cups, juice, ice cream and cake. They also throw in party hats, favors and tickets for a Carrousel ride for each child. The price includes admission to the Zoo and Children's Zoo. By prearrangement, box lunches can be provided. What a deal!

CAPACITY: Varies from 10–500 people. Call for specific area capacities.

FEES & DEPOSITS: For special events the rental fees are $1000–5000. Picnic areas are $40 and up. Call for specific rates. A deposit of 10% of the rental fee is required. Children's birthday parties cost $7.50/child and $12.50/adult.

CANCELLATION POLICY: Your deposit is refunded in full if you cancel 30 days prior to your event.

AVAILABILITY: Year-round; special events can be arranged for day or evening hours.

SERVICES/AMENITIES:

Restaurant Services: no
Catering: provided, or BYO
Kitchen Facilities: no
Tables & Chairs: BYO, some provided
Linens, Silver, etc.: BYO, some provided
Restrooms: wca
Dance Floor: yes

Parking: on street
Overnight Accommodations: no
Telephone: pay phones
Outdoor Night Lighting: in certain areas
Outdoor Cooking Facilities: CBA, approval needed
Cleanup: whoever caters event

RESTRICTIONS:

Alcohol: provided, no BYO
Smoking: restricted
Music: restricted

Wheelchair Access: yes
Insurance: required

THE SHERMAN HOUSE

2160 Green Street between Webster & Fillmore
San Francisco, CA 94123
(415) 563-3600
Reserve: 3 months in advance

This tastefully and artfully decorated house, originally built in 1876 by the founder of the Sherman/Clay Music Company, opened as a hotel 6 years ago with a private dining room. This is an elegant place for a business or special event. The Sherman House butler ushers guests into the house through a separate entry for private functions. Guests then move on to the music room featuring wood paneling, fireplace, leaded glass skylight, mirrors and a double staircase that descends into the room from an upper level gallery. The musicians' balcony, overlooking the music room, is a perfect spot for a harpist, guitarist or trio. The lush gardens in the back of the house are quite lovely, with a cobbled courtyard, gazebo and fountain. If you want a place that is really private, quiet and sophisticated, ask to see the Garden Suite. These quarters can be rented separately, and come with private salon, bedroom, bath and two private gardens. The Sherman House staff offers personal, attentive service and will help you with flowers, cake or other party planning details.

CAPACITY: The house can accommodate up to 80 for an hors d'oeuvres reception, carried by silver tray butler service. Capacity for seated meals is 45. No buffets are allowed.

MEETING ROOM: The Garden Suite can accommodate up to 14 for a conference-style meeting.

FEES & DEPOSITS: A refundable deposit is required to secure your event date. The rental fee for use of the music room and gallery is $500–$1500 depending on the number of guests, season and time of day. Use of the Garden Suite is $700. Food service costs range from hors d'oeuvres receptions $35-$55/person to seated functions ranging from $55–$80/person. Gratuity at 18% and a 7.25% tax are added to the final bill. The final balance is due at least 30 days prior to the function.

CANCELLATION POLICY: Cancellation is required 30 days prior to your event to receive a refund and 45 days prior to your party during peak periods.

AVAILABILITY: Not restricted. Guests must vacate the premises by 10pm during the week, 10:30pm on weekends.

SERVICES/AMENITIES:
Restaurant Services: yes
Catering: provided, no BYO
Kitchen Facilities: n/a
Tables & Chairs: provided
Linens, Silver, etc.: provided
Restrooms: wca
Dance Floor: no

Parking: valet CBA
Overnight Accommodations: 14 guestrooms
Telephone: house phone
Outdoor Night Lighting: no
Outdoor Cooking Facilities: no
Cleanup: provided

RESTRICTIONS:
Alcohol: provided
Smoking: outside only
Music: no amplified

Wheelchair Access: yes
Insurance: not required

SHOWPLACE DESIGN CENTER

2 Henry Adams Street
San Francisco, CA 94103
(415) 864-1500 Donna or David
Reserve: 3–6 months in advance

Built in the early 1900s, this historic building has survived two major earthquakes. The main event area has a western ambiance with white shutters, rough-hewn wood, and brick walls. One entire side of the room has floor-to-ceiling multi-paned windows that flood the space with natural light during the day. Small palms add a touch of greenery. The Cabaret's sunken dance floor has first-rate sound and stage lighting, and guests can appreciate the festivities from seating arranged around the dance floor and on the mezzanine. Another space available at the Showplace is The Penthouse. It's a large, sunny living room environment for intimate parties, meetings and dinners with a glass-enclosed meeting/dining area on the roof terrace.

CAPACITY, FEES & DEPOSITS:

Area	Seated	Reception	Rental Fees
Cabaret	250	500	$1500/day
Penthouse	80	125	$850/day
Penthouse & Meeting Rooms	—	—	$350/day for meetings

A nonrefundable deposit of 50% of the rental fee is required when the contract is submitted. The balance is due 30 days prior to the event. Fees include a house technician.

MEETING ROOMS: 1 meeting room for 20–125 seated participants.

CANCELLATION POLICY: The fees and deposits can be applied toward another event within a 90-day period.

AVAILABILITY: Year-round. The Cabaret Monday–Thursday after 3pm, Sunday from 8am; no Friday or Saturday nights. The Penthouse every day from 8am.

SERVICES/AMENITIES:

Restaurant Services: no
Catering: in-house caterer or BYO w/approval, extra fee
Kitchen Facilities: minimal
Tables & Chairs: provided
Linens, Silver, etc.: BYO
Restrooms: no wca
Dance Floor: yes

Parking: street, adjacent lot
Overnight Accommodations: no
Telephone: pay phones
Outdoor Night Lighting: no
Outdoor Cooking Facilities: no
Cleanup: provided
Other: event coordination, technician for shows

RESTRICTIONS:

Alcohol: provided, no BYO
Smoking: allowed
Music: amplified ok

Wheelchair Access: limited
Insurance: certificate required

SS JEREMIAH O'BRIEN

Fort Mason
San Francisco, CA 94123
(415) 441-3101 Marci Hooper
Reserve: 1—6 months in advance

This is America's last unaltered Liberty Ship. Out of more than 2,700 nearly identical ships, the Jeremiah O'Brien is the only known Liberty Ship that is in original and full operating condition! Preserved as a National Historic Landmark, the 441-foot long ship is now docked at Fort Mason and is available for Bay charter cruises, tours and special events. The forward gun tub and deck are great party places because the views of Alcatraz, Angel Island and Aquatic Park are sensational. This is a wonderful spot (especially if you're a World War II buff) and there is an additional bonus—during events the ship's staff is available to give highly interesting tours of the multiple decks and machine rooms.

CAPACITY: The ship can accommodate 300 standing guests and 220 for seated functions.

FEES & DEPOSITS: A $125 cleaning deposit is required. There's a flat rental fee of $65—250 (depending on which space is reserved) plus an additional $3/person.

CANCELLATION POLICY: A 10-day advance notice is required for a full refund.

AVAILABILITY: 9:30am to midnight. No events on New Year's, Christmas, Easter or Thanksgiving holidays.

SERVICES/AMENITIES:

Restaurant Services: no
Catering: BYO
Kitchen Facilities: no
Tables & Chairs: provided
Linens, Silver, etc.: BYO
Restrooms: no wca
Dance Floor: yes

Parking: large lot
Overnight Accommodations: no
Telephone: office phone
Outdoor Night Lighting: yes
Outdoor Cooking Facilities: no
Cleanup: caterer

RESTRICTIONS:

Alcohol: BYO
Smoking: outside preferred
Music: amplified ok

Wheelchair Access: no
Insurance: sometimes required
Other: gangway entry steep & narrow

THE STANFORD COURT

905 California Street
San Francisco, CA 94108
(415) 989-3500
Reserve: 1 week–12 months in advance

When you arrive at this 5-star hotel on prestigious Nob Hill, you don't just walk through the front door—you drive through an imposing stone arch, park in an enclosed brick courtyard and then walk into the elegant lobby. The floor is alabaster marble accented by oriental carpets, and overhead is a stunning stained glass domed skylight, the focal point of the room. Its green, white and orange geometric pattern softly diffuses incoming rays. The adjacent lounge is also out of the ordinary with wood paneling, marble pillars and a grandfather clock. The hotel offers numerous meeting and event spaces. The Ballroom, traditional in decor, is highlighted by Baccarat chandeliers acquired from the Grand Hotel in Paris. A smaller room, The India Suite, features hand-painted murals depicting scenes from India. The hotel has recently added three new burlwood-paneled rooms for multi-purpose functions and four private rooms in the restaurant for board meetings, luncheons or dinners.

	Room	*Reception*	*Seated*	*Classroom-Style*	*Theater-Style*
CAPACITY:	Stanford Ballroom	800	400	350	700
	India Suite	250	180	150	275
	Telegraph Hill Room	40	30	20	30
	Russian Hill	50	40	25	40
	Nob Hill	90	70	40	50
	Fournou's Ovens Private Rooms (4)	—	10–24	—	—

FEES & DEPOSITS: A refundable deposit of 25% of the estimated food and beverage cost is payable when reservations are confirmed. For functions without food service, rental fees range from $150–3500. All or a portion of the rental fees may be waived with a minimum level of service. The balance and final guest count are due 2 days–1week prior to the event. Invoicing can be arranged. Per person rates: seated breakfasts start at $19.50, luncheons at $22, dinners at $32, buffets (for 75 min) start at $32–46, and hors d'oeuvres at $15. Tax of 7.25% and gratuity of 15% are additional.

CANCELLATION POLICY: If the space(s) can be rebooked, the deposit will be refunded.

AVAILABILITY: Year-round, every day, any time.

SERVICES/AMENITIES:
Restaurant Services: yes
Catering: provided, no BYO
Kitchen Facilities: n/a
Tables & Chairs: provided

Linens, Silver, etc.: provided
Restrooms: wca
Dance Floor: yes
Parking: valet

Overnight Accommodations: 400 guestrooms
Telephone: pay phones
Outdoor Night Lighting: no

RESTRICTIONS:
Alcohol: provided, no BYO
Smoking: designated areas
Music: amplified w/approval

Outdoor Cooking Facilities: no
Cleanup: provided
Other: event & conference coordination, piano

Wheelchair Access: yes
Insurance: sometimes required
Other: no open flames

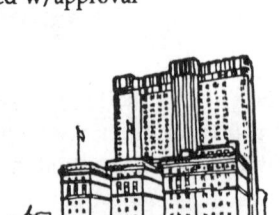

THE ST. FRANCIS HOTEL

335 Powell Street, Union Square
San Francisco, CA 94102
(415) 774-0126   Catering Manager
Reserve: 1 day–12 months in advance

Named the Westin St. Francis in 1982, this famous San Francisco landmark has been the hotel of choice for internationally prominent guests since its inception. From royalty to presidents and society notables to Hollywood stars, the St. Francis has offered first class dining and lodging for almost 100 years. This stately, 12-story building facing Union Square was one of the few structures to survive the 1906 earthquake. Considerably damaged by fire, it was quickly refurbished using California's most skilled artists and craftsmen to recreate the ornate and opulent interior. Marble Corinthian columns, paneled ceilings with gold leaf trim and crystal chandeliers are highlights of the Main Lobby. Innovations were added to make it the most sophisticated hotel of its time. Still a grand and impressive place, the St. Francis is more than qualified to host your business functions or special celebrations.

CAPACITY: The St. Francis has 29 rooms that can accommodate events. Here are a few:

Room	Theater-Style	Classroom-Style	Seated
Grand Ballroom	1500	1000	1150
Colonial Room	400	250	340
California Ballroom	600	450	600
4 Elizabethan Rooms (ea)	125	80–100	100–110
12 Parlor Meeting Rooms	30–70	15–45	20–60
City Club (3 sections)	110	70	100

FEES & DEPOSITS: A nonrefundable $500–1000 deposit is payable when you confirm your reservation and 25% of the estimated event total is due 2 weeks prior to the function. Rental fees vary from $75–$3000 for a 4-hour rental. Deposits and fees vary with guest count, type of function and room(s) rented. The balance is invoiced, payable 30 days following the function. If food service is provided, rental fees are reduced. Per person rates: continental breakfasts range from $11–15, breakfasts $16–23, luncheons $23–50, dinners $34–70, hors d'oeuvres start at $10 and buffets range from $27-65. Coffee service for meetings starts at $3.25/person. Tax of 7.25% and 15% gratuity are added to the final bill.

AVAILABILITY: Year-round, every day, any time up to 2am.

SERVICES/AMENITIES:

Restaurant Services: yes

Catering: provided, no BYO

Kitchen Facilities: n/a

Tables & Chairs: provided

Linens, Silver, etc.: provided

Restrooms: wca

Dance Floor: yes

Parking: hotel garage or adjacent lots

Overnight Accommodations: 1200 guestrooms

Telephone: pay phone

Outdoor Night Lighting: no

Outdoor Cooking Facilities: no

Cleanup: provided

Other: event coordination, grand piano

Special. theme party coordination

RESTRICTIONS:

Alcohol: provided, BYO WB $12/bottle

Smoking: allowed

Music: amplified ok

Wheelchair Access: yes

Insurance: not required

THE TROCADERO

Sigmund Stern Grove Clubhouse
19th Ave. and Sloat Blvd.
San Francisco, CA 94116
(415) 666-7035 Recreation & Parks
(415) 776-4104 S. F. Croquet Club
Reserve: 1–12 months in advance

Tucked in the middle of Stern Grove, approached from a lovely entry drive flanked by eucalyptus and stone walls, sits The Trocadero Clubhouse. This turn-of-the-century, two-story Victorian is available for special events, and features a spacious veranda, river rock fireplace, hardwood floors, old fashioned bar, and fully equipped industrial kitchen. Adjacent park amenities include a pond, redwood grove, bridge, meadow, outdoor stone fireplaces and picnic tables. (This is also the home of the San Francisco Croquet Club, located on 19th Ave., adjacent to the Wawona Club House. Plan your corporate or social event to include a 3-hour croquet program with world-class equipment, fast lawns and an unmatched coach-to-player ratio. Rivaling the offerings of the West's best croquet resorts, it's a terrific Club for novices.) In Stern Grove, you can ignore the fact that you're in urban San Francisco; this is an oasis in the heart of the City.

CAPACITY: The Trocadero can hold up to 175 guests for a standing reception and 100 for seated meals. Outdoor picnic tables can seat 400 for an informal affair.

FEES & DEPOSITS: The fees and a refundable cleaning/security deposit of $150 are due 30 days prior to your event. The rental fee is $200 for a 6-hour function on weekdays. From 5pm Friday to 11pm Sunday and holidays, the fee is $300.

CANCELLATION POLICY: If you cancel 30 days prior to your event, you will receive 90% of your deposit; if less than 10 working days in advance, no refund.

AVAILABILITY: Rental times are 10am–4pm and 5–11pm in 6-hour blocks any day of the week. Extended hours 8–10am and 11am–1pm can be arranged with advance notice.

SERVICES/AMENITIES:

Restaurant Services: no

Catering: BYO

Kitchen Facilities: moderate

Tables & Chairs: provided

Linens, Silver, etc.: BYO

Restrooms: multiple, wca

Dance Floor: yes

Parking: 50–75 cars

Overnight Accommodations: no

Telephone: distant pay phone

Outdoor Night Lighting: yes

Outdoor Cooking Facilities: stone fireplaces

Cleanup: caterer

Other: wooded area and gardens nearby

RESTRICTIONS:

Alcohol: BYO

Smoking: allowed

Music: amplified until 11pm

Wheelchair Access: yes

Insurance: not required

TUBA GARDEN

3634 Sacramento Street
San Francisco, CA 94118
(415) 921-8822   Ben or Anthony
Reserve: 1 week in advance

Located in Presidio Heights and tucked away on a quiet semi-residential street, this charming Victorian mansion and nearby carriage house is enhanced by an English garden with classical statues and a bubbling fountain. Its atmosphere and cuisine are reminiscent of a lovely European cafe. Individual rooms for private parties can be arranged for celebrations, business meetings and luncheons.

CAPACITY: 60 people can be accommodated for a sit-down affair and up to 120 for a standing hors d'oeuvres reception.

FEES & DEPOSITS: A $150 refundable deposit is required one month prior to the function. Food service is provided. Luncheons start at $7/person and dinners at $22/person. Hors d'oeuvres start at $20/person. Tax is 7.25% and service charge is 15%.

AVAILABILITY: Year-round, any day, any time.

SERVICES/AMENITIES:

Restaurant Services: yes

Catering: provided, no BYO

Kitchen Facilities: n/a

Tables & Chairs: provided

Linens, Silver, etc.: extra charge

Dance Floor: yes

Parking: valet recommended

Overnight Accommodations: no

Telephone: pay phone

Outdoor Night Lighting: yes

Outdoor Cooking Facilities: no

Cleanup: provided

Special: full event planning

RESTRICTIONS:
Alcohol: provided, $7/BYO bottle corkage
Smoking: outside only
Music: no amplified

Wheelchair Access: yes
Insurance: not required

THE WATTIS ROOM
At Davies Symphony Hall

201 Van Ness Avenue
San Francisco, CA 94102
(415) 552-4089
Reserve: 1–6 months in advance

Most folks don't know that the Wattis Room, the private dining room in Davies Symphony Hall, is available for business functions and social events. Well, luckily for us, it is. This is a space tucked away on the first floor, approached through the main doors on Grove Street. As you enter the room, you'll notice the large art pieces on the walls, rotating exhibits from the San Francisco Museum of Art. The lighting is subdued and the room's decor is sophisticated and understated. From cocktail parties to formal seated dinners, the Wattis Room is versatile enough to handle any type of crowd.

CAPACITY: The Wattis Room can hold 100 seated guests and 200 guests for a reception.

FEES & DEPOSITS: No deposit is required. The rental fee covers a 4-hour block and is $450 for a nonprofit group/individual or $650 for businesses. Rental includes event manager, flowers, piano and custodial services. Any hours over 4 cost $100/hour. Food service is provided. Seated breakfasts $10/person, buffets range $12–18/person, luncheons start at $12/person, dinners at $18/person and hors d'oeuvres start at $3/person. Tax is 7.25% and the production charge is 20%.

AVAILABILITY: Year-round, any day, any time. Overtime will be charged for functions past midnight. Dates in June, July, August and Christmas holidays are more available because the symphony is in recess.

SERVICES/AMENITIES:
Restaurant Services: no
Catering: in-house caterer has first right of refusal
Kitchen Facilities: fully equipped
Tables & Chairs: some provided
Linens, Silver, etc.: provided, extra fee
Dance Floor: CBA

Parking: Grove & Franklin garage
Overnight Accommodations: no
Telephone: pay phone
Outdoor Night Lighting: no
Outdoor Cooking Facilities: no
Cleanup: provided

RESTRICTIONS:
Alcohol: provided, $3.50-5/BYO
bottle corkage negotiable
Smoking: allowed
Music: amplified ok

Wheelchair Access: yes
Insurance: not required
Other: red wine at seated events only, votive candles only

WHITE SWAN INN

845 Bush Street
San Francisco, CA 94108
(415) 775-1755
Reserve: 3–12 months in advance

Ideally located in the heart of San Francisco, the White Swan Inn blends the charm of an English country house with the cosmopolitan bustle of the City. This building is a distinctive 4-story bed and breakfast, constructed in 1908 and completely renovated in 1985. The Inn offers a variety of rooms that can be set up for private parties. Guests are ushered through the Art Nouveau beveled-glass entry doors into an English-style interior, complete with delicate floral wallpaper and handsome antiques. Downstairs rooms can be reserved for private parties. The Dining Room has wood parquet floors, antiques, marble-topped tables and a small bar. The Library, reached through a set of French doors, is similar to an English gentleman's club with wood paneling, working fireplace and comfy furniture. The adjacent Conference Room has mirrors, built-in bar with audio visual equipment and doors leading to a back garden. It's like being in London: sophisticated and stylish but with all the comforts of home.

CAPACITY: The downstairs rooms can hold up to 70 standing and 30 seated guests.

FEES & DEPOSITS: A refundable deposit of 50% of the total estimated cost is payable when you make your reservation. The rental fees range from $250–750 depending on the length of the event and the number of guests. The Inn caters all events. Hors d'oeuvres start at $20–$30/person and seated meals range from a low of $30 to a high of $70/person for a 7-course dinner. A 7.25% sales tax and 15% gratuity are added to the final bill which is payable at the completion of your party.

CANCELLATION POLICY: Your deposit is refunded in full if you cancel 30 days prior to your event.

AVAILABILITY: Every day, from noon–4pm and 7pm–10pm. The Inn can be flexible with these hours, especially if your group books guest rooms.

SERVICES/AMENITIES:
Restaurant Services: no
Catering: provided, no BYO
Kitchen Facilities: ample
Tables & Chairs: provided
Linens, Silver, etc.: provided
Restrooms: no wca
Dance Floor: no dancing

Parking: public garage nearby
Overnight Accommodations: 26 guestrooms
Telephone: house phone
Outdoor Night Lighting: CBA
Outdoor Cooking Facilities: no
Cleanup: whoever caters event

RESTRICTIONS:
Alcohol: provided or BYO at $4/bottle corkage
Smoking: allowed
Music: amplified restricted

Wheelchair Access: no
Insurance: not required

WHITTIER MANSION

2090 Jackson Street
San Francisco, CA 94109
(415) 567-1848 Corinne Abbott
Reserve: 1–3 months in advance

The Mansion was completed in 1896 for William Whittier, paint mogul and founding father of the Fuller O'Brien Paint Company. Reflecting a blend of influences, the architecture mixes Richardsonian Romanesque, late Queen Anne and Classic Revival styles. One of the key elements here is wood. The foyer glows with its golden oak stairway, parquet floor and arched entryways to adjacent rooms. The Parlor features a stunning oversized fireplace hewn from deep rose, dusky pink and white marble. It is surrounded by carved wood from floor to ceiling, and is completed by a beautiful wooden mantle. Wood pillars, trim, and wainscotting add a rich warmth throughout. The Turkish Lounging Room, in a rounded corner of the building, is unique. A molded plaster ceiling in a colorful red, green, blue and gold design, and striking brass fixtures from Turkey create an unusual and vibrant setting in which to hold small meetings and for larger groups, meetings can be held in the spacious ballroom. Other noteworthy features are the Dining Room walls, fashioned from an unknown but rare wood, and the original lighting fixtures in the reception room downstairs. The Whittier Mansion is a turn-of-the-century jewel that will add a special ambiance to any event.

CAPACITY: The Mansion can seat 150 guests, 300 for receptions (all 3 floors) and 200 guests using just 2 floors.

FEES & DEPOSITS: A refundable deposit of 50% of the rental fee is payable when the contract is submitted and a refundable $500 security deposit is also required. The balance is due 1 month prior to the event. The rental fees are $1500 first floor, $1800 first and second floors and $2200 for the entire house. For a small function with no kitchen use the rate is $150/hour, the daily rate is $1000. For tours of the building the cost for 2 docents is $25.

CANCELLATION POLICY: With 60 days' notice you'll receive a full refund. The security deposit is usually returned after an event; however, if you cancel it's forfeited.

AVAILABILITY: Year-round, every day, any time.

SERVICES/AMENITIES:

Restaurant Services: no
Catering: preferred list, BYO with approval
Kitchen Facilities: ample
Tables & Chairs: BYO
Linens, Silver, etc.: BYO
Restrooms: no wca
Dance Floor: Ballroom

Parking: nearby lot $2/car
Overnight Accommodations: no
Telephone: house phone
Outdoor Night Lighting: no
Outdoor Cooking Facilities: no
Cleanup: caterer
Other: docents and tours

RESTRICTIONS:

Alcohol: BYO
Smoking: outside only
Music: amplified ok to 11:30pm

Wheelchair Access: yes
Insurance: not required
Other: votive candles only

Half Moon Bay

DOUGLAS BEACH HOUSE

Miramar Beach
Half Moon Bay, CA 94018
(415) 726-4143   Carol Christen
Reserve: 1 week in advance

You can't get much closer to the ocean than this. On a secluded stretch of coast just north of Half Moon Bay lies the Douglas Beach House, famous for its concerts otherwise known as The Bach Dancing and Dynamite Society. It's actually a rambling complex of a house with recital/music hall, decks, and dining rooms. The proprietor is a character. Pete Douglas is well known for his jazz and classical programs presented regularly on Fridays and Sundays. Saturdays and weekdays are set aside for private parties. The decor has been described as "comfy-funky in that rustic Northern California style of hanging ferns, dark wood and stained glass." The multiple decks and ocean vistas make this a great place to have a fun gathering or an out-of-the-ordinary business meeting.

CAPACITY: The concert room can hold up to 180 guests theater-style, the dining area, 95 for seated meals. The entire facility can accommodate up to 150.

FEES & DEPOSITS: For meetings, no deposit is required. For social events, a refundable deposit of 50% of the total estimated rental fee is due on confirmation. The rental fee for meetings is $120–225, depending on the number of guests. For social events, the fee is $650–1000, depending on the date, time and number of guests.

CANCELLATION POLICY: Any setup for meetings will be charged if the date is cancelled. Refunds for meetings require a 24-hour advance notice. For social events, refunds will be made only if the space can be rebooked on the event date.

AVAILABILITY: Year-round, except for major holidays. Parties are scheduled for Saturdays 2pm–8pm; and occasional Friday nights may be scheduled if available. Business functions Monday-Friday 8am–6pm.

SERVICES/AMENITIES:

Restaurant Services: no
Catering: BYO
Kitchen Facilities: ample
Tables & Chairs: provided
Linens, Silver, etc.: BYO
Restrooms: no wca
Dance Floor: yes

Parking: parking lot
Overnight Accommodations: no
Telephone: pay phone
Outdoor Night Lighting: yes
Outdoor Cooking Facilities: BYO
Cleanup: provided

RESTRICTIONS:
Alcohol: BYO, no kegs
Smoking: allowed
Music: amplified ok

Wheelchair Access: limited
Insurance: not required

MILL ROSE INN ★

615 Mill Street
Half Moon Bay, CA 94019
(415) 726-9794
Reserve: 1 month in advance

The Mill Rose is more than just a bed and breakfast. It's an outstanding location for business retreats, seminars or awards ceremonies. From the gingerbread detailing and blue and white Victorian features, to the sensational floral palette of the garden, the Mill Rose offers a first rate experience. Every room is appealing, many with excellent floral arrangements composed by the owner. The dining room is light and fresh, with rose carpets, fireplace and decorative wallpaper. The parlor is warm and inviting with lots of color and appointments that express attention to detail. The library is a small jewel-of-a-room that features a beautifully painted fireplace and window alcove with benchseat overlooking the magnificent blooms outside. Framed by handsome oaks, the courtyard is a sheltered and lovely space for an outdoor luncheon, comfortable and spacious, yet small enough to lend intimacy to any gathering. There's no doubt why the Mill Rose Inn is so popular. It delivers that extra, intangible quality that's hard to describe but immediately recognizable when felt.

CAPACITY: Indoor areas can hold up to 25 seated guests; 40–60 for outdoor functions.

FEES & DEPOSITS: Payment in full is required when reservations are confirmed. For groups of over 8 guests, the business rate is $80/person for 8 hours which includes continental breakfast, lunch, unlimited beverages, afternoon fruit, wine and cheese, business equipment and rental space. For under 8 guests, the rental rate is $600/day. Overtime runs $50/hour. Commercial discounts can be arranged for Sunday–Thursday overnight stays.

CANCELLATION POLICY: No refunds. If you cancel, credit can be applied towards another meeting.

AVAILABILITY: Year-round, any day in an 8-hour block, usually 9am–5pm.

SERVICES/AMENITIES:
Restaurant Services: no
Catering: provided, BYO ok
Kitchen Facilities: n/a
Tables & Chairs: provided
Linens, Silver, etc.: provided
Restrooms: no wca
Dance Floor: no
Parking: on street, off street

Overnight Accommodations: 8 guestrooms
Telephone: house & guest phones
Outdoor Night Lighting: yes
Outdoor Cooking Facilities: yes
Cleanup: provided
Other: event coordination
Special: spa, massage service

RESTRICTIONS:
Alcohol: BYO
Smoking: outside only
Music: amplified ok

Wheelchair Access: yes
Insurance: not required

STRAWBERRY RANCH

Redondo Beach Rd. at Highway 1
Half Moon Bay, CA 94019
(415) 726-5840   Shelly Gill
Reserve: 2 weeks–6 months in advance

Strawberry Ranch is a bit off the beaten path, but well worth the effort if you're looking for a unique retreat or mini-conference environment. Follow the bumpy and largely unpaved Redondo Beach Road to the end and turn left. Sitting by itself, within 100 yards of the ocean, is an attractive, 2-story gray and blue wood structure with decks and garden. The original building was constructed in the early 1900s, and has seen a colorful past, from rum runners during prohibition to military operations through World War II. Remodeled and restored, it provides unobstructed panoramic views of the ocean through wall-to-wall windows while getting down to business in a comfortable and casual workshop setting. Strawberry Ranch offers its guests an outstanding oceanfront location with quiet and privacy, away from phones and the bustle of the office.

CAPACITY: Strawberry Ranch can accommodate up to 50 guests.

MEETING ROOMS: Downstairs conference room, 12 guests (6 person min), upstairs room, 50 guests (20 person min).

FEES & DEPOSITS: Half of the estimated cost of the conference is due when reservations are confirmed. The rental fee is $55/person which includes meeting space, continental breakfast, deli-buffet lunch, all beverages throughout the day, all conference-related equipment, tax and gratuity. For the upstairs room, the minimum rental cost is $1100 for up to 20 guests. The fee for each additional guest is $55. Dinners and hors d'oeuvres, wine, beer and BBQ events can be arranged.

CANCELLATION POLICY: With 30 days' notice, the deposit is fully refundable.

AVAILABILITY: Year-round, 8am–9pm. Closed the last 2 weeks of December.

SERVICES/AMENITIES:
Restaurant Services: no
Catering: provided, no BYO
Kitchen Facilities: n/a
Tables & Chairs: provided
Linens, Silver, etc.: provided
Restrooms: no wca
Dance Floor: no

Parking: large lot
Overnight Accommodations: no
Telephone: house phones
Outdoor Night Lighting: CBA
Outdoor Cooking Facilities: BBQ
Cleanup: provided

RESTRICTIONS:

Alcohol: WB provided or BYO, no hard liquor
Smoking: outside only
Music: amplified subject to approval

Wheelchair Access: limited
Insurance: required

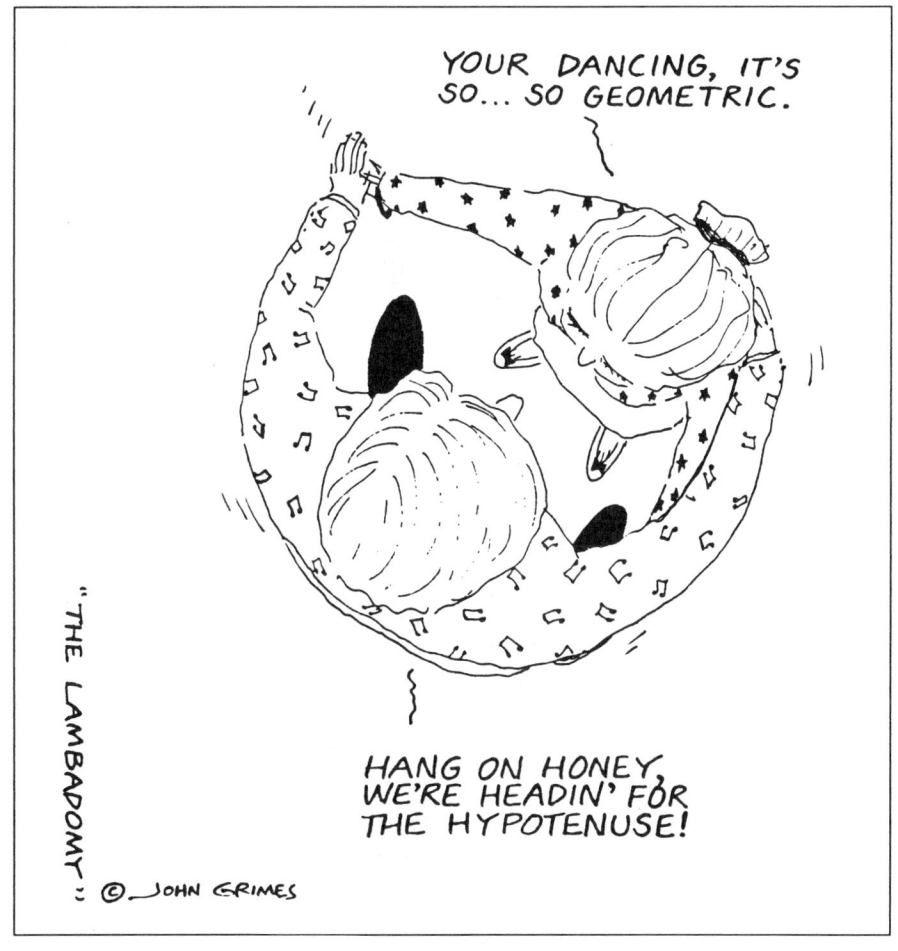

Belvedere

CHINA CABIN

54 Beach Road
Belvedere, CA
(415) 435-2251 Beverly Bastian
Reserve: 10 days in advance

In 1866, the Pacific Steamship Company commissioned W.M.Webb to construct a sidewheel steamer. Unfortunately, with a wood hull, the ship was destined for a short career and was burned for scrap metal in 1886. The China Cabin, the First Class social salon, was removed intact from the ship and set on pilings in the Belvedere Cove. The Cabin consists of a large room and two small state rooms. Its plain exterior belies the ornate and regal appointments inside. This place is impressive. The walls and domed ceiling are panels of elaborately carved wood that have been painted a crisp white and highlighted with gold leaf. Along the sides of the Cabin are a series of small, delicately etched glass windows; handsome crystal chandeliers hang at each end of the room. The Cabin also has decks on three sides that have wonderful views of the Cove and boats of the nearby yacht club. The China Cabin offers a glimpse of old world elegance and attention to detail; the result is a rich, sophisticated appearance that makes this a very unique setting for a significant corporate event or special party.

CAPACITY: The Cabin can hold up to 55 standing and 48 seated guests. The outdoor deck will allow 65 guests during summer months.

FEES & DEPOSITS: A $100 deposit is required when you make your reservation. The rental fee is $520/hour for a 5-hour minimum rental block, and $100 for each additional hour. The total fee is due 10 days prior to your party.

CANCELLATION POLICY: Should you cancel 2 weeks before the event, your deposit will be refunded.

AVAILABILITY: Any day, any time until midnight.

SERVICES/AMENITIES:

Restaurant Services: no
Catering: BYO, must be approved
Kitchen Facilities: no
Tables & Chairs: chairs provided
Linens, Silver, etc.: some provided
Restrooms: wca
Dance Floor: yes

Parking: CBA
Overnight Accommodations: no
Telephone: house phone
Outdoor Night Lighting: limited
Outdoor Cooking Facilities: no
Cleanup: caterer

RESTRICTIONS:

Alcohol: BYO
Smoking: not allowed
Music: no amplified

Wheelchair Access: yes
Insurance: proof of liability required
Other: decorations restricted

SAN FRANCISCO YACHT CLUB

98 Beach Road
Belvedere, CA 94920
(415) 435-9133 Cathy Larson
Reserve: 12 months in advance

Established in 1869, the San Francisco Yacht Club is the oldest yacht club on the West Coast. Located on Belvedere Cove, the Club offers an enchanting view of blue-trimmed sail boats and the sound of lapping waves. The Club has a variety of settings for private parties. The spacious Main Dining Room and Bar have warm, dark woods, comfortable chairs and large glass windows that overlook the deck and marina. The Commodore Room has a similar decor but can accommodate a smaller, more intimate party. It offers access to a wide deck overlooking the marina. The Cove House, a designated historical landmark, was originally built as a private residence in 1915 and its interesting arched entry was incorporated from the 1914 Pan-Pacific Exhibition. The interior features a large fireplace, delicate chandeliers and shiny hardwood floors; the overall mood is cool, sophisticated and elegant. In front of the House is a piazza of patterned brick and a well manicured lawn with benches. Beautiful, wide stones steps lead up to a spacious terrace that flows gracefully into the main structure. Note that this is a private club and that you must have a member sponsor your group.

CAPACITY, FEES & DEPOSITS: Half of the rental fee is required as a deposit to secure your date.

Area	Standing	Seated	Fees
Main Dining Room & Bar	300	185	$1200
Commodore Room (winter)	40	40	250
Commodore Room (summer)	60	40	400
Cove House Only	50-75	60	800
Cove House w/Piazza	—	—	1600

Food service is provided. Hors d'oeuvres are $20/person and seated meals start at $25/person. Bar service runs an additional $8.75-12/person plus a bartender charge of $12/hour. A 6.25% sales tax and 15% gratuity are added to the final total which is billed, net 30 days.

CANCELLATION POLICY: The deposit will be fully refunded with written notice 3 months prior to your party.

AVAILABILITY: The Main Dining Room and Bar are available Monday, Tuesday and Wednesday any time after 11am. Cove House 11:30am-8pm every day, April-October with a maximum of 60 guests.

SERVICES/AMENITIES:

Restaurant Services: yes
Catering: provided, no BYO
Kitchen Facilities: n/a
Tables & Chairs: provided
Linens, Silver, etc.: provided
Restrooms: wca
Dance Floor: yes

Parking: lot, on street
Overnight Accommodations: no
Telephone: pay phones
Outdoor Night Lighting: Cove House only
Outdoor Cooking Facilities: yes
Cleanup: provided

RESTRICTIONS:

Alcohol: provided, no BYO
Smoking: allowed
Music: amplified until 8pm

Wheelchair Access: yes
Insurance: not required
Other: $200 fee if confetti thrown

Fairfax

DEER PARK VILLA

367 Bolinas Road
Fairfax, CA 94930
(415) 456-8084
Reserve: 1–6 months in advance

The Villa is nestled among 4 acres of redwoods, oaks and lush hydrangeas. This homey Italian restaurant is supported by a very professional catering and restaurant staff which has plenty of experience hosting parties and business events. The facility includes a front garden with outdoor dance area, bar, covered and heated patio, towering redwood trees and a small Japanese pagoda and foot bridge. The main dining area is decorated in muted pinks and dark mint green with windows on three sides; adjacent to the dining area is a full bar. The split level, back deck is intimate and surrounded by dense greenery. Operated by the Ghiringhelli family since 1937, the Deer Park Villa is a Marin County dining and banquet tradition.

CAPACITY: The Redwood Grove holds up to 300 guests; the Redwood Deck and adjoining indoor room, 125. The Villa can accommodate up to 225, but can be partitioned so that smaller groups have privacy.

FEES & DEPOSITS: For luncheons the deposit is $2/person, for banquets $3/person and for special events $375-575 depending on the type of function. The deposit secures your date and is required when you make your reservation. The rental fee for special events is $375–900, depending on the combination of spaces desired. Per person rates: event hors d'oeuvres start at $15, buffets at $18.50 and seated meals at $19.50. Sales tax of 6.25% and a 15% gratuity will be applied to the total food and bar service bill, excluding rental fees.

For group meetings or parties taking place in the Villa's regular dining areas, there is no rental fee. Group rates for brunch and lunch are each $13.50/person and dinners are $16.75/person. Tax and gratuity are included in these rates.

CANCELLATION POLICY: If your date can be rebooked, the deposit will be refunded in full.

AVAILABILITY: For a group of 150 or more, any day, any time. For groups of 25 to 125, Wednesday–Sunday all day.

SERVICES/AMENITIES:

Restaurant Services: yes

Catering: provided, no BYO

Kitchen Facilities: n/a

Tables & Chairs: provided

Linens, Silver, etc.: provided

Restrooms: wca limited

Dance Floor: yes

Parking: large lot

Overnight Accommodations: no

Telephone: pay phone

Outdoor Night Lighting: yes

Outdoor Cooking Facilities: BBQs

Cleanup: provided

RESTRICTIONS:

Alcohol: provided, BYO W&C corkage $5.50/bottle

Smoking: allowed

Music: amplified until 8pm, restricted

Wheelchair Access: yes

Insurance: not required

Greenbrae

JOE LO COCO'S RESTAURANTE

300 Drake's Landing Road
Greenbrae, CA 94904
(415) 925-0808
Reserve: 1 month in advance

Known for its distinctive Northern Italian cuisine and friendly staff, Joe Lo Coco's also offers a private banquet room in addition to its main dining room. This room has clean lines and a spare decor, making it perfect for 'dressing up'. The day we visited this facility, it was being decorated for a bar mitzvah. The walls are all glass, making the room light and cheerful for daytime functions. During large receptions, guests can spill out into the adjacent courtyard, which is just a stone's throw from one of Greenbrae's many canals.

CAPACITY: The Banquet Room can hold 130 seated guests, 250, for a reception. For luncheons Monday–Friday, the minimum is 25 guests, on weekends 100 guests. The minimum for dinner is 25 guests.

FEES & DEPOSITS: A refundable deposit of 25% of the estimated food cost, or $250 is due when reservations are confirmed. The room rental is $100, and a bartender fee is $100. The balance is payable the day of the event. Per person rates: seated or buffet luncheons $15–25, seated or buffet dinners $20–30, and hors d'oeuvres $12–15. Tax of 6.25% and a 17% gratuity are additional.

CANCELLATION POLICY: If the space can be rebooked within 6 months, the deposit will be refunded.

AVAILABILITY: Year-round, every day 11:30am–midnight. Closed most major holidays.

SERVICES/AMENITIES:

Restaurant Services: yes

Catering: provided, no BYO

Kitchen Facilities: n/a

Tables & Chairs: provided

Linens, Silver, etc.: provided

Restrooms: wca

Dance Floor: yes

Parking: large lot

Overnight Accommodations: no

Telephone: pay phone

Outdoor Night Lighting: no

Outdoor Cooking Facilities: no

Cleanup: provided

RESTRICTIONS:

Alcohol: provided, no BYO

Smoking: allowed

Music: amplified ok

Wheelchair Access: yes

Insurance: not required

Other: decorations require approval

Larkspur

THE LARK CREEK INN ★★

234 Magnolia Avenue
Larkspur, CA 94939
(415) 924-1602 or 924-7766 Banquet Manager
Reserve: 1–2 months in advance

A refreshing vision, The Lark Creek Inn sits back from the road, shaded by coast redwoods and nestled next to Lark Creek. Inside, the yellow 1888 Victorian country home is painted in muted colors and appointed with taste and a sense of understatement. The walls are adorned with original watercolors and in the main dining room there's a brick oven open for viewing. The Garden Patio, adjacent to the creek and approached through either the well-tended garden or Sun Porch, is a little bit of heaven. It's a tranquil and private spot for a reception or a lovely garden party. We'd like to mention that the food here is exceptionally good, some of the best we've ever had. Add that to the outstanding ambiance and you'll understand why any business or personal event here turns into a celebration. The Lark Creek Inn rates high on our list.

CAPACITY, FEES & DEPOSITS:

Area	Reception	Seated	Fees/event
Private Dining Room	50	32	$50
Garden	100	60	100
Sun Porch	65	44	100
Main Dining Room	150	116	100
Sun Porch & Garden	150	100	100

A refundable deposit of 50% of the estimated food and beverage total is due when reservations are confirmed. The entire restaurant can be reserved, with rates ranging from $2000–$25,000 depending on the day of week, time and guest count. The Private Dining Room minimum is $600 for luncheons and Sunday Brunch, $900 for dinners. The balance is due the day of the function. Tax of 6.25% and an 18% gratuity are additional.

CANCELLATION POLICY: 50% of the deposit is refundable with 30 days' written notice.

AVAILABILITY: Year-round, every day, any time. Closed Christmas day and eve, New Year's day and July 4th.

SERVICES/AMENITIES:

Restaurant Services: yes

Catering: provided, no BYO

Kitchen Facilities: n/a

Tables & Chairs: provided

Linens, Silver, etc.: provided

Restrooms: wca

Dance Floor: yes

Parking: large lot

Overnight Accommodations: no

Telephone: pay phone

Outdoor Night Lighting: yes

Outdoor Cooking Facilities: BBQs

Cleanup: provided

Other: in-house pastry chef

RESTRICTIONS:

Alcohol: provided, BYO corkage $10/bottle

Smoking: bar and patio only

Music: amplified w/approval

Wheelchair Access: yes

Insurance: not required

Mill Valley

THE MILL VALLEY OUTDOOR ART CLUB

1 West Blithedale
Mill Valley, CA
(415) 383-2582
Reserve: 6–12 months in advance

The Outdoor Art Club, located in downtown Mill Valley, is one of Marin's favorite event spots. You enter through a wooden arch into a restful garden patio that immediately removes you from the bustle of everyday life. Centered in the large patio is a sprawling grand oak that provides a canopy, allowing dappled light to filter through. The flowers and other landscaping add to the serenity of this outdoor space. The clubhouse, designed in 1904 by Bernard Maybeck, displays his trademark peaked roof line. Inside, the main hall is spacious and majestic with a very high ceiling of dark exposed beams. Windows across the south side lighten the room and can be opened to admit breezes. There's a large stage at one end of the clubhouse for a dance band and a smaller room, running the full length of the clubhouse, which is perfect for a lavish buffet. There's no question why the Outdoor Art Club is so popular—this is a great location.

CAPACITY: The facility can hold up to 200 standing and 120 seated guests. The sun room holds an additional 40 seated guests.

FEES & DEPOSITS: A refundable deposit of 50% of the rental fee is required to reserve a date. A security deposit of $500 is also required and is refunded after the keys are returned. The Club's rental fee is $1000. The remaining 50% is due 10 days before your function.

CANCELLATION POLICY: The deposit is refunded only if the date can be rebooked.

AVAILABILITY: Weekends 8am–1am. Weekdays are negotiable.

SERVICES/AMENITIES:

Restaurant Services: no
Catering: BYO
Kitchen Facilities: ample
Tables & Chairs: most provided
Linens, Silver, etc.: some provided
Restrooms: wca
Dance Floor: yes

Parking: street only
Overnight Accommodations: no
Telephone: pay phone
Outdoor Night Lighting: yes
Outdoor Cooking Facilities: no
Cleanup: caterer
Other: caretaker provided

RESTRICTIONS:

Alcohol: BYO
Smoking: allowed
Music: amplified until midnight, indoors only

Wheelchair Access: yes
Insurance: not required

MOUNTAIN HOME INN

810 Panoramic Highway
Mill Valley, CA 94941
(415) 381-9000
Reserve: 1–6 months in advance

Perched on the eastern slope of Mt. Tamalpais is a modern wooden structure with spectacular views of Marin, San Francisco Bay and Mt. Diablo. The decor in the main dining room is simple, but elegant. Furniture and rugs are in muted pastels and a large stone fireplace enhances a feeling of cozy intimacy. The Mountain Home Inn also features a bar area which is light and airy with high ceilings adorned with natural redwood tree trunks. Nearby is a large deck that takes full advantage of the panoramic views below. An additional dining room downstairs uses mirrors to draw the light through double glass doors off the neighboring deck.

CAPACITY:	Area	Season	Standing	Seated
	Upper & Lower Floor and Deck	March–Oct	110	40–110
	Upper Floor & Deck	Oct–March	80	80
	Lower Floor	—	40	35

FEES & DEPOSITS: A nonrefundable deposit in the amount of your rental fee is required to secure your date. The Upper & Lower Floor rental rate is $1500. The Lower Floor rental fee is $250. The rate for each of the 10 guestrooms ranges from $112–178/night. Food service is provided. Food costs run $20/person for hors d'oeuvres or light meals, $25-30/person for buffets and seated meals. Bar service, 6.25% sales tax and 15% gratuity are added to the final bill.

AVAILABILITY: Every day, from 11:30am-4pm and 5:30-11pm.

SERVICES/AMENITIES:

Restaurant Services: yes

Catering: provided, no BYO

Kitchen Facilities: n/a

Tables & Chairs: provided

Linens, Silver, etc.: provided

Restrooms: wca

Dance Floor: yes

Parking: easy eves, difficult weekend days

Overnight Accommodations: 10 guestrooms

Telephone: pay phone

Outdoor Night Lighting: yes

Outdoor Cooking Facilities: no

Cleanup: provided

RESTRICTIONS:

Alcohol: provided, WBC only, BYO corkage $8/bottle

Smoking: allowed

Music: amplified until 11pm

Wheelchair Access: yes

Insurance: not required

Muir Beach

PELICAN INN

Muir Beach, CA 94965
(415) 383-6000
Reserve: 3–6 months in advance

Capturing the spirit of a 16th century English country inn, the Pelican Inn's romantic illusion is enhanced by sea-blown fog, a touch of forest and the fragrance of honeysuckle and jasmine in the air. The merry Tudor bar serves an impressive selection of foaming brews, wines and sherries. The dining room, with its authentic great brick Inglenook (fireplace) is rustic, dark and cozy. The adjoining patio, surrounded by stone and vines, and topped with a glass roof, is light and convivial. In the tradition of English country inns, the food is hearty and succulent with a slight American accent. The outdoor patio is wonderful for meetings and special events, and if you're considering spending the night here, don't worry. The Inn has seven rooms with private baths, English antiques and canopy beds. For weekday meetings, the Inn can accommodate small groups in their 'Snug' (cozy) Room.

CAPACITY: The Inn's patio can accommodate 45 guests for meetings; the Snug up to 12 people. The dining room can hold up to 45 guests.

FEES & DEPOSITS: Half of the rental fee is required to reserve your date. The dining room with patio and use of the bar is $500. The fee for use of the patio or Snug is $100. Food service is provided. Hors d'oeuvres start at $6/person and buffets start at $15/person. Bar service, 6.25% tax and 15% gratuity will be applied to the final bill, payable the day of the party.

CANCELLATION POLICY: The deposit is refunded if you cancel 30 days or more in advance.

AVAILABILITY: Mondays 8am–11pm. Other weekdays, 8am-10pm by arrangement.

SERVICES/AMENITIES:

Restaurant Services: yes

Catering: provided, no BYO

Kitchen Facilities: n/a

Tables & Chairs: provided

Linens, Silver, etc.: provided

Restrooms: wca

Dance Floor: CBA

Parking: big lot

Overnight Accommodations: 7 guestrooms

Telephone: pay phone

Outdoor Night Lighting: no

Outdoor Cooking Facilities: no

Cleanup: provided

RESTRICTIONS:

Alcohol: provided, WBC only, BYO corkage $10/bottle

Smoking: allowed

Music: acoustical until 10pm

Wheelchair Access: yes

Insurance: not required

Nicasio

THE SHADOWS

1901 Nicasio Valley Road
Nicasio, CA 94946
(415) 662-2012
Reserve: 2–4 months in advance

Ensconced in a circle of towering redwoods, The Shadows is a woodsy and private spot for small social and business groups looking for something a bit different. A cultural and educational retreat, perfectly suited for overnight stays, it's located in a secluded redwood forest in West Marin County. It's a quiet getaway for an undisturbed meeting, workshop, seminar or gathering of any sort. The buildings here are new, tastefully designed in an elegant yet rustic style with stone fireplaces and beamed ceilings. There's also a pool house and pool which can be used for meetings or parties. Close by are wooded hiking and biking trails leading to adjoining State and Federal parks or to a nearby golf course. Although just 19 miles from the Golden Gate Bridge, The Shadows has that intangible quality of making you feel like you're in another world.

CAPACITY: The Shadows has indoor meeting rooms which can accommodate 15–30 people. Outdoor facilities can hold up to 120 guests.

FEES & DEPOSITS: A $200 refundable deposit secures your date and is due when reservations are made. Rental fees: $400/day for the outdoor picnic and BBQ areas, $300/day for the pool and pool house, $300–400 for other indoor facilities.

CANCELLATION POLICY: With 60 days' notice, the deposit is refunded in full.

AVAILABILITY: Year-round, every day 10am–10pm unless you are an overnight guest.

SERVICES/AMENITIES:

Restaurant Services: no
Catering: BYO or CBA
Kitchen Facilities: ample
Tables & Chairs: BYO or CBA
Linens, Silver, etc.: BYO or CBA
Restrooms: wca
Dance Floor: outdoor
Parking: big area

Overnight Accommodations: 15 bedrooms
Telephone: guest phone
Outdoor Night Lighting: yes
Outdoor Cooking Facilities: BBQ
Cleanup: whoever caters event
Other: audio-visual equipment
Special: kids' play area

RESTRICTIONS:

Alcohol: BYO
Smoking: outside only
Music: amplified, DJ ok

Wheelchair Access: yes
Insurance: certificate required
Other: no pets

Ross

MARIN ART AND GARDEN CENTER
Caroline Livermore Room

30 Sir Francis Drake Blvd.
Ross, CA 94957
(415) 454-1301 Phyllis Ongaro
Reserve: 1–2 months in advance

The Caroline Livermore Room is located in a small building set way back into the lovely ten acres of the Marin Art and Garden Center. Just off Sir Francis Drake Blvd. in Ross, this special indoor-outdoor space is perfectly suited for meetings, seminars and workshops as well as events. The indoor space has a large party room with multiple glass doors opening out onto the deck and stone patio. The adjacent outdoor gravel and paved areas are surrounded by large trees and flowers which provide spots of color. This facility, a favorite among Marin residents because of its park-like setting, attracts groups from all over the Bay Area.

CAPACITY: This facility can accommodate 225 standing and 140 seated guests. In combination with the outdoor areas, it can hold up to 500 guests. For lectures or workshops, it can seat between 120 and 160 people.

FEES & DEPOSITS: For special events, a $200 nonrefundable deposit is required to secure your date; for business events, the deposit is a nonrefundable $20. For special events, the fees vary depending on season and guest count:

Number of Guests	Winter Fee	Spring/Summer Fee
50-200	$550	$650
200-300	—	750
300-400	—	800

For business meetings of less than 50 people, the rental fee is $45/day; over 50 people, $75/day. For all-day business functions, nonprofits are charged $200/day and others $300/day. Fees must be received 10 days prior to an event or meeting.

AVAILABILITY: Year-round. Wintertime indoor functions: Friday eves, Saturday and Sunday until 11pm. Spring/Summer outdoor events: weekends until dusk. Weekday functions until 11pm.

SERVICES/AMENITIES:

Restaurant Services: no

Catering: BYO, must be licensed

Kitchen Facilities: ample

Tables & Chairs: provided

Linens, Silver, etc.: caterer

Restrooms: wca

Dance Floor: yes

Parking: large lot

Overnight Accommodations: no

Telephone: pay phone

Outdoor Night Lighting: yes

Outdoor Cooking Facilities: no

Cleanup: caterer

Other: security guard

RESTRICTIONS:

Alcohol: BYO, caterer must serve

Smoking: allowed

Music: inside only

Wheelchair Access: yes

Insurance: liability required

MARIN ART AND GARDEN CENTER
Ross Garden Restaurant

30 Sir Francis Drake Blvd.
Ross, CA 94957
(415) 457-2151
Reserve: 2 weeks in advance

Within the Marin Art and Garden Center located in lovely residential Ross, is the Ross Garden Restaurant. Parties can take place indoors or on the spacious patio which has umbrella-shaded tables for balmy al fresco dining. Converted from a 1930s home and set off from the rest of the garden complex, the restaurant derives its secluded, woodsy ambiance from the surrounding canopy of trees and the adjacent ten acres of beautiful gardens. Consequently, it's a wonderful place for a relaxed, comfortable outdoor function, especially during spring and summer months. In wintertime, enjoy the fireplace indoors.

CAPACITY: The restaurant and garden patio can accommodate 150 guests spring through fall. The private dining room can hold 75 guests year-round.

FEES & DEPOSITS: The $200–500 rental fee is the deposit required to secure your date for a 4-hour function. For outdoor parties, there's a security guard fee of $75. Meals start at $18/person; a 6.25% tax and 15% gratuity are additional. The event balance is payable by the end of the function.

CANCELLATION POLICY: The deposit is nonrefundable unless the space can be rebooked.

AVAILABILITY: Luncheons, every day Tuesday–Friday 11:30am–2pm. For outdoor functions, weekdays, 4pm to dusk; Saturdays and Sundays, any time to dusk. Indoor events 4pm–10pm Friday–Sunday. The restaurant is closed two weeks over the Christmas holiday.

SERVICES/AMENITIES:

Restaurant Services: yes
Catering: provided, no BYO
Kitchen Facilities: n/a
Tables & Chairs: provided
Linens, Silver, etc.: provided
Restrooms: wca
Dance Floor: yes

Parking: large lot
Overnight Accommodations: no
Telephone: pay phone
Outdoor Night Lighting: no
Outdoor Cooking Facilities: no
Cleanup: provided

RESTRICTIONS:

Alcohol: provided, WBC only, BYO corkage $5/bottle
Smoking: allowed
Music: amplified restricted

Wheelchair Access: ramp
Insurance: not required

San Rafael

DOMINICAN COLLEGE

50 Acacia Avenue
San Rafael, CA 94901
(415) 485-3228
Reserve: 2–12 months in advance

This facility is situated in a quiet residential area of San Rafael, on an 80-acre wooded campus developed at the turn of the century. For an outdoor affair, the Ann Hathaway Garden provides a lovely lawn, ringed with roses and other annuals, which can be equipped with a dance floor or decorated with night lighting. Housed in a modern building nearby, the Shield and Creekside Rooms offer spaces for smaller parties and meetings. Also located on campus is Meadowlands, a grand, three-story Victorian structure that has been meticulously maintained. Broad steps lead up to a sunny veranda, and the massive front door seems a threshold into another era. Spacious and inviting, the interior entry hall and dining room feature polished wood paneling and patterned ceilings. Downstairs you'll see the dance hall and stage alcove lit by brilliant sunlight coming through stained glass windows. The Meadowlands can accommodate a very large group by offering variety—the veranda and grounds for sun, the main floor for quiet dining and conversation and the downstairs for lively dancing. The campus is also a popular spot for conferences, seminars, workshops, and retreats. During the summer, the college offers overnight accommodations for business guests.

CAPACITY, FEES & DEPOSITS: The full rental fee is the deposit required to secure your date.

Area	Standing	Seated	Rental Fee
Meadowlands	250	150	$600
Ann Hathaway Garden	200	100	150
Shield Room	500	340	500-600
Creekside Room	100	50-75	300-350

CANCELLATION POLICY: If you cancel 60 days or more in advance of your event, you'll receive a full refund. Weekday meetings may require less notice.

AVAILABILITY: Meadowlands: Mid-May to mid-June, Christmas school break and early September before the school session begins. Hathaway Garden: weekends only. The Creekside Room is available any time; however, the Shield Room has restricted hours.

SERVICES/AMENITIES:

Restaurant Services: no

Catering: BYO except Shield & Creekside Rooms, preferred caterer

Kitchen Facilities: varies

Tables & Chairs: some provided

Linens, Silver, etc.: BYO

Restrooms: wca

Dance Floor: yes or CBA

Parking: large lot, on street

Overnight Accommodations: summer only

Telephone: varies

Outdoor Night Lighting: CBA

Outdoor Cooking Facilities: yes

Cleanup: caterer

Other: baby grand piano

RESTRICTIONS:

Alcohol: BYO, permit required

Smoking: allowed

Music: amplified ok

Wheelchair Access: mostly yes

Insurance: certificate required

FALKIRK MANSION

1408 Mission Street
San Rafael, CA 94901
(415) 485-3328
Reserve: 6–8 months in advance

The historic Falkirk Mansion, built in 1888, is a lovely Queen Anne Victorian. Spacious foyer, parlor and dining room lend themselves beautifully to elegant parties, receptions, change-of-pace business meetings, small seminars, workshops and special events. The interior's redwood paneling, shiny hardwood floors and elegant wall coverings are stunning. The dining area has a huge fireplace and floor-to-ceiling windows overlooking the deck. Curving around two sides of the Mansion is a wide veranda bordered by colorfully planted flower boxes. Nestled on the hill above San Rafael's City Hall and surrounded by lawns and tall, stately trees, this century-old Victorian mansion has a charm and intimacy along with a central location to be found nowhere else in Marin.

CAPACITY: Parlor, 50 seated guests; dining room 30 seated. The entire Mansion can hold up to 100 for a standing reception and 50 seated guests. The summer capacity, with veranda, is 125.

FEES & DEPOSITS: A nonrefundable deposit of 50% of the rental fee is required to reserve your date. From October 15-April 15, there is a $90/hour rental fee for a 6-hour minimum block. From April 16–October 14, the fee is $115/hour for a 6-hour minimum. Ask about special holiday rates. The total balance is payable 45 days in advance of your event.

CANCELLATION POLICY: The deposit and any additional fees paid will be forfeited if cancellation occurs within 45 days of the event.

AVAILABILITY: Year-round.

SERVICES/AMENITIES:

Restaurant Services: no
Catering: select from approved list
Kitchen Facilities: minimal
Tables & Chairs: CBA, extra charge for chairs
Linens, Silver, etc.: BYO
Restrooms: wca
Dance Floor: yes

Parking: large lot
Overnight Accommodations: no
Telephone: pay phone
Outdoor Night Lighting: CBA
Outdoor Cooking Facilities: BBQ
Cleanup: caterer

RESTRICTIONS:

Alcohol: BYO, caterer must serve
Smoking: outside only
Music: amplified to 90 decibels

Wheelchair Access: yes
Insurance: extra liability for alcohol
Other: no candles, decorations restricted

SAN RAFAEL IMPROVEMENT CLUB

Corner of 5th and H Streets
San Rafael, CA 94901
(415) 459-9955
Reserve: 2 weeks–6 months in advance

The San Rafael Improvement Club is one of the few structures remaining from the 1914 San Francisco Pan Pacific Exhibition. The building, designed by William B. Faville, was brought over to San Rafael in 1915 and purchased by the Improvement Club. It's now an historic landmark, ensconced in a small garden setting with an adjacent brick patio. Its interior is sophisticated and attractive, accented with scalloped pillars, large windows and a sculpted ceiling. Light and airy, this facility is great for parties of any kind.

CAPACITY: The Club can hold up to 160 for a buffet and 125 seated guests.

FEES & DEPOSITS: A $200 refundable security deposit is required to reserve a date. On weekends, the rental fee is $350 and on weekdays, the fee for business meetings is $100 for a 2-hour minimum. The rental fee for luncheons during the week is $225, evening events $275. The final rental balance is due 10 days prior to the event.

CANCELLATION POLICY: The deposit for weekend events is fully refundable with 60 days' notice. For weekday functions, a 2-week notice is required.

AVAILABILITY: Weekends, 10am–midnight. During the week, 8am–midnight. Thursdays and Fridays from 10am–5pm are not available for bookings.

SERVICES/AMENITIES:

Restaurant Services: no
Catering: BYO
Kitchen Facilities: minimal
Tables & Chairs: provided
Linens, Silver, etc.: BYO
Restrooms: wca
Dance Floor: yes

Parking: lot and street
Overnight Accommodations: no
Telephone: pay phone
Outdoor Night Lighting: yes
Outdoor Cooking Facilities: no
Cleanup: caterer

RESTRICTIONS:

Alcohol: BYO
Smoking: not allowed
Music: amplified until 10pm

Wheelchair Access: yes
Insurance: liability required
Other: decorations restricted, no candles

Sausalito

THE ALTA MIRA

125 Bulkley Avenue
Sausalito, CA 94965
(415) 332-1350
Reserve: 2 weeks–6 months in advance

The Alta Mira is one of Marin's oldest and most renowned hotels. The property was originally the residence of Thomas Jackson, who later converted his villa into a hotel. After the original structure was lost in a fire, Jackson's son rebuilt the Alta Mira as a Spanish-style villa. The main dining room has a huge deck, reminiscent of the Riviera with its round tables and bright umbrellas. The deck also has one of the most spectacular panoramic views of the San Francisco skyline, Sausalito Harbor and Angel Island. It's understandably a very popular spot for business as well as private gatherings. The main dining area is relaxed but elegant, highlighted with leaded glass mirrors and floral designs. A private dining room called the Fiesta Room has high ceilings, chandeliers and a gorgeous fireplace with hand-painted tiles displaying a country garden. Large mirrors extend the open, sunny feeling of this beautiful room and the adjoining deck has a lovely view of the San Francisco skyline. Rooms at the hotel are available, including a suite in an adjacent Victorian house that includes sitting room, kitchen and deck.

CAPACITY: The Annex Dining Room and Deck can hold 200 standing guests and 150 seated. There is a 130-guest minimum requirement for this space. The Fiesta Room can accommodate 110 for a buffet and 100 seated guests, with a 35-guest minimum. The Outdoor Patio seats 150 maximum.

FEES & DEPOSITS: For special events, a $500 refundable deposit is required to reserve a date and is applied towards the food and beverage bill. For a luncheon or dinner, there is no rental fee. 50% of the anticipated total is due 30 days prior to your function and the balance is due the day of the event. Food service is provided. Hors d'oeuvres/receptions run $35–40/person and seated meals $30–45/person, including bar service. A 6.25% tax and 15% gratuity will be applied towards the final bill.

For weekday business meetings, the rental fee is $200. The fee is used as a deposit and is due 10 days prior to the function. Continental breakfasts and coffee service can be arranged.

CANCELLATION POLICY: If you give notice 4 months in advance, your deposit will be returned. Business functions require less notice.

AVAILABILITY: The Annex and Deck are available Saturdays, 2:30pm–6:30pm. The Fiesta Room is available anytime during the week, noon–5pm and 6:30pm–11pm Saturday and 4pm–9pm Sunday.

SERVICES/AMENITIES:

Restaurant Services: yes
Catering: provided, no BYO
Kitchen Facilities: n/a
Tables & Chairs: provided
Linens, Silver, etc.: provided
Restrooms: limited wca
Dance Floor: yes

Parking: valet CBA, on street
Overnight Accommodations: yes
Telephone: pay phone
Outdoor Night Lighting: patio only
Outdoor Cooking Facilities: no
Cleanup: provided
Special: event planning services

RESTRICTIONS:

Alcohol: provided, BYO corkage $10/bottle
Smoking: allowed
Music: no amplified

Wheelchair Access: limited, entry CBA
Insurance: sometimes required

CASA MADRONA

801 Bridgeway
Sausalito, CA 94965
(415) 332-0502
Reserve: 1–2 months in advance

Located in the hills of Sausalito, the Casa Madrona Hotel is a haven of comfort and retreat. Built in 1885, the original Victorian mansion has been expanded to include three cottages and the New Casa. The result is a grand establishment that offers a variety of services and settings. The Casa Madrona Restaurant has a dramatic, glass-enclosed terrace with a retractable roof and sliding glass windows that create an open, outdoor feeling. It is situated high on the hill and has spectacular views. The North East Alcove, adjacent to the main dining area, is a smaller semi-private dining room perfect for small business dinners. Below the restaurant is a 1300 square foot tiled terrace. Again, views of Angel and Belvedere Islands and the harbor are unsurpassed. The Cafe Madrona is located next door, in the newly remodeled Village Fair. Though a more informal atmosphere, you still have the advantages of superb views. Indirect lighting and pinkish stone floor tiles further enhance the relaxed but stylish motif. The Villa Madrona Suite is a terrific location for a meeting, with its three verandas overlooking the Bay, a private terrace and fireplace.

CAPACITY, FEES & DEPOSITS: A refundable deposit in the amount of your rental fee is due when you reserve your date and space.

Room	Standing	Seated	Fee
Restaurant (min 75 guests)	140	110	$750
Cafe Madrona	110	80	500
Northeast Alcove	—	36	—
Tiled Terrace	120	40	100
Villa Madrona Suite (business retreats)	25-60	30	300

For any time beyond your event deadline, a fee of $50/15 minutes will apply. Food service is provided. Meals run $25-30/person minimum and approximately $7–10/person for alcohol. The food and beverage total is due 30 days prior to your event. Any remaining balance is due the day of the event.

CANCELLATION POLICY: The deposit is refunded if the space can be rebooked.

AVAILABILITY: Cafe Madrona: 6pm–11pm every day.
Restaurant/Alcove: Mon-Fri, 11:30am–2:30pm; Mon-Sun, 6–10pm; Sunday, 10am–2:30pm.
Villa Madrona Suite: Every day from 2–10pm, 5-hour block maximum.

SERVICES/AMENITIES:

Restaurant Services: yes
Catering: provided, no BYO
Kitchen Facilities: n/a
Tables & Chairs: provided
Linens, Silver, etc.: provided
Restrooms: wca
Dance Floor: yes

Parking: City lot nearby, valet CBA
Overnight Accommodations: 33 guestrooms
Telephone: pay and guest phones
Outdoor Night Lighting: tile terrace
Outdoor Cooking Facilities: no
Cleanup: provided
Other: superb cakes

RESTRICTIONS:

Alcohol: provided, BYO corkage $10/bottle
Smoking: in designated areas
Music: amplified until 9pm

Wheelchair Access: Restaurant: no; Suite & Cafe: yes
Insurance: not required

SAUSALITO WOMAN'S CLUB ★

120 Central Ave.
Sausalito, CA 94965
(415) 332-0354
Reserve: 2–6 months in advance

This is a Sausalito landmark building, a classic craftsman-style Julia Morgan building nestled in the hills overlooking the Bay. Dedicated in 1918, and built as a woman's club, it's been a preferred place for meetings and social functions through the years. The structure is clad in brown shingles and is designed with simple and understated detailing. The large auditorium room has a stage, original fixtures, hardwood floor and large paned windows, perfect for receptions or business presentations. Multiple doors open onto a small brick patio sheltered by mature oaks. The landscaping is well maintained and the canopy of trees surrounding the Woman's Club filters glimpses of the Bay beyond. Unpretentious yet stately, this structure fits into the hillside landscape perfectly. It's a bit hard to find, but worth the exploratory trip into the always interesting and visually stimulating Sausalito hills.

CAPACITY: The Club can hold 150–175 seated guests, 200–225 for buffets and 250–275 theater-style.

FEES & DEPOSITS: For weekend events, a refundable $500 deposit is due when the rental contract is submitted. The rental fee is $775 for 48 hours for both Saturday and Sunday. For weekday events the deposit is $200 and the rental fee is $250 for 12 hours. The rental balance is due 10 days prior to the function.

CANCELLATION POLICY: The deposit is refunded with 6 months' notice.

AVAILABILITY: Year-round, every day until midnight except Thursdays.

SERVICES/AMENITIES:

Restaurant Services: no

Catering: BYO

Kitchen Facilities: setup only

Tables & Chairs: provided

Linens, Silver, etc.: BYO

Restrooms: wca

Dance Floor: yes

Parking: street, shuttle encouraged

Overnight Accommodations: no

Telephone: house phone

Outdoor Night Lighting: no

Outdoor Cooking Facilities: no

Cleanup: whoever caters event

RESTRICTIONS:

Alcohol: BYO

Smoking: outside only

Music: amplified within limits, until 10pm

Wheelchair Access: limited

Insurance: certificate required

Other: decorations restricted

Tiburon

CORINTHIAN YACHT CLUB

End of Main Street
Tiburon, CA 94920
(415) 435-4771 Linda Gow
Reserve: 2–12 months in advance

Reminiscent of a ship captain's parlor, the Corinthian Yacht Club Ballroom is a spacious room that is popular for receptions, business luncheons and banquets. It features wood paneling with hardwood floors plus high ceilings which are draped with nautical flags and lit by two chandeliers made from wooden ship wheels. There is an enormous stone fireplace above which soars a majestic bronze eagle. Adjacent is a glass-enclosed solarium with a fantastic view of the Tiburon Harbor and San Francisco Bay. When there's a full moon, this panoramic view is absolutely breathtaking (not to mention romantic). Downstairs, the newly remodeled main dining room is also available for parties. The neighboring deck overlooks the picturesque marina and has a similar, sensational view of the harbor and Bay. Note that this is a private club and that you must be sponsored by a member.

CAPACITY: The Ballroom can accommodate 250 standing guests and 150–200 seated guests. The Main Dining Room can hold between 50–100.

FEES & DEPOSITS: A refundable $750 deposit (applied towards the fee) is required to secure your date and is payable when you reserve. The rental fee for the Ballroom for up to 150 guests, is $1650, for over 150, $2,200. The Dining Room fee is $500. For less than 100 guests, a $95 cleaning fee is required. These fees are for a 5-hour maximum rental and are payable 1 week prior to your function.

Food service is provided. Prices range from $25–35/person. A $400 minimum for bar service is required; an open bar usually costs 12.50–16.50/person. A 6.25% tax and 17% gratuity are applied to the final bill. Note that rental discounts of up to 50% are available Monday-Friday for events.

CANCELLATION POLICY: With 4 months' advance notice in writing, you will receive a full refund. Less than 4 months, the deposit is forfeited.

AVAILABILITY: The Ballroom is available every day from 9am–midnight. The Dining Room Monday-Thursday, from 9am–midnight.

SERVICES/AMENITIES:

Restaurant Services: yes
Catering: provided, no BYO
Kitchen Facilities: n/a
Tables & Chairs: provided
Linens, Silver, etc.: provided
Restrooms: limited wca downstairs
Dance Floor: yes

Parking: public lot nearby
Overnight Accommodations: no
Telephone: pay phone
Outdoor Night Lighting: yes
Outdoor Cooking Facilities: no
Cleanup: provided

RESTRICTIONS:

Alcohol: provided, BYO possible
Smoking: allowed
Music: amplified restricted

Wheelchair Access: downstairs only
Insurance: not required

CHARLOTTE MAILLARD SWIG
San Francisco Director of Protocol

It was the 1983 opening of Otello when tenor Carlo Cossutta lost his voice and cancelled at the last minute. I was working on the pre-opera supper at the Museum of Modern Art when we got the message that Placido Domingo, who was in New York, would fly to San Francisco to substitute. Obviously, he was going to be late! I went to the phone and got Walt Tolleson's band to come over and play for dancing. People had a wonderful time. About every 45 minutes, they'd give us an update about what city Placido was flying over. There was great anticipation. When the opera finally happened, it wasn't over until the wee hours.

It all made for an exciting evening. People loved the fact that they didn't have to hurry through dinner. They figured that after all the effort of getting ready for the opera opening, with the clothes, the dinner, and the tickets, their expenses got pro-rated into many more hours, so the evening just got gayer and happier. No one dared leave, since there was no telling what might happen next. Getting the dance music must have been a good idea, because now it has become part of the Museum's pre-opera supper tradition. Later on, I flew to New York to give Placido the key to our City in thanks.

Reprinted with permission from "San Francisco Focus" September 1990

Bodega

SCHOOLHOUSE INN

17110 Bodega Lane
Bodega, CA 94922
(707) 867-3257
Reserve: 1 month in advance

The Schoolhouse Inn is probably best known for its role as the schoolhouse in the movie, "The Birds." Before becoming a movie star, however, it served as Potter School between 1873 and 1961. Five years later, the current owners purchased it and have used it as a residence, art gallery and restaurant. Two large classrooms were transformed into four guest rooms, all of which still retain the basic character of the original structure. The spacious hall upstairs is used for workshops, parties, local theater and other special events. It's a delightful room with a high ceiling, beautiful fir floor, fireplace and plenty of light.

CAPACITY: The facility can accommodate 100 people.

FEES & DEPOSITS: The function space at the Inn rents for $350, with an additional fee of $65 for use of the kitchen. A $200 deposit is due at the time of booking and the balance is due on arrival.

CANCELLATION POLICY: $100 is refunded with 30 days' notice; with less than 30 days' notice, $100 is refunded only if the space is rebooked.

AVAILABILITY: Every day, 11am–10pm.

SERVICES/AMENITIES:

Restaurant Services: no
Catering: BYO
Kitchen Facilities: ample
Tables & Chairs: chairs 50¢ each up to 80
Linens, Silver, etc.: caterer
Restrooms: no wca
Dance Floor: yes

Parking: on street
Overnight Accommodations: 4 guestrooms
Telephone: house phone
Outdoor Night Lighting: no
Outdoor Cooking Facilities: no
Cleanup: caterer

RESTRICTIONS:

Alcohol: BYO BW only
Smoking: outside only
Music: volume restricted

Wheelchair Access: yes
Insurance: liability required
Other: no children or pets

Bodega Bay

BAY HILL MANSION

3919 Bay Hill Road
Bodega Bay, CA 94923
(800) 526-5927 or (707) 875-3577 Fran Miller
Reserve: 2–3 months in advance

This contemporary Queen Anne Victorian bed and breakfast sits high, overlooking a sweeping panorama of Bodega Bay, its sand dunes and marinas. The main rooms are spacious and inviting, warmed by abundant natural light, comfortable furniture and a lovely fireplace. Marble and hardwood floors, high ceilings and soft colors create an elegant interior. All of the guestrooms have ocean views and fresh flowers from the surrounding hills. Whether you're planning a reunion, seminar, or reception, the Bay Hill Mansion will provide a serene and intimate setting.

CAPACITY: The facility has a maximum capacity of 50.

MEETING ROOMS: The Parlor and Dining Room accommodate 30 each.

FEES & DEPOSITS: The entire facility must be reserved, and a $500 deposit is due at the time of booking. The balance is due on arrival. In-house catering runs $15 to $30 per person.

CANCELLATION POLICY: A full refund will be given with 1 month's notice. With less than a month's notice, the deposit is forfeit unless the inn is rebooked.

AVAILABILITY: Year-round, every day.

SERVICES/AMENITIES:

Restaurant Services: no
Catering: provided or BYO
Kitchen Facilities: ample
Tables & Chairs: provided to 24
Linens, Silver, etc.: provided to 24
Restrooms: wca
Dance Floor: living room or deck

Parking: off street
Overnight Accommodations: 5 guestrooms
Telephone: common area
Outdoor Night Lighting: yes
Outdoor Cooking Facilities: yes for a fee
Cleanup: caterer
Special Services: massage room

RESTRICTIONS:

Alcohol: BYO, corkage $5/bottle
Smoking: outside or designated areas only
Music: approval required

Wheelchair Access: limited
Insurance: not required

TERRA NOVA INSTITUTE

PO Box 985
Bodega Bay, CA 94923
(707) 865-2377 Richard Murphy
Reserve: 1–2 months in advance

The Institute is a truly unique facility. Situated at the convergence of natural springs, white sandy beaches, acres of dunes, Salmon Creek and the ocean, it is a place for people to meditate, rest, commune with nature and generally disengage. The main house was built in the mid 1800s, but the current focal point of the Institute is the floral solarium, added nearly 40 years ago. A 2,000 square foot greenhouse, it houses dozens of varieties of coastal and semi-tropical plants. It is here, in the midst of greenery and sunlight, that people participate in workshops and seminars. The Institute is only available for use by nonprofit organizations involved in educational, spiritual or holistic pursuits.

CAPACITY: The facility can accommodate 50 people.

MEETING ROOMS: The Solarium has a capacity of 30.

FEES & DEPOSITS: The Solarium and grounds rent for $200 per day, $500 per weekend. If the entire house is rented, including overnight accommodations, the fee is $750. A $200 deposit is due at the time of booking and the balance is payable on arrival. Catering fees need to be arranged.

CANCELLATION POLICY: A full refund is given with 30 days' notice. Otherwise, a refund is given only if the space is rebooked.

AVAILABILITY: Every day.

SERVICES/AMENITIES:
Restaurant Services: no
Catering: provided from preferred list
Kitchen Facilities: n/a
Tables & Chairs: caterer
Linens, Silver, etc.: caterer
Restrooms: no wca
Dance Floor: no
Parking: on and off street

Overnight Accommodations: 4 guestrooms, 5 nearby homes
Telephone: house phone
Outdoor Night Lighting: no
Outdoor Cooking Facilities: BBQ
Cleanup: caterer, renter

RESTRICTIONS:
Alcohol: not permitted
Smoking: outside only
Music: no amplified

Wheelchair Access: yes
Insurance: not required
Other: no shoes worn in house

Cazadero

TIMBERHILL RANCH ★

35755 Hauser Bridge Road
Cazadero, CA 95421
(707) 847-3258
Reserve: 4–6 months in advance

Timberhill Ranch is a little like Shangri-la—a place steeped in beauty and harmony, far removed from the rest of the world. Set on a sunlit ridge, surrounded by high meadows and towering redwoods, Timberhill is an oasis of tranquility. The Main Lodge provides an intimate yet open space for get-togethers. Floor-to-ceiling windows and skylights bring the outdoors in, and the warmth of a parquet floor, wood and stone fireplace, exposed beams and comfortable seating invite guests to relax and stay a while. Ten private cottages work a similar magic: each has its own fireplace, private deck and tiled bath, and is fragrant with scents of cedar and fresh flowers. Add tennis courts, a swimming pool, a jacuzzi and exceptional cuisine, and you have a resort that is, perhaps, the ultimate escape.

CAPACITY: The Dining Room and Main Room in the Lodge can accommodate 26 people. This number is negotiable depending on the function.

MEETING ROOMS: A Conference Center that can accommodate 30 will be completed in Spring 1991.

FEES & DEPOSITS: Use of the facility is only available to overnight guests. Rates for accommodations are $148 per person/double occupancy on weekends, and $133 per person/double occupancy on weekdays. Fees include breakfast and dinner. There are special policies for holidays. A one night deposit is required at the time of booking, and the balance is due on departure.

CANCELLATION POLICY: With 7 days' notice, a full refund less a 5% processing fee is given. With less than 7 days' notice, a full refund less a 10% processing fee is given only if the accommodations are rebooked.

AVAILABILITY: Every day except 2 weeks in January.

SERVICES/AMENITIES:

Restaurant Services: yes
Catering: provided, no BYO
Kitchen Facilities: n/a
Tables & Chairs: provided
Linens, Silver, etc.: provided
Restrooms: no wca
Dance Floor: CBA

Parking: off street
Overnight Accommodations: 10 cottages
(5 more in Spring 91)
Telephone: house phone
Outdoor Night Lighting: minimal
Outdoor Cooking Facilities: no
Cleanup: provided

RESTRICTIONS:

Alcohol: BW provided, BYO in cottages only
Smoking: designated areas only
Music: with approval

Wheelchair Access: limited
Insurance: not required

Fort Bragg

MENDOCINO COAST BOTANICAL GARDENS

18220 N. Highway 1
Fort Bragg
(707) 964-4352
Reserve: 2–3 months in advance

It is hard to believe that a garden as spectacular as this exists a mere 500 feet from the highway. When you walk through the entrance, a seemingly endless landscape of colorful and varied plants unfolds before you. Meandering paths take you past plant species from all over the world—the Mediterranean, South Africa, Australia and more! Nestled between the pine forest and the main garden is the Meadow Lawn, a lovely, semi-private clearing surrounded by trees, bushes and flowers. On a sunny day the setting is just right for a small reception or intimate party. With 47 acres of garden and pine forest to explore, this is a one-of-a-kind event location.

CAPACITY: The Meadow Lawn accommodates 50.

FEES & DEPOSITS: A fee of $50 for up to 25 people and $100 for 26–50 people is payable at the time of booking.

CANCELLATION POLICY: A full refund will be given with 30 days' notice.

AVAILABILITY: Every day except Thanksgiving, Christmas, and New Years. Hours are 9am–5pm, March–October; 10am–4pm, November–February. The rainy season is mid-October through mid-March.

SERVICES/AMENITIES:

Restaurant Services: no
Catering: BYO
Kitchen Facilities: no
Tables & Chairs: BYO
Linens, Silver, etc.: BYO
Restrooms: wca
Dance Floor: no

Parking: lot
Overnight Accommodations: no
Telephone: pay phone
Outdoor Night Lighting: no
Outdoor Cooking Facilities: no
Cleanup: renter or caterer

RESTRICTIONS:

Alcohol: BYO
Smoking: designated areas only
Music: with approval

Wheelchair Access: yes
Insurance: not required
Other: no vehicle access to site; 500-foot walk from lot

Gualala

ST. ORRES ★

36601 S. Highway 1
Gualala, CA 95445
(707) 884-3303 Jan Harris
Reserve: 6 months in advance

St. Orres is a feast for the eyes as well as the palate. As you approach this fantastic structure along the coast, you realize that you've never seen anything quite like it. Built from rough-hewn redwood, with intricately carved railings and large onion-shaped copper domes, it evokes the Russian countryside. Inside, the Lobby welcomes guests with a blazing fire. The Dining Room, with its soaring cathedral ceiling, massive beams, and 30-foot high wall of windows provides the perfect setting for the inn's renowned cuisine. Named one of Northern California's 100 best restaurants by *Epicurean* magazine, St. Orres' ever-changing menu showcases fresh local and home-grown ingredients. The inn is also an interesting spot for a retreat, private party or business function. Groups can gather in the larger cottages, on the grounds or in the Dining Room (when available). Ensconced among acres of woods, facing the spectacular Mendocino coast, St. Orres is one of the most remarkable inns you are likely to encounter.

CAPACITY: The facility accommodates 50 inside and 100 outside.

MEETING ROOMS: The Dining Room is available daily until 3:30pm and has a capacity of 55; Pinehaven Cottage can hold up to 30.

FEES & DEPOSITS: Rental fees are based on the number of accommodations reserved. A 2-night minimum is required on weekends (Fri–Sun). 50% of the estimated cost is due within 5 days of making reservations and the balance is payable 1 month before the event. Catering fees run $40+ per person.

CANCELLATION POLICY: With 3 weeks' notice or more, a full refund is given minus a fee of $10 per accommodation. With shorter notice, a refund will be given for the lodging that is rebooked minus a $10 per accommodation fee.

AVAILABILITY: Lodging is available every day except for holiday weekends. The restaurant is closed for 3 weeks in December.

SERVICES/AMENITIES:

Restaurant Services: yes
Catering: provided, no BYO
Kitchen Facilities: n/a
Tables & Chairs: provided for a fee or BYO
Linens, Silver, etc.: provided
Restrooms: wca
Dance Floor: spa deck only

Parking: off street
Overnight Accommodations: 8 rooms, 11 cottages
Telephone: pay phones
Outdoor Night Lighting: no
Outdoor Cooking Facilities: no
Cleanup: provided

RESTRICTIONS:

Alcohol: BW provided, no BYO
Smoking: not permitted in dining room
Music: reasonable amplified ok

Wheelchair Access: limited
Insurance: not required
Other: children in cottages only

Jenner

MURPHY'S JENNER INN

10400 Coast Highway 1
Jenner, CA 95450
(707) 865-2377
Reserve: 3–6 months in advance

Jenner by the Sea is surrounded by fifteen miles of sandy beaches and hundreds of acres of state parks. And if you're planning a meeting, seminar or special event, the Inn can address all your needs. It's conveniently located right off of the coastal highway, has its own restaurant and offers a variety of overnight accommodations. The Salon, used for all types of functions, has a rustic charm. Wood, antiques, fireplace and cut flowers give the room a relaxed, warm ambiance. Two of the larger cabins can also be used for small meetings.

CAPACITY: This facility accommodates 60.

MEETING ROOMS: The Salon holds up to 50, the Captain's Cabin 10-15 and the Pelican 10–15 guests.

FEES & DEPOSITS: Meeting room fees are $75/hr (with a 2–hr minimum) up to $350 per day. If 5 or more overnight accommodations are booked with the meeting, the room rental fee is $100/day. For special events, the Inn rents for $100/hr with a maximum of $500 per day. This includes one staff person and beverage service. Catering fees run $10–15 for lunch and $15–25 for dinner. 50% of all fees are due at the time of booking and the balance is payable on the day of the event.

CANCELLATION POLICY: A full refund is given (minus a small handling fee) with 30 days' notice. With less notice, the refund is determined by how much space is rebooked.

AVAILABILITY: Every day.

SERVICES/AMENITIES:

Restaurant Services: yes
Catering: provided or BYO if rent whole inn
Kitchen Facilities: ample
Tables & Chairs: provided
Linens, Silver, etc.: provided
Restrooms: no wca
Dance Floor: yes

Parking: on and off street
Overnight Accommodations: 10 rooms,
several rental homes
Telephone: pay phone
Outdoor Night Lighting: no
Outdoor Cooking Facilities: no
Cleanup: caterer

RESTRICTIONS:

Alcohol: provided or BYO
Smoking: outside only
Music: no restrictions if entire inn rented

Wheelchair Access: no
Insurance: not required

Little River

GLENDEVEN

8221 N. Highway 1
Little River, CA 95456
(707) 937-0083
Reserve: 4–6 months in advance

Glendeven is a delightful small country inn located in a restored 1867 farmhouse. Set back on a headland meadow with the bay of Little River in the distance, the inn's two acres of tended grounds invite you to have a picnic, take a walk, or sunbathe on the brick terrace. The innkeepers have blended antiques with contemporary ceramics, paintings and prints, creating an appealing and interesting decor. Gallery Glendeven on the premises is separate from the main building, and is available for limited special events. A conference room above the gallery is an excellent place for small meetings.

CAPACITY: The gallery accommodates up to 40, and the maximum for the entire facility is 50.

MEETING ROOMS: 2 meeting rooms have a capacity of 12–15.

FEES & DEPOSITS: A refundable deposit of 50% of the total anticipated rental is due when reservations are confirmed. The balance is due upon departure. For Friday, Saturday or Sunday, the entire facility rents for $1350/night and midweek $1200/night. Individual areas of Glendevon are available for functions. Call for rates. Breakfast is included in these fees. Room and breakfast tax and 15% gratuity are additional.

CANCELLATION POLICY: With 30 days' notice the deposit is returned, less a service charge.

AVAILABILITY: Every day.

SERVICES/AMENITIES:

Restaurant Services: no
Catering: preferred list or BYO
Kitchen Facilities: moderate
Tables & Chairs: some provided
Linens, Silver, etc.: some provided
Restrooms: no wca
Dance Floor: no

Parking: off street
Overnight Accommodations: 10 guestrooms, 1 suite
Telephone: house & conference phone
Outdoor Night Lighting: minimal
Outdoor Cooking Facilities: no
Cleanup: provided, extra fee

RESTRICTIONS:

Alcohol: BYO
Smoking: outside only
Music: with approval

Wheelchair Access: limited
Insurance: not required
Other: no pets

INN AT SCHOOLHOUSE CREEK

7051 N. Highway 1
Little River, CA 95456
(707) 937-5525   Linda Wilson
Reserve: 2–6 months in advance

Once part of a large coastal ranch, the Inn has offered lodging to visitors since the 1930s. Quaint cottages built at the turn of the century are surrounded by tall cypress trees and wild flowers. White picket fences add old-fashioned charm. Other accommodations have ocean views, wood-burning stoves, and small decks and the main building offers a relaxed space for meetings, receptions, and dining. Redwood walls and ceilings, wide plank fir floors, and a brick fireplace create a warm, homey ambiance. The dining room has views of the sea and the adjacent forest. Businesses will appreciate the fact that the Inn can provide all meals, enabling guests to focus on work without interruption. This writer also had an opportunity to sample the Inn's hospitality and clam chowder, and found them both to be exceptional.

CAPACITY: The Inn accommodates 50 standing and 20 seated indoors, and 50 outdoors.

MEETING ROOMS: There are 5 rooms with a capacity of 6–30.

DEPOSITS & FEES: If you are reserving the entire inn, a deposit of one night's stay is due at the time of booking, and the balance is due on arrival. Use of the main building usually requires rental of the whole Inn. Fees vary depending on the use of the facilities and whether food is included with the event. Catering costs run about $7–20 for lunch and $15–25 for dinner.

CANCELLATION POLICY: A full refund is given with 1 month's notice or if the rooms are rebooked.

AVAILABILITY: Every day.

SERVICES/AMENITIES:

Restaurant Services: yes
Catering: provided, BYO licensed
Kitchen Facilities: ample
Tables & Chairs: provided, extra fee if BYO caterer
Linens, Silver, etc.: provided, extra fee if BYO caterer
Restrooms: no wca
Dance Floor: no

Parking: off street
Overnight Accommodations: 6 cottages, 7 rooms
Telephone: house phone
Outdoor Night Lighting: no
Outdoor Cooking Facilities: no
Cleanup: caterer

RESTRICTIONS:
Alcohol: provided BW only
Smoking: designated areas only
Music: amplified ok if rent entire inn

Wheelchair Access: no
Insurance: not required

RACHEL'S INN

8200 N. Highway 1
Little River, CA 95456
(707) 937-0088 Rachel Binah
Reserve: 3 months in advance

The first thing you notice when you drive up to the Inn is the old-fashioned garden. Rachel has a way with flowers—they blossom wildly, creating a tapestry of color all around the grounds. Inside, the Inn is fresh and tasteful. The fireplace in the dining room, piano in the parlor and newly-cut flowers everywhere are the kinds of touches that make guests feel right at home. The space in the Inn is also very flexible, and can be arranged to accommodate your business or special event needs.

CAPACITY: The facility accommodates 30 seated, 125 standing.

MEETING ROOMS:	*Room*	*Capacity*
	Dining Room & Parlor	30 at tables, 60 assembly
	Sitting Rooms (3)	10

FEES & DEPOSITS: When you hold an event at the Inn, your reservation also includes all overnight accommodations. A deposit for one night's lodging ($1,050) is due at the time of booking. Catering runs $15 and up per person, and a 20% deposit for catering is required. The balance of all fees is due on departure.

CANCELLATION POLICY: A full refund is given with 1 month's notice or more. Otherwise a refund is only given if the rooms are rebooked.

AVAILABILITY: Every day.

SERVICES/AMENITIES:
Restaurant Services: no
Catering: provided, no BYO
Kitchen Facilities: n/a
Tables & Chairs: provided
Linens, Silver, etc.: provided
Restrooms: wca
Dance Floor: no

Parking: off street
Overnight Accommodations: 6 guestrooms
Telephone: house phone
Outdoor Night Lighting: yes
Outdoor Cooking Facilities: no
Cleanup: provided for a fee

RESTRICTIONS:
Alcohol: provided, BYO corkage $5/bottle
Smoking: ok
Music: amplified ok

Wheelchair Access: yes on 1st floor only
Insurance: not required

STEVENS WOOD

8211 Highway 1
Little River, CA 95460
(707) 937-2810
Reserve: 1 month or more in advance

Stevens Wood is located two miles south of Mendocino. Named for Isaiah Stevens, pioneer settler and postmaster of historic Little River, Stevens Wood blends the natural beauty of its setting by forest and sea with an elegant and spacious contemporary lodge design. The result of meticulous planning, the inn offers a custom Executive Conference Room, an inviting lounge with a warm wood floor and fireplace, and all the amenities you could want for an overnight stay. The inn also serves as a first-rate gallery, exhibiting paintings and sculpture throughout.

CAPACITY:

Room	Capacity
Executive Conference Room	10 (with conference table)
Lounge	30–40
Suites (2)	3 each

The Inn can accommodate 250 people maximum in the Lounge, Foyer, and outdoors combined.

FEES & DEPOSITS: These vary according to how many guestrooms are booked with your event. 25% of the cost is due at the time of booking, an additional 50% is due 1 month before the event and the rest is due the day of the event. Catering runs about $10-50 per person.

CANCELLATION POLICY: The amount of notice required to receive a refund depends on the number of rooms reserved. Generally it is 72 hours for 2 rooms, 1 week for 3 rooms, and 2 weeks for over 4 rooms. Some events require a nonrefundable deposit.

AVAILABILITY: Every day.

SERVICES/AMENITIES:

Restaurant Services: no
Catering: provided
Kitchen Facilities: n/a
Tables & Chairs: provided
Linens, Silver, etc.: provided
Restrooms: wca
Dance Floor: yes
Parking: off street

Overnight Accommodations: 9 suites, 1 guestroom
Telephone: guest phones
Outdoor Night Lighting: yes
Outdoor Cooking Facilities: yes
Cleanup: provided for fee
Special Services: concierge service, gallery, complimentary wine bar, airport pickup

RESTRICTIONS:

Alcohol: provided, can BYO with permission
Smoking: outside only
Music: amplified ok

Wheelchair Access: yes
Insurance: not required
Other: limited kinds of functions allowed

Marshall

MARCONI
CONFERENCE CENTER

18500 Highway 1
Marshall, CA 94940
(415) 663-9020
Reserve: 3–6 months in advance

Situated on 62 acres of wooded hillside overlooking Tomales Bay, the Center is the perfect setting for productive conferences. Meeting areas are designed with break-out rooms and in-house AV equipment. Overnight accommodations support the purpose of the center by providing a smoke-free environment, study desks and a simple, uncluttered decor. The Center prepares all meals and has games, books, films and snacks for evening relaxation.Tranquil and free from urban distractions, the Marconi Conference Center is a great place in which to think. (Note: a substantial expansion is planned for 1991-92).

CAPACITY:

Room	Informal Seating	Classroom	Room	Informal Seating	Classroom
Pine Lodge	30	60	Cypress Lodge	30	60
Break-Out A	6	12	Break-Out A	6	14
Break-Out B	6	10	Pelican Shores	12	24

FEES & DEPOSITS: Rates include lodging, use of meeting spaces, 3 meals and all conference center amenities. The range per person/day is $39–97 depending on the type of accommodation and the room occupancy. A booking deposit is required to hold your space.

CANCELLATION POLICY: The deposit is refundable, less a $25 processing fee, with written notice 120 days prior to the conference date.

AVAILABILITY: Every day.

SERVICES/AMENITIES:

Restaurant Services: yes
Catering: n/a
Kitchen Facilities: n/a
Tables & Chairs: provided
Linens, Silver, etc.: provided
Restrooms: wca
Dance Floor: n/a

Parking: off street
Overnight Accommodations: 40 guestrooms
Telephone: pay phones
Outdoor Night Lighting: no
Outdoor Cooking Facilities: no
Cleanup: provided

RESTRICTIONS:

Alcohol: BYO
Smoking: outside only
Music: with approval

Wheelchair Access: yes, hilly terrain
Insurance: not required

Mendocino

AMES LODGE

42287 Little Lake Road
Mendocino, CA 95460
(707) 937-0811
Reserve: 2–3 months in advance

Located in a secluded forest near Mendocino, this casual, comfortable family-run lodge is a unique facility for retreats, workshops, reunions and other group getaways. Guests can relax in the main room with its fireplace, stereo, library and piano or gather on the sundeck beneath surrounding redwoods. Nearby trails meander through redwood and pygmy forests or to the river. Only minutes from town and the coast, Ames Lodge provides privacy and intimacy in a truly rustic setting.

CAPACITY: This facility can accommodate day groups up to 30, overnight up to 18 guests.

MEETING ROOMS: The Living Room accommodates 20.

FEES & DEPOSITS: You must rent the entire facility. A 2-night deposit for all 7 rooms ($648) is due at the time of booking. The balance is due on arrival. Day use rates are $100/day.

CANCELLATION POLICY: A full refund will be given with 1 month's notice. A sliding fee is imposed on short notice cancellations.

AVAILABILITY: Every day except for occasional closures.

SERVICES/AMENITIES:

Restaurant Services: no
Catering: BYO, vegetarian only
Kitchen Facilities: ample
Tables & Chairs: provided
Linens, Silver, etc.: provided
Restrooms: wca
Dance Floor: no

Parking: off street
Overnight Accommodations: 7 rooms
Telephone: house phone
Outdoor Night Lighting: yes
Outdoor Cooking Facilities: no
Cleanup: provided except for kitchen

RESTRICTIONS:

Alcohol: BYO BW, hard alcohol discouraged
Smoking: outside only
Music: no amplified

Wheelchair Access: no
Insurance: not required
Other: no pets, no meat

HILL HOUSE

10701 Palette Drive
Mendocino, CA 95460
(707) 937-0554
Reserve: 1–2 months in advance

Although Hill House is a relatively new inn, its style is reminiscent of 19th century New England. Set atop a knoll in the village of Mendocino, the inn has dramatic coastal views through grand windows in the dining room. With its two banquet/meeting rooms and 44 guestrooms, Hill House can accommodate large groups for the day as well as for an overnight stay. Its central location in the village of Mendocino gives guests easy access to local shops, state parks, boating, fishing, wine tasting and whale watching.

CAPACITY: The facility has a maximum capacity of 100.

MEETING ROOMS: 2 Banquet/meeting rooms can accommodate 50–100

FEES & DEPOSITS: A deposit of $125 for the smaller room and/or $250 for the larger is required 30 days prior to the event. The balance is due upon departure.

CANCELLATION POLICY: A full refund will be given with 1 month's notice.

AVAILABILITY: Every day.

SERVICES/AMENITIES:

Restaurant Services: yes
Catering: provided
Kitchen Facilities: n/a
Tables & Chairs: provided
Linens, Silver, etc.: provided
Restrooms: wca
Dance Floor: yes
Parking: off street

Overnight Accommodations: 44 guestrooms
Telephone: guest phones
Outdoor Night Lighting: no
Outdoor Cooking Facilities: no
Cleanup: provided
Special Services: complete event planning

RESTRICTIONS:

Alcohol: provided or BYO, corkage $5/bottle, no kegs
Smoking: designated areas only
Music: approval required

Wheelchair Access: yes
Insurance: not required

MENDOCINO HOTEL

45080 Main St.
Mendocino, CA 95460
(800) 548-0513 or (707) 937-0511
Reserve: 6–12 months in advance

The Mendocino Hotel occupies a select spot on the village's Main Street—directly overlooking the rugged Mendocino coast. Built in 1878, the hotel was recently remodeled. While the original Victorian style is maintained with antiques, rich wood detailing and stained glass, guests can appreciate the hotel's many modern amenities. In the main hotel, the Garden Room is an unusual place to hold an event. Once an outdoor patio, it is now enclosed by a translucent "ceiling" which lets in plenty of light. Plants abound, increasing the sensation of being outside. Meeting rooms, located in separate buildings, are comfortable and private. And the hotel's location couldn't be better—visitors not only have the ocean right across the street, but the entire town with its shops, galleries and distinctive architecture!

CAPACITY: The Garden Room seats 110.

MEETING ROOMS: The Conference Room seats 75 theater-style, 40 conference-style; the Meeting Room seats 20.

FEES & DEPOSITS: Rental rates are: Conference Room $125/day, Meeting Room $125/day and Garden Room rates vary. Catered luncheons run $8–15/person, dinners $15–30/person, hors d'oeuvres start at $5/person, and buffets can be arranged. 50% of the estimated cost is due 30 days prior to the event and the balance is due on departure.

CANCELLATION POLICY: The cancellation policy depends on the number of rooms reserved.

AVAILABILITY: Year-round, every day.

SERVICES/AMENITIES:

Restaurant Services: yes
Catering: provided, no BYO
Kitchen Facilities: n/a
Tables & Chairs: provided
Linens, Silver, etc.: provided
Restrooms: wca
Dance Floor: yes

Parking: on and off street
Overnight Accommodations: 51 guestrooms
Telephone: guest phones
Outdoor Night Lighting: limited
Outdoor Cooking Facilities: no
Cleanup: provided

RESTRICTIONS:

Alcohol: provided, no BYO
Smoking: not in Garden or Meeting Rooms
Music: with approval

Wheelchair Access: yes
Insurance: not required
Other: children not encouraged

WINNING IMAGES

PO Box 1883
Mendocino, CA 95460
(707) 964-1444
Reserve: 2–3 months in advance

If you have ever wanted to experience the ocean as close as your front door, Winning Images has what you have been looking for. Most of their homes are less than 100 feet from the water's edge! Each home is unique and the majority have decks, barbecues, hot tubs, fireplaces and panoramic views of the coast. Families, businesses and organizations can rent one or more homes—usually just a short walk from one another—depending on the size of the group. The Mendocino coast offers unlimited quiet, privacy and salt air along with a wide variety of activities: hiking, horseback riding, fishing, and of course, whale watching. Whether you're planning a vacation, retreat or casual get-together, Winning Images can arrange a getaway that meets your needs.

CAPACITY: Winning Images manages approximates 18 homes which range in capacity from 2–15 guests.

MEETING ROOMS: The Granny Hill Retreat will be completed in Fall, 1990 and will accommodate 40.

FEES & DEPOSITS: The homes rent for $125–275/night. The Granny Hill Retreat will be $850/night for the entire facility. A holding deposit is due within 10 days of booking. The balance along with bed tax, cleaning fee and refundable security deposit are due any time prior to arrival. However, if payment is by check, the check must arrive 3 weeks before arrival. Call for exact fees.

CANCELLATION POLICY: A full refund is given with 2 weeks' notice. With less than 2 weeks' notice, there is a $150 fee, refundable only if the space is rebooked. No refunds with less than 48 hours' notice.

AVAILABILITY: Every day.

SERVICES/AMENITIES:

Restaurant Services: no
Catering: BYO
Kitchen Facilities: adequate
Tables & Chairs: provided
Linens, Silver, etc.: provided
Restrooms: some wca
Dance Floor: n/a

Parking: off street
Overnight Accommodations: varies
Telephone: house phone
Outdoor Night Lighting: varies
Outdoor Cooking Facilities: yes
Cleanup: provided
Special: food baskets, child care w/advance notice

RESTRICTIONS:

Alcohol: BYO
Smoking: designated areas only
Music: with approval
Wheelchair Access: yes

Insurance: required
Other: children under 12, smoking & pets allowed in some homes

Monte Rio

HUCKLEBERRY SPRINGS

8105 Old Beedle Rd.
Monte Rio, CA 95462
(707) 865-2683
Reserve: 1–2 months in advance

With its fresh, regional cuisine and natural hot springs, Huckleberry Springs gives guests the advantages of the French auberge and the Japanese ryokan. Located high above the Russian River on 56 heavily wooded acres, the inn enjoys spectacular views of the surrounding hills. The main lodge is comfortable and airy with lots of light from windows and skylights. Guests can sunbathe on the deck and at the swimming pool, or totally relax in the spa. Each cabin is unique in design, but all offer privacy, wood stoves and the soothing, restful feeling that comes from communing in the forest.

CAPACITY: The facility accommodate a maximum of 50 people.

MEETING ROOMS: The Dining Room and Solarium in the main lodge have a total capacity of 35.

FEES & DEPOSITS: Most events require that you also reserve all the overnight accommodations. If you book the entire inn, the fee is $600 per night (double occupancy for 4 cabins). For Mon–Fri day use only the fee is $450 for a 4.5-hour period. A 2-night minimum is required for business events on weekends. For both special events and meetings, 50% of the fee is due at the time of booking and the balance is payable on departure. Catering costs run $10.50–18.50/person.

CANCELLATION POLICY: For 1-day meetings, 2 weeks' notice is required for a full refund. All other events require 30 days' notice for a full refund.

AVAILABILITY: Wednesday–Sunday, closed Monday & Tuesday. Closed to the public January and February, with some exceptions made for business functions.

SERVICES/AMENITIES:

Restaurant Services: no
Catering: provided, BYO for fee
Kitchen Facilities: ample
Tables & Chairs: provided
Linens, Silver, etc.: provided or BYO
Restrooms: wca, main building only
Dance Floor: pool area or deck

Parking: off street
Overnight Accommodations: 4 cabins
Telephone: house phone
Outdoor Night Lighting: limited
Outdoor Cooking Facilities: BBQ
Cleanup: caterer

RESTRICTIONS:

Alcohol: BW provided, no BYO
Smoking: outside only
Music: all ok

Wheelchair Access: limited
Insurance: required for day use
Other: no children under 14 or pets

Occidental

HEART'S DESIRE INN

3657 Church Street
Occidental, CA 95465
(707) 874-1311
Reserve: 2 months in advance

Heart's Desire Inn, nestled against a hillside of berries and fruit trees, is a two-story Victorian built in the 1860s. The interior is light and airy, with lots of windows overlooking the nearby greenery. Glistening fir floors, white wainscotting and flowers from the garden add a fresh, homey quality. The first floor and garden provide lovely areas for private affairs, while the downstairs conference room, with fireplace, offers the privacy and the special features needed for business functions.

CAPACITY:

Area	Capacity	Area	Capacity
Conference Room	30	entire facility, indoors	50
Dining & Parlor combined	40	entire facility, outdoors	150

FEES & DEPOSITS:

Area	Fee
Conference Room	$150/4 hrs, $300/8 hrs, $350/12 hrs
Garden & Porch	$350/4hrs (up to 50 people)
	$500/4hrs (51–100 people)
Parlor & Dining Room	$350/4–6 hrs
Parlor, Dining Room, Kitchen	$500/4–6 hrs

50% of the rental charges plus a refundable cleaning and damage deposit for the same amount are due at the time of booking. The balance is payable the day of the event. There are no rental fees for the downstairs conference facility if all rooms are reserved mid-week. Catering can be provided by the Inn and runs $9–15/ person for lunch and $14–25/person for dinner or you can arrange for your own caterer.

CANCELLATION POLICY: A full refund minus a $10 handling fee with 7 days' notice when you have reserved just a function area, or 1 month's notice when you have reserved the entire Inn. Otherwise, a refund will be granted only if the space is rebooked.

AVAILABILITY: Every day.

SERVICES/AMENITIES:

Restaurant Services: no
Catering: provided, BYO ok
Kitchen Facilities: ample
Tables & Chairs: some provided
Linens, Silver, etc.: some provided

Restrooms: wca
Dance Floor: portable CBA for fee
Parking: on and off street
Overnight Accommodations: 8 rooms
Telephone: guest phones

Outdoor Night Lighting: yes

Outdoor Cooking Facilities: no

RESTRICTIONS:

Alcohol: BYO

Smoking: outside only

Music: amplified restricted

Cleanup: whoever caters event

Special Services: horse & buggy tours CBA

Wheelchair Access: yes

Insurance: not required

Other: no children or pets

Atherton

HOLBROOK PALMER PARK

150 Watkins Avenue
Atherton, CA 94027
(415) 688-6534
Reserve: 2 weeks–6 months in advance

Holbrook Palmer Park is what's left of an old estate, complete with numerous old buildings, mature oak trees and an old water tower. Located on Watkins Avenue near Middlefield Road, the park is a sizable piece of open space in exclusive residential Atherton. The main house rests in the center of the property and has wide, gracious steps that lead from the main reception room down to a spacious patio framed by large trees. The patio and steps are perfect for an outdoor luncheon or twilight dinner. Inside are several interconnecting rooms appropriate for receptions. Nearby is the Jennings Pavilion, a modern structure which can accommodate large events and bands. Outside the Pavilion is another patio which is appropriate for outdoor seated functions. Although you might think that a facility in Atherton would require formality, just the opposite is true. The house and Pavilion both lend themselves to outdoor functions on warm days and the feeling here is one of relaxed informality.

CAPACITY: The Main House, with outdoor seating, can accommodate 100 guests, the Jennings Pavilion 250 guests with outside seating included. The entire facility can hold up to 500.

FEES & DEPOSITS: A $250 refundable security/damage deposit is required when reservations are made. The rental fee is payable 1 month before the event.

Social Functions		Business Functions			Business Functions		
Guests	*Fee*	*Guests*	*Jennings Pavilion*		*Guests*	*Main House*	
			(4 hrs)	(8 hrs)		(4 hrs)	(8 hrs)
1–100	$450						
101–200	825	1–100	$115	$175	1–50	$100	$120
201–300	1325	101–150	175	230	51–100	115	175
to 500	call	150–200	230	290	70+ outside use required		

For each 1/2 hour over 4 hours, you must have advance approval and a charge of $50 will apply. An additional 3 hours are set aside for setup and cleanup and $25/hour will be charged for more than 3 hours.

CANCELLATION POLICY: With 6 months' notice, the deposit is refunded; with 4–6 months' notice, $200; and 2–3 months' notice, $175 is refunded.

AVAILABILITY: Weekends, noon–4pm and 7pm–11pm. For weekday meetings, 7:45am–11pm. After 5pm, there is an extra charge.

SERVICES/AMENITIES:

Restaurant Services: no

Catering: BYO

Kitchen Facilities: yes

Tables & Chairs: some provided

Linens, Silver, etc.: BYO

Restrooms: wca in Pavilion only

Dance Floor: CBA

Parking: several lots

Overnight Accommodations: no

Telephone: pay phone

Outdoor Night Lighting: yes

Outdoor Cooking Facilities: BYO

Cleanup: caterer

RESTRICTIONS:

Alcohol: BYO, cannot sell in park

Smoking: outside only

Music: amplified inside only

Wheelchair Access: yes

Insurance: provided at extra charge

Belmont

RALSTON HALL

1500 Ralston Avenue
Belmont, CA 94002
(415) 593-1601 ext. 201
Reserve: 1–12 months in advance

Ralston Hall is a stunning Victorian mansion, completed in 1867 by William Chapman Ralston, founder of the Bank of California. Ralston purchased the land in 1864 and modified the original Italian villa with touches of Steamboat Gothic and Victorian details to create a lavish and opulent estate. The exterior of this three-story mansion is meticulously maintained. The front doors have delicately etched glass panes. Inside, the decor is outstanding. The first floor consists of a large ballroom, several parlors, dining rooms and a sun porch. Each room is decorated with beautiful antiques, stunning crystal chandeliers and elegant oriental rugs. The ballroom is particularly sensational. The patterned hardwood floors are encircled by mirrored walls. Three delicate chandeliers hang gracefully from the huge skylight. At the far end of the ballroom is a large bay window with a curving red velvet bench seat and regal red brocade curtains. Musicians can set up in a Ballroom alcove without interfering with the grandeur and flow of the ballroom floor. The spacious dining rooms are decorated with an attention to detail that is mind-boggling. Because of its size and layout, you can choose from a variety of setups that include the entire first floor, or the West or East wings. This facility is a special and outstanding location for memorable parties, business dinners, awards ceremonies or promotional events.

CAPACITY: The entire facility can accommodate 250 guests. The East Wing, 150 seated guests and the West Wing, 100 guests with partial seating.

FEES & DEPOSITS: A $500 refundable deposit is required when you make reservations. The entire facility, $3300-3800/8 hours; East Wing, $2800/8 hours; West Wing, $1500/8 hours. Fees include 2 hours for setup and 1-hour cleanup. For weekday business functions, call for rates, which are lower for blocks of 4 hours or less.

CANCELLATION POLICY: If you cancel 120 days prior to your party, your deposit minus a $50 administration fee is refunded.

AVAILABILITY: Ralston Hall is open for events every day 9am-1am, except Thanksgiving Day, December 25th and December 31st.

SERVICES/AMENITIES:

Restaurant Services: no

Catering: BYO from approved list

Kitchen Facilities: ample

Tables & Chairs: CBA, extra charge

Linens, Silver, etc.: BYO

Restrooms: wca

Dance Floor: yes except for West Wing

Parking: ample

Overnight Accommodations: no

Telephone: local calls only

Outdoor Night Lighting: no

Outdoor Cooking Facilities: BBQ

Cleanup: caterer

Other: hostess included

RESTRICTIONS:

Alcohol: BYO

Smoking: not permitted

Music: amplified ok

Wheelchair Access: limited

Insurance: extra liability required

Other: candles not permitted

Burlingame

KOHL MANSION ★

2759 Adeline Drive
Burlingame, CA 94010
(415) 343-3631
Reserve: 12 months in advance

Commissioned by C. Frederick Kohl and his wife in 1912, the Kohl Mansion was built on 40 acres of oak woodlands in Burlingame. Kohl, heir to a shipping fortune, loved to entertain and created this grand estate to include manor house, tennis court, pool, green houses, rose garden, large carriage house and 150,000-gallon reservoir. The elegant rosebrick Tudor mansion is again available for parties and has many spectacular rooms for events and business functions. The wood-paneled Library, with large granite fireplace, book cases and graceful French doors opening to a center courtyard, ends in a Gothic bay window which catches the light filtered through the oaks on the lawns outside. The sizable Great Hall, a copy of the Arlington Tudor Hall in Essex, England, was built for music and entertaining. It has very high ceilings and a stage, plus its paneling and walnut floors create a fine acoustical setting for music. A lighter twin of the Library, the spacious and airy Dining Room has delicate, pristine white plaster relief on the walls and ceiling. This marvelous dining environment is complete with views of oaks and lawns from bay windows. Guests can roam outdoors, surrounded by a courtyard combination of green lawns, red brick and an immaculate gravel terrace. The Kohl Mansion is a perfect facility for those who want to party in grand style.

CAPACITY: Indoors, the Mansion can hold 450 standing and 250 seated guests. The indoor facilities plus outdoor tents can hold up to 600 for a reception and 350 seated guests. Monday–Thursday, 100 guests maximum.

MEETING ROOMS: 5 rooms that can accommodate 10–200 people. Call for specifics.

FEES & DEPOSITS:

Social Functions:	*Saturday and Sunday*				*Friday*	
	Guests	*Oct–Mar*	*Apr–Sept*	*Guests*	*Oct–Mar*	*Apr–Sept*
Morning/Dining Room	80–100	$2200	$2400	80–100	$1800	$2000
Great Hall & Clock Hall	—	—	—	101–150	2100	2300
Great Hall and Library	100–150	2500	2700	—	—	—
The Entire House	150–200	2700	3000	150–250	2300	2500
	201–250	3000	3300	251–350	2500	2700
	251–350	3200	3600			

Alumnae rate for immediate family includes a 50% discount. Hourly rates: entire Mansion $300/hour, Great Hall and Library $200/hour, Dining and Morning Rooms $200/hour.

Business Functions: Fridays, Saturdays and Sundays: $4500 for over 200 guests, $4000 for under 200. Weekdays $3500. Alumnae rate 15% discount. Hourly rates: entire Mansion $400/hour, Great Hall and Library $300/hour, Dining and Morning Rooms $300/hour.

The deposit is 50% of the rental fee, due when you reserve your date. The final balance is due 30 days in advance of the party. There is also a $10/table setup charge and a $50 fee for use of the baby grand piano. The rental fee for tents is $1200.

CANCELLATION POLICY: The deposit, minus $50, will be refunded only if the date can be rebooked.

AVAILABILITY: From Sept–June, parties can be held after 4pm on Fridays and any time on Saturday and Sunday. June–August, every day, any time. Weekdays, business functions after 4pm on school days.

SERVICES/AMENITIES:

Restaurant Services: no

Catering: BYO, select from list

Kitchen Facilities: ample

Tables & Chairs: provided

Linens, Silver, etc.: BYO

Restrooms: wca

Dance Floor: yes

Parking: lot or on street

Overnight Accommodations: no

Telephone: pay phone

Outdoor Night Lighting: yes

Outdoor Cooking Facilities: BBQ

Cleanup: caterer

Other: baby grand

RESTRICTIONS:

Alcohol: BYO, bartender required

Smoking: outside only

Music: amplified until 10pm

Wheelchair Access: yes

Insurance: required

Hillsborough

THE CROCKER MANSION

6565 Skyline Boulevard
Hillsborough, CA 94010
(415) 348-2272
Reserve: 6–12 months in advance

The Crocker Mansion, a palatial estate designed by the architect of San Francisco's Opera House and City Hall, was built for W.W. Crocker in the 1930s. The large white facade and arches create an atmosphere of permanence and stability. Guests are ushered into the Mansion through impressive wood double doors into a round foyer and second set of double doors leading into the Ballroom. The Ballroom, complete with lofty arched glass doors and fireplace with mantel, is light and airy. A grand piano is available for functions. The room has a wide stone balcony with sensational views of the adjacent property that is landscaped with orange and olive trees. The building is bordered by impeccably kept gardens and a serene woodland running 35 acres along Hillsborough's Skyline Ridge. Several areas are especially well suited for outdoor parties: the wide lawns joined by a winding fieldstone stairway and a cloistered courtyard are graced by manicured hedges and bright flowers. The Italian Renaissance-style mansion, now a private school for children, is a beautiful and versatile event setting for large parties.

CAPACITY: In summer, the Mansion can accommodate 300 guests using both indoor and outdoor spaces. In the winter, 100–150 guests depending on use.

DONATION: The donation is $2800; it covers an 8-hour block of time.

AVAILABILITY: Saturday and Sunday only. No weekdays available.

SERVICES/AMENITIES:

Restaurant Services: no
Catering: BYO, select from preferred list
Kitchen Facilities: moderate
Tables & Chairs: provided for 150 guests
Linens, Silver, etc.: caterer
Restrooms: no wca
Dance Floor: yes

Parking: large lot
Overnight Accommodations: no
Telephone: pay phone
Outdoor Night Lighting: limited
Outdoor Cooking Facilities: CBA
Cleanup: caterer
Other: baby grand piano

RESTRICTIONS:

Alcohol: BYO, service by caterer only
Smoking: outside only
Music: amplified ok

Wheelchair Access: limited
Insurance: recommended
Other: decorations restricted

Menlo Park

LATHAM HOPKINS GATEHOUSE

555 Ravenswood
Menlo Park, CA 94025
(415) 858-3470
Reserve: 3–6 months in advance

The Gatehouse is a Victorian structure that has been tastefully restored to its former splendor. This facility is rather small, and lends itself to more intimate gatherings. With mansard roof and decorative Victorian shingling, the Gatehouse is an attractive reminder of days gone by. The main entrance for functions is from the back of the house, where a circular lawn is ringed by large oaks. Beyond the small lawn is a much larger lawn backdrop, separating the Gatehouse from City Offices. At the lawn's edge is an old-fashioned fountain supported by two Mermen (as opposed to Mermaids), with water spouting out of the mouths of fanciful turtles and lion-like animals. The Gatehouse has a medium-sized wood deck with stairs gracefully cascading down to the lawn. Its interior is decorated with understated floral wallpaper and attractive appointments. The dining room, living room and kitchen are available for functions. Even though the Latham Hopkins Gatehouse can accommodate only very small parties, it has considerable charm and appeal.

CAPACITY: In the winter, the Gatehouse can accommodate 45 guests including 15 seated. In the summer, the facility can hold up to 100 total for a standing buffet with 45 seated guests using the patio area.

FEES & DEPOSITS: The total rental fee is required as a refundable deposit: $400 cleaning/security deposit plus the $45–54/hour rental fee multiplied by the number of hours anticipated. The cleaning/security deposit is usually returned 2–3 weeks after your event. The rental fee for Saturday and Sunday is $45/hour for Menlo Park residents and $54/hour for nonresidents. Monday through Friday the rates are $35 and $42, respectively. This fee includes a staff person for your function and applies to a 3-hour block minimum. For functions Monday through Friday between 5pm–10pm, a staff charge of $8.50/hour is applied.

CANCELLATION POLICY: If you give more than 2 weeks' notice, the total deposit is refunded less $25.

AVAILABILITY: Monday-Friday noon–10pm; Saturday and Sunday, all day to 8pm.

SERVICES/AMENITIES:

Restaurant Services: no
Catering: BYO
Kitchen Facilities: minimal
Tables & Chairs: BYO
Linens, Silver, etc.: BYO
Restrooms: no wca
Dance Floor: no

Parking: on street, lot
Overnight Accommodations: no
Telephone: no
Outside Night Lighting: limited
Outdoor Cooking Facilities: BBQ
Cleanup: caterer

RESTRICTIONS:
Alcohol: BYO, WBC only
Smoking: outside only
Music: no amplified

Wheelchair Access: no
Insurance: not required

Portola Valley

THOMAS FOGARTY WINERY AND VINEYARDS ★★

19501 Skyline Blvd.
Portola Valley, CA 94028
(415) 851-1946
Reserve: 2–12 months in advance

If we were to rate facilities on a scale from 1 to 10, the Fogarty Winery would be deemed a 10! Located off Skyline Boulevard, this has got to be one of the best places we've seen for parties and business functions. Commanding an extraordinary view of the Bay and Peninsula, the Winery sits high on a ridge in a quiet, vineyard setting. A small, lovely pond with circling swans and vineyards all around greet you as you drive in. At the top of the ridge is a large lawn, beautifully landscaped around the perimeter—a perfect spot for an outdoor reception. The building steps down the hill, and is designed with incredible attention to detail, with stone fireplaces, fine woodwork, skylights and lots of decks. The Tasting Room is light and airy, arranged with custom-built 'barrel' tables, handcrafted leather chairs, wood burning stove and full kitchen. In the restroom, there's even a bluegreen slate and stone bath tub! The Hill House is at the lower level. It has a semi-enclosed deck, stone fireplace, wine bar and professional kitchen. This is an exceptionally pleasant environment for an executive retreat, seminar or workshop, with wood parquet floors, comfortable seating and windows overlooking the adjacent vineyard and distant Bay. The Tasting Room and Hill House both reflect the ambiance of the surrounding environment with taste and sophistication. We can't recommend it more highly.

CAPACITY: The Hill House can hold 20–100 for business functions, 225 guests for social events. The Tasting Room can hold 10–45 guests for business, up to 150 for social functions. The lawn can accommodate up to 150 for receptions.

FEES & DEPOSITS: A nonrefundable deposit of 25% of the rental fee is due when reservations are confirmed. The balance is invoiced, payable within 30 days.

Area	Months	Days	No time limit	4 hours	8 hours
Total Facility	April–Nov	weekends	$3000	—	—
Tasting & Lawn	April–Nov	weekends	$2000	—	—
Tasting & Conference	Dec–Mar	weekdays	—	$350	$500
	Dec–Mar	weekends	—	500	750
Hill House	Dec–Mar	weekdays	—	$600	$1200
	Dec–Mar	weekends	—	750	1500

CANCELLATION POLICY: With 1 month's notice, the deposit is fully refunded.

AVAILABILITY: Year-round, every day from 7am–midnight. Closed Thanksgiving, Christmas Day and January 1.

SERVICES/AMENITIES:

Restaurant Services: no
Catering: preferred caterer or BYO with approval
Kitchen Facilities: fully equipped
Tables & Chairs: some provided
Linens, Silver, etc.: BYO
Restrooms: no wca
Dance Floor: deck or lawn
Parking: large lots or valet

Overnight Accommodations: no
Telephone: pay phone
Outdoor Night Lighting: yes
Outdoor Cooking Facilities: CBA
Cleanup: caterer
Other: audio-visual equipment, event coordination
Special: wine tasting

RESTRICTIONS:

Alcohol: WC provided, no BYO
Smoking: outside only
Music: no amplified

Wheelchair Access: no
Insurance: certificate required

LADERA OAKS

3249 Alpine Road
Portola Valley, CA 94028
(415) 854-3101 Annie
Reserve: 1–6 months in advance

Located off Alpine Road in Portola Valley, the Ladera Oaks' shingled clubhouse and beautifully landscaped grounds provide a really pleasant indoor and outdoor event facility. The building's exterior is covered with vines and the courtyard garden between clubhouse and pools has an extremely attractive interior garden, with two-tiered lawn areas, surrounded by oak trees, flowering annuals and perennials. The clubhouse Ballroom offers a sizable space for indoor dining, with hardwood floors and large picture windows overlooking the garden. An adjoining Lounge can be used in conjunction with the Ballroom or separately for smaller gatherings. Private and quiet, this is a great location for indoor/outdoor celebrations.

CAPACITY: The Ballroom can seat 100-150 guests in the daytime, 180 in the evening and, in combination with the garden, 350 seated guests. Alone, the Courtyard Garden can accommodate 200 seated guests. The Lounge can hold up to 35 seated.

FEES & DEPOSITS: To make a reservation, a partially refundable $400–500 deposit is required, the amount based on the estimated total use fee. A 4-hour block of time is usually provided with 2 additional hours for preparation and 1 hour for cleanup.

	Month	*Hours Available*	*Fee*
Mon–Thurs	year-round	7am–6pm	$5/guest
		6pm–10pm	$6/guest ($600 min)
Fri–Sun	Jan, Feb, Nov	7am–1am	$9/guest ($900 min)
Sundays	December	7am–10pm	$9/guest ($900 min)
Saturdays	December	7am–4pm	$9/guest ($900 min)
Fri & Sat Eves.	December	5pm–1am	$9/guest ($1200 min)
Fri–Sun	March–October	7am–5pm	$9/guest ($1350 min)
		5pm–1am	$9/guest ($1800 min)*
		7pm–1am	$9/guest ($1000 min)

* *evening block of time which includes any hours between 5pm and 7pm*

CANCELLATION POLICY: If you cancel within 5 days of making the reservation, 50% of your deposit will be refunded. If you cancel thereafter, 50% of the deposit will be refunded only if your date can be rebooked.

AVAILABILITY: Year-round, every day.

SERVICES/AMENITIES:

Restaurant Services: no

Catering: BYO

Kitchen Facilities: ample

Tables & Chairs: provided

Linens, Silver, etc.: BYO

Restrooms: wca

Dance Floor: yes

Parking: large lots, limited weekdays

Overnight Accommodations: no

Telephone: pay phone

Outdoor Night Lighting: yes

Outdoor Cooking Facilities: BBQ

Cleanup: caterer and club staff

RESTRICTIONS:

Alcohol: BYO

Smoking: allowed

Music: amplified inside only

Wheelchair Access: yes

Insurance: not required

Alameda

GARRATT MANSION

900 Union Street
Alameda, CA 94501
(415) 521-4779
Reserve: 1 week–6 months in advance

The Garratt Mansion, built in 1893 for a turn-of-the-century industrialist, is one of the exceptional Victorian houses of Alameda. Here you can have a fundraiser, office party, business meeting or afternoon tea party. Stained glass windows, antiques and an abundance of woodwork not only provide an interesting and rich interior, but practically eliminate the need for decoration. Worthy of note are an elegant staircase and landing, softly illuminated by natural light. The variety of rooms, which flow nicely together, give guests plenty of space in which to dine, dance, and mingle. Outside, a garden area is available during good weather. And because the Garratt Mansion is also a bed and breakfast inn, guests have the option of staying overnight, and the innkeepers are always available to assist in making your event worry-free and warmly remembered.

CAPACITY: The facility can accommodate up to 75 for events; 5–30 people for meetings.

FEES & DEPOSITS: A deposit of half the total fee is required to reserve a date. The balance plus a refundable damage and cleaning deposit is due 3 weeks before the event. Deposits are not refundable after 7 days unless the date can be rebooked.

	Fee	*Hours*	*Time Period*
Special Events	$800	4 hours	Fri–Sat
Meetings	75	4 hours	Mon–Fri, 9am–5pm
Weekday Special Events	200	3 hours	Mon–Thurs, noon–10pm

AVAILABILITY: Parties and special events can be on Friday evenings to 10pm and Saturdays from 11am to 10pm.

SERVICES/AMENITIES:

Restaurant Services: no
Catering: provided or BYO
Kitchen Facilities: moderate
Tables & Chairs: some provided
Linens, Silver, etc.: some provided
Restrooms: wca
Dance Floor: yes

Parking: on street, driveway (6 cars)
Overnight Accommodations: 6 guestrooms
Telephone: pay & house phone
Outdoor Night Lighting: yes
Outdoor Cooking Facilities: no
Cleanup: provided
Other: event planning assistance

RESTRICTIONS:

Alcohol: WC only, no open bar
Smoking: outside only
Music: amplified ok inside

Wheelchair Access: no
Insurance: not required

Albany

THE TURF CLUB

1100 East Shore Highway (Golden Gate Fields)
Albany, CA 94706
(415) 527-8900 Diane Hisey
Reserve: 4–5 months in advance

Where can you find a sweeping vista of both the San Francisco skyline, Golden Gate Bridge, *and* the Golden Gate Fields Racetrack? At The Turf Club. Located at the edge of the Bay, this facility can handle large groups with ease. The lounge-in-the-round overlooking the ocean offers a dazzling view of San Francisco at night, and is ideal for cocktails and mingling. The dining area has a view onto the racetrack, and even though there are never any races during private events, you still feel as though horses may appear on the track at any time. True to its name, the main color of the interior is green, and "racetrack" pictures adorning the walls add to the character of the place. Off-season, July through December, are good times to have business conferences and seminars here.

CAPACITY: The Turf Club (main dining area) can accommodate 150 to 1500 seated guests, the Director's Lounge holds 50 to 70 seated.

FEES & DEPOSITS: A $500 nonrefundable rental deposit is due at the time of booking.

Room	Fee		Fee
Turf Club	$500	Security guard	$175 each
Director's Room	$100	Coat check	$100 (optional)

The balance of the fees is due within 5 days of the event. Per person catering costs run $13-$17 for hors d'oeuvres and $20-$34 for a sit-down dinner. A 7.25% sales tax and 15% gratuity are additional.

AVAILABILITY: 8am to 3am daily, from July through December.

SERVICES/AMENITIES:

Restaurant Services: no
Catering: provided
Kitchen Facilities: ample
Tables & Chairs: provided
Linens, Silver, etc.: provided
Restrooms: wca
Dance Floor: yes

Parking: lot
Overnight Accommodations: no
Telephone: house phone
Outdoor Night Lighting: no
Outdoor Cooking Facilities: no
Cleanup: provided

RESTRICTIONS:

Alcohol: provided, BYO corkage $7.50/bottle, WC only
Smoking: allowed

Music: amplified ok
Wheelchair Access: yes
Insurance: not required

Benicia

CAMEL BARN MUSEUM

2024 Camel Road
Benicia, CA 94510
(707) 746-0189 or 745-5435
Reserve: 3–12 months in advance

Once a military storehouse, the building acquired some distinction in 1864 when 35 camels were housed there pending auction. They stayed in the storehouse for approximately 6 weeks, during which time folks started referring to the place as the Camel Barn. Needless to say, the name stuck. Today, the museum is housed upstairs, and social events take place on the first floor. The building's interior is cool, with 22"-thick sandstone walls. Down the center of the first floor are a series of graceful arches which support the upper level, and arched windows along the length of one side let in some natural light. White and unadorned, the room lends itself to decoration. Way off the beaten path, the Camel Barn Museum is an interesting and little known part of Benicia's history.

CAPACITY: The Camel Barn can accommodate 200 guests, maximum.

FEES & DEPOSITS: A refundable deposit of 1/3 the rental fee is due when reservations are confirmed, and is applied towards the fee. The rental fee Monday–Friday is $200 for public or private parties, and $300 on Saturday or Sunday. Local nonprofits $150 Monday–Friday, and $300 Saturday or Sunday. The balance is due 1 month before the function.

CANCELLATION POLICY: With 3 months' notice, the deposit will be returned.

AVAILABILITY: Year-round, every day 8am–midnight.

SERVICES/AMENITIES:

Restaurant Services: no
Catering: BYO
Kitchen Facilities: moderate
Tables & Chairs: provided
Linens, Silver, etc.: BYO
Restrooms: wca
Dance Floor: wood floor

Parking: large lot
Overnight Accommodations: no
Telephone: restricted, emergencies only
Outdoor Night Lighting: no
Outdoor Cooking Facilities: BYO
Cleanup: caterer or renter
Other: piano $50/event, raised platforms

RESTRICTIONS:
Alcohol: BYO, license required
Smoking: outside only
Music: amplified ok

Wheelchair Access: yes
Insurance: not required

CAPTAIN DILLINGHAM'S INN

145 East 'D' Street
Benicia, CA 94510
(707) 746-7164 or (800) 544-2278
Debbie or Denny
Reserve: 3 months in advance

If you would like to make a novel entrance at your party, arrange to have a horse-drawn carriage and coachman escort you to the picturesque Captain Dillingham's Inn. Centered in Benicia's waterfront-historical district, this bright yellow clapboard inn was built in the 1850s by a New England sea captain. Set back from the street amid Eucalyptus trees, the redwood gazebo and decks, brick walkways and balmy sea breezes provide a lovely outdoor setting. Inside, the French country dining room with its cherrywood floors, wooden ceiling beams and flower-filled windows is ideal for buffets or small winter parties. And for those who wish to stay overnight, the Inn offers 10 spacious, period-furnished rooms. The staff here emphasize the personal touch and are available to help you with every detail of your event.

CAPACITY: The deck and patio hold 150 seated or 180 standing guests; the dining room up to 20 seated or 50 standing guests.

FEES & DEPOSITS: A $250 deposit plus a $50 refundable cleaning deposit are due at the time of booking. The rental fees are as follows: less than 50 guests, the fee is negotiable; 51 to 100 guests $750; 101 to 150 guests $950.

CANCELLATION POLICY: Handled on an individual basis.

AVAILABILITY: Small indoor events, year-round; large outdoor events, May 1st through mid-October, from 12:30pm to sundown.

SERVICES/AMENITIES:
Restaurant Services: no
Catering: BYO
Kitchen Facilities: minimal
Tables & Chairs: provided
Linens, Silver, etc.: BYO
Restrooms: no wca
Dance Floor: yes

Parking: on street, lot
Overnight Accommodations: 9 guestrooms, 1 suite
Telephone: restricted
Outdoor Night Lighting: no
Outdoor Cooking Facilities: BYO
Cleanup: caterer
Other: horse-drawn carriage CBA

RESTRICTIONS:
Alcohol: BYO
Smoking: allowed
Music: amplified 'til dusk, restricted volume

Wheelchair Access: limited
Insurance: not required

CLOCK TOWER

1187 Washington Street
Benicia, CA 94510
(707) 746-4285   Facility Reservations
Reserve: 3–6 months in advance

There was a time back in the 1850s when people worried about an Indian attack. So they built a munitions fort on a spit overlooking the Carquinez Straits. Originally it was three stories high, constructed of locally mined sandstone blocks. But around 1912, some munitions exploded, blowing the top story of the building into the sky. It was never replaced. The current two-story version has a medieval clock tower, and a 16,000 square foot second floor where all events are held. It is a cavernous space with a high-gloss hardwood floor. The steel structure is visible, but there are no posts, columns or other supports obstructing the space. From most windows you have a view of the straits, the bridge, Martinez, the hills, and the oil tankers passing by. You probably never will see any Indians, though.

CAPACITY: This facility can hold up to 350 seated and 700 standing guests for a reception.

FEES & DEPOSITS: A refundable $250 security deposit is payable when the contract is submitted. The rental fee is due 10 days prior to the event. Setup/takedown will cost $50/each.

Rental Fees	Resident Nonprofit	Resident	Non Resident Nonprofit	Non Resident
Monday–Thursday	$12/hr	$20/hr	$20/hr	$45/hr
Fri, Sat & Sunday	$20/hr	$40/hr	$30/hr	$65/hr

CANCELLATION POLICY: With 21 (business) days' notice, the deposit will be refunded less $25. With less than 21 days, $25 plus 1/3 of the total rental fee will be forfeited. The security deposit will be refunded after the event if the facility is left in good condition.

AVAILABILITY: Year-round, every day until 1am unless pre-approved for additional hours. Closed all major holidays.

SERVICES/AMENITIES:

Restaurant Services: no
Catering: BYO
Kitchen Facilities: moderate, $5/hour use fee
Tables & Chairs: provided
Linens, Silver, etc.: BYO
Restrooms: wca
Dance Floor: yes

Parking: large lot
Overnight Accommodations: no
Telephone: pay phone
Outdoor Night Lighting: no
Outdoor Cooking Facilities: CBA w/approval
Cleanup: caterer or renter
Other: PA system, coffee urns, podium

RESTRICTIONS:

Alcohol: BYO
Smoking: allowed
Music: amplified ok

Wheelchair Access: yes
Insurance: certificate required

Berkeley

BERKELEY CITY CLUB

2315 Durant Avenue
Berkeley, CA 94704
(415) 848-7800
Reserve: 3–6 months in advance

The Berkeley City Club is a sensational landmark building, located just one block from the U.C. Berkeley campus. It's a private social club, designed in 1927 by Julia Morgan in a Venetian-Mediterranean style with inner landscaped courtyards and fountains. The Club includes a 75-foot swimming pool, dining room, bar lounges, conference and reception rooms, many of which are available for private or business functions. Throughout, the detailing and craftsmanship are impressive. The Drawing and Patio Rooms are large, gracious rooms with beamed ceilings, fireplaces, wall tapestries, tile floors, oriental carpets and sizable leaded glass windows. The Auditorium is a large, spacious theater-like space with stage, parquet floor, and leaded glass windows. A wonderful, outdoor spot on a warm day for a cocktail party, the Terrace is an appealing reception area that has a terra cotta-colored canopy overhead. Berkeley campus and downtown life bustles all around the City Club, yet it remains a quiet, old world haven of comfort.

CAPACITY, FEES & DEPOSITS: A $500 deposit is required when the reservations are confirmed and is applied toward the rental fee.

Room	Theater-style	Reception	Seated	Fees
Drawing Room	100	80	60	$200
Patio Room	50	30	20	200
Drawing Rm, Patio & Courtyard	—	125 total	—	500
Courtyard	40	30	25	100
Loggia Court	—	—	12	50–75
Ballroom	300	275	250	300
Venetian Room	—	50	—	100
Ballroom & Venetian Rooms	—	325 total	300	400
The Terrace	150	120	100	200
Julia Morgan Room	—	25	40	100

All fees cover a 4-hour rental period. An additional flat fee of $200 is applied to all Sunday events; $400 additional to all holiday events. The balance and a final guest count are due 10 days prior to the function. For events with public access, security attendants are required on each floor, $75/each if provided. For a separate bar setup, there's a $50 bartender fee.

Food service is provided. Per person rates are: hors d'oeuvres buffet $18, seated luncheons $8.50–15.50, dinner buffets $23–27, luncheon buffets $14–18, breakfast meetings $5.50–10 and seated dinners by arrangement.

CANCELLATION POLICY: With 30 days' notice, all but $150 of the deposit is refundable.

AVAILABILITY: Year-round, every day from 6am–10pm; extra hours can be arranged. Closed Christmas and Thanksgiving.

SERVICES/AMENITIES:

Restaurant Services: yes
Catering: provided, no BYO
Kitchen Facilities: n/a
Tables & Chairs: provided
Linens, Silver, etc.: provided
Restrooms: wca
Dance Floor: yes
Parking: $4/car if reserved City Club spaces, lots nearby, street

Overnight Accommodations: 18 guestrooms
Telephone: pay and guest phones
Outdoor Night Lighting: yes
Outdoor Cooking Facilities: no
Cleanup: provided
Other: full event coordination
Special: stage lighting, business equipment, candelabras

RESTRICTIONS:

Alcohol: provided, no BYO
Smoking: designated areas
Music: amplified ok

Wheelchair Access: yes
Insurance: sometimes required
Other: security sometimes required

BERKELEY CONFERENCE ★ CENTER

2105 Bancroft Way
Berkeley, CA 94704
(415) 848-3957
Reserve: 1–2 months in advance

Don't let the modest, understated entry on Bancroft fool you. The Berkeley Conference Center has remarkable facilities for both business and social events. Housed in a historic, 4-story landmark building, the Center has over 11,000 sq. ft. of meeting and banquet space. Built in 1905 as a Masonic Temple, this building has an amazing assortment of highly detailed, classically beautiful spaces great for parties, awards ceremonies or big receptions. The Ballroom is magnificent. This is an enormous and elegant room with high ceilings, diffused lighting and a color palette that is superb. The Carleton and Haste Rooms are also large, with lots of wood mouldings and high ceilings. The Board Room is at the top, featuring bay views out of a long wall of windows. This is a medium-sized room, equipped with a small bar. Throughout, the facility maintains a high standard of excellence, not only in the decor, but in the high level of staff support. The Berkeley Conference Center is an unexpected and delightful surprise.

CAPACITY:

Room	Seated	Standing	Room	Seated	Standing
Grand Ballroom	250	350	Haste	150	250
Carleton	150	250	Board Room	70	125
Bancroft	50	85	Ashby	40	50
Evans	30	45	Channing	20	30

FEES & DEPOSITS :

Room	4-hour fee	8-hour fee	Room	4-hour fee	8-hour fee
Grand Ballroom	$400	$800	Haste	$200	$400
Carleton	200	400	Board Room	150	250
Bancroft	125	200	Ashby	100	150
Evans	80	120	Channing	80	120

A deposit equal to the room rental is required to secure the date. Half of the estimated food and beverage balance is due 2 months prior to the event, the remaining balance due 2 weeks before the event. For extended hours, there are additional fees.

CANCELLATION POLICY: For meetings or short term events, 30 days' advance notice is required for a full refund. For social events, 60 days is required.

AVAILABILITY: Year-round, every day from 6am–1am.

SERVICES/AMENITIES:

Restaurant Services: no
Catering: provided, no BYO
Kitchen Facilities: n/a
Tables & Chairs: provided
Linens, Silver, etc.: provided
Restrooms: mostly wca
Dance Floor: yes

Parking: lot nearby
Overnight Accommodations: Shattuck Hotel
Telephone: pay phone
Outdoor Night Lighting: no
Outdoor Cooking Facilities: no
Cleanup: provided
Other: full event planning and coordination

RESTRICTIONS:

Alcohol: provided, BYO corkage $6/bottle
Smoking: restricted
Music: amplified ok

Wheelchair Access: yes
Insurance: not required
Other: security guards sometimes required

BRAZILIAN ROOM

Tilden Park
Berkeley, CA 94708
(415) 540-0220 Jeri Honderd
Reserve: 2–12 months in advance

Once a part of the 1939 Golden Gate Exposition on Treasure Island, the Brazilian Room was presented as a gift to the East Bay Regional Park District by the country of Brazil. The original interior hardwood paneling and parquet flooring were kept intact, while a new exterior of local rocks and timber was constructed to permanently house the room. Natural light flows through the floor-to-ceiling leaded glass windows that run the length of the room on both sides, and a huge stone fireplace gives the space an added charm and warmth. Outside, the large flagstone patio overlooks a sloping lawn and the adjacent botanical garden. Located in Tilden Park, nestled high in the Berkeley Hills above UC Berkeley, the serene, pastoral surroundings offer an environment free from noise and distraction—perfect for business retreats, workshops, award dinners or private parties of all kinds.

CAPACITY: The Main Room holds 250 standing guests, 150 seated at tables and 200 theater-style.

MEETING ROOMS: 1 conference room with audio-visual equipment

FEES, DEPOSITS & AVAILABILITY: A $150 deposit, applied toward the rental fee, is due at the time of booking. A refundable cleaning/damage deposit of $200 is also required.

Weekend Rates (min. 5 hours)	*Fee*	*Time Blocks*
Saturday, Sunday, holidays	$500	10am–3pm or 6pm–11pm
Friday evening	500	6–11pm
One additional hour to 4pm or midnight	75	
Weekday Rates (min. 3 hours)		
Monday, Wednesday, Thursday	150	8am–midnight
Friday day (any 3-hour block)	150	8am–4pm
Each additional hour costs $50		
Special all day rate	200	8am–4pm
2 consecutive days	350	8am–4pm
3 consecutive days	500	8am–4pm
Seasonal Sunday Rates (min. 6 hours)		
November through April, any 6-hour block	600	10am–midnight
Each additional hour costs $50		

The fee balance is due 90 days prior to the event. Optional services are available for a fee. If using a non-preferred caterer, add $75. For non-residents of Alameda and Contra Costa counties, add $100 on weekends and holidays only.

CANCELLATION POLICY: If written notice is provided 120 days prior to the event, a full refund minus a $25 cancellation fee will be given. If less than 120 days' notice is given, you will receive the cleaning/ damage deposit along with any optional service fees you may have paid. If your date is rebooked, the balance you paid will be refunded minus a $25 cancellation fee.

SERVICES/AMENITIES:

Restaurant Services: no
Catering: provided or BYO
Kitchen Facilities: ample
Tables & Chairs: some provided
Linens, Silver, etc.: BYO
Restrooms: wca
Dance Floor: yes

Parking: lot
Overnight Accommodations: no
Telephone: pay phone
Outdoor Night Lighting: yes
Outdoor Cooking Facilities: yes
Cleanup: caterer

RESTRICTIONS:

Alcohol: WCB only, kegs of beer restricted to patio and kitchen
Smoking: outside only
Music: amplified inside only

Wheelchair Access: yes
Insurance: extra liability required
Other: decorations restricted

CRYSTAL ROOM
At the Sedona Grill

2086 Allston Way
Berkeley, CA 94704
(415) 841-3848
Reserve: 1 week–6 months in advance

What a find! Who would ever think that behind the trendy Sedona Grill lies a beautiful and elegant private dining room, perfect for receptions and special events? Reminiscent of a turn-of-the-century ballroom, it's large, simple and elegant. The color palette is soft and subdued, with two-tone cocoa colored walls and cream trim. There are also two mirrored arches running the length of the room, reflecting light from three large, historic crystal chandeliers. Mostly carpeted, the room boasts an oak dance floor making it a perfect spot for a dance party. Housed in the landmark Shattuck Hotel building, and entered from the Sedona lounge, this room comes as a wonderful surprise. For a special celebration or business event, this is an unusual and very appealing space. We highly recommend it.

CAPACITY: The Crystal Room can hold 100 seated guests and 150 for a reception. There is a minimum of 25 guests.

FEES & DEPOSITS: A $175 refundable deposit, applied toward the rental fee, is required when reservations are confirmed. The rental fee is $175 for up to 6 hours. Per person rates for meals: luncheons $17–20, dinners $25–30, buffets $20–35 and hors d'oeuvres start at $10. 50% of the estimated food and beverage total is payable 1 week prior to the function; the balance is due the day of the event. Business breakfasts can be arranged. A 15% service charge and 7.25% tax are additional.

CANCELLATION POLICY: With 30 days' notice, the deposit will be refunded.

AVAILABILITY: Every day 7:30am–1am except major holidays and Mother's Day.

SERVICES/AMENITIES:

Restaurant Services: yes

Catering: provided, no BYO

Kitchen Facilities: n/a

Tables & Chairs: provided

Linens, Silver, etc.: provided

Restrooms: wca

Dance Floor: yes

Parking: adjacent lots

Overnight Accommodations: 145 guestrooms

Telephone: pay phones

Outdoor Night Lighting: no

Outdoor Cooking Facilities: no

Cleanup: provided

Other: floral arrangements CBA

RESTRICTIONS:

Alcohol: provided , BYO corkage $10/bottle, WC only

Smoking: outside or in lounge only

Music: amplified ok

Wheelchair Access: yes

Insurance: not required

GRAMMA'S INN

2740 Telegraph Avenue
Berkeley, CA 94705
(415) 549-9167
Reserve: 1 week–6 months in advance

Two beautifully restored turn-of-the-century mansions constitute Gramma's Inn. The main house, built in 1900, is a sunny, Tudor-style manor. Furnished with antiques, this comfortable, sprawling house opens onto a large deck and garden. The 1905 Fay House is a stately mansion. Some of its original hand-painted gold leaf ceilings, stained glass windows and mahogany wood trim have not changed since the house was constructed. French doors open onto a spacious deck. Event areas include the parlor, dining room, sunporch, deck and garden area. Gramma's specializes in corporate retreats and can accommodate meetings as well. It's also a bed and breakfast inn, so guests can extend their stay in rooms featuring antiques, private decks and fireplaces.

CAPACITY: The Main House can accommodate up to 200 people standing and 140 seated when the garden is used. Indoor capacity is 100 standing and 70 seated. The Fay House can accommodate 150 standing and 140 seated when the deck is used, and 100 standing and 75 seated for inside events.

MEETING ROOMS: Pavilion Room, 65 participants seated classroom-style, 40 with tables. Greenhouse Room, 40 classroom-style, 25 with tables. Spacious suites for casual meetings and audio-visual equipment are available.

FEES & DEPOSITS: For events, a $400 deposit is due upon receipt of contract. It is refundable after the event. For business functions, there is a $100 deposit.

# of Guests	Main House	Fay House
0–20	$150	$150
21–39	200	200
40–50	300	300
51–60	300	465

# of Guests	Main House	Fay House
61–70	$350	$525
71–99	400	575
100–200	450	615

If your event precludes rental of hotel rooms to the public, those rooms affected would have to be rented as part of the event, and would be available to the guests of that event. For business functions: $25/hour with a minimum of 4 hours for any meeting room. Catering is provided and includes chairs, tables, silverware, glassware, dishes, linens, servers, setup and cleanup. Per person menu prices range from $10 to $50. A 15% service charge is added plus 7.25% tax.

CANCELLATION POLICY: There is no penalty for cancellation 90 days prior to the event. If written notice is not received 90 days prior, the deposit will be refunded only if the date is rebooked. For business functions the policy varies, so call for details.

AVAILABILITY: Any day, any time.

SERVICES/AMENITIES:

Restaurant Services: no
Catering: provided
Kitchen Facilities: n/a
Tables & Chairs: provided
Linens, Silver, etc.: provided
Restrooms: wca
Dance Floor: yes

Parking: lot, offstreet, valet
Overnight Accommodations: 30 guestrooms
Telephone: pay and house phones
Outdoor Night Lighting: yes
Outdoor Cooking Facilities: no
Cleanup: provided
Other: event planning & coordination

RESTRICTIONS:

Alcohol: provided, BYO corkage fee
Smoking: outside and guestrooms only
Music: amplified inside until 9pm

Wheelchair Access: yes
Insurance: not required

HILLSIDE CLUB

2286 Cedar Street
Berkeley, CA 94709
(415) 848-3227
Reserve: 1 month in advance

The Hillside Club was founded by a group of Berkeley citizens who wished to protect the hills of their town from "unsightly grading and the building of unsuitable and disfiguring houses." The original 1906 Club building was designed by renowned architect Bernard Maybeck. Destroyed in the great fire of 1923, it was redesigned by Maybeck's partner, John White, and rebuilt that year. Its style is that of an English Tudor hall, featuring a high wood-beamed ceiling, and massive fireplace. Afternoon light traverses the tall, multi-paned windows, warming the dark wood interior. Recitals often make use of the stage, piano and newly improved lighting system. The hardwood floor is perfect for dancing. An integral part of Berkeley's history, the Hillside Club is a casual, no-frills place to host your event.

CAPACITY: The hall accommodates 150 standing and 120 seated.

FEES & DEPOSITS: $100 or 50% of the fee, whichever is larger, is due at the time of booking. Weekdays and evenings (except Friday evening) the facility rents for $175. Friday evening, Saturday or Sunday it rents for $200. The balance of the fee is due a week before the event. The basic rental is for a 4-hour block of time. For each hour over 4 hours, there is a $40 charge. There are additional fees for use of certain items.

CANCELLATION POLICY: Cancellations are handled on an individual basis.

AVAILABILITY: Until 11pm every day.

SERVICES/AMENITIES:

Restaurant Services: no
Catering: BYO
Kitchen Facilities: minimal
Tables & Chairs: provided
Linens, Silver, etc.: BYO
Restrooms: no wca
Dance Floor: yes

Parking: on street
Overnight Accommodations: no
Telephone: no
Outdoor Night Lighting: no
Outdoor Cooking Facilities: no
Cleanup: caterer
Other: sound system, movie screen, piano

RESTRICTIONS:

Alcohol: BYO, BWC only
Smoking: not allowed
Music: amplified ok

Wheelchair Access: no
Insurance: not required
Other: no confetti

Crockett

CROCKETT COMMUNITY CENTER

850 Pomona
Crockett, CA 94525
(415) 787-2414   Melanie Rich Perkins
Reserve: 1–12 months in advance

Looking at the modest, rustic wooden exterior of the Center, one is surprised by the spacious vaulted auditorium inside. Designed by San Francisco architect William Crim for the C&H Sugar Company, the building is constructed on a grand scale, featuring a post and beam style ceiling, hardwood floors, an enormous (and functional) stone fireplace, a monumental bar, and a stage. In addition to the main hall, there are two smaller rooms, one with kitchenette, that can be rented separately. A park area is also available for outdoor activities.

CAPACITY: The Main Hall accommodates 350–400 people. The other, smaller rooms have varying capacities.

MEETING ROOMS: The multi-purpose room can accommodate 50.

FEES & DEPOSITS: A $200 cleaning and damage deposit is required for all rentals.

Auditorium including park area (10-hour rental): $315 residents, $365 non-residents. This includes $6.50/hr. for in-house security. For rentals over 10 hours, add $25/hr. for overtime. The rental is $55/hr.

Kitchen facilities: Add $50 to above rates for use of large kitchen.

Multi-purpose Room (4-hour rental): Room and kitchenette rental is $50 (includes security). Add $50 for use of large kitchen. For rentals over 4 hours, add $12.50/hr. for overtime.

Park and Restroom facilities: $50

CANCELLATION POLICY: Cancellations must be submitted in writing. Refund of the rent portion of the fees will be returned to the renter upon receipt of the written notice of cancellation. Refund of the total deposit is based upon the following time frame: 30 days' notice—75% refund; 14-29 days' notice—50% refund; less than 14 days—forfeiture of entire deposit.

AVAILABILITY: All year, 24 hours a day.

SERVICES/AMENITIES:

Restaurant Service: no

Catering: BYO

Kitchen Facilities: ample

Tables & Chairs: provided

Linens, Silver, etc.: BYO

Restrooms: wca

Dance Floor: yes

Parking: on street

Overnight Accommodations: no

Telephone: pay phone

Night Lighting: no

Outdoor Cooking Facilities: yes

Cleanup: caterer and renter, or provided for a fee

Other: podium, sound system, VCR & screen

RESTRICTIONS:

Alcohol: BYO

Smoking: allowed

Music: amplified ok

Wheelchair Access: yes

Insurance: not required

Other: decorations restricted

Danville

BEHRING MUSEUM ★★

3750 Blackhawk Plaza Circle
Danville, CA 94506
(415) 735-8511 Kahle-McCann
Reserve: 2–6 months in advance

The Behring Museum is a study in glass, granite and stainless steel. Overlooking Blackhawk Plaza, this multi-million dollar museum showcases rare classic automobiles in elegant, sumptuous surroundings. The lobby is impressive with its soaring skylights and dusty rose Italian marble floors and walls. As the sun sets through the tinted glass facade, the entire space is bathed in a warm hazy glow. The juxtaposition of metal and stone with soft rich colors creates a subtle excitement. The dining room presents a striking contrast: black from its granite floor to unadorned ceiling, it offers an unusual backdrop for your own color theme. Vintage car galleries border the dining area, and can be illuminated or rendered invisible by a network of computerized lights. Whether you come here to savor Ken Behring's ultra-modern vision or you simply like the idea of a private celebration amidst classic cars, the Behring Museum will make your event unforgettable.

CAPACITY: The Dining Room accommodates up to 500 seated guests. For more than 300 guests, additional fees may be required for a special dining room setup. The Lobby holds 600 standing.

FEES & DEPOSITS: A $1000 nonrefundable rental deposit for museum use and a nonrefundable $2500 deposit for event planning are due when the date is booked. These fees are credited to the final bill. The facility rental is $2000 for up to 200 guests; for every additional 50 people or part thereof, add $500. Catering is provided or you can select from a preferred list. Although any arrangements can be made, a popular, all-inclusive package includes: all food, staff, linens, china and silver, flower arrangements for tables and lobby, a quartet during cocktails, full bar and wine with the meal and service charges. Package rates run approximately $125/person for seated buffet dinners, $70/person for substantial hors d'oeuvres, $50/person for light cocktail hors d'oeuvres, $40/person for wine, pate and cheese. A 7.25% sales tax is applied to the final bill.

AVAILABILITY: 5pm to midnight.

SERVICES/AMENITIES:

Restaurant Services: no

Catering: provided or preferred list

Kitchen Facilities: in progress

Tables & Chairs: provided

Linens, Silver, etc.: provided

Restrooms: wca

Dance Floor: yes

Parking: lot

Overnight Accommodations: no

Telephone: pay phone

Outdoor Night Lighting: yes

Outdoor Cooking Facilities: yes

Cleanup: caterer

RESTRICTIONS:

Alcohol: no red wine except in dining room, no alcohol allowed in galleries

Smoking: outside only

Music: amplified ok

Wheelchair Access: yes

Insurance: liability required

GRACE SLICK

Singer, Songwriter, Performer; formerly of the Jefferson Airplane

My house is the best party place—if you happen to be a raccoon. I serve between 25-30 raccoons every night! You can get as many Oreos as you want (with extra stuff), grapes, cat food, pasta— anything you want that is left over from dinner. You can swim in the pool and do anything you want. It happens every night; it's at my house, and if you have a bandit mask across your eyes, and seven rings on your tail, be my guest.

Emeryville

CHALKERS BILLIARD CLUB

5900 'S' Hollis Street
Emeryville, CA 94608
(415) 658-5821 Sue or Hal
Reserve: 1–3 weeks in advance

Chalkers is an upscale pool hall. The decor is reminiscent of an art gallery: clean lines, dressed in sophisticated colors with good art work on the walls. Chalkers not only provides its customers with billiard and snooker lessons, it also serves champagne, wine, beer, hors d'oeuvres and fine pastries, too. Located in the back of a renovated industrial complex near Hollis and 59th Street, Chalkers offers an interesting and fun event venue for those who want to play pool or snooker. There are two floors of pool tables. The upper floor, private VIP room or the entire facility can be made available for your private party. Impress your friends or workmates—bring your own custom-made cue.

FEES, DEPOSITS & CAPACITY: A deposit in the amount of the first hours rental is required to secure your date. If you rent the entire facility, the deposit will increase.

Area	Hours	Fee	Capacity
Entire Facility	until 6pm	$175/hour	225
	after 6pm	$250/hour	
Upper Floor	until 6pm	$135/hour	150
	after 6pm	$190/hour	
VIP Room	any time	$30/hour	15

Capacities are for standing affairs only. There is a 3-hour minimum for group rentals.

CANCELLATION POLICY: A 72-hour notice is required for events with food or if the entire facility is rented. Small parties with no food service require a 24-hour notice.

AVAILABILITY: Any day, noon–9pm; Tues, Wed and Sun from noon–2am.

SERVICES/AMENITIES:

Restaurant Services: no
Catering: provided or BYO with approval
Kitchen Facilities: no
Tables & Chairs: stools provided or BYO
Linens, Silver, etc.: provided
Restrooms: wca
Dance Floor: no

Parking: large lot
Overnight Accommodations: no
Telephone: pay phone
Outdoor Night Lighting: no
Outdoor Cooking Facilities: no
Cleanup: caterer

RESTRICTIONS:

Alcohol: WBC provided, BYO $5/corkage, no hard alcohol
Smoking: designated areas

Music: amplified ok
Wheelchair Access: yes
Insurance: not required

Fremont

ARDENWOOD HISTORIC PRESERVE

34600 Ardenwood Blvd.
Fremont, CA 94555
(415) 462-1400 Kathy Barlow
Reserve: 3–12 months in advance

Ardenwood is a 205-acre working farm, established during the last half of the 19th century. Here, you can travel back in time—draft horses still pull wagons, ladies wear Victorian dresses and the land still grows the kinds of crops it did 100 years ago. Guests can stroll through the beautiful gardens, tour the impressive Patterson Mansion and enjoy historic farm demonstrations and other remnants of a past way of life. Ardenwood offers a unique atmosphere for group picnics and special events. A short ride on the horse-drawn railroad brings you to the Deer Park Picnic Areas, where your group can relax and enjoy the simple pleasures of a time gone by.

CAPACITY: The Deer Park Picnic Areas can hold groups between 75–1200 people.

FEES & DEPOSITS: A nonrefundable reservation deposit, ranging from $100–1200 (depending on the group size) is required to secure your date. The deposit is due when the date is booked and is credited to the final billing. Picnic site rental includes sports and recreation activities, tours, demonstrations and wagon rides. Site rental ranges from $395–$2900 depending on the size of the site(s) rented. Purchase of beverages is required (beer, wine, soft drinks, coffee & tea) at $3.25/person. Catered all-you-can-eat meals, BBQ-style, range from $3.65–$13.95/person. Moonlighting Parties start at $17.95/person with rental, food and beverages included.

AVAILABILITY: May–October, Saturday and Sunday from 10am–5pm. Moonlighting Party hours are 6:30pm–midnight.

SERVICES/AMENITIES:

Restaurant Services: no
Catering: provided or cater yourself, no outside caterer
Kitchen Facilities: n/a
Tables & Chairs: provided
Linens, Silver, etc.: provided
Restrooms: wca
Dance Floor: CBA, extra fee

Parking: ample lots
Overnight Accommodations: no
Telephone: pay phone
Outdoor Night Lighting: yes
Outdoor Cooking Facilities: BBQs
Cleanup: provided
Other: horse-drawn carriage CBA, complete event services

RESTRICTIONS:
Alcohol: provided , no BYO
Smoking: allowed
Music: amplified after 5pm only

Wheelchair Access: yes, restricted vehicle access
Insurance: not required
Other: park open to public from 10am to 4pm

THE PALMDALE ESTATE

159 Washington Blvd.
Fremont, CA 94539
(415) 651-8908
Reserve: 2–12 months in advance

The Palmdale Estate is an unexpected jewel in Fremont. Towering palm trees, lakes, rose gardens and expansive lawns grace this 23-acre estate. Best House (built by Mrs. Best) is a white, brown-trimmed Tudor-style home. Built in 1915, it features a large ballroom with burgundy drapes, hardwood floors and murals on the walls and ceilings. The Music room is decorated in gold leaf and also has artwork everywhere you look. French doors, chandeliers, hardwood and marble floors make this an attractive and special spot to hold a celebration, business seminar or retreat.

CAPACITY: The gardens can hold 1000 guests for a reception and Best House can hold 150 seated indoors and combined with outdoor spaces, up to 500 guests.

FEES & DEPOSITS: To rent the house and garden, a $250 refundable security deposit is due when the rental agreement is submitted. Rental fees are as follows:

	Fees	*Timeframe*
Weekend	$1250/8 hours	8am–midnight
Weekday	$500/8 hours or $100/hour	9am–5pm
Weekday Evenings	$150/hour	5pm–midnight

CANCELLATION POLICY: The security deposit is forfeited if you cancel.

AVAILABILITY: Year round, every day except Easter and Christmas.

SERVICES/AMENITIES:
Restaurant Services: no
Catering: BYO
Kitchen Facilities: minimal
Tables & Chairs: provided to 150 guests
Linens, Silver, etc.: BYO or CBA
Restrooms: wca
Dance Floor: Ballroom

Parking: large lot
Overnight Accommodations: no
Telephone: lounge phone
Outdoor Night Lighting: CBA
Outdoor Cooking Facilities: no
Cleanup: whoever caters event
Other: event coordination

RESTRICTIONS:
Alcohol: BYO WCB only, hard alcohol restricted
Smoking: outside only
Music: amplified within limits

Wheelchair Access: yes
Insurance: sometimes required

Livermore

RAVENSWOOD

2647 Arroyo Road
Livermore, CA 94550
(415) 373-5700 Park District Office
Reserve: 3–12 months in advance

Ravenswood is one of those places you want to explore the minute you see it. A pepper tree-lined driveway draws your eye straight up to the two houses set far back from the main road. The Cottage House, built in 1885, looks out over a lovely little garden. As you walk toward the main house, the fragrance of roses accompanies you. A Queen Anne Victorian, the larger house on the estate has real old-fashioned charm. A comfortable wrap-around veranda encourages lazy afternoon socializing, and the palm-ringed front lawn is a perfect spot for an al fresco repast. Inside, high ceilings, a fireplace, hardwood floors and simple decor make you feel right at home. Behind both houses is grassy area with a gazebo. Surrounded by a dozen trees, it rests in dappled shade completing a picture of country serenity.

CAPACITY:

Area	Standing	Seated
Main House	150	71
Grounds	150	150
Billiard Room	75	50

The facility accommodates a maximum of 150 guests.

FEES & DEPOSITS : A $50 rental deposit is required to secure a date. The balance of the rental fee and a $150 cleaning deposit are due 30 days prior to the event. The rental fee is $436 for Livermore residents, and $654 for non-residents. There is also a $30 liquor permit charge.

CANCELLATION POLICY: If the event is canceled three months or more prior to the event, 50% of the rental deposit is returned. If you cancel within 3 months of the event, the deposit will be forfeited. For either period, any prepaid rental charges in excess of the facility rental deposit are refunded. With less than one month's notice, only the cleaning deposit is returned.

AVAILABILITY: Every day 8am–9pm, except Tuesdays.

SERVICES/AMENITIES:

Restaurant Services: no
Catering: BYO
Kitchen Facilities: moderate
Tables & Chairs: some provided
Linens, Silver, etc.: BYO

Parking: lot
Overnight Accommodations: no
Telephone: restricted use
Outdoor Night Lighting: no
Outdoor Cooking Facilities: no

Restrooms: wca
Dance Floor: yes

RESTRICTIONS:
Alcohol: WCB only with license
Smoking: outside only
Music: no amplified music

Cleanup: caterer and renter
Other: horse-drawn carriage CBA

Wheelchair Access: yes
Insurance: damage and liability required
Other: decorations restricted

WENTE BROS. ESTATE WINERY

5565 Tesla Road
Livermore, CA 94550
(415) 447-3603
Reserve: 6–12 months in advance

The Estate Winery is located in the scenic Livermore Valley in a lovely vineyard setting. This 100-year-old winery has charm and a rustic ambiance perfect for leisurely brunches, luncheons or evening dinners in the banquet room or on the adjacent patio.

CAPACITY: The banquet room holds up to 100 standing guests and 70 seated; the patio up to 500 standing and 250 seated guests.

FEES & DEPOSITS: A deposit of 50% of the estimated total plus a $250 security deposit are due at the time of reservation. The remainder is due 30 days prior to the event. For events of up to 200 people there is a $200 fee for the use of any part of the facility. For over 200 people add $2 per person. Per person catering costs run between $25–40 and do not include wine. A 15% gratuity and 7.25% sales tax are additional.

CANCELLATION POLICY: With 90 days' notice, the deposit minus $200 will be refunded. With less than 90 days' notice, the deposit is forfeited.

AVAILABILITY: The facility is available every day from 10am–midnight.

SERVICES/AMENITIES:
Restaurant Services: no
Catering: provided, no BYO
Kitchen Facilities: n/a
Tables & Chairs: provided
Linens, Silver, etc.: provided
Outdoor Night Lighting: yes
Outdoor Cooking Facilities: no

Restrooms: wca
Dance Floor: no
Parking: lot
Overnight Accomodations: no
Telephone: pay phone
Cleanup: provided

RESTRICTIONS:
Alcohol: provided, WC only
Smoking: outside only
Music: amplified ok

Wheelchair Access: yes
Insurance: not required

WENTE BROS. SPARKLING WINE CELLARS

5050 Arroyo Road
Livermore, CA 94550
(415) 447-3023
Reserve: 6–12 months in advance

For private parties or special events, the Wente Brothers' spacious patio and lawn area are perfect. There's also a Visitor's Center and a casually elegant restaurant which serves top-notch cuisine. Both are white, Spanish-style stucco buildings. Tile roofs and floors, terra cotta pots full of flowers, and acres of vineyards convey a strong Mediterranean feeling. For businesses, there's even a full service conference center here, with 4 state-of-the-art meeting rooms. Shimmering white and green in the soothing afternoon sun, this winery is an oasis in the midst of dry California hills.

CAPACITY: *Area*	*Standing*	*Seated*	*At Tables*	*Theater Style*
Restaurant (min 60 guests)	200	120	—	—
Visitor's Center	300	160	—	—
Garden Area	—	700	—	—
Veranda Area	—	120	—	—
Conference Center Rooms A–D	—	—	25–80	35–120

FEES & DEPOSITS: A deposit of 50% of the estimated total plus a $250 security deposit are due at the time of reservation. The remainder is due 30 days prior to the event. For over 200 people, add $2 per person. The Visitor's Center Building/Patios rents for $200. Meals run between $20–40/person and do not include wine. A 15% gratuity and 7.25% sales tax will be added. Meeting room fees range from $75–150/day.

CANCELLATION POLICY: If you cancel up to 90 days in advance, the deposit minus $200 will be refunded. With less than 90 days' notice, the deposit is forfeited.

AVAILABILITY: The facility is available every day from 10am–midnight. The restaurant Wednesday–Sunday.

SERVICES/AMENITIES:

Restaurant Services: yes
Catering: provided, no BYO
Kitchen Facilities: n/a
Tables & Chairs: provided
Linens, Silver, etc.: provided
Outdoor Night Lighting: yes
Outdoor Cooking Facilities: no

Restrooms: wca
Dance Floor: yes
Parking: lot
Overnight Accommodations: no
Telephone: pay phone
Cleanup: provided
Other: audio-visual equipment

RESTRICTIONS:

Alcohol: provided, WC only
Smoking: outside only
Music: amplified ok

Wheelchair Access: yes
Insurance: not required

Moraga

HACIENDA DE LAS FLORES

2100 Donald Drive
Moraga, CA 94556
(415) 376-2520
Reserve: 2–12 months

An authentic Spanish-style mansion, the Hacienda de las Flores sits on land that was once the hunting ground for Miwok Indians. The rambling structure is painted white with blue trim, and is surrounded by park grounds. A large lawn spreads out behind the building, enhanced by blue spruce trees, weeping willows, palms and flowers. A circular flower bed and fountain in the middle of the yard serve as the backdrop for special celebrations. Guests can relax on the stone patio, ringed by tropical plants and shrubs. Inside the building, hardwood floors, beamed ceilings, a fireplace and red leather furniture create a warm and inviting setting. Tranquil and secluded, the Hacienda is a favorite event and business meeting spot not only among local residents, but for people all over the Bay Area.

CAPACITY: The Hacienda accommodates 200 guests outdoors and 128 for a sit-down meal indoors. The Pavilion seats 40 inside and has an outdoor capacity of 85. For business functions, see the chart below.

FEES & DEPOSITS: For special events, a security deposit is due at the time of booking and will be refunded within 30 days after the event provided all conditions have been met. Completed rental packet and final fees are due 60 days before the event. Additional hours can be arranged for a fee. June–Sept there is a $100 surcharge.

	Weekend Special Events				Weekday Business Functions		
	Residents		*Non Residents*				
Friday (6 hr)	*Deposit*	*Fee*	*Deposit*	*Fee*	*Capacity*	*4 Hr.-Fee*	*8 Hr.-Fee*
Hacienda	$475	$605	$675	$935	—	—	—
Pavilion	350	440	575	770	40 w/tables 60 theater-style	$150	$200
Hacienda & Pavilion	700	880	1050	1430	—	—	—

	Weekend Special Events				Weekday Business Functions		
	Residents		*Non Residents*				
Sat/Sun (5 hr)	*Deposit*	*Fee*	*Deposit*	*Fee*	*Capacity*	*4-Hr. Fee*	*8-Hr. Fee*
Hacienda	$475	$700	$675	$1025	—	—	—
Pavilion	350	525	575	875	—	—	—
Hacienda & Pavilion	700	1075	1050	1700	—	—	—
Terrace Room	—	—	—	—	20 w/tables 32 theater-style	$125	$150
La Sala	—	—	—	—	60 w/tables 75 theater-style	$150	$200

The deposit for weekday functions is the same as the rental fee, payable when reservations are made.

CANCELLATION POLICY: Cancellations must be made in writing. Special event refunds will be made as follows: over 120 days' notice—100% of deposit less a $50 bookkeeping fee; 90-120 days' notice—50% returned. For weekday functions, 2 weeks' notice is required to receive a full refund.

AVAILABILITY: Weekdays from 10am–5pm, Fridays from 5–11pm, Saturdays and Sundays, 10am–11pm.

SERVICES/AMENITIES:

Restaurant Services: no

Catering: BYO, must be licensed

Kitchen Facilities: ample

Tables & Chairs: provided

Linens, Silver, etc.: BYO

Restrooms: wca

Dance Floor: yes

Parking: on street and lot

Overnight Accommodations: no

Telephone: pay phone

Outdoor Night Lighting: no

Outdoor Cooking Facilities: no

Cleanup: provided

RESTRICTIONS:

Alcohol: BYO, WCB only

Smoking: outside only

Music: no outdoor amplified music

Wheelchair Access: yes

Insurance: extra insurance required

Other: decorations restricted

Oakland

CAMRON-STANFORD HOUSE

1418 Lakeside Drive
Oakland, CA 94612
(415) 836-1976   Elizabeth Way
Reserve: 1–6 months in advance

Gracing the shore of Lake Merritt, the Camron-Stanford House is the last of the grand Victorian homes that once ringed the lake. Constructed in 1876, it derives its name from the Camrons who built it, and the Stanfords who occupied it for the longest period. When the building was scheduled for demolition in the late 1960s, concerned citizens formed the Camron-Stanford House Preservation Association and spent the intervening years raising funds to return the home to its former splendor. Elaborate molding, authentic wallpaper and fabrics have all been restored to match the original as closely as possible. Rooms filled with period artifacts, antiques and photos take you back to the turn of the century. The only operational gas lamp in Northern California is located here. Outside, an enormous rear veranda overlooks Lake Merritt. Events and celebrations can take place in the house or on the large, fenced in lawn that extends to the lake. The outside veranda is popular for business functions. An iron fence enclosing the site ensures privacy while allowing guests to appreciate the colorful tapestry of boats, birds, and joggers that surrounds them.

CAPACITY: The facility accommodates 125 guests inside, and 250 outside.

MEETING ROOMS: The Dining Room can hold 45–80 guests; one other room up to 20.

FEES & DEPOSITS: Half the rental fee and a refundable $50 cleaning deposit are due at the time of booking.

Area	Fee
Veranda, Hall, Dining Room, Kitchen (2 hours)	$ 275
Veranda, Hall, Dining Room, Kitchen (4 hours)	475
Additional time	100/hr.
Period Room (maximum 2 hours)	50/hr.

CANCELLATION POLICY: If less than 30 days' notice is given, 50% of the rental fee will be forfeited. The remainder of the fee and the cleaning deposit are usually returned.

AVAILABILITY: To 10pm weekdays, and to 11pm Saturdays.

SERVICES/AMENITIES:

Restaurant Services: no
Catering: BYO licensed
Kitchen Facilities: moderate
Tables & Chairs: BYO
Linens, Silver, etc.: BYO
Restrooms: wca
Dance Floor: CBA, extra fee

Parking: on street, lot
Overnight Accommodations: no
Telephone: emergencies only
Outdoor Night Lighting: CBA
Outdoor Cooking Facilities: BYO
Cleanup: caterer
Other: Lake tour on Merritt Queen paddleboat CBA

RESTRICTIONS:

Alcohol: allowed
Smoking: outside only
Music: amplified outside only
Wheelchair Access: limited

Insurance: proof required
Other: decorations restricted, no candles, flame-heated chafing dishes, confetti

MARTIN YAN
TV Personality Chef

I am not much of a caterer, but once a year for the KQED Auction, I offer to cook a dinner for 10. This particular dinner was very special—it had a price tag of $15,000! That's perhaps the most expensive Chinese dinner in the world. The planning of the menu was the first step. What could I possibly serve that would meet a $15,000 expectation? Wontons and egg rolls just wouldn't do. How many courses would I have to prepare? I took 4 1/2 months to plan the menu.

Dinner began at 6pm and the last course was served as 12:30pm—6 1/2 hours! A total of 18 courses were served, accompanied by 12 vintage wines. And amazing as it may seem, there were no leftovers. They ate all 18 courses! I guess they liked the dinner. But after all that wine, I am wondering if they could tell the difference between the Sizzling Spicy Lobster on a Hot Plate from the Chilled Seasonal Greens with Exotic Mushrooms.

I must admit that after this experience, I'm glad I'm only a humble Chinese cook and not an ambitions Chinese caterer. Can you imagine all the dirty dishes after 18 courses? My apron never looked the same after that evening.

THE CLAREMONT RESORT, SPA & TENNIS CLUB

Ashby and Domingo Avenues
Oakland, CA 94623
(415) 843-3000 Jan Hager
Reserve: 1–12 months in advance

The Claremont rises up from the Oakland/Berkeley Hills where it has been a Bay Area landmark for decades. Hotel, resort, and spa, it offers an extensive range of services and amenities, and numerous rooms for business conferences and special events. This is a full-service conference site with over 32,000 sq. ft. of meeting space. You can choose from among private rooms, balconies, trellised patios or lawns and gardens. The Claremont can cater a small cocktail party, a formal sit-down feast for hundreds, or anything in between. If you need help with any aspect of your event, the Claremont has the staff to assist you—there's even a conference service department as well as an on-site audio-visual company. So whether you want an affair on a grand scale, or a small informal gathering of business associates, the Claremont Resort can accommodate your needs.

CAPACITY: Two of the ballrooms can accommodate 400 guests standing, and 350 seated. The 20 other available rooms have varying capacities.

MEETING ROOMS: 22 meeting rooms

FEES & DEPOSITS: For special events, a $500 nonrefundable deposit, which is applied toward the fee, is due at the time of booking. 80% of the total estimated bill is due 5 days prior to the event, and the balance is due at the conclusion. For business functions, deposits and fees vary. The fee schedule is based on the room(s) selected and the number of guests in attendance.

AVAILABILITY: Any day between 6am and 1am.

SERVICES/AMENITIES:

Restaurant Services: yes
Catering: provided, no BYO
Kitchen Facilities: n/a
Tables & Chairs: provided
Linens, Silver, etc.: provided
Restrooms: wca
Dance Floor: yes
Parking: lot, valet

Overnight Accommodations: 239 guestrooms
Telephone: pay phone
Outdoor Night Lighting: no
Outdoor Cooking Facilities: yes
Cleanup: provided
Special: spa, tennis courts, swimming pool
Other: full conference amenities

RESTRICTIONS:

Alcohol: provided
Smoking: allowed
Music: no music at poolside

Wheelchair Access: yes
Insurance: not required
Other: receptions held inside only

DUNSMUIR HOUSE ★★

2960 Peralta Oaks Court
Oakland, CA 94605
(415) 562-0328
Reserve: 1–3 months in advance

Nestled in the East Bay foothills, the historic Dunsmuir House and Gardens offer a lovely and secluded setting featuring a turn-of-the-century white mansion and a 40-acre expanse of lawn and trees, evoking the serenity of a bygone era. The House was a romantic wedding gift from Alexander Dunsmuir to his bride on the occasion of their marriage in 1899. The full estate can accommodate up to 3000 guests and is glorious on a sunny day. This is one of the most exceptional sites in the Bay Area for an outdoor party, corporate event or private celebration.

CAPACITY:

Area	Standing	Seated
Mansion	80 (by special arrangement)	—
Carriage House	200	100 or more
Greenhouse	350	200
Pond area	—	300
Grounds	3,000	—

FEES & DEPOSITS: 50% of the rental fee is due at the signing of the rental contract. The balance of the fee and an additional refundable cleaning deposit of $300 are due four weeks prior to the event. Use fees (min. 3 hrs) are determined by location or combination of locations and event time span. During business functions, tours can be arranged, docent charge $300/hour. Parking can be rented for $100/event.

Area	Fee/Hour	Area	Fee/Hour
Mansion	$350	Pond area	$150
Carriage House	$175	Meadow	$200
Greenhouse	$200	Dinklespiel	$125

CANCELLATION POLICY: No refund will be given after a reservation is confirmed. All deposits are considered payment for services rendered after 72 hours.

AVAILABILITY: Year-round, any day.

SERVICES/AMENITIES:

Restaurant Services: no
Catering: provided or BYO extra fee
Kitchen Facilities: no
Tables & Chairs: provided
Linens, Silver, etc.: provided
Restrooms: wca
Parking: lot

Dance Floor: CBA, extra fee
Overnight Accommodations: no
Telephone: pay phone
Outdoor Night Lighting: CBA
Outdoor Cooking Facilities: CBA
Cleanup: provided

RESTRICTIONS:

Alcohol: provided or BYO, BWC only
Smoking: outside only
Music: amplified ok

Wheelchair Access: yes
Insurance: may be required
Other: decorations limited

JACK LONDON'S ★ FESTIVAL CENTER

Foot of Broadway at Jack London Waterfront
Oakland, CA 94607
(415) 444-5969 Banquet Services
Reserve: 1 month in advance

Jack London's Pavilion is being developed into the Festival Center. Designed by Esherick (the architect that developed the Monterey Bay Aquarium), this new, terra cotta-colored structure is situated close to the waterfront. From outside the building you can watch ships and sail boats cruise by in the Oakland Estuary. There's an attractive, well-designed plaza, equipped with a sea urchin-shaped fountain and flower-filled planters. The Festival Center will be outfitted to serve private and public parties, special events and business functions. A permanent bakery/delicatessen and old fashioned ice cream parlor are envisioned along with a large open area and stage for movable party props and special events decor. If you'd like a theme party, all the details can be professionally produced and catered by the Jack London Festival Center. This flexible and large event space can serve all types of gatherings: charity benefits, classic auto shows, jazz concerts, bridal fairs, company parties, etc. An added treat is a memorial antique carrousel that will operate in the plaza, providing both a festive atmosphere and an attractive element for kids' parties.

CAPACITY: Inside, the Festival Center can hold 200–1500 seated guests, for receptions 200–2000 guests. The Plaza can also be used for outdoor functions.

FEES & DEPOSITS : Rates are being formulated. Please call for specifics.

CANCELLATION POLICY: If the space(s) can be rebooked, the deposit will be refunded.

AVAILABILITY: Year-round, every day, any time.

SERVICES/AMENITIES:

Restaurant Services: no
Catering: provided
Kitchen Facilities: fully equipped
Tables & Chairs: provided
Linens, Silver, etc.: provided
Restrooms: wca
Dance Floor: provided

Parking: adjacent garage
Overnight Accommodations: no
Telephone: pay phones
Outdoor Night Lighting: yes
Outdoor Cooking Facilities: CBA
Cleanup: provided
Other: full event coordination, theme parties

RESTRICTIONS:

Alcohol: provided, BYO corkage $7.50/bottle
Smoking: designated areas
Music: amplified ok

Wheelchair Access: yes
Insurance: sometimes required

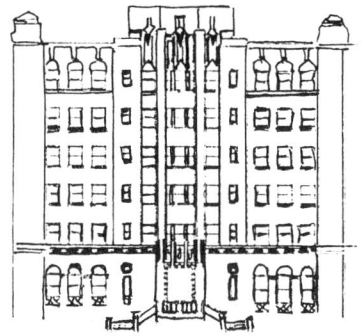

THE LAKE MERRITT HOTEL

1800 Madison Street at Lakeside
Oakland, CA 94612
(415) 832-2300
Reserve: 3–12 months in advance

Totally enclosed in twenty-foot floor-to-ceiling windows, the Lake Merritt Hotel's Restaurant presents a spectacular panorama of Lake Merritt, Lakeside Park and the Oakland hills. At night, the lake glitters below, reflecting the Necklace of Lights gracing its perimeter. Wrought iron window castings, symmetrical design and restaurant entrance are pure 1927 Art Deco. Over $1.5 million has recently been spent to turn the hotel and restaurant into one of Oakland's premier entertainment sites.

CAPACITY: The Restaurant accommodates 300 standing and 250 for a seated affair.

MEETING ROOMS: Can accommodate 80 standing guests, 50 seated.

FEES & DEPOSITS: A $250 security deposit is required to reserve space. 50% payment is required 1 month prior to the event date; the balance due 1 week prior to your event. For events, the room rental fee is $1500 with substantial reductions for each hotel room booked. The meeting rental fee is $250–350 with reductions made for each hotel room booked.

AVAILABILITY: The banquet and meeting rooms are available every day from 7am–2am.

SERVICES/AMENITIES:

Restaurant Services: no
Catering: provided
Kitchen Facilities: n/a
Tables & Chairs: provided
Linens, Silver, etc.: provided
Restrooms: no wca
Dance Floor: yes

Parking: on street, valet CBA
Overnight Accommodations: suites and packages available
Telephone: pay phone
Outdoor Night Lighting: no
Outdoor Cooking Facilities: no
Cleanup: provided

RESTRICTIONS:

Alcohol: provided, no BYO
Smoking: allowed
Music: amplified restricted

Wheelchair Access: limited
Insurance: not required

MILLS COLLEGE ★
CONFERENCE FACILITIES

5000 MacArthur Blvd.
Oakland, CA 94613
(415) 430-2145   Conference Center
Reserve: 1–12 months in advance

When you're here, it's hard to believe you are in the midst of a city. The 127-acre, tree-shaded Mills College Campus offers a phenomenal site for social, business or cultural events. This quiet and secluded retreat in the hills east of San Francisco Bay offers an extensive and eclectic array of distinctive meeting facilities. Developed here in 1871, Mills has many historic buildings; some Victorian, some Craftsman and others designed in a grand Mediterranean style with light stucco walls and terra cotta tile roofs. Seminar rooms, lounges, classrooms, lecture halls and an incredibly beautiful theater are available for formal or informal gatherings. Areas for outdoor events include the Art Complex grounds and a meadow equipped with stage and power. Business seminar equipment, meal service and overnight accommodations are no problem. There's an on-site professional conference staff to meet the multiple needs of any group.

CAPACITY, FEES & DEPOSITS:

Area	Capacity	Fee/Day	Area	Capacity	Fee/Day
Concert Hall	500	$800	Student Union	200	$350
Bender Room	100	350	Danforth Hall	80	275
Ensemble Room	50	250	Alderwood Hall	60–100	125–200
Faculty Lounge	100	350	Toyon Meadow	500	500–1500
Faculty Dining Room	120	250	Art Complex Grounds	500	500–1500
Wetmore Lodge	75	150			

The deposit for day meetings is equal to the rental fee; for overnight conferences the deposit is 25% of the estimated total event cost. Both are refundable and are due when the contract is submitted. A confirmed guest count is due 30, 60 and 90 days in advance of the function. The balance is invoiced, payable within 15 days of the billing date. Overnight stays can be arranged for $67/night which includes 3 cafeteria-style meals per day. Catering can be provided. Per person rates: dinners $9.50–18.50, buffets $10–13, box lunches $7.50–11, hors d'oeuvres $30–60/tray and continental breakfasts/coffee service starting at $5.

CANCELLATION POLICY: With 90 days' notice, the deposit less $150 is refundable.

AVAILABILITY: Year-round, every day, any time.

SERVICES/AMENITIES:

Restaurant Services: yes
Catering: preferred list, BYO w/approval
Kitchen Facilities: no
Tables & Chairs: provided or BYO
Linens, Silver, etc.: provided or BYO
Restrooms: some wca
Dance Floor: BYO

Parking: large lots
Overnight Accommodations: 48 guestrooms, 800 summer
Telephone: pay phone
Outdoor Night Lighting: no
Outdoor Cooking Facilities: BBQ
Cleanup: whoever caters event
Other: business conference equipment

RESTRICTIONS:

Alcohol: CBW provided, setup fee $2/person
Smoking: outside only
Music: amplified ok

Wheelchair Access: limited
Insurance: sometimes required
Other: no sale of alcohol, no pets

OAKLAND MUSEUM

1000 Oak Street
Oakland, CA 94607
(415) 273-2264   Harriet Y. Wright
Reserve: 6 months in advance

Ensconced in the heart of downtown Oakland, the museum and grounds provide a surprisingly quiet and bucolic setting. Business meetings, events and receptions can be held in the Restaurant or on the adjacent tree-lined terraces and patios. The Restaurant, with its carpeting and comfy chairs, has a casual, relaxed ambiance. There's even a baby grand piano in here for your use. The rambling spaces outdoors, however, are what make the museum a special site. Guests can enjoy the openness of a tree-shaded lawn or wander off for a little solitude among the many levels of terraces.

CAPACITY: The Museum Restaurant accommodates 240 standing guests and 145 seated. The Gardens and Terraces have space for a sizable party.

FEES & DEPOSITS: 25% of the total estimated fee plus a refundable cleaning/damage deposit are required when the contract is signed. The Restaurant rents for $850–1020 for up to 4 hours and $1050–1260 for more than 4 hours, depending on whether you're a profit or nonprofit organization. Call for Garden and Terrace fee information. You are billed for the balance after the event, and payment is due within 30 days of the invoice date.

CANCELLATION POLICY: If notice of cancellation is received by the Museum within 5 working days of the event, the 25% deposit will be refunded. Regardless of the time of notification, however, any direct costs incurred in preparing for the event will be charged to the renting party.

AVAILABILITY: Monday–Tuesday, 10am–9pm. Wednesday–Sunday, 6pm–midnight. You may be able to arrange other times during the hours the Museum is open to the public.

SERVICES/AMENITIES:

Restaurant Services: Restaurant is open during hours of public access
Catering: provided or BYO
Kitchen Facilities: ample, $175 kitchen use fee
Tables & Chairs: some provided
Linens, Silver, etc.: BYO
Restrooms: wca
Dance Floor: outside terrace or CBA, extra charge

Parking: garage and on street
Overnight Accommodations: no
Telephone: pay phone
Outdoor Night Lighting: CBA
Outdoor Cooking Facilities: no
Cleanup: caterer and renter
Other: baby grand piano

RESTRICTIONS:
Alcohol: provided or corkage fee required
Smoking: allowed
Music: amplified with restrictions

Wheelchair Access: yes
Insurance: damage and liability required or indemnity clause

OTIS SPUNKMEYER AIR
Sentimental Journey

8433 Earhart Road
Oakland, CA 94578
(415) 667-3800
Reserve: 1 week in advance

Enjoy the Bay Area's most popular landmarks from a very different vantage point—in a classic DC-3 from 1000 feet in the air! The romance, adventure and excitement of the 1940s is captured in this vintage aircraft, serviced by a 1940s-attired staff. Your business meeting, special event or office party can be enhanced with music, wine and champagne and catered hors d'oeuvres. You can walk about the plane and even visit the cockpit. If you're looking for nostalgia or you're a World War II buff, this journey will be distinctly memorable.

CAPACITY: 18 passenger first class seating

FEES & DEPOSITS: For any group under 18 passengers, the flight is $100/person. To rent the entire plane for your private party, the fee is $1600. Half is due when the reservation is made, the remaining half is payable 1 week in advance of the sky tour. An 8% tax is additional.

CANCELLATION POLICY: If cancellation is necessary due to weather or mechanical reasons, your flight will be rescheduled.

AVAILABILITY: Year-round. 1-hour flights available weekend afternoons and Friday, Saturday and Sundays at twilight.

SERVICES/AMENITIES:
Catering: provided, no BYO
Linens, Silver, etc.: provided
Parking: large lot

Cleanup: provided
Other: 1940s tunes provided

RESTRICTIONS:
Alcohol: WBC provided
Smoking: not allowed

Wheelchair Access: no

PARAMOUNT THEATRE

2025 Broadway
Oakland, CA 94612
(415) 893-2300 Lisa Van Slyke
Reserve: 6 months in advance

Standing in the grand lobby of this spectacular theater is an experience. The sweeping scale, sultry lighting and arresting floor-to-ceiling colors overwhelm the eye. A pair of staircases flows beneath a shimmering curtain of green light down to a vast floral patterned carpet. Amber illumination glows through towering frosted glass wall panels, and emanates from the "fountain of light," a monumental green and yellow glass sculpture rising above the entrance. Beautifully restored in 1972-73, all the fixtures and furnishings reflect the Art Deco style of the period. It's easy to imagine a 1930 crowd of slinky women and brilliantined men mingling in a smoky haze. Any event here automatically takes on this one-time movie palace's mystique, and will be, as the huge lettering over the entrance proclaims, "THE BEST SHOW IN TOWN."

CAPACITY: The lobby accommodates 500 standing and 200 seated guests. The auditorium seats 2998.

FEES & DEPOSITS : Both vary depending on use, with the average rental plus expenses costing about $5000, not including catering. Catering fees run $15-$20/person for a buffet. A 7.25% sales tax and 15% gratuity are additional.

CANCELLATION POLICY: Cancellations are handled on an individual basis.

AVAILABILITY: Any time, 24 hours a day.

SERVICES/AMENITIES:

Restaurant Services: no
Catering: provided, no BYO
Kitchen Facilities: no
Tables & Chairs: some provided
Linens, Silver, etc.: caterer provides
Restrooms: wca
Dance Floor: CBA
Parking: on street, lot

Overnight Accommodations: no
Telephone: pay phone
Outdoor Night Lighting: n/a
Outdoor Cooking Facilities: no
Cleanup: caterer
Other: totally equipped for presentations, films, etc.

RESTRICTIONS:

Alcohol: no beer or red wine
Smoking: not allowed
Music: amplified ok

Wheelchair Access: yes
Insurance: extra insurance required
Other: union stage hands required

SAILBOAT HOUSE

1520 Lakeside Drive in Lakeside Park
Oakland, CA 94612
(415) 273-3187 Parks and Recreation Office
Reserve: 11 months in advance

Resting on the edge of Lake Merritt, the Sailboat House offers a wonderful view of the water and its inhabitants. The large upstairs room that is available for parties, meetings and receptions is totally enclosed in glass, and has an outdoor deck which runs the length of the lake side of the building. The atmosphere is especially light and airy during sunny afternoons, and at night the lakeside necklace of lights lends an added sparkle to events.

CAPACITY: The room accommodates 225 standing and 155 seated.

FEES & DEPOSITS: A deposit of $100 (or $200 if the facility is to be used after 11:30pm) is due when reservations are made. The facility rents for $30/hr, during the week and $35/hr from Friday at 6pm to midnight, or Saturday and Sunday until midnight. On Friday and Saturday there is a $100 charge for use from midnight to 1am, and a $150/hr penalty for use after 1am. There is a 4-hour minimum rental; setup and cleanup are available for $50 each.

CANCELLATION POLICY: With 30 days' notice, the entire deposit minus a $75 cancellation fee will be refunded. With less than 30 days' notice, only the deposit is refunded unless the facility is rebooked, in which case the $75 cancellation fee is charged.

AVAILABILITY: The facility is available from 8am–midnight Monday–Friday and until 1am on Friday and Saturday nights.

SERVICES/AMENITIES:

Restaurant Services: no
Catering: BYO
Kitchen Facilities: moderate
Tables & Chairs: provided
Linens, Silver, etc.: BYO
Restrooms: no wca
Dance Floor: yes

Parking: lot ($1.50/car)
Overnight Accommodations: no
Telephone: pay phone
Outdoor Night Lighting: no
Outdoor Cooking Facilities: no
Cleanup: whoever caters event
Other: piano

RESTRICTIONS:

Alcohol: BYO ($50 permit fee)
Smoking: outside only
Music: amplified ok

Wheelchair Access: no
Insurance: usually not required

SCOTT'S SEAFOOD
GRILL & BAR

#2 Broadway at Jack London's Waterfront
Oakland, CA 94607
(415) 444-5969   Banquet Services
Reserve: 1 day in advance

Surprise! Scott's has great private facilities that are not part of their main dining room. Located on the Oakland Estuary, the Harbor View Rooms and Bay View Terrace have views of Alameda, San Francisco and passing ships. Recently developed, the Harbor View rooms are sophisticated in color and decor, plus they have the advantage of multiple folding doors, which can create various combinations of rooms. Scott's has full conference capability and a support staff for private parties. If you're looking for a waterfront location for a special business or social function in Oakland, this is an unexpected find.

CAPACITY:

Room	Seated	Standing
Harbor View A	70	120
Harbor View B	50	80
Harbor View C	60	80
Combined ABC	180	280
Bay View/Terrace	35	75

FEES & DEPOSITS: A deposit of $250/room is required to secure your date. For meetings without food, the rental is $50/hour per room. No rental fee is required with meal service. Per person prices: breakfasts/brunch $7.50–16, luncheons $11–19.50, dinners $11–25, buffets $20–25 and hors d'oeuvres $10–25. Tax of 7.25% and 17% service charge are additional.

CANCELLATION POLICY: Deposits will be refunded only if the space(s) rented can be rebooked.

AVAILABILITY: Year-round, closed Christmas day. Every day from 7am–2am.

SERVICES/AMENITIES:

Restaurant Services: yes
Catering: provided, no BYO
Kitchen Facilities: n/a
Tables & Chairs: provided
Linens, Silver, etc.: provided
Restrooms: wca
Dance Floor: yes, extra charge
Parking: valet or parking lot

Overnight Accommodations: no
Telephone: pay phone
Outdoor Night Lighting: yes
Outdoor Cooking Facilities: BBQ
Cleanup: provided
Other: full event coordination

RESTRICTIONS:

Alcohol: provided, BYO corkage $7.50/bottle
Smoking: allowed
Music: amplified ok

Wheelchair Access: yes
Insurance: not required

SEQUOIA LODGE

2666 Mountain Blvd.
Oakland, CA
(415) 273-3187 Parks and Recreation Office
Reserve: 11 months in advance

This facility has the feel of a mountain lodge, cloaked in its own redwood and pine forest. The interior features rustic wood paneling, a raised stone fireplace and a high pitched roof with skylight. A sunken seating area in front of the fireplace gives guests an intimate spot for conversation, and the large porch encourages them to sample the outdoors. Firewood is provided along with a "tot lot" for kids. If you're lucky you may glimpse a local deer who visits Sequoia Lodge on a regular basis.

CAPACITY: The Lodge accommodates 150 standing and 100 seated guests.

FEES & DEPOSITS: A deposit of $100 (or $200 if the facility is to be used after 11:30pm) is due at the time of booking. The facility rents for $30/hr during the week, $35/hr Friday 6pm to midnight, or Saturday and Sunday until midnight. On Friday and Saturday there is a $100 charge for use from midnight to 1am, and a $150 penalty for use after 1am. Setup and cleanup are available for $50 each. There is a 4-hour minimum rental.

CANCELLATION POLICY: With 30 days' notice, the entire rental fee minus a $75 cancellation fee will be refunded. With less than 30 days' notice, only the deposit will be refunded unless the facility can be rebooked, in which case the $75 cancellation fee is charged.

AVAILABILITY: Monday through Friday after 3:30pm., Saturday 9 am to 1am, and Sunday 9am to midnight.

SERVICES/AMENITIES:

Restaurant Services: no
Catering: BYO
Kitchen Facilities: ample
Tables & Chairs: provided
Linens, Silver, etc.: BYO
Restrooms: wca
Dance Floor: yes

Parking: on and off street, lot
Overnight Accommodations: no
Telephone: pay phone
Outdoor Night Lighting: yes
Outdoor Cooking Facilities: BYO BBQ
Cleanup: whoever caters event

RESTRICTIONS:

Alcohol: BYO for $50 fee
Smoking: outside only
Music: amplified ok

Wheelchair Access: yes
Insurance: usually not required

Piedmont

PIEDMONT
COMMUNITY CENTER

711 Highland Ave.
Piedmont, CA 94611
(415) 420-3081 Penny Robb
Reserve: 3–6 months in advance

Brick steps lead down to the Center, situated in a park-like setting. Mediterranean in style, the white building with its tile roof and landscaped plaza is surrounded by redwood and flowering cherry trees. Azaleas and camellias provide splashes of color near the round patio and behind the building, a stream and more trees complete the circle of greenery. Starting this year, different seasonal plantings of annuals will highlight the entry patio circle. The Center's interior is a great party room; it has a high, beamed ceiling and chandeliers. Floor-to-ceiling windows allow lots of natural light, and ensure that the feeling of the park carries over into your event, whether it be a fundraiser, business meeting, seminar or retreat.

CAPACITY: The Hall accommodates 223 standing and 104 seated guests. The patio area holds 300 standing and 150 seated guests.

FEES & DEPOSITS: A security deposit of $200 is due two weeks after booking, and is refundable four weeks after the event. The facility is rented in 6-hour blocks on Saturday and Sunday. The fee for residents is $550, and for non-residents it is $700. Weekday rates for 4-hour blocks are $250 for residents and $350 for non-residents. For nonprofits: M–F; $200 for a 6-hour block. Additional time can be scheduled at $50/hour. Payment is due 30 days prior to the event.

CANCELLATION POLICY: If notification of cancellation is given 2 months prior to the event, $100 of the security deposit will be refunded. A full refund minus $20 will be given with 6 months' notice.

AVAILABILITY: The Center is available (one event per day) from 8am to midnight daily, with extensions possible if requested in writing 30 days in advance. The summer months are booked quickly.

SERVICES/AMENITIES:

Restaurant Services: no
Catering: BYO
Kitchen Facilities: minimal
Tables & Chairs: provided
Linens, Silver, etc.: BYO
Restrooms: wca
Dance Floor: yes

Parking: on and off street
Overnight Accommodations: no
Telephone: pay phone
Outdoor Night Lighting: yes
Outdoor Cooking Facilities: BYO
Cleanup: whoever caters event

RESTRICTIONS:

Alcohol: BYO, must have controlled bar
Smoking: not allowed
Music: amplified ok

Wheelchair Access: yes
Insurance: included in weekend rates, you must provide for weekday use

Pleasanton

CENTURY HOUSE

2401 Santa Rita Road
Pleasanton, CA 94566
(415) 484-8160
Reserve: 2–9 months in advance

Set far back from the main street, Century House is an unexpected sight. It's a white Victorian farmhouse, which underwhelms with its modest proportions and simple country detailing. The path leading up to the house is flanked by two expansive lawns and lined with rose bushes in bloom. A decorative iron fence surrounds the site, enclosing a brick patio stretching the entire length of the house front. Like many homes built in the 1870s, this one has an oversized veranda, leaded glass panels in the front door, and white latticework along the base of the building. Inside, the rooms are small but softly decorated in muted colors. On the south side of the house, a large brick patio and white gazebo shaded by Chinese elm trees provide a perfect setting for an outdoor celebration. The Century House exudes an old-fashioned warmth that stirs memories of "the old days." Guests will feel that they've been transported out of suburban Pleasanton and into a different place and time altogether.

CAPACITY: October–March 50 guests; April–September 125 guests.

FEES & DEPOSITS: A $50 nonrefundable deposit is required to secure your date with full payment due 4 weeks prior to the event. The rental fee is for 6 hours of use and includes setup and cleanup.

	Resident		Non-Resident	
	Basic Fee	*Add. Hourly*	*Basic Fee*	*Add. Hourly*
up to 50 guests	$200	$25	$250	$35
51 to 125 guests	$250	$35	$300	$50

CANCELLATION POLICY: Cancellations must be made in writing at least 4 weeks prior to the date reserved and will incur a cancellation fee of $50. If less than 4 weeks' notice is given, the rental deposit and up to 50% of the rental fee will be forfeited.

AVAILABILITY: 10am to 10pm Friday and Saturday, 10am to 9pm Sunday through Thursday.

SERVICES/AMENITIES:

Restaurant Services: no
Catering: BYO
Kitchen Facilities: moderate
Tables & Chairs: some provided
Linens, Silver, etc.: BYO
Restrooms: wca
Dance Floor: limited

Parking: lot, on street
Overnight Accommodations: no
Telephone: pay phone
Outdoor Night Lighting: limited
Outdoor Cooking Facilities: not allowed
Cleanup: some provided, renter provides the rest

RESTRICTIONS:
Alcohol: BYO
Smoking: outside only
Music: no amplified or DJs

Wheelchair Access: yes
Insurance: bodily injury and damage liability required
Other: decorations restricted

THE PLEASANTON HOTEL

855 Main St.
Pleasanton, CA 94566
(415) 846-8106 Catering
Reserve: 6–12 months in advance

The Pleasanton Hotel sits in the center of Pleasanton's old downtown. The building, flanked by stately palm trees, is a turn–of–the–century Victorian with typical "gingerbread" detailing. Given that this building has been a hotel for over 100 years, it is in remarkably good shape. The recently decorated interior boasts a large dining room and several adjacent rooms which can be connected together via folding doors to make room for larger parties. The decor is vintage 1890s, with heavy window draping and colors in ivories, burgundies and pastels. There are numerous chandeliers and Victorian appointments. Outside are a patio shaded by a large magnolia, a BBQ, outdoor bar and raised brick stage available for either DJ or band setup.

CAPACITY: The hotel can seat a maximum of 200 guests.

FEES & DEPOSITS: A $100 deposit is required to secure your date and is applied towards the final bill. Some rental fees may be required, and are determined by day of week and size of the event. Full meal service is provided. Luncheons range from $10.50-15/person and dinners $15-21/person. A 7.25% tax and 15% gratuity will be applied to the final bill, which is due and payable upon completion of the event.

CANCELLATION POLICY: The deposit is not refundable unless the space can be rebooked with an equal or larger party.

AVAILABILITY: Monday–Friday, any time. Saturdays 11am–4pm and 6am–11pm; Sunday 5pm–10pm.

SERVICES/AMENITIES:
Restaurant Services: yes
Catering: no BYO
Kitchen Facilities: n/a
Tables & Chairs: provided
Linens, Silver, etc.: provided
Restrooms: wca
Dance Floor: yes
Parking: lot

Overnight Accommodations: no
Telephone: pay phone
Outdoor Night Lighting: yes
Outdoor Cooking Facilities: BBQ
Cleanup: provided
Other: event coordination

RESTRICTIONS:
Alcohol: provided, BYO corkage $5/bottle
Smoking: allowed
Music: amplified ok

Wheelchair Access: yes
Insurance: not required

Point Richmond

EAST BROTHER ★
LIGHT STATION

117 Park Place
Point Richmond, CA 94801
(415) 233-2385
Reserve: 12 months in advance

A short but exhilarating boat ride takes you to the island. On this one-acre, sun-washed speck in the Bay sits the oldest operational lighthouse in or around San Francisco Bay. Constructed in 1873-74, the light station continues to preserve a little bit of maritime history. From the island one has a clear, unobstructed view of the San Francisco skyline and the Marin coast. Gone are the telephone poles, cars, crowds, and noise of the mainland. The main house, with its lace curtains, wooden floors and fireplaces, is relaxed and homey. Surrounded by seagulls, the sea and the foghorn, this is an exceptional place for an event.

CAPACITY: The island can accommodate a maximum of 200 people.

FEES & DEPOSITS: A deposit of $200 is required to secure an event date. The island rents for $2000. This includes $820 for use of the facility and $1180 for dinner and bed and breakfast for up to 8 guests. Guests are not obligated to stay, but room reservation is part of the package. Note that fees for boat transportation, catering, and all other services are extra and are not provided by East Brother Light Station.

CANCELLATION POLICY: All fees are potentially refundable. If, however, the date canceled is not rebooked, the bed and breakfast portion of the fees will be forfeited.

AVAILABILITY: 11am to dusk, Thursday through Sunday. Weather is best between April and October.

SERVICES/AMENITIES:

Restaurant Services: no
Catering: provided or BYO
Kitchen Facilities: limited
Tables & Chairs: some provided
Linens, Silver, etc.: BYO
Restrooms: no wca
Dance Floor: no

Parking: n/a
Overnight Accommodations: 4 guestrooms
Telephone: house phone
Outdoor Night Lighting: no
Outdoor Cooking Facilities: yes
Cleanup: caterer

RESTRICTIONS:

Alcohol: provided or BYO
Smoking: outside only
Music: amplified ok

Wheelchair Access: difficult
Insurance: not required

LINSLEY HALL

235 Washington Ave.
Point Richmond, CA 94801
(415) 235-7338 Donna Powers
Reserve: 2 weeks–6 months in advance

Linsley Hall, built in 1904 as a church, is now a distinctive, multi-use facility located in historic Point Richmond. With its vaulted ceiling, wood paneling and lovely original stained glass windows, the Chapel offers its guests turn-of-the-century warmth and dignity. The sanctuary's acoustics are so outstanding that it's rented quite often for concerts and recitals. Downstairs, the Reception Room has a custom-built oak bar, and guests can flow out into the attractive flower garden which has shade trees, gazebo, brickwork and lawn. This spot is ideal for special occasions such as holiday parties and family reunions. And, if you're here for a business seminar, workshop or class, you can walk just a few blocks into the center of town to sample some good Point Richmond restaurants.

CAPACITY: The Hall can hold up to 110 guests, the Reception Room 10–60 and the Garden 50.

MEETING ROOMS: The Reception Room can hold meetings up to 60 people.

FEES & DEPOSITS: A nonrefundable deposit (25% of the rental fee) is due when reservations are made. For special events, the rental fee is $100/hour, minimum 3 hours. For business functions the fee is $50/hour, minimum 2 hours.

AVAILABILITY: All year, every day from 9am to 11pm.

SERVICES/AMENITIES:

Restaurant Services: no
Catering: BYO
Kitchen Facilities: moderate
Tables & Chairs: most provided
Linens, Silver, etc.: BYO
Restrooms: no wca
Dance Floor: yes

Parking: on street
Overnight Accommodations: no
Telephone: local calls only
Outdoor Night Lighting: no
Outdoor Cooking Facilities: yes
Cleanup: caterer
Special: box lunches CBA

RESTRICTIONS:

Alcohol: WCB only
Smoking: outside only
Music: no amplified music outdoors

Wheelchair Access: limited
Insurance: not required

San Leandro

BEST HOUSE

1315 Clarke Street
San Leandro, CA 94577
(415) 351-0911
Reserve: 1–6 months in advance

This yellow Victorian is a bright spot in the city. The yard, where business lunches and parties are held, is shaded by a variety of trees, and the brick patio and low decks give guests plenty of room to unwind. A working water wheel and miniature street lamps add quaint touches to this quiet setting. Personalized service and a relaxed atmosphere make this facility terrific for small business meetings and private functions. Best House is also a bed and breakfast inn, and guests are welcome to stay the night.

CAPACITY: The grounds accommodate a maximum of 150 people.

FEES & DEPOSITS: A deposit of 50% of the rental fee is required to reserve your date. An additional $200 damage/cleaning deposit is due 30 days before your event, and is refundable within 1 week of your event. The total rental fee is $850 for a 5-hour block of time; shorter rental times can be arranged at a reduced fee. The remaining balance is due 30 days prior to the event.

CANCELLATION POLICY: With less than 30 days' notice, deposits are not refundable unless the date can be rebooked.

AVAILABILITY: For small meetings or gatherings of under 50 people, year-round. For larger groups, anytime between April and October. Reserve early for summer.

SERVICES/AMENITIES:

Restaurant Services: no
Catering: BYO, licensed only
Kitchen Facilities: moderate
Tables & Chairs: provided up to 50, over that BYO
Linens, Silver, etc.: BYO
Restrooms: wca in garden
Dance Floor: brick patio

Parking: lot and on street
Overnight Accommodations: 5 guestrooms
Telephone: pay phone, emergencies only
Outdoor Night Lighting: yes
Outdoor Cooking Facilities: no
Cleanup: caterer

RESTRICTIONS:

Alcohol: WCB only
Smoking: outside only
Music: no amplified

Wheelchair Access: outdoors only
Insurance: not required

San Pablo

ROCKEFELLER LODGE

2650 Market St.
San Pablo, CA 94806
(415) 235-7344 Joyce or Deborah
Reserve: 1–3 months in advance

Have you always wanted to celebrate a bit differently? Maybe have a Victorian or Western theme party? Or perhaps treat your friends to milk and cookies baked on the spot. Whatever your fantasy, the owner and staff of the Rockefeller Lodge love the challenge of making it a reality. And with its variety of rooms and outdoor areas, the Lodge can accommodate a wide range of creativity. Once a Japanese Buddhist Temple, the Rockefeller Lodge still offers a fragrant, woodsy serenity. The brown-shingled building derives its secluded feeling from the surrounding trees and quiet neighborhood. Winding brick paths and wisteria-covered arbors invite leisurely, relaxed strolls through the grounds. The outdoor patios are popular for both business and private parties. The interior rooms are spacious, featuring hardwood floors, hand-hewn ceiling beams and a noteworthy fireplace constructed from burnt bricks from the 1906 earthquake.

CAPACITY: The Lodge and grounds accommodate 350 seated guests, the Lodge alone holds 150 seated; the entire site, 500 total for a standing reception.

MEETING ROOMS: Garden Room 75 seated; Fireplace Room 40 seated; Rockefeller Room 40 seated. Outdoor meetings: front garden, 150 seated; total outdoors, 100 seated.

FEES & DEPOSITS:

	Deposit/Rental Fee	*Food Service*
Weekdays	$200 if luncheon involved	$10–15/person
	$50/hour, no luncheon	includes coffee service

		Luncheons or Buffets
Friday & Sunday Eves	$200	50–99 guests starts at $12.50/person
Saturday–Sunday	$600	Over 100 guests, $7.95–20/person
		Seated meals start at $14/person

For special events, the rental fee is used as the refundable deposit, and is required to secure your date. There is a 50-guest minimum. Food service is provided. The $200 deposit includes a $100 rental fee and $100 janitorial fee.

CANCELLATION POLICY: With 4 months' notice, a full refund minus a 20% bookkeeping charge is given. Less than 4 months, the deposit will be forfeited.

AVAILABILITY: Any day from 6am–midnight. No bookings on Christmas.

SERVICES/AMENITIES:

Restaurant Services: no
Catering: provided
Kitchen Facilities: n/a
Tables & Chairs: provided
Linens, Silver, etc.: provided
Restrooms: wca
Dance Floor: yes

Parking: 2 lots
Overnight Accommodations: no
Telephone: pay phone
Outdoor Night Lighting: yes
Outdoor Cooking Facilities: yes
Cleanup: provided
Other: full event planning

RESTRICTIONS:

Alcohol: BYO, $2.50/person service fee
Smoking: allowed
Music: amplified inside only, 4-piece band limit

Wheelchair Access: yes
Insurance: not required

Sunol

ELLISTON VINEYARDS

463 Kilkare Road
Sunol, CA 94586
(415) 862-2377
Reserve: 2 weeks–12 months in advance

This is a family-owned winery, tucked in a sheltered valley between the Pleasanton and Sunol ridges. Elliston Vineyard was founded in 1983 and named after the Gold Rush pioneer, Henry Hiram Ellis, who built the stately 3-story stone mansion here in 1890. Built of thick sandstone from nearby Niles Canyon, and featuring graceful stone arches over window and entrances in a Romanesque style, this landmark structure and acres of vineyards greet guests as they enter the site. The adjacent Carriage House is used for wine production and for aging wines below, while upstairs a reception room and deck are used for private parties. Although close to civilization, it seems like you're a million miles away. The quiet, country atmosphere makes a nice contribution to any celebration, wine tasting party or business function. When you want to get away, but not go very far, this is the spot.

CAPACITY: The Terrace Room and Buffet Room combined can hold 125 seated guests and up to 200 for a reception.

FEES & DEPOSITS: A refundable deposit of $300 for weekday functions or $500 for weekend events is required when reservations are confirmed. Monday–Friday the rental fee for business functions is $300 for 4 hours. For social functions on Friday evenings–Sunday, the minimum event cost is $3500, which includes rental and reception buffet service. 50% of the estimated event or meeting cost is due 2 months prior to the event and the balance is due with a confirmed guest count 1 week prior to the function. Invoicing can be arranged for business-related events. Additional staff charges may apply for seated functions.

CANCELLATION POLICY: With 4 months' notice, deposits are refunded.

AVAILABILITY: Year-round, Monday–Saturday until 10pm, Sunday until 6pm.

SERVICES/AMENITIES:

Restaurant Services: no
Catering: provided, no BYO
Kitchen Facilities: n/a
Tables & Chairs: provided
Linens, Silver, etc.: provided
Restrooms: wca
Dance Floor: yes
Parking: large lot, parking attendants

Overnight Accommodations: no
Telephone: office phone
Outdoor Night Lighting: yes
Outdoor Cooking Facilities: no
Cleanup: provided
Other: event planning, tours and tastings

RESTRICTIONS:

Alcohol: WC provided, BYO $5/bottle corkage
Smoking: outside only
Music: amplified inside only

Wheelchair Access: yes
Insurance: not required

Vallejo

CALIFORNIA MARITIME ACADEMY

200 Maritime Academy Drive
Vallejo, CA 94590
(707) 648-4150   Robin Gilbaugh
Reserve: 2 months in advance

The Academy occupies an enviable location—set in the Vallejo hills while facing the water, boats and sea breezes of the Carquinez Straits. It is an ideal environment for nonprofit and educational organizations to hold classes, meetings and seminars. Private parties are not permitted. Traditional classrooms and a large auditorium, complete with audio-visual equipment, provide flexibility for your presentations. The Commons Complex is an especially lovely area for functions in the summer. This multipurpose building overlooks the water through a wall of windows. A lawn, palm trees and picnic tables make the surrounding grounds perfect for outdoor activities.

MEETING ROOMS:

Room	*Capacity*
Auditorium	500*
Classrooms (6)	25 each
Ward Room	100
Sick Bay	25

The Auditorium can be divided into 3 areas with capacities of 305, 98 and 98, respectively.

FEES & DEPOSITS: A refundable deposit of 10% of the total event cost is required when reservations are confirmed. Rental fees ranging from $45–375 are charged after the event and are based on space(s) rented and the final guest count.

CANCELLATION POLICY: With 30 days' notice, the deposit will be refunded.

AVAILABILITY: Every day.

SERVICES/AMENITIES:

Restaurant Services: cafeteria style
Catering: provided w/restrictions or BYO
Kitchen Facilities: no
Tables & Chairs: CBA
Linens, Silver, etc.: CBA
Restrooms: wca
Dance Floor: yes

Parking: limited
Overnight Accommodations: summer & winter only
Telephone: pay phones
Outdoor Night Lighting: yes
Outdoor Cooking Facilities: BBQs
Cleanup: renter outside, provided inside
Special: tours of campus and ship

RESTRICTIONS:

Alcohol: BYO with approval
Smoking: outside only
Music: amplified ok

Wheelchair Access: yes
Insurance: required

FOLEY CULTURAL CENTER
Dan Foley Park

East end of N. Camino Alto
Vallejo, CA 94589
(707) 648-4630   Eileen Brown
Reserve: 6–11 months in advance

This community park has a multipurpose auditorium and several smaller rooms which are available for meetings. The auditorium, known as The Lake Room, overlooks the large man-made Chabot Lake. Hexagonal in shape, it has a high beamed ceiling and a wall of windows with a view. The interior is light and airy and is designed for a wide variety of uses. Outside, a wide deck runs along one side of the building, providing relaxed, breezy seating right off the lake. The whole facility is situated inside a lovely 65-acre park, making a nice setting for casual get-togethers.

CAPACITY:

Room	Seated	Reception	Theater-style
Lake Room	500	600	600
Vista Room	50	75	75

MEETING ROOMS: 4 rooms that can hold 20–49 guests.

FEES & DEPOSITS: A $100 deposit, applied toward the rental fee, is due when the use permit is submitted. The balance and a $100 cleaning/damage deposit is payable 60 days prior to the event. The rental for private parties is approximately $500/10 hours. The rental for Monday–Friday business functions varies depending on hours rented and the type of function.

CANCELLATION POLICY: If you cancel, 10% of the total fees and charges will be forfeited; with 30 days' notice or less, 50% will be forfeited.

AVAILABILITY: Year-round, Friday–Sunday from 10:30am–2am, Monday–Thursday, only if there is a cancellation in a regularly scheduled program. Closed most major holidays.

SERVICES/AMENITIES:

Restaurant Services: no

Catering: BYO

Kitchen Facilities: fully equipped

Tables & Chairs: provided

Linens, Silver, etc.: BYO

Restrooms: wca limited

Dance Floor: yes

Parking: large lots

Overnight Accommodations: no

Telephone: pay phone

Outdoor Night Lighting: no

Outdoor Cooking Facilities: in adjacent park

Cleanup: renter or CBA ext. fee

Other: stage, setup service, pianos, PA system

RESTRICTIONS:

Alcohol: BYO, sales need permit, surcharge $25

Smoking: designated areas

Music: amplified ok

Wheelchair Access: yes

Insurance: not required

HERBERT HOUSE

1 Kentucky Street
Vallejo, CA 94540
(707) 646-3587 or 642-8722   Steve Morgan
Reserve: 1–6 months in advance

This 1898 city landmark is a classic pearl-grey Victorian situated on the Mare Island Channel. It was once the home of a prominent Vallejo family. All of the rooms have rich redwood molding which has been recently restored, and of special note is an elegantly carved staircase bannister. Another interesting feature are the original gas and electric chandeliers still hanging in the main rooms. Upstairs, three small rooms decorated with pictures of early Vallejo history are available for meetings. The Dining and Living Rooms can be used together, or separately by closing the pocket doors between them. The space is most lovely in late afternoon, when the waning sunlight filters in through lace curtains and bathes the house in a honey-yellow glow.

CAPACITY: The House can accommodate 55–70 seated guests and 85 for a reception.

FEES & DEPOSITS: A refundable $200 cleaning deposit is due when reservations are confirmed; the rental balance is payable 7 days prior to the event. The rental fee is $200 for the entire house from 8am–midnight.

CANCELLATION POLICY: With 14 days' notice, the deposit is refunded.

AVAILABILITY: Year-round, every day from 8am–midnight except the 1st and 3rd Wednesdays and 2nd and 4th Tuesdays of the month.

SERVICES/AMENITIES:
Restaurant Services: no
Catering: BYO
Kitchen Facilities: setup only
Tables & Chairs: some provided
Linens, Silver, etc.: BYO
Restrooms: no wca

RESTRICTIONS:
Alcohol: BYO, BWC only
Smoking: outside only
Music: amplified w/in limits

Dance Floor: CBA
Parking: street, on site
Overnight Accommodations: no
Telephone: house phone
Outdoor Night Lighting: no
Outdoor Cooking Facilities: no
Cleanup: renter or caterer

Wheelchair Access: yes
Insurance: proof required
Other: no open flames

Walnut Creek

THE HOUSTON
Key Tours

1390 S. Main St., Suite 312
Walnut Creek, CA 94596
(415) 945-8687 Christopher Kyte
Reserve: 2 weeks–6 months in advance

Built in 1926, The Houston is a time capsule of plush 1920s train travel. Once reserved for the very rich or very famous, this elegantly understated private railcar epitomized first class business travel before the advent of commercial airlines. It has the traditional open-air observation platform and a wood-paneled observation lounge which is the center of daytime activity, from mid-morning coffee to pre-dinner cocktails. For overnight trips, there is a bedroom with upper and lower berths and a 8 ft x 17 ft master suite with large closets and built-in dressers. Morning coffee, bathrobes, nightcap and chocolate mint on your pillow are all part of your non-stop impeccable service. Also on board is a formal dining room with antique chairs, wood paneling and table seating for eight. Aft is a fully equipped kitchen complete with charcoal broiler. The Houston is one of the few cars to feature 'track lights' which illuminate the passing scene at night. This railcar can be attached to any AMTRAK train or can be 'parked' in a number of cities for stationary special events. For a nostalgic and exciting environment, The Houston is ideal for special celebrations, corporate meetings or promotional events. Pamper your friends or associates by inviting them aboard! It'll be the highlight of their lives.

CAPACITY: For day trips, up to 12 passengers; overnight stays, up to 5 passengers.

FEES & DEPOSITS: For trips, a deposit of 20% of the total estimated cost is required. For stationary functions, a $500 deposit is required. Both are nonrefundable and due when the contract is submitted. For an event with extended travel, costs will run $3400/day, which includes chef, butler, all meals, snacks, wine, cocktails, transportation costs, rental fees, operational charges, personalized stationary and flowers. To 'park' nearby (primarily Oakland and San Francisco locations) the cost is $500–$1000 for 4–5 hours depending on whether it's for afternoon tea, cocktails or a formal, seated dinner. The balance is payable 7 days prior to any event or departure.

AVAILABILITY: Year-round, every day with no hourly restrictions.

SERVICES/AMENITIES:

Restaurant Services: no

Catering: provided on board

Kitchen Facilities: n/a

Tables & Chairs: provided

Linens, Silver, etc.: provided

Restrooms: no wca

Dance Floor: no

Parking: available

Overnight Accommodations: for 5 guests

Telephone: cellular

Outdoor Night Lighting: no

Outdoor Cooking Facilities: no

Cleanup: provided

RESTRICTIONS:

Alcohol: provided, no BYO

Smoking: rear platform only

Music: amplified ok

Wheelchair Access: no

Insurance: not required

THE MANSION ★
AT LAKEWOOD

1056 Hacienda Drive
Walnut Creek, CA 94598
(415) 946-9075   Sharyn McCoy
Reserve: 1–3 months in advance

Hidden away behind white wrought iron gates, the Mansion is a modern day Camelot. This 1861 Victorian country manor rests on three lovely acres of trees and flowers that change colors every season. The secluded location provides a thoughtful and quiet atmosphere for your company activities. Training seminars can take place in the majestic library, away from ringing phones and the demanding office. The gardens and gazebo offer the perfect setting for an outdoor party. The interior of The Mansion is also delightful. Whether you're relaxing in front of a glowing fire in the library, or spending the night in any of the uniquely appointed guestrooms, the century-old charm of The Mansion envelopes you. Antiques, harmonious colors and flowers combined with high ceilings, hardwood floors and abundant natural light create an elegant and gracious retreat.

CAPACITY: The house and grounds can accommodate a maximum of 20 guests.

FEES & DEPOSITS: A security deposit in the amount of the anticipated rental fee is required when you make your reservation. Rental of the entire Mansion, including 7 guestrooms, is $1000. Rental on weekdays is $40/hour and on weekends, $100/hour.

CANCELLATION POLICY: There is a $25 service charge for any canceled event. A full refund of the initial deposit will be given only if the function is rebooked and/or if 30 days' prior notice is given.

AVAILABILITY: Monday–Friday, 8am–5pm. Saturdays and Sundays, 8am–9pm.

SERVICES/AMENITIES:

Restaurant Services: no
Catering: provided
Kitchen Facilities: ample
Tables & Chairs: some provided
Linens, Silver, etc.: provided
Restrooms: wca
Dance Floor: "barefoot" dancing only in library

Parking: on grounds
Overnight Accommodations: 7 guestrooms
Telephone: restricted use
Outdoor Night Lighting: no
Outdoor Cooking Facilities: no
Cleanup: caterer

RESTRICTIONS:

Alcohol: not allowed
Smoking: outside only
Music: amplified not allowed

Wheelchair Access: outside only, will provide assistance inside
Insurance: sometimes required

PETER BARSOTTI
Production Manager for Bill Graham Presents

Cairo, 1978. On the third night of a Grateful Dead appearance in Egypt, located at the base of the Great Pyramid adjacent to the Sphinx, Bill Graham decided to throw a party celebrating the conclusion of the last show. He asked me to pull together this gala at the end of the performance. After making preliminary plans, it appeared that nobody was interested in having a party—so I canceled it.

The word got around that a party was happening, and an hour and a half before the show concluded, all of a sudden everybody wanted to go, and I was the only one who knew that there was no party! So I grabbed our cab driver and hot-footed it 5 miles into the Sahara desert to a tented tourist trap called the Oasis (Oh yes, we accept American Express!). Here I made arrangements for 100 revelers to arrive sometime after midnight, with appropriate belly dancing, food and drink. As soon as these plans were finalized, I dashed to a local village in Giza, and implored Omar the camel driver at 10pm to instantly come up with 50 horses and 50 camels for our post-show ride into the desert. This he did by waking up every relative and friend in the village, for it seems that every horse and camel had to have a person accompanying it.

At the conclusion of the musical performance, over the dunes came Omar with 100 four-footed animals and what seemed to be the entire village. They proceeded to march up to the stage and kneel in the sand to await our command. Everybody, musicians, friends and crew, jumped on horses and camels from the stage, and followed-the-leader out into the desert. What a sight—a Hell's Angel hopping on a donkey, Ken Kesey and Jerry Garcia on camels, all riding off into the night. Since the horses were the most popular mode of transport, I got the last camel, of course. Everybody had an absolute ball, riding around, looking for the lights of the distant oasis. We pulled in, drank Egyptian beer 'til dawn and watched the sun rise behind the pyramids.

Campbell

CAMPBELL HOUSE RESTAURANT

106 E. Campbell Ave.
Campbell, CA 95008
(408) 374-5757
Reserve: 1–4 weeks in advance

A quaint old stucco house that you could easily drive right by, Campbell House is one of those unexpected little gems. Aesthetically it has its charms: beautiful multi-paned windows, wood trim around everything, tables set elegantly with white cloth over dark green and illustrations of different grape varieties on the walls. It's a small, very homey restaurant which serves good food. The chef here, however, improves on a good thing by adding his special touch. For a party of no more than 16, he will set up a long table in the middle of the main room and grace it with candelabras. The effect is romantic and intimate, the service highly personalized. If your guest list is short, the Campbell House merits consideration.

CAPACITY: The Campbell House will seat 16 guests for a private party.

FEES & DEPOSITS: No deposit or rental fees are required for group functions. Luncheons range from $15–20/person and dinners from $35–40/person. Menus for groups are prearranged at least 1 week prior to the event.

AVAILABILITY: Year-round, closed Monday and Tuesday. Luncheons are served Wednesday–Friday, dinners Wednesday–Sunday.

SERVICES/AMENITIES:

Restaurant Services: yes
Catering: provided, no BYO
Kitchen Facilities: n/a
Tables & Chairs: provided
Linens, Silver, etc.: provided
Restrooms: no wca
Dance Floor: no

Parking: rear lot
Overnight Accommodations: no
Telephone: office phone
Outdoor Night Lighting: no
Outdoor Cooking Facilities: no
Cleanup: provided

RESTRICTIONS:

Alcohol: WBC provided, BYO corkage $13/bottle
Smoking: not allowed
Music: no amplified

Wheelchair Access: limited
Insurance: not required

MARTHA'S VINEYARD

1875 S. Bascom Avenue #2400
Campbell, CA 95008
(408) 371-5060 David Peacock
Reserve: 1–6 months in advance

Martha's Vineyard is located on the second floor of the Pruneyard, where it overlooks the courtyard below. One of the nicest attributes of this restaurant is the 'greenhouse' terrace with glass on three sides and overhead, allowing light to flood the dining room and affording great views of the hills beyond and the courtyard's century-old palm tree. The interior's cane chairs and white tablecloths contribute to the decor, along with pictures of coastal scenes and replicas of ships relating to the famous Martha Vineyards on the Eastern Seaboard, hence the restaurant's name. A separate room for functions is the Fireplace Lounge and there's also a small, but appealing room for business functions called the Library. It has an arched white ceiling and glass cases filled with wine racks and books. The ship replicas on the walls and long conference table with green chairs give this room a pleasant, nautical feeling.

CAPACITY: The entire facility can accommodate 175 seated guests; the Lounge 100 standing.

MEETING ROOMS: The Library can hold up to 40 seated.

FEES & DEPOSITS: A $100 refundable deposit is due when reservations are confirmed. There is a rental charge of $50 if the group is under 15 guests. The Library fee is $100/event if no food service is provided. Per person rates are: luncheons $9–16, dinners $14–25 and hors d'oeuvres starting at $3. A 7.25% tax and 15% gratuity are additional.

CANCELLATION POLICY: One month's advance notice is required for a refund.

AVAILABILITY: Year-round, every day from 8am–1am except Sundays (unless the group is over 100 guests). Closed major holidays.

SERVICES/AMENITIES:
Restaurant Services: yes
Catering: provided, no BYO
Kitchen Facilities: n/a
Tables & Chairs: provided
Linens, Silver, etc.: provided
Restrooms: wca
Dance Floor: yes

Parking: large lot
Overnight Accommodations: no
Telephone: pay phone
Outdoor Night Lighting: no
Outdoor Cooking Facilities: no
Cleanup: provided

RESTRICTIONS:
Alcohol: provided, BYO corkage $8/bottle
Smoking: allowed
Music: amplified ok

Wheelchair Access: yes, elevator
Insurance: not required

PRUNEYARD INN

1995 S. Bascom Avenue
Campbell, CA 95008
(408) 559-4300   Marilyn Echols
Reserve: 1 week–6 months in advance

A relatively new facility, The Pruneyard Inn is already becoming a popular spot for special events and business functions. The spacious Lobby and Lobby Cafe area provide elegant and inviting surroundings. Abundant natural light, high ceilings, glass, marble and soothing tones of cream and tan create a pleasant, understated ambiance. Well placed art and plants add accents of bright color. For events on the main floor, the nearby Board Room can be set up with a dance floor. There are two additional rooms for business meetings on the second and third floors; both are bright and airy.

CAPACITY: The Lobby and Lobby Cafe can accommodate 120.

MEETING ROOMS: Boardroom seats 35 guests, Harvest Room 90 and Orchard Room 50.

FEES & DEPOSITS: No deposit is required for business functions. Rental fees are $175–200 for 8 hours, $100–125 for 4 hours. Discounts are available with overnight stays. For special events, 50% of the estimated food and beverage total is due upon confirmation. For social functions, there is no rental fee with meal service. Hors d'oeuvres are $20/person, buffets start at $30/person and luncheons, $13/person. The balance is due upon the completion of the event. Tax of 7.25% and 15% gratuity are added to the final total.

CANCELLATION POLICY: Deposits are partially refundable if the spaces can be rebooked.

AVAILABILITY: Year-round, every day 6am–1am.

SERVICES/AMENITIES:

Restaurant Services: no
Catering: provided, no BYO
Kitchen Facilities: n/a
Tables & Chairs: provided
Linens, Silver, etc.: provided
Restrooms: wca
Dance Floor: yes

Parking: large lot
Overnight Accommodations: 116 rooms
Telephone: pay phone
Outdoor Night Lighting: limited
Outdoor Cooking Facilities: no
Cleanup: provided
Other: full event coordination

RESTRICTIONS:

Alcohol: provided, BYO corkage $7/bottle
Smoking: designated areas
Music: no amplified

Wheelchair Access: yes
Insurance: not required

SEBASTIAN'S & CLUB JENINE'S

1901 South Bascom Avenue
Campbell, CA 95008
(408) 377-8600
Reserve: 1 week–2 months in advance

If you want to feel like you're on top of the world, Sebastian's is the place to go. A quick elevator ride brings you to this unique high-rise restaurant. The main U-shaped dining room has mirrored walls in its center and glass "walls" on three exterior sides. This expanse of windows offers unparalleled panoramas of the entire valley. Parties often take place upstairs at Club Jenine's, a more intimate area with cocktail lounge, discotheque and dance floor. Guests can relax in comfortable upholstered chairs or stroll around this circular space, appreciating the 360-degree visibility. With subtle shades of cream, tan and brown, and unpretentious decor, Sebastian's low-key ambiance invites you stay awhile and enjoy the view.

CAPACITY, FEES & DEPOSITS:

Room	Seated Guests	Standing Guests	Weekend (F & Sat Eve) Food Service Min.	Weekday Food Service Min.
Mt. View	8–30	—	$1400	$1000
Airport	50	—	2000	1800
Valley	80	—	3400	avail. for large party only
Club Jenine's	160	170	6500	negotiable

The above food service minimums are approximate. If the food and beverage service is less than the minimum, the difference will be the room rental charge. A refundable deposit of 10% of the estimated food service total is required to confirm your reservation. The balance is due the day of the event. Invoicing can be arranged. For groups, set menus are prepared. Per person rates: luncheons $12–20, dinners $28–42, hors d'oeuvres $14 and buffets start at $19.50. A 7.25% tax and 18% gratuity are additional.

CANCELLATION POLICY: With 30 days' notice, the deposit is refundable.

AVAILABILITY: Year-round, daily until 2am. Closed Christmas day and New Years day.

SERVICES/AMENITIES:

Restaurant Services: yes
Catering: provided, no BYO
Kitchen Facilities: n/a
Tables & Chairs: provided
Linens, Silver, etc.: provided
Restrooms: wca
Dance Floor: yes
Parking: large lot

Overnight Accommodations: no
Telephone: pay phone
Outdoor Night Lighting: no
Outdoor Cooking Facilities: no
Cleanup: provided
Special: live entertainment, DJ dancing, event coordination

RESTRICTIONS:

Alcohol: provided, BYO corkage $10/bottle
Smoking: designated areas
Music: amplified ok

Wheelchair Access: yes, elevator
Insurance: not required
Other: no confetti, dress code enforced

Cupertino

DE ORO CLUB

20441 Homestead Road
Cupertino, CA 95014
(408) 252-9130 Arleen Walton
Reserve: 6–12 months in advance

A remnant of the past, this historic Victorian schoolhouse is one of the few structures left from the large South Bay farming community of the early 20th century. It became a women's club in the 1920s, a place for the wives of local orchard owners to have their meetings. Still a women's club, much of the original structure and atmosphere remain: decorative exterior detailing, antique fixtures and a turn-of-the-century kitchen. The main auditorium with its rose-colored backdrop and flowered drapes provides ample space for a reception or any type of large gathering.

CAPACITY: The Club can accommodate up to 150 guests.

FEES & DEPOSITS: A $100 refundable deposit, applied toward the rental fee, is required when your rental contract is submitted. The rental fee is $600 for an entire day up to midnight. The balance of the rental fee plus a refundable $200 security and damage deposit are payable with the issuance of the key, one day prior to the event.

CANCELLATION POLICY: With 12 weeks' notice, the deposit is fully refundable.

AVAILABILITY: Weekends only. Saturday or Sunday, never both during the same week. Guests must vacate the premises by midnight.

SERVICES/AMENITIES:

Restaurant Services: no
Catering: BYO
Kitchen Facilities: minimal
Tables & Chairs: provided
Linens, Silver, etc.: BYO
Restrooms: no wca
Dance Floor: yes

Parking: large lot
Overnight Accommodations: no
Telephone: pay phone
Outdoor Night Lighting: no
Outdoor Cooking Facilities: no
Cleanup: caterer or renter

RESTRICTIONS:

Alcohol: BYO
Smoking: outside only
Music: amplified within limits

Wheelchair Access: limited
Insurance: not required
Other: decorations restricted

SUNRISE WINERY

13100 Montebello Road
Cupertino, CA 95014
(408) 741-1310   Rolayne Stortz
Reserve: 6–9 months in advance

Sunrise Winery, part of the historic Picchetti Brothers Ranch, is located at the base of the Santa Cruz Mountains. This is one of the last intact turn-of-the-century wineries in California. Originally developed by the Picchettis in the 1870s, the old stone and brick winery and adjacent ranch structures offer guests a rare glimpse of early California ranch life. In 1982, Ronald and Rolayne Stortz leased the winery ranch and have since been involved in restoring the property. The winery's interior is rustic, with wood floor, brick walls, and small wood-paned windows. The Stortz's hold many formal parties, yet they're open to creative and innovative events. They have organized quite a few theme parties, such as a western winery celebration where guests wore period costumes, arrived by horse-drawn conveyance and checked their "guns" at the bar upon entry. Square dancing with dance caller can easily be arranged. The outdoor area in front of the winery can be attractively set up with tables and umbrellas for large informal buffets or elegant affairs. The Sunrise Winery and Ranch, great for wine tastings, picnics and business functions, offers guests a unique event space conducive to relaxed and friendly gatherings.

CAPACITY: The winery building can hold up to 100 guests. If both indoor and outdoor facilities are used, the capacity is 200.

FEES & DEPOSITS: A nonrefundable deposit of $600 is required when your date is booked. Fees are $4/person with a $600 minimum rental required. Additional costs include a $6/person (Sunrise) wine fee. All remaining fees are due at the completion of your event.

CANCELLATION POLICY: A full refund is made if you cancel 2 months prior to the event.

AVAILABILITY: Friday, Saturday and Sunday from 4pm–10pm. Monday through Thursday, any time up to 10pm.

SERVICES/AMENITIES:

Restaurant Services: no
Catering: BYO, must be approved
Kitchen Facilities: no
Tables & Chairs: BYO
Linens, Silver, etc.: BYO
Restrooms: wca
Dance Floor: yes

Parking: large lot
Overnight Accommodations: no
Telephone: emergency only
Outdoor Night Lighting: yes
Outdoor Cooking Facilities: no, BYO
Cleanup: caterer

RESTRICTIONS:

Alcohol: Sunrise wine only, no champagne
Smoking: allowed
Music: amplified ok

Wheelchair Access: limited
Insurance: not required
Other: no children's parties

Gilroy

FORTINO WINERY

4525 Hecker Pass Highway
Gilroy, CA 95020
(408) 842-3305
Reserve: 1–2 months in advance

Established in 1970, this family-owned winery is the product of three generations of winemaking. Events are held in the same rooms where the wine is crushed, bottled or stored. The largest room has barrels of wine stacked up 15 feet high on two sides. The space is left completely natural with plywood walls and tin roof. The only additions are the white and burgundy tablecloths and flower arrangements on each table. This room and two others are kept cool to protect the wine and are a refreshing retreat from the valley heat. Immediately adjacent is "the shed," an area open to the outdoors overlooking the vineyards. And right next to the rows of grapes are the BBQ facilities. Fortino is noted for great barbecues, and people can do their own cooking, dance and enjoy themselves in the company of fragrant eucalyptus trees, vineyards and sun. For a relaxed and casual party in the heart of the South Bay's wine country, try sampling the Fortino family's hospitality.

CAPACITY: The Winery can hold up to 250 guests.

FEES & DEPOSITS: A $300 nonrefundable fee (cleaning, setup and rental fee) is required when reservations are confirmed.

AVAILABILITY: Spring and summer, every day 5pm–midnight. Closed major holidays.

SERVICES/AMENITIES:

Restaurant Services: no
Catering: BYO
Kitchen Facilities: no
Tables & Chairs: provided
Linens, Silver, etc.: provided
Restrooms: wca
Dance Floor: yes

Parking: large lot
Overnight Accommodations: no
Telephone: office phone
Outdoor Night Lighting: yes
Outdoor Cooking Facilities: BBQs
Cleanup: provided
Other: tastings and tours

RESTRICTIONS:

Alcohol: WBC provided, no BYO
Smoking: allowed
Music: amplified ok

Wheelchair Access: yes
Insurance: not required
Other: no hard alcohol

GILROY
HISTORICAL MUSEUM
Carnegie Library

195 Fifth Street
Gilroy, CA 95020
(408) 847-2685 Pat Snar
Reserve: 2 weeks–3 months in advance

Designed by noted architect, William H. Weeks, this Classical Revival style building has housed the Museum since 1963. The space is only available for cultural events and consists of a round foyer with skylight flanked by rectangular rooms on either side. Glass cases in both rooms house museum artifacts, and overhead spots highlight the artwork displayed throughout. A cool, subdued pale green, the interior offers an interesting backdrop for art shows, music, historical and theater receptions.

CAPACITY: The Museum can accommodate 75 guests for a reception.

FEES & DEPOSITS: A $25 refundable deposit is required when reservations are confirmed. The rental fee is $50/event for 3 hours.

CANCELLATION POLICY: With 5 working days' notice, the deposit is refunded.

AVAILABILITY: Year-round, every day 9am–midnight.

SERVICES/AMENITIES:

Restaurant Services: no
Catering: BYO
Kitchen Facilities: no
Tables & Chairs: provided
Linens, Silver, etc.: BYO
Restrooms: no wca
Dance Floor: no

Parking: street, parking lot
Overnight Accommodations: no
Telephone: office phone
Outdoor Night Lighting: no
Outdoor Cooking Facilities: no
Cleanup: provided
Other: tours of historic district

RESTRICTIONS:

Alcohol: BYO WBC only
Smoking: outside only
Music: no amplified

Wheelchair Access: no
Insurance: not required
Other: no hard alcohol

HECKER PASS
A Family Adventure

3050 Hecker Pass Highway
Gilroy, CA 95020
(408) 842-2121
Reserve: 6–12 months in advance

Once the private park for Nob Hill employees, this facility is now open for social events such as corporate picnics, seminars, day retreats, concerts or theme festivals. Eighty acres of the 600-acre site are being transformed into a large theme park, scheduled to open in 1993. There's a plant nursery on site, hence Hecker Pass is beautifully landscaped, with a multitude of trees, shrubs and flowers. One of the big benefits of having a nursery here is that plant materials can be moved to divide spaces and enhance the ambiance of different areas. The recreation complex includes a pool, spa and gym, racquetball, volleyball and tennis courts, weight room, softball diamonds and horseshoes. There's also a fishing lake and lots of picnic areas. The serene and peaceful Creekside Terrace Pavilion is a lovely spot for concerts or gatherings such as wine auctions. On a hot sunny day, this facility is a terrific destination for any gathering.

CAPACITY: This facility is large! It can accommodate between 100-5000 guests.

FEES & DEPOSITS: A nonrefundable deposit of $1/guest is due when reservations are confirmed. Rental fees range from $15–30/person based on space(s) reserved, type of function, food and beverages or entertainment selected and use of recreation facilities. A 50% deposit is payable either 30 or 60 days prior to the event. The balance is due the day of the event.

AVAILABILITY: April–October, every day from 10am–8pm.

SERVICES/AMENITIES:

Restaurant Services: no
Catering: provided, BYO with approval
Kitchen Facilities: fully equipped
Tables & Chairs: provided
Linens, Silver, etc.: some provided
Restrooms: wca
Dance Floor: Pavilions

Parking: large lots
Overnight Accommodations: no
Telephone: pay phones
Outdoor Night Lighting: minimal
Outdoor Cooking Facilities: BBQ
Cleanup: provided
Other: event coordination

RESTRICTIONS:

Alcohol: BWC provided, no hard alcohol
Smoking: allowed
Music: amplified within limits

Wheelchair Access: yes
Insurance: certificate required

Los Gatos

VILLAGE HOUSE AND GARDEN RESTAURANT

320 Village Lane
Los Gatos, CA 95030
(408) 354-1040
Reserve: 2 weeks in advance

The first thing you notice about the Village House and Garden Restaurant is the large outdoor patio, a wonderful area for al fresco dining during warm weather. Trees and flowers border the patio, while a trellis provides shade and the added beauty of hanging plants and wind chimes. The restaurant's interior also conveys a feeling of spring. Decorated in white and green, the ambiance is fresh and relaxed. The main dining room and patio combined make a popular setting for receptions. The Copper Corner, a smaller room with brick fireplace and copper "hood," is suitable for groups of up to 36 people, and is often used for business meetings and luncheons.

CAPACITY:	Area	Season	Seated	Minimum Required
	Main Dining Room	all	90	50 (days), 60 (eves)
	Copper Corner	all	36	16
	Inside/Outside	Oct 1–May 14	130	100
	Inside/Outside	May 15–Sept 30	130	100

FEES & DEPOSITS: For weekday functions, no deposit is required. A confirmed guest count is due 4 days prior to the event. For evening or Saturday functions, a nonrefundable $250 deposit is required when reservations are confirmed. No rental fees are required for evening functions if food is served; Saturday rental is $400 for 3 hours. The balance is due at the end of the event. Per person rates: luncheons $12, dinners $20 and Saturday luncheons start at $15. Hors d'oeuvres and business breakfasts by arrangement. A 7.25% tax and 15% gratuity are additional.

AVAILABILITY: Year-round, Mon–Fri 9am–3pm, Saturday 11am–6pm. Closed Sundays for group functions, major holidays and the week between Christmas and New Years day.

SERVICES/AMENITIES:

Restaurant Services: yes
Catering: no BYO
Kitchen Facilities: n/a
Tables & Chairs: provided
Linens, Silver, etc.: provided
Restrooms: no wca
Dance Floor: yes

Parking: street, public parking lot nearby
Overnight Accommodations: no
Telephone: pay phone
Outdoor Night Lighting: no
Outdoor Cooking Facilities: no
Cleanup: provided

RESTRICTIONS:

Alcohol: WB provided, BYO $4/bottle corkage
Smoking: allowed
Music: amplified ok

Wheelchair Access: yes
Insurance: not required

Morgan Hill

THE FLYING LADY

Morgan Hill, CA 95037
(408) 779-4136 or 778-0410
Reserve: 1 month in advance

The Flying Lady Restaurant sits on a knoll overlooking a golf course, with great panoramic views of the hills beyond and the valley below. The entryway is eye-catching, with the Marx Brothers, Charlie Chaplin, Laurel and Hardy, Al Jolson and others carved into sections of logs that look like totem poles. The restaurant is a humorous mix of styles—a unique blend of wild west and aviation themes. One room boasts a life-size replica of the Wright Brothers' plane suspended from a vaulted ceiling. Other rooms feature clowns and a western town facade with paraphernalia like branding irons, saddles and wagon wheels. For visual interest, there's a moving track that runs throughout the restaurant, with small replicas of different types of flying machines. The hospitality here is great, and the environment lends itself to theme parties. Colorful and unique, The Flying Lady is a good choice for a fun party.

CAPACITY:	*Room*	*Seated Capacity*
	Upstairs Banquet Room (private)	250
	Lower Level Banquet Room (private)	500
	Clown Room (private)	80
	Main Dining Room	500

MEETING ROOMS: 3 rooms from 10–80 guests.

FEES & DEPOSITS: A refundable $200 deposit is required when reservations are confirmed. For meetings without food service, the rental fee is $50–350. Meeting coffee service runs $2–5/person, continental breakfasts, $6/person. For social functions, per person rates are: seated luncheons or dinners $14–16, luncheon or dinner buffet in main dining room $8–10. The balance is due at the end of the event. Tax of 7.25% and 12% gratuity are additional.

CANCELLATION POLICY: With 1 month's notice, the deposit is refunded.

AVAILABILITY: Year-round, every day 9am–midnight except Monday, Tuesday and Christmas.

SERVICES/AMENITIES:

Restaurant Services: yes

Catering: provided, no BYO

Kitchen Facilities: n/a

Tables & Chairs: provided

Linens, Silver, etc.: provided

Restrooms: wca

Dance Floor: yes

Parking: large lots

Overnight Accommodations: no

Telephone: pay phones

Outdoor Night Lighting: no

Outdoor Cooking Facilities: no

Cleanup: provided

RESTRICTIONS:

Alcohol: provided, BYO WC only, corkage $3/bottle

Smoking: designated areas

Music: amplified ok

Wheelchair Access: yes, elevator

Insurance: not required

EMILIO GUGLIELMO WINERY

1480 E. Main Avenue
Morgan Hill, CA 95037
(408) 779–2145
Reserve: 1 month in advance

The name looks difficult, but it's easy if you pronounce it as Gool-yell-mo. This winery is a family affair, with the three grandsons of the winery's founder carrying on the business. It's a modest, very informal setting where the proprietors make you feel right at home. For outdoor events, the winery has a large patio bordered by vineyards. Simple round picnic tables can be used as is or spruced up with tablecloths. If you prefer a cooler place, steeped in the smells and the tools of the winemaking trade, try the Winery Building. Here you're surrounded by bottling equipment on one side and storage barrels on the other. It's a great escape from the summer heat, and a unique place to hold an event. The Guglielmo brothers are very flexible, going out of their way to accommodate your needs. They'll even cater your event—provided you stick to uncomplicated fare such as pasta feasts or BBQ luncheons. You'd be hard put to find a more relaxed and friendly atmosphere.

CAPACITY: Outdoor events, 80 seated guests; indoor functions, 50 seated.

FEES & DEPOSITS: A new fees and deposits policy is being developed. Call for details.

AVAILABILITY: April–October, any day to 9pm.

SERVICES/AMENITIES:

Restaurant Services: no

Catering: provided or BYO

Kitchen Facilities: moderate

Tables & Chairs: provided

Linens, Silver, etc.: provided or BYO

Restrooms: no wca

Dance Floor: patio

Parking: large lot

Overnight Accommodations: no

Telephone: pay phone

Outdoor Night Lighting: yes

Outdoor Cooking Facilities: BBQ

Cleanup: provided

Other: tours and tastings

RESTRICTIONS:

Alcohol: WC provided, no BYO
Smoking: allowed
Music: amplified ok

Wheelchair Access: yes
Insurance: sometimes required
Other: no hard alcohol

THE GOLDEN OAK RESTAURANT

16695 Condit Road
Morgan Hill, CA 95038
(408) 779-8085 Matthew Mirazarafi
Reserve: 1 week–12 months in advance

Once a winery, the Golden Oak Restaurant derives its name from the impressive oak tree which dominates the restaurant entrance and spreads its branches over a lovely patio. Even when the temperature soars, the oak keeps its domain breezy and temperate. The main patio is linked to a smaller patio by a long grape vine-covered trellis. Overlooking a vineyard, this patio sits in full sun and can be set up with attractive umbrella-shaded tables. The restaurant's interior is cool and subdued, offering a variety of rooms from the small and intimate to a larger banquet facility. Wood beams and tile floors add a touch of "old California" to an otherwise contemporary decor.

CAPACITY:

Area	Seated	Reception
Garden Patio	200	400
Main Dining Room	140	150
Oak Room	30	—
Lazzerini Room	30	—
Mediterranean Room	250	400
Veranda	20	30

FEES & DEPOSITS: A $300 nonrefundable deposit, applied toward the event total, is required when the rental agreement is submitted. For meetings or other functions with no food service, rental fees are $100 for the Mediterranean Room, $40 each for the smaller rooms. The balance is due the day of the function. Per person rates: seated breakfasts $8–13, luncheons $8–14, seated dinners $16–29, hors d'oeuvres start at $4, and a range of buffets are available from $15–45. A 7.25% tax and 15% gratuity are additional.

AVAILABILITY: Year-round, every day from 10am–1:30am. Closed Christmas day.

SERVICES/AMENITIES:

Restaurant Services: yes
Catering: provided, no BYO
Kitchen Facilities: n/a

Tables & Chairs: provided
Linens, Silver, etc.: provided
Restrooms: wca

Dance Floor: yes
Parking: large lots
Overnight Accommodations: no
Telephone: pay phone

RESTRICTIONS:
Alcohol: provided, BYO $6/bottle corkage
Smoking: designated areas
Music: amplified ok

Outdoor Night Lighting: yes
Outdoor Cooking Facilities: CBA
Cleanup: provided
Other: event coordination, piano, bartenders CBA

Wheelchair Access: yes
Insurance: not required
Other: no drinking in parking lot

San Jose

ABIGAIL'S PUB
AND FLOWERS

265 North First Street
San Jose, CA 95113
(408) 294-4111
Reserve: 2 weeks–12 months in advance

Look for the British flags flying in front of this historic Victorian building and you'll know you've located Abigail's, San Jose's only British restaurant and flower shop. Located close to downtown, this place is unusual because to enter the restaurant you've got to go through the flower store. Abigail's entertains all sorts of groups, serving such fare as prime rib with Yorkshire pudding, pasty's, pot pies, bangers and 'mash', beef Wellington, mixed grills and raspberry trifle. If you want, have high tea here with sandwiches, scones and fruit compote. The interior boasts high ceilings, pleasant decor and a friendly, warm ambiance—a perfect setting for a business breakfast or an evening celebration.

CAPACITY: The Pub's dining room can hold up to 50 seated guests, 75 for a standing reception.

FEES & DEPOSITS: A $75 refundable deposit secures your date. For functions without food service, the fee is $300/4 hours. With food, there is no rental charge. Per person rates: luncheons start at $12, dinners at $17, brunches at $9, and hors d'oeuvres at $5. Buffets and breakfast meetings can be arranged. A 7.25% tax and 15% gratuity are additional.

CANCELLATION POLICY: With 1 month's notice, you'll receive a full refund.

AVAILABILITY: Year-round, every day 6am–midnight, except Christmas.

SERVICES/AMENITIES:
Restaurant Services: yes
Catering: provided, BYO extra $300 fee
Kitchen Facilities: fully equipped

Tables & Chairs: provided
Linens, Silver, etc.: provided
Restrooms: no wca

Dance Floor: no
Parking: on street, parking lots nearby
Overnight Accommodations: no
Telephone: office phone

RESTRICTIONS:
Alcohol: WB provided, BYO $5/bottle corkage
Smoking: designated areas
Music: amplified ok

Outdoor Night Lighting: no
Outdoor Cooking Facilities: no
Cleanup: provided
Other: flowers, decorations, entertainment

Wheelchair Access: yes
Insurance: not required

THE BRIAR ROSE

897 East Jackson Street
San Jose, CA 95112
(408) 279-5999
Reserve: 2 weeks–1 month in advance

The Briar Rose Inn is a very attractive old Victorian home located in a quiet residential neighborhood five minutes from downtown San Jose. You enter under a vine-covered trellis and stroll up the rose-lined walkway past a small, white pitched-roof gazebo shaded by an old elm in the front yard. With a decorative wrought iron fence, lace curtains and pastel-painted exterior, the Inn presents an inviting face. Wide stairs lead you past the veranda into a warm and comfortable interior with lots of charm and Victorian detailing. The back yard has a well-tended garden and amenities for outdoor parties. Beautifully restored by its present owners, the Inn offers a variety of carefully appointed rooms for small parties, receptions and overnight guests. The good news is that with the purchase of the adjacent property, Briar Rose now offers additional facilities for business functions, too.

CAPACITY: The Inn can hold up to 50 guests indoors; outdoors 125. The total capacity is 150.

FEES & DEPOSITS: For weekday business functions, a $75 deposit is required when reservations are confirmed. The rental fee is $75/hour, the total payable 1 week prior to the function. For special events, a $200 deposit is required upon reservation. The rental is $650 for 4 hours, payable 1 week in advance of the event.

CANCELLATION POLICY: With 2 weeks' notice, you'll receive a full refund.

AVAILABILITY: Year-round, every day.

SERVICES/AMENITIES:
Restaurant Services: no
Catering: provided or BYO
Kitchen Facilities: setup only
Tables & Chairs: CBA
Linens, Silver, etc.: CBA
Restrooms: no wca
Dance Floor: brick portico

Parking: street
Overnight Accommodations: 5 guestrooms, 2 cottages
Telephone: guest phone
Outdoor Night Lighting: yes
Outdoor Cooking Facilities: no
Cleanup: provided
Other: event coordination

RESTRICTIONS:

Alcohol: WCB only, provided or BYO
Smoking: outside only
Music: no amplified

Wheelchair Access: garden only
Insurance: sometimes required

CHILDREN'S DISCOVERY ★ MUSEUM

180 Woz Way
San Jose, CA 95110
(408) 298-5437 Museum Rental
Reserve: 1–4 months in advance

Open for 'hands-on' adventure during private parties, the new Children's Discovery Museum is a marvel of delights for adults as well as kids. The spacious layout enables guests to enjoy a wide range of activities and interactive exhibits. The major theme of the Museum is "connection to the community," with an emphasis on our relationship to the infrastructure that exists all around us. Here it is articulated by exhibits relating to typical public services on a city street. The major circulation arteries in the Museum are designed as a street scene, complete with fire hydrants, traffic lights and manholes. You can assume the role of a fireman or ambulance driver by donning the appropriate attire and hopping onto an awaiting vehicle. The Museum highlights community elements by making each a learning experience. For example, there's a cross-section of a street showing what occurs underground, plus exhibits focusing on communications, health care and an art recycle center. It's a stimulating event environment, inviting interaction and discussion, movement and flexibility. Although the Museum is more conducive to informal gatherings, black tie events have been held here, too.

CAPACITY: The Museum can hold up to 200 seated guests and 800 for a reception indoors; with outdoor spaces, the total capacity is 1200 guests.

FEES & DEPOSITS: A $600 nonrefundable deposit is due when reservations are confirmed. The fee is $10/person or a minimum of $1200/event. The nonprofit rate is $8 per person, minimum $1200/event. For corporate Museum members, discounts are available.

AVAILABILITY: Year-round. Mondays are for large groups only. Tuesday–Sunday 5pm–midnight. Closed Thanksgiving and Christmas.

SERVICES/AMENITIES:

Restaurant Services: no
Catering: BYO with approval
Kitchen Facilities: setup only
Tables & Chairs: BYO
Linens, Silver, etc.: BYO
Restrooms: wca
Dance Floor: no

Parking: large lots
Overnight Accommodations: no
Telephone: pay phone
Outdoor Night Lighting: limited
Outdoor Cooking Facilities: BYO
Cleanup: whoever caters event
Other: Discovery Guides included

RESTRICTIONS:

Alcohol: BYO
Smoking: outside only
Music: amplified ok

Wheelchair Access: yes
Insurance: certificate required

EULIPIA RESTAURANT & BAR

374 South First Street
San Jose, CA 95113
(408) 280-6161
Reserve: 2 weeks in advance

Eulipia translates as an artist's version of utopia. When the restaurant first opened as a jazz club 13 years ago, the owners named it after a song by Rahsaan Roland Kirk, who actually made up the word. Now a trendy eatery in downtown San Jose, Eulipia offers fresh and attractive spaces for events, along with creative American cuisine. With lots of contemporary art on the walls, modern appointments and a light pastel interior, this restaurant is a great place for small business or private parties. For more privacy, try The Gallery and Bar upstairs, featuring ever-changing contemporary works of art. For corporate dinner meetings and private events, the Eulipia offers a very appealing environment.

CAPACITY: The Gallery can hold up to 100 seated guests; 200 for a reception. The Bar 65 seated; 150 standing. The Eulipia downstairs can hold up to 24 seated for a private party.

FEES & DEPOSITS: A nonrefundable deposit totaling 50% of the food and beverage estimate is payable when reservations are confirmed. The balance and confirmed guest count are due 5 days prior to the event. Per person rates: business breakfasts/brunches range $8–15, luncheons start at $13, dinners at $18, buffets at $25 and hors d'oeuvres at $10.

AVAILABILITY: Year-round, every day, any time. Closed Christmas day.

SERVICES/AMENITIES:

Restaurant Services: yes
Catering: provided, no BYO
Kitchen Facilities: n/a
Tables & Chairs: provided
Linens, Silver, etc.: provided
Restrooms: wca
Dance Floor: yes

Parking: street or public lot, $3 at night
Overnight Accommodations: no
Telephone: pay phone
Outdoor Night Lighting: no
Outdoor Cooking Facilities: no
Cleanup: provided
Other: event coordination, piano

RESTRICTIONS:

Alcohol: provided, BYO corkage $7/bottle
Smoking: allowed
Music: amplified restricted

Wheelchair Access: first floor only
Insurance: not required

EVENT CENTER
At San Jose State University

290 S. 7th Street at San Carlos
San Jose, CA 95192
(408) 924-6300
Reserve: 1–6 months in advance

Although mostly recognized as a venue for sports and concerts, the Event Center is also available for corporate and special events. This is a relatively new brick and concrete structure, built near the Student Union in the heart of the San Jose State Campus. During the day, students predominate. But at night and on weekends, this facility is a great location for fashion shows, large business functions, fundraisers or awards ceremonies. The interior is a state-of-the-art mini-arena, with stadium-style tiered seating facing a center floor. The flooring can be changed to suit different functions, from a basketball hardwood court to a dance floor. You may never have thought of this place for your next party, but it's a winner for large events where theatrical lighting, good sound and great visibility are required. Check it out.

CAPACITY:

Type of Function	Guest Count
Concert-style w/ seating above and on center floor	6500
Concert-style, seating in tiers only	5400
Athletic and social events	4600

FEES & DEPOSITS: A nonrefundable deposit totaling a percentage of the rental fees and services is due when reservations are confirmed. The deposit amount is based on the type of function and its total estimated cost. The rental fee for functions where tickets are sold is $2000 or 10% of gross ticketed sales, whichever is greater. A service fee for setup is $1000/day. The minimal rental for banquets or events without ticket sales is $3500. Other fees, such as security, box office, ticket takers, AV and setup/cleanup, are negotiable. The final balance or estimated direct costs are due 10 days prior to the event.

AVAILABILITY: Year-round, any day. All private functions are planned around scheduled sports events.

SERVICES/AMENITIES:

Restaurant Services: no
Catering: BYO extra fee, approval required
Kitchen Facilities: fully equipped
Tables & Chairs: some provided or BYO
Linens, Silver, etc.: BYO
Restrooms: wca
Dance Floor: yes, extra fee

Parking: adjacent garage, extra fee
Overnight Accommodations: no
Telephone: pay phone
Outdoor Night Lighting: no
Outdoor Cooking Facilities: no
Cleanup: caterer and janitorial
Other: professional lighting & sound

RESTRICTIONS:

Alcohol: provided or BYO with restrictions
Smoking: designated areas
Music: amplified ok

Wheelchair Access: yes
Insurance: certificate required
Other: no open flames

D. P. FONG GALLERIES

383 South First Street
San Jose, CA 95113
(408) 298-4141   Keiko Mochizuki Spratt
Reserve: 1 month in advance

Located across the street from the Eulipia Restaurant, this gallery space is like an empty canvas. Consisting of two connected, large and virtually unadorned storefront spaces with white walls, contemporary art and high ceilings, the d.p. Fong Galleries are perfect places to "dress up" for a gala party or business event. Because the rooms have minimal appointments, the spaces lend themselves to a wide range of decorating possibilities. This gallery is very popular for Christmas and New Year's parties, so reserve well in advance.

CAPACITY: For receptions 150–175 guests; seated functions 75 guests.

FEES & DEPOSITS: As a refundable deposit, 50% of the $250 rental fee is due when reservations are confirmed. The balance is due the day of the event. The rental fee covers a 4-hour block.

CANCELLATION POLICY: With 3 days' advance notice, the deposit is refunded.

AVAILABILITY: Year-round, every day. Sunday and Monday 10am–10pm; Tuesday–Saturday 6pm–10pm. Not available on Thursdays.

SERVICES/AMENITIES:

Restaurant Services: no
Catering: BYO
Kitchen Facilities: no
Tables & Chairs: BYO
Linens, Silver, etc.: BYO
Restrooms: no wca
Dance Floor: no

Parking: street, adjacent lots $3/car
Overnight Accommodations: no
Telephone: office phone
Outdoor Night Lighting: no
Outdoor Cooking Facilities: no
Cleanup: caterer

RESTRICTIONS:

Alcohol: BYO
Smoking: outside only
Music: no amplified

Wheelchair Access: yes
Insurance: required

HENSLEY HOUSE

456 N. Third Street
San Jose, CA 95112
(408) 298-3537
Reserve: 2 weeks in advance

Centrally located near the heart of downtown San Jose, this Queen Anne Victorian known as 'The Hensley House' was built about 1884 for the controversial educator and superior Court Judge, Perley Gosbey. Occupying a prominent corner in San Jose's downtown historic residential district, the House is now a bed and breakfast inn, catering to small business functions and private parties. Parts of the interior were remodeled in the Craftsman style around 1906, however there are original beamed ceilings,1880s woodwork and hardware and built-in leaded glass cabinets from the early 1890s. Restored over a 5-year period, The Hensley House provides a warm ambiance and lovely Victorian-style environment for any type of gathering.

CAPACITY: The House can hold up to 20 guests for seated dinners, 25–30 for seminars, 50–70 for receptions and the outdoor areas up to 100. The total capacity for any one event is 150.

FEES & DEPOSITS: 50% of the estimated total is due when reservations are confirmed. For business functions, the $100/hour rental fee includes beverage service, hors d'oeuvres, fax, computer and outside telephone line. Seated luncheons start at $12/person, dinners $18–23/person including tax and tip.

For special events, the rental fee is $100/hour. This is sometimes waived depending on the total food and beverage service provided. Per person rates: hors d'oeuvres and wine $10, luncheons start at $10, dinners start at $10 and buffets start at $15. Tax at 7.25% and gratuity 15% are additional. Menus can be customized.

CANCELLATION POLICY: For business functions, 5 working days' notice is required for a refund; for events, 2 weeks' notice is required. There's a $25 charge for any cancellation.

AVAILABILITY: Year-round, every day from 7: 30am–5pm.

SERVICES/AMENITIES:

Restaurant Services: no
Catering: provided, no BYO
Kitchen Facilities: n/a
Tables & Chairs: provided
Linens, Silver, etc.: provided
Restrooms: no wca
Dance Floor: no

Parking: street or rear lot
Overnight Accommodations: 4 guestrooms
Telephone: house phone
Outdoor Night Lighting: yes
Outdoor Cooking Facilities: BBQ
Cleanup: provided
Other: event coordination, grand piano

RESTRICTIONS:

Alcohol: W provided or BYO corkage $3/bottle
Smoking: outside only
Music: no amplified

Wheelchair Access: no
Insurance: sometimes required

HOCHBURG
VON GERMANIA

261 N. Second Street
San Jose, CA 95112
(408) 295-4484
Reserve: 1 week–2 months in advance

What's a Bavarian Inn doing in downtown San Jose? Providing its guests with an unusual setting for wining, dining and dancing. This 101-year-old historic landmark greets you with colorful flags, family crests and the intricate "gingerbread" woodwork reminiscent of the Old Country. The Ballroom continues the festive theme with multicolored lighting inset in a huge wooden disk suspended from the ceiling and Christmas lights strung around the perimeter. A small stage with a mural of a Bavarian field of flowers adds a final touch to the unique decor. And for beer lovers, the Hochburg has a separate menu offering over 50 varieties of German beer! The ambiance here is loose, informal and fun.

CAPACITY: The Ballroom can seat 250 guests, the dining room 65.

MEETING ROOMS: 1 room, 50 people.

FEES & DEPOSITS: 25% of the estimated food total is required as the deposit, due when reservations are confirmed. There's a $150 rewaxing charge for the Ballroom if the event includes dancing and a $200 refundable cleaning deposit. There are no rental fees with food service. Per person rates are: buffets $13–17, seated dinners, $12–20 and seated luncheons $5–10. Buffet luncheons can be arranged. For functions without food service, the rental fee is $600 for 6 hours.

CANCELLATION POLICY: With 3 weeks' notice, you'll receive a full refund. If the facility does not provide cleanup for your event, the cleaning deposit is returned.

AVAILABILITY: Year-round, every day from 9am–2am. Closed Christmas and Thanksgiving.

SERVICES/AMENITIES:

Restaurant Services: yes
Catering: provided, or BYO with approval
Kitchen Facilities: setup only
Tables & Chairs: provided
Linens, Silver, etc.: provided
Restrooms: no wca
Dance Floor: yes

Parking: adjacent lots
Overnight Accommodations: no
Telephone: pay phone
Outdoor Night Lighting: yes
Outdoor Cooking Facilities: no
Cleanup: provided or renter
Other: event coordination, movie screen

RESTRICTIONS:

Alcohol: provided, BYO corkage $5/wine bottle, $6/champ. bottle
Smoking: allowed

Music: amplified ok
Wheelchair Access: no
Insurance: not required

KATIA LACOSTE GALLERY

227 N. First Street
San Jose, CA 95113
(408) 295-5706
Reserve: 1 month in advance

In this gallery, housed in a historic building not far from the downtown center, everything has been remodeled with taste and attention to detail. As you step inside the building's Sculpture Atrium, you'll find yourself standing on a chic gray marble floor looking two stories up to a well-designed skylight from which light filters into the office and gallery spaces below. The Katia Lacoste Gallery on the first floor provides a contemporary setting with glass walls, gray neutral carpeting, mirrors, spot lighting and white walls. Sculpture and paintings also add interest to an already appealing event site. It's an intimate space that appears larger as a result of the careful layout. The Main Gallery, Annex and Sculpture Atrium combined make a great spot for business or private cocktail receptions.

CAPACITY: The Main Gallery, Annex and Sculpture Atrium can hold up to 200 guests for a reception.

FEES & DEPOSITS: none

CANCELLATION POLICY: 2 weeks' notice of cancellation is required.

AVAILABILITY: Year-round, every day. Smaller functions 10am–6pm, larger functions 6pm–9pm. Closed major holidays.

SERVICES/AMENITIES:

Restaurant Services: no
Catering: BYO
Kitchen Facilities: minimal
Tables & Chairs: BYO
Linens, Silver, etc.: BYO
Restrooms: wca
Dance Floor: no

Parking: rear lot
Overnight Accommodations: no
Telephone: office phone
Outdoor Night Lighting: no
Outdoor Cooking Facilities: no
Cleanup: caterer

RESTRICTIONS:

Alcohol: BYO
Smoking: allowed
Music: no amplified

Wheelchair Access: yes
Insurance: required

LE PETIT TRIANON
Center for the Arts

72 North Fifth Street
San Jose, CA 95112
(408) 998-0834
Reserve: 2 weeks–1 month in advance

Le Petit Trianon is what we call an unusual 'find'. Built in 1922 as a church, it's now a residence hotel as well as a place for special functions. We were surprised to learn that it was designed to resemble Le Trianon, Marie Antionette's home at Versailles! It houses some unique and impressive interior spaces, with dual curved staircases, vintage light fixtures, decorative molding and arched windows and doorways. Of special interest are the auditorium and small theater—absolutely terrific spots for business lectures, music recitals, symposiums, awards ceremonies or small fashion shows. These rooms have theater seating, hardwood floors and multi-paned windows. There's a lovely conference room upstairs: light and airy with interesting details, ceiling skylights, small dance floor and kitchen. The exterior of this structure is a bit imposing, but don't let that deter you. We were very impressed by the unusual layout and the range of distinctive rooms.

CAPACITY:

Room	Theater-style	Seated	Standing
Small Theater	132 fixed	—	—
Large Auditorium	342 fixed	—	—
Banquet/Conference Room	—	135	—
Grand Reception Hall	—	—	200–350
Courtyard	650	400	500

FEES & DEPOSITS: One third of the total rental fee is due as a nonrefundable deposit when reservations are confirmed. Two weeks prior to the event another third is payable. The final third is due 3 days prior to the event. Rental fees range from $100–400 depending on which room(s) are reserved, the guest count and day of the week. Discounts are available for nonprofits. Extra rooms can be arranged for an additional fee.

AVAILABILITY: Year-round, every day from 9am–11pm.

SERVICES/AMENITIES:

Restaurant Services: no
Catering: BYO
Kitchen Facilities: limited
Tables & Chairs: provided
Linens, Silver, etc.: BYO
Restrooms: no wca
Dance Floor: yes

Parking: 2 lots
Overnight Accommodations: 15 guestrooms
Telephone: pay phone
Outdoor Night Lighting: yes
Outdoor Cooking Facilities: BBQ
Cleanup: renter or caterer

RESTRICTIONS:

Alcohol: BYO
Smoking: outside only
Music: amplified ok

Wheelchair Access: yes
Insurance: sometimes required

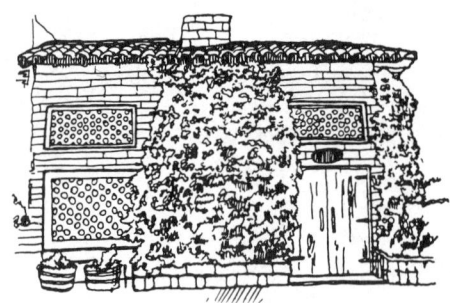

MIRASSOU

3000 Aborn Road
San Jose, CA 95135
(408) 274-4000 Melanie Bacon
Reserve: 2–6 months in advance

This winery offers businesses and private parties a chance to savor Mirassou wines during events. Two Conference Rooms provide comfortable meeting space with all the necessities, including light food service. Wine bottles line the walls and in one room there are views of giant wine barrels. The Tasting Room is a popular place: spacious, with an oversized suspended mirror for cooking demonstrations, windows fashioned out of bottles and a backdrop of huge wine barrels. Mirassou's two patios can accommodate either simple wine and cheese affairs or full course meals with guests seated at umbrella-shaded tables. For a slightly more formal affair, the Heritage House has two light, airy rooms with views of the back garden. Whether you're planning a meeting, secretary's luncheon, or sunset dinner, Mirassou provides versatility and a beautiful, tranquil setting.

CAPACITY:	*Area*	*Month*	*Capacity*
	Outdoor Patios	June–Sept	120
	Tasting & Dining Room	October	80
	Tasting Room	Nov–March	65
	Tasting Room & Patio	April–May	80
	Conference Room	year-round	18
	(There is a 15-guest minimum)		

FEES & DEPOSITS: Deposits are sometimes required; in December a refundable $250 deposit is required when reservations are confirmed. There are no rental fees with food service. Per person rates for meals, including wine, tax and tip: $45 for dinners and $25 for luncheons. The Conference Room Lunch Program rate is $250/day for 10 guests, which includes meeting space, business equipment, lunch, tax, tip and wine. For each guest over 10, the rate is $22/person. Seminars, minimum 25 participants, can be arranged for a $50 setup fee. Food service is $5–10/person for fruit, cheese and paté.

CANCELLATION POLICY: One month's notice is required for a refund.

AVAILABILITY: Year-round, every day except for major holidays.

SERVICES/AMENITIES:

Restaurant Services: no
Catering: provided, no BYO
Kitchen Facilities: n/a
Tables & Chairs: provided
Linens, Silver, etc.: provided
Restrooms: wca
Dance Floor: no

Parking: large lot
Overnight Accommodations: no
Telephone: pay phone
Outdoor Night Lighting: yes
Outdoor Cooking Facilities: CBA
Cleanup: provided
Other: wine tasting, tours

RESTRICTIONS:

Alcohol: CW provided, no BYO
Smoking: allowed
Music: amplified within limits

Wheelchair Access: yes
Insurance: sometimes required
Other: no hard alcohol or guests under 21

SAN JOSE ATHLETIC CLUB

196 N. Third Street
San Jose, CA 95112
(408) 292-1141 Ken Surber
Reserve: 1–10 months in advance

Located in the heart of old downtown San Jose, the San Jose Athletic Club is a striking and imposing Neoclassic structure with huge columns, large urns and broad steps up to the massive front doors. Inside you'll find a variety of rooms available for your private party. Large functions are usually held in the Main Dining Room which has very high ceilings and stage. It has recently undergone a $400,000 renovation which includes additional event lighting, huge palm trees and tasteful appointments. The Room's new faux marble finish is extraordinary. For formal or informal parties, The Club is an impressive building with interior spaces to match.

CAPACITY:

Room	Standing	Seated	Room	Standing	Seated
Discus Lounge	250	—	Main Dining Rm	400	250
Olympia Room	—	80	Gold, Silver, Bronze Rm	200	125

FEES & DEPOSITS: A $500 refundable deposit secures your date and is due when the reservation is made. It is only refundable if the event date can be rebooked. The rental fee for the Main Dining Room is $500 for a 5-hour block. The fee for the Olympia Room is $75. There is no charge for use of the Discus Lounge or the Gold, Silver, Bronze Room which is sometimes used for business meetings. Full payment is due 2 weeks prior to your event. Per person rates: hors d'oeuvres $15–25 and seated meals run $19–35. Sales tax of 7.25% and a 17% service charge will be applied to the final bill.

AVAILABILITY: Saturdays and Sundays 9am–1am. Weekdays from 4pm–1am.

SERVICES/AMENITIES:

Restaurant Services: yes
Catering: provided, BYO CBA
Kitchen Facilities: n/a
Tables & Chairs: provided
Linens, Silver, etc.: provided
Restrooms: wca
Dance Floor: yes

Parking: street or nearby garage
Overnight Accommodations: no
Telephone: pay phone
Outdoor Night Lighting: no
Outdoor Cooking Facilities: no
Cleanup: provided

RESTRICTIONS:
Alcohol: provided, BYO corkage $6/bottle
Smoking: allowed
Music: amplified ok
Wheelchair Access: yes

Insurance: not required
Other: no helium balloons or confetti
in Main Dining Room

SAN JOSE HISTORICAL MUSEUM

Kelley Park between Story & Tully on
Senter Road
San Jose, CA 95112
(408) 287-2290 Events Dept.
Reserve: 1–3 months in advance

Housed on 25 acres in the southernmost section of Kelley Park, the Historical Museum Complex offers a unique glimpse of the old homes and businesses that once graced the streets of early San Jose. This is a recreation of old San Jose, with historically significant buildings and exhibits depicting the history of Santa Clara Valley. Whether restored or reconstructed, each building in Kelley Park is placed as nearly as possible in its original relation to other structures. The Museum Complex features an operating, turn-of-the-century trolley with costumed conductor, a scaled-down 115-foot high replica of the San Jose 1881 Electric Light Tower, a 1927 gas station and decorative 1890-style park bandstand. In addition to various outdoor spaces for parties, there are facilities in the Firehouse and Pacific Hotel for indoor functions. This is an interesting and unusual site for an event. Dress up and arrive in style aboard a vintage trolley or horse-drawn carriage! The Museum staff can help you be creative—period costumes, trolley rides, museum tours and ice cream parlor parties for kids can be arranged.

CAPACITY: The Pacific Hotel's meeting room can hold up to 40 seated guests, 80 standing and the Firehouse upstairs reception room can accommodate 60 seated guests, 125 standing. Outdoor functions up to 1000.

FEES & DEPOSITS: A nonrefundable deposit of 50% of the estimated use fee is required when the reservation is made. A refundable maintenance deposit of $150 (indoor events) or $250 (outdoor events) is due 30 days prior to your function and is returned 2-3 weeks afterwards.

Indoor Functions: $50/hour 8am–5pm, $75/hour 5pm-midnight. A 3-hour minimum block is required. The security requirement of 1 off-duty police officer is required, rate varies. For daytime business meetings or retreats, there's a flat fee of $125, 8am–5pm.

Outdoor Functions:

Guest Count	Rates	Guest Count	Rates
0–100	$360	401–600	$1350
101–200	510	601–800	1710
201–300	675	801–1000	2100
301–400	900	over 1000	quoted

Up to 600 guests, the maximum rental is 8 hours; over 600 guests, the maximum is 10 hours. The outdoor security requirement of 1 or more off-duty police officers is required, rate varies. The total balance is due 5 days prior to the event.

AVAILABILITY: Indoor functions: 8am–midnight. Outdoor events: 8am–10pm. Events are in either 8 or 10-hour blocks.

SERVICES/AMENITIES:

Restaurant Services: no
Catering: BYO
Kitchen Facilities: minimal
Tables & Chairs: some provided
Linens, Silver, etc.: BYO
Restrooms: wca varies
Dance Floor: at plaza outside, indoors CBA

Parking: large lots
Overnight Accommodations: no
Telephone: pay phone
Outdoor Night Lighting: limited
Outdoor Cooking Facilities: BBQs
Cleanup: caterer
Other: trolley, costumes & tours CBA

RESTRICTIONS:

Alcohol: BYO, BWC only
Smoking: outside only
Music: amplified restricted

Wheelchair Access: yes
Insurance: sometimes required

VICTORIAN GARDEN RESTAURANT

476 South First Street
San Jose, CA 95113
(408) 286-1770 Event Coordinator
Reserve: 1 day–12 months in advance

Filled with an eclectic collection of antiques, Tiffany style lamps, art work and leaded glass windows, the Victorian Garden Restaurant is a fun, upbeat place with lots of character. A wonderful patio in the back has an overhead canopy structure and sunscreen, lots of plants and a bubbling fountain. For evening parties, heat lamps are well situated to make al fresco dining comfortable. Private and inviting, the patio is a lovely spot for outdoor receptions.

CAPACITY: The restaurant can hold 200 guests total; 105 seated inside, 105 on the Patio.

FEES & DEPOSITS: A $200–500 security deposit is required depending on group size. The deposit is credited toward the final bill. A nonrefundable facility fee may be charged depending on group size. Per person rates: breakfasts start at $8, brunches at $12, luncheons $9–15, dinners $15–30, buffets start at $17. The balance is due at the time of the event. Tax of 7.25% and a 15% gratuity are additional.

CANCELLATION POLICY: Refunds are made only if the space can be rebooked.

AVAILABILITY: Year-round, every day, any time. Closed July 4th, Labor Day and Memorial Day.

SERVICES/AMENITIES:

Restaurant Services: yes
Catering: provided, no BYO
Kitchen Facilities: n/a
Tables & Chairs: provided
Linens, Silver, etc.: provided
Restrooms: no wca
Dance Floor: CBA

Parking: valet
Overnight Accommodations: no
Telephone: pay phone
Outdoor Night Lighting: yes
Outdoor Cooking Facilities: no
Cleanup: provided
Other: event coordination

RESTRICTIONS:

Alcohol: provided, BYO corkage $10–15/bottle
Smoking: designated areas
Music: amplified ok

Wheelchair Access: yes
Insurance: not required

WINCHESTER MYSTERY HOUSE

525 S. Winchester Blvd.
San Jose, CA 95128
(408) 247-2000
Reserve: 3–6 months in advance

The Winchester Mystery House is a 160-room Victorian mansion designed and built from 1884–1922 by Sarah Winchester, heir to the Winchester rifle fortune. Allegedly distraught by the loss of her only child and early death of her husband, she funneled all of her energy and money into the continuous construction of this extraordinary structure in order to stay her own death. Reports note that she spent the astronomical sum of $5.5 million on the house from the late 1800s to the early 1920s. Today the Mansion is open to the public for tours and private functions. The house is enormous, with incredible 'gingerbread' detailing and craftsmanship throughout. The grounds are formal, with meticulously manicured lawns, flower beds, courtyard fountains and towering palm trees. Your guests will be thrilled to attend a private party surrounded by the unique product of an eccentric who had unlimited wealth and the freedom to spend it as she pleased.

CAPACITY:

Area	Standing	Seated	Area	Standing	Seated
Front Garden	1000	450	Central Courtyard	300	150
Central Garden	300	150	Winchester Room	65	65

For private parties of 200 guests or more, the Mansion will open for self-guided tours for up to 2 hours. For under 200, 35-minute guided tours are available.

FEES & DEPOSITS: A $500 deposit is due with the rental agreement 30 days prior to your event. The Garden and Courtyard fees: $1500 for the first 100 guests, based on 10/table seating, and $150 for each additional table of 10; $1600 for the first 100 guests, based on 8/table seating, with $160 for each additional table of 8. The Winchester Room fee is $500 for the first 48 guests, based on 8/table seating plus $10/person for each additional guest. These fees cover a 4-hour rental period.

Food and beverage service can be provided and will be catered on an individual basis. Prices will vary accordingly. Tax is 7.25% and gratuity is normally 15%.

CANCELLATION POLICY: With 2 or more weeks' notice, you'll receive a full refund; with 1 week's notice, a 50% refund.

AVAILABILITY: Gardens and grounds available every day, April, May and September from 7pm–11pm; June, July and August 8pm–midnight. The Winchester Room is available year-round.

SERVICES/AMENITIES:

Restaurant Services: no

Catering: provided, can BYO but will be charged 20% of gross

Kitchen Facilities: minimal

Tables & Chairs: provided

Linens, Silver, etc.: BYO

Restrooms: wca

Dance Floor: CBA

Parking: large lots

Overnight Accommodations: no

Telephone: pay phone

Outdoor Night Lighting: yes

Outdoor Cooking Facilities: no

Cleanup: whoever caters event

Other: mini tours, flashlight tours & murder mystery events

RESTRICTIONS:

Alcohol: provided, BYO corkage $2/bottle

Smoking: garden and courtyard only

Music: amplified until 11pm

Wheelchair Access: to garden only

Insurance: not required

Santa Clara

DECATHLON CLUB

3250 Central Expressway
Santa Clara, CA 95051
(408) 738-8743 Catering Department
Reserve: 2–12 months in advance

One of Silicon Valley's finest private athletic clubs, the Decathlon Club is ingeniously designed to accommodate private parties without disturbing its membership. As you enter, there is a shaded garden setting with a bubbling stream which flows through the building, beautifully separating the social function spaces from the club's athletic areas. The dining area is large and open, yet it gives guests a feeling of privacy. It opens onto a wide deck overlooking a lush, sloping lawn and tennis court below. This is one of the nicest, most sophisticated combination of facilities we've seen—the deck, lawn and private tennis court combo allows a private group to design their own tournament for fundraising, corporate fun or just a private tennis match. For unique corporate events, all of the Club's sports facilities are available for rental. Corporate challenges or inter-office games can be played here, all supported by a helpful and experienced staff.

CAPACITY: Indoors, the Club can hold 700 guests for receptions with dancing; 400 seated. The outdoor stadium tennis court and outside deck areas can hold 200 guests. The combination of different sports facilities can accommodate 300 guests.

MEETING ROOMS: 2 rooms, 10–22 people conference seating; 25–50 classroom seating.

FEES & DEPOSITS: A nonrefundable $500 deposit is required when reservations are confirmed. The fees for events range from $150–$20,000 depending on the function, area(s) reserved and guest count. Rental fees cover a 4 1/2-hour period. Overtime is available at an additional charge. Meeting room fees are $200/8 hours for the large room, $150/8 hours for the small room. Invoicing for business meetings can be arranged. Special events utilizing a combination of different sports facilities (gym, swimming pool, volleyball, tennis, racquet & squash courts) can be arranged for corporations. Call for rates.

Food service is provided. Per person rates: luncheons start at $12, dinners at $20, buffets at $25, hors d'oeuvres at $12 and BBQs at $15. For meetings, continental breakfast, lunch and coffee service can be arranged starting at $6/person. A 7.25% tax and 17% gratuity are additional.

AVAILABILITY: Year-round, daily 7am–1am for group events. Closed major holidays.

SERVICES/AMENITIES:

Restaurant Services: yes
Catering: provided, no BYO
Kitchen Facilities: n/a
Tables & Chairs: provided
Linens, Silver, etc.: provided
Restrooms: wca
Dance Floor: yes

Parking: large lots
Overnight Accommodations: no
Telephone: pay phone
Outdoor Night Lighting: yes
Outdoor Cooking Facilities: BBQ
Cleanup: provided
Other: event coordination, theme parties

RESTRICTIONS:

Alcohol: provided, no BYO
Smoking: allowed
Music: amplified ok

Wheelchair Access: yes
Insurance: not required

MADISON STREET INN

1390 Madison Street
Santa Clara, CA 95050
(408) 249-5541
Reserve: 2 weeks in advance

The Madison Street Inn is an inviting bed and breakfast establishment offering an unusual blend of 1890s Victorian charm with modern amenities. The house, with its white picket fence, antique furnishings, authentic wallpaper and lace curtains, maintains its period authenticity. Soothing colors, an intimate parlor with fireplace and a warm and airy dining area make guests feel right at home. The grounds offer a more contemporary setting with swimming pool and brick patio. In the summer, the trellis over the patio is ablaze with fuchsia and colorful bougainvillea; the adjacent lawn area is perfect for small outdoor gatherings.

CAPACITY: The Inn can hold up to 20 guests indoors and 75 outdoors.

FEES & DEPOSITS: A nonrefundable $200 deposit, applied toward the rental fee, is required when reservations are confirmed. The rental fee is $100–400 depending on the total guest count. The total estimated balance of both rental and food service is due 1 week before the event. The Inn provides catering: hors d'oeuvres run $5–20/person, luncheons $10–15/person and dinners $15–25/person. Tax of 7.25% and a 15% gratuity are additional.

AVAILABILITY: Year-round, every day 11am–7pm for group events.

SERVICES/AMENITIES:

Restaurant Services: no
Catering: provided or BYO with approval
Kitchen Facilities: setup only
Tables & Chairs: some provided
Linens, Silver, etc.: some provided
Restrooms: wca
Dance Floor: yes

Parking: on street
Overnight Accommodations: 5 guestrooms
Telephone: house phone
Outdoor Night Lighting: limited
Outdoor Cooking Facilities: BBQ
Cleanup: whoever caters event
Other: event coordination

RESTRICTIONS:

Alcohol: BYO, BWC only
Smoking: outside only
Music: no amplified

Wheelchair Access: limited to garden
Insurance: not required

TRITON MUSEUM OF ART ★★

1505 Warburton Ave.
Santa Clara, CA 95050
(408) 247-3754 Ruth Kaplan
Reserve: 6 weeks–6 months in advance

Fine art is exhibited in a building that captivates with stunning simplicity. As you walk through the main entrance into the Rotunda, you are bathed in light from the huge pyramid-shaped skylight overhead. Plain cement pillars provide structural support and a neutral concrete floor enhances the feeling of unclutteredness. Floor-to-ceiling glass draws your attention to a lovely sculpture garden with redwood trees and well-tended grass, flanked by large-scale palms. To the left of the Rotunda, the meeting room is spacious with white walls and a high ceiling; to the right are two gallery spaces. The Museum is available for business and organization functions only.

CAPACITY: The Rotunda plus the 2 galleries can accommodate 500 standing guests, combined with the S.H. Cowell Room, 750. For indoor/outdoor receptions, the facility holds up to 1500. The sculpture garden can be rented separately; call to make arrangements. Seated functions can be arranged on an individual basis.

MEETING ROOMS: The S.H. Cowell Room, theater-style 150 participants.

FEES & DEPOSITS: A partially refundable $500 security/cleaning deposit is required when reservations are confirmed. The Museum rental is $1600, payable 2 weeks prior to the event. The rental fee covers a 6 1/2-hour block, including setup and breakdown. By arrangement, you can extend hours for approximately $250/hour. Nonprofits may receive some discount or the fee may be waived depending on the type of function. Corporate members of the Museum have one free rental per year.

AVAILABILITY: Year-round, every day, primarily evenings after 5pm for group events. An occasional weekend afternoon reception can be arranged. Meetings in the S.H. Cowell Room Monday–Friday 9am–5pm, Saturday and Sunday noon–5pm.

SERVICES/AMENITIES:

Restaurant Services: no

Catering: BYO with approval

Kitchen Facilities: setup only

Tables & Chairs: some provided

Linens, Silver, etc.: BYO

Restrooms: wca

Dance Floor: no dancing

Parking: adjacent City lot

Overnight Accommodations: no

Telephone: pay phone

Outdoor Night Lighting: yes

Outdoor Cooking Facilities: no

Cleanup: caterer and/or custodial service

RESTRICTIONS:

Alcohol: BYO, no red wine

Smoking: outside only

Music: amplified restricted

Wheelchair Access: yes

Insurance: certificate required

Other: walk-through with renter required

Saratoga

CINNABAR VINEYARDS

23000 Congress Springs Road
Saratoga, CA 95070
(408) 741-5858
Reserve: 2 weeks –1 month in advance

High in the Santa Cruz Mountains, Tom Mudd and Melissa Frank own a little piece of paradise. These new vineyards and winery are located on a ridgetop 1600 feet above the Santa Clara Valley. There's no tasting room, and in fact, Cinnabar is not open to the public. However, private parties, conferences or special events are welcome. This winery is an inspirational environment for catered picnics or indoor dinners. Although the first harvest was in 1986, Tom and Melissa are already receiving accolades for their products. Cinnabar is a casual and friendly facility, offering guests a chance to taste highly regarded wines and a place to relax with sensational views. Here, you feel like you're on top of the world.

CAPACITY: Cinnabar can accommodate 24 seated guests indoors. Indoor and outdoor areas, combined, 100 guests maximum.

FEES & DEPOSITS: A deposit of 25% of the estimated total rental fee plus a $500 refundable damage deposit for non-corporate events are due when reserving your date. Rental fees are $20/person.

CANCELLATION POLICY: With 2 weeks' notice, the rental deposit will be refunded. The damage deposit will be refunded with less than 2 weeks' notice.

AVAILABILITY: Year-round, except for wine harvest season. Every day 8am–10pm.

SERVICES/AMENITIES:

Restaurant Services: no

Catering: CBA or BYO with approval

Kitchen Facilities: fully equipped

Tables & Chairs: some provided

Linens, Silver, etc.: BYO

Restrooms: wca limited

Dance Floor: no

Parking: limited

Overnight Accommodations: no

Telephone: office phone

Outdoor Night Lighting: limited

Outdoor Cooking Facilities: CBA

Cleanup: caterer

Other: winery tours, tastings, picnic tables

RESTRICTIONS:

Alcohol: W provided, no BYO, champagne by arrangement

Smoking: outside only

Music: amplified restricted

Wheelchair Access: limited

Insurance: certificate of insurance required

Other: no hard alcohol

CONGRESS SPRINGS WINERY

23600 Congress Springs Road
Saratoga, CA 95070
(408) 867-1409 Barbara Jonsson
Reserve: 1 week –12 months in advance

You have to drive a bit into the Santa Cruz foothills to get to Congress Springs, but it's well worth the effort. Approached from below by a shaded road studded with redwoods, you drive out of the trees onto a surprisingly sun-drenched knoll. Here you are surrounded by grape vines and teased by the aromas of fine wines in-the-making. The Villa sits at the highest point and has brilliant and colorful views of the adjacent vine-dotted hillsides, valleys and Congress Springs vineyards. The lawn in front of the Villa is a lovely and perfectly situated spot for outdoor celebrations and meetings on warm days. This is where tables with umbrellas are informally arranged for seated meals. The views from the lawn, looking down on the panorama below, are breathtaking. Ample guest parking is provided near the top, as well as overflow parking near the wine tasting building below. This charming site lends itself to relaxed gatherings of good friends and business associates.

CAPACITY: The lawn in front of the Villa can hold up to 250 guests for a buffet and 200 for a seated function. Indoors, the Tasting Hall can hold up to 80.

FEES & DEPOSITS: A nonrefundable deposit of 50% of the estimated total fee is due when reserving your date. A $250 refundable security deposit is due 1 month prior to the event and is returned within 4 weeks following the party. The rental fee is $5/person. There is a $250 minimum for events or business functions, which includes use of the grounds for 4 hours, a prefunction meeting, assistance during the event, parking attendant, wine glasses and champagne flutes plus wine service. A $100/hour fee applies to each additional hour over 4 hours.

AVAILABILITY: Outdoor spaces any time, from the third week in April through the third week in October. The Tasting Hall is available year-round after 5pm.

SERVICES/AMENITIES:

Restaurant Services: no
Catering: preferred list
Kitchen Facilities: minimal
Tables & Chairs: provided
Linens, Silver, etc.: caterer
Restrooms: wca
Dance Floor: yes, also can rent parquet floor

Parking: large lots
Overnight Accommodations: no
Telephone: office phone
Outdoor Night Lighting: limited
Outdoor Cooking Facilities: no
Cleanup: caterer
Other: event consultant

RESTRICTIONS:

Alcohol: must purchase Congress Springs wine, case discount prices
Smoking: allowed
Music: amplified within limits

Wheelchair Access: yes
Insurance: certificate of insurance required
Other: no beer or hard alcohol

HAKONE GARDENS ★

21000 Big Basin Way
Saratoga, CA 95070
(408) 867-3438 Marlene
Reserve: 3–12 months in advance

If guests don't miss the small blue and white Hakone Gardens entry sign, they are in for a treat. The gardens are located on a secluded hillside, reached by a narrow, winding and shaded road. At the top, you are beckoned through a formal gate into lush Japanese gardens complete with an arched foot-bridge over carp-filled ponds and a waterfall. Several Japanese buildings in the garden are set against a backdrop of stately pine trees. Although not used for events, the upper structure is visually striking with bamboo wood siding and classic, curved roof line. Guests step on large, well-placed stones to enter the lower teahouse through a small, formal dry gravel garden. The house's medium-sized main room provides a unique setting for indoor receptions, with hardwood floors and shoji panels which open onto exterior garden spaces. The large gravel courtyard leading to the lower house is often used for events. Another excellent place for a celebration is to the side of the teahouse where there's a nicely shaded and mounded gravel area, dotted with majestic madrones and oaks. If you want to have a noisy bash, the Hakone Gardens are not for you. If a quiet and serene setting is more your style, give this spot serious consideration.

CAPACITY: The lower house can accommodate 60 seated guests. The combination of the house and the garden space can hold up to 150 guests.

FEES & DEPOSITS: A $250 deposit is required when you book your reservation and a security and damage deposit of $300 is due 30 days prior to your event. For Saratoga residents, the fee for use of the garden is $350 for 3 hours maximum. For non-residents, the fee is $400. Other fees include use of the lower house at $100. All fees are due 30 days in advance of your party.

CANCELLATION POLICY: You must cancel 90 days prior to your event to receive a full refund.

AVAILABILITY: Exclusive use must occur between 8am–11am or 5pm–8pm because the site is open to the public at all other times. No bookings are made on holidays.

SERVICES/AMENITIES:

Restaurant Services: no
Catering: BYO
Kitchen Facilities: moderate
Tables & Chairs: limited quantity provided
Linens, Silver, etc.: BYO
Restrooms: wca
Dance Floor: no

Parking: large lot
Overnight Accommodations: no
Telephone: no
Outdoor Night Lighting: no
Outdoor Cooking Facilities: no
Cleanup: caterer

RESTRICTIONS:

Alcohol: BYO, BWC only
Smoking: outside only
Music: recorded only, 60 dba within 15 ft of source

Wheelchair Access: no
Insurance: indemnity clause required
Other: no nails, tacks or staples

THE MOUNTAIN WINERY

14831 Pierce Road
Saratoga, CA 95070
(408) 741-0763
Reserve: 2 weeks in advance

Way up in the Santa Cruz mountains, with spectacular views of the Santa Clara Valley, rests the famous Mountain Winery. Because the Winery hosts a summer entertainment program, reservations are limited June through September. If you can plan your event during the other months of the year, it's a terrific spot. The winery is part of a lovely outdoor natural setting with multicolored vineyards dotting the landscape. The historic winery building, built in 1905, is stone masonry with its three levels built into the side of the mountain to maintain an even, cool temperature for wine barrel storage. Inside are large wood beams, oak casks and the appealing aroma of aging wine. Outdoors are lawns, large oaks and magnificent views. Paul Masson's original home, Chateau La Cresta, is now available for meetings or dining. Events can also take place on a large wood deck overlooking the valley floor. Here, umbrella-shaded tables can be arranged for an open-air buffet or seated reception. At 1400 feet up, this "vineyard in the sky" provides a tranquil and unusual setting for an unforgettable business or social function.

CAPACITY: The Mountain Winery can accommodate up to 1000 guests depending on how the facility is used.

FEES & DEPOSITS: As a nonrefundable deposit, 50% of the total estimated cost along with the signed agreement and confirmed guest count are required at the time of confirmation. The average cost per person for wine, rental and meal service is $50. The final balance is invoiced, payable within 30 days after the event.

AVAILABILITY: Events are not held June–September. October through May, functions are allowed between 10am-noon and 4pm–8pm on non-performance days only.

SERVICES/AMENITIES:

Restaurant Services: no
Catering: BYO, must select from list
Kitchen Facilities: moderate
Tables & Chairs: provided
Linens, Silver, etc.: caterer
Restrooms: limited wca
Dance Floor: CBA
Parking: large lot

Overnight Accommodations: no
Telephone: pay phone
Outdoor Night Lighting: yes
Outdoor Cooking Facilities: BBQ
Cleanup: caterer
Other: hosts available
Special: free wine service

RESTRICTIONS:

Alcohol: provided, WC only, no BYO
Smoking: not allowed
Music: amplified with volume control

Wheelchair Access: limited
Insurance: certificate required
Other: no confetti or streamers

SARATOGA FOOTHILL CLUB

20399 Park Place
Saratoga, CA 95070
(408) 867-3428 Dianna
Reserve: 9–12 months in advance

In a spot you'd never expect, on a quiet residential street near the crossroads of Big Basin and Sunnyvale/ Saratoga Roads, lies the Foothill Club. This decorative 1915 Arts and Crafts-style historic landmark was designed by Julia Morgan as a women's club. The old-fashioned brown-shingled facade has a wisteria-covered trellis framing unusually shaped windows. An adjoining paved courtyard is dotted with Japanese maples. It's small but very pretty and private. The Club's formal entry is all in redwood and ushers you into a room that is perfect for a buffet arrangement. The interior's largest room has 30-foot high ceilings, a raised platform stage, hardwood floors and an elaborate window through which glorious sunlight filters in and sets the room aglow. The Foothill Club offers a formal entry space, two interior rooms and an exterior courtyard for fundraisers, business meetings or recitals. All are pleasant, intimate spaces. The final impression is one of old-world comfort and warmth.

CAPACITY: From November–May, the Club's indoor and outdoor combined maximum capacity is 150 guests. From June-October the combined capacity is 185. The indoor maximum seated capacity is 126 guests.

FEES & DEPOSITS: A $200 refundable security deposit is required when reservations are made.

	Business Functions & Private Parties	Nonprofits	Piano Recitals
Food Served	$300	$225	$225
No Food Served	250	175	175

There is a 4-hour maximum for events and business functions.

AVAILABILITY: Tuesday through Sunday, 9:30am–9pm.

SERVICES/AMENITIES:

Restaurant Services: no

Catering: BYO

Kitchen Facilities: moderate

Tables & Chairs: provided

Linens, Silver, etc.: BYO

Restrooms: wca

Dance Floor: yes

Parking: adjacent church lot, $50 donation

Overnight Accommodations: no

Telephone: house phone

Outdoor Night Lighting: no

Outdoor Cooking Facilities: no

Cleanup: caterer

Other: baby grand available

RESTRICTIONS:

Alcohol: BYO, WC only

Smoking: outside only

Music: amplified restricted

Wheelchair Access: no

Insurance: not required

VILLA MONTALVO ★★

15400 Montalvo Road
Saratoga, CA 95071
(408) 741-3421
Reserve: 1 month in advance

The Villa is a stately Mediterranean-style estate nestled against a wooded slope in the private and secluded Saratoga hills. Built in 1912 as the private home of one of San Francisco's former mayors, Villa Montalvo, with its terra cotta tile roofs and light stucco exterior, is now an arboretum and a center for the arts. The Villa is approached from below by a narrow, one-way road offering a striking view of the structure as you round the last turn. Its fine interior rooms are available for events with use of the Spanish Courtyard and another wisteria-laden outdoor courtyard. The tiled and paved verandas are also impressive spots for outdoor receptions. These have sweeping views down the grand steps and main lawn corridor to the Love Temple. Villa Montalvo is an extraordinary site for elegant and sophisticated celebrations.

CAPACITY: The maximum capacity for outdoor functions is 350 guests, indoor capacity 200 guests.

FEES & DEPOSITS: A nonrefundable 50% deposit of the total fee is required when you book your event date. A $1000 security deposit is payable 30 days prior to the event and is usually returned 2 weeks after the event. The special event fee for 8 hours' use is $2400.

AVAILABILITY: Year-round

SERVICES/AMENITIES:

Restaurant Services: no

Catering: BYO, select from list

Kitchen Facilities: ample

Tables & Chairs: provided, extra charge

Linens, Silver, etc.: caterer

Restrooms: no wca

Dance Floor: dancing permitted w/dance floor

Parking: 125 cars, carpooling encouraged

Overnight Accommodations: no

Telephone: pay phone

Outdoor Night Lighting: yes

Outdoor Cooking Facilities: no

Cleanup: caterer

RESTRICTIONS:

Alcohol: BYO, BWC only

Smoking: discouraged, not allowed inside Villa

Music: no amplified

Wheelchair Access: yes

Insurance: not required

STEVE HENDRICKSON
1989 49er Superbowl Champ

My favorite party is a drinking game traditionally held every year on the UC Berkeley campus. First, car keys are put in a community helmet to eliminate drinking and driving. Then the 'Tape Party' begins! Guests draw pieces of trainer's tape marked with football player's names, football plays and miscellaneous things like 'crowd shot' from behind a covering so that nobody can see what's marked. A sip of beer is mandatory when your player, play or miscellaneous part is shown on the TV monitor.

This tradition originated with only 15 guys—this past season 200 people crammed themselves into a 3-bedroom apartment (also called the house of strength). The whole University football team was there, plus baseball players, cheerleaders and other celebs such as Keith Cards (Denver Broncos), David Zewatson (New York Jets) and Dale Ingram (Minnesota Vikings). The apartment is equipped with 7 TV sets including a TV set in the bathroom! It's like being on the New York Stock Exchange—something happening every moment.

Alexander Valley

CHATEAU SOUVERAIN

Independence Lane
Alexander Valley, CA 95441
(707) 433-3141
Reserve: 2–6 months in advance

Slightly north of Healdsburg, Chateau Souverain is beautifully situated on a vine-covered hill which commands a spectacular view of Sonoma's Alexander Valley. The Chateau is one of the few California premium wineries to offer year-round gourmet dining. The main building is approached from a grand staircase that leads from a tree-lined drive below to the large upper courtyard and fountain. The buildings are architecturally striking, designed in the shape of hop kilns with high-peaked slate roofs and extensive window detailing. Inside, Chateau Souverain's two dining rooms are connected by double glass doors. The Main Dining Room with its large fireplace and cathedral ceilings, opens onto the terrace, while the smaller dining area has a view of the fountain. Both are decorated in muted pastels and are well-adorned with stunning flower arrangements. A bit off the beaten path, this winery makes a lovely setting for a quiet and relaxed party or a truly elegant business dinner.

CAPACITY: Chateau Souverain can hold up to 100 guests for private parties, but their main focus is on smaller gatherings. To open during hours when normally closed requires a minimum of 40 guests.

FEES & DEPOSITS: A refundable deposit of $15/person for lunch or brunch, $25/person for dinner is required for any group reservation of 15 guests or more. Deposits are credited to the final bill. For any party larger than 15 guests, a set menu with a minimum of 3 courses is required. A final guest count guarantee is needed 5 working days prior to your function. A 6.25% sales tax and 15% gratuity will be applied to the closing bill. Payment is due in full the day of the event. Special decorations can be provided at an extra charge. Food service is provided for full, seated meals only: brunches and luncheons start at $20/person, dinners at $35.

CANCELLATION POLICY: With 14 days' written notice in advance of your function, your deposit will be refunded.

AVAILABILITY: Functions can take place on Sundays after 5pm.

SERVICES/AMENITIES:

Restaurant Services: yes
Catering: no BYO
Kitchen Facilities: n/a
Tables & Chairs: provided
Linens, Silver, etc.: provided
Restrooms: wca
Dance Floor: CBA

Parking: large lots
Overnight Accommodations: no
Telephone: pay phone
Outdoor Night Lighting: no
Outdoor Cooking Facilities: no
Cleanup: provided

RESTRICTIONS:

Alcohol: provided, WC only, BYO $5/bottle corkage
Smoking: not allowed
Music: no amplified after 9:45pm

Wheelchair Access: yes
Insurance: indemnification clause required
Other: decorations restricted

Calistoga

CALISTOGA INN
Napa Valley Brewing Co.
1250 Lincoln Ave.
Calistoga, CA 94515
(707) 942-4101
Reserve: 1 week in advance

The historic Inn reflects the personality of Calistoga, renowned for its hot springs and spas. A landmark structure built in the early 1900s, the Calistoga Inn provides a nice combination of garden patio with comfortable interior rooms, well-prepared food and a friendly atmosphere. The 'beer garden' is very inviting, with trellis-shaded tables, awning-striped tablecloths and lattice work intertwined with grape leaves. Even the creek adjacent to the patio adds to the relaxed ambiance. The Napa Valley Brewing Co., a microbrewery located in the old water tower in the garden, is receiving acclaim for its home brew. Tasty and cold, it's making lots of people deliriously happy when temperatures soar over 90. If you'd like to plan a celebration or business retreat in this area, we recommend the Inn for a guaranteed pleasant experience.

CAPACITY: The Main Dining Room can seat 80–100 guests, the Annex 35 and the Beer Garden up to 175 seated, 250 for a reception. The indoors maximum is 152 seated.

FEES & DEPOSITS: A $50 refundable deposit is due when reservations are confirmed. No rental fees are required with food service. For business functions without food, the rental is $50–150 depending on group size. Luncheons range from $5–9/person, dinners from $10–18/person. The balance is due at the end of the function. Buffet and hors d'oeuvres parties can be arranged.

CANCELLATION POLICY: A 48-hour notice is requested for a deposit refund.

AVAILABILITY: Year-round, every day 10am–midnight, except for Christmas Day.

SERVICES/AMENITIES:

Restaurant Services: yes
Catering: provided, no BYO
Kitchen Facilities: n/a
Tables & Chairs: provided
Linens, Silver, etc.: provided
Restrooms: wca limited
Dance Floor: CBA

Parking: street
Overnight Accommodations: 17 guestrooms
Telephone: pay phone
Outdoor Night Lighting: yes
Outdoor Cooking Facilities: large grill
Cleanup: provided
Special: beer tastings, event coordination

RESTRICTIONS:
Alcohol: provided, BYO $5/bottle corkage
Smoking: outside only or in Pub
Music: amplified until 11pm

Wheelchair Access: yes
Insurance: not required

CLOS PEGASE ★

1060 Dunaweal Lane
Calistoga, CA 94515
(707) 942-4981
Reserve: 3 weeks in advance

Both controversial and architecturally dramatic, Clos Pegase was designed as a temple to celebrate the marriage of wine and art. The terra cotta-roofed and earth-toned buildings bring to mind ancient images—a bit of Egyptian grandeur and classic Roman symmetry. This site is impressive, indeed. Although no private parties are permitted, the winery is available for corporate functions, food and beverage industry and arts groups events. The Dining Room is clean, stylish and sophisticated with detailed wood cabinets, high ceiling and subtle colors. For a very unique experience, have your group meet in the new underground 'Cave', a tunnel into the mountainside created for cool and controlled wine storage. Softly lit and appointed with ancient artifacts nestled into alcoves along the Cave's corridors, the Cave is extraordinary for a business lecture or cocktail party. There's a room with a stage for formal presentations, too.

CAPACITY: The Dining Room can seat 50–70 guests, The Cave 140 seated and the Garden 400 seated.

FEES & DEPOSITS: A $250 refundable deposit is due when reservations are confirmed. For groups, there is a winery charge of $10 plus 1/2 bottle per guest. Catered dinners range from $25–55/person including tour and tasting. Tax and tip are additional.

CANCELLATION POLICY: With 7 days' notice, you will receive a full refund.

AVAILABILITY: Year-round, except for New Year's and Christmas days, and Thanksgiving. Any time until midnight.

SERVICES/AMENITIES:
Restaurant Services: no
Catering: preferred list or BYO with approval
Kitchen Facilities: fully equipped
Tables & Chairs: provided
Linens, Silver, etc.: provided
Restrooms: wca
Dance Floor: no

Parking: large lots
Overnight Accommodations: no
Telephone: pay phone
Outdoor Night Lighting: yes
Outdoor Cooking Facilities: BBQ
Cleanup: Clos Pegase and caterer
Special: wine tours & tastings, wine & art slide show

RESTRICTIONS:
Alcohol: W provided, no BYO
Smoking: outside only
Music: with approval

Wheelchair Access: yes
Insurance: not required

ONCE IN A LIFETIME BALLOON COMPANY

1458 Lincoln Ave. #12
Calistoga, CA 94515
(800) 722-6665
Reserve: 1–2 months in advance

Up, up and away in your beautiful balloon! What a magnificent way to have a party—in a 7-story high hot air balloon. For one hour, you and your select group of friends, family or workmates can soar above the colorful tapestry of Napa Valley. Share an air current with a local bird, and breathe in the cool, crisp air of high altitudes. When your flight is over and your appetite whetted, you and your guests can reminisce about your "uplifting" adventure over a gourmet breakfast in quaint Calistoga. You have to get up with the sun and dress warmly, but it's worth it for this once-in-a-lifetime experience.

CAPACITY: Two balloon sizes are available; one holds 6, the other 8 passengers. The pilot is additional.

FEES & DEPOSITS: The total fee is payable when the reservation is made. Usually a group reserves the entire balloon. If there are only 2 of you, you'll probably share the balloon with strangers. The 6-passenger balloon rental is $930 and the 8-passenger is $1116. This includes the one-hour flight, a gourmet brunch at the Cinnabar Restaurant in Calistoga following the flight, a color photo, and flight certificate. For each person over the 6 or 8 in the balloon party, add $15 for brunch.

CANCELLATION POLICY: If you cancel with 30 days' notice, you'll receive a full refund. Between 2–4 weeks' notice, 50% will be refunded.

AVAILABILITY: Weather permitting, daily from 5am–7am, when air currents are best.

SERVICES/AMENITIES:
Parking: ample

RESTRICTIONS:
Alcohol: not allowed in balloon
Smoking: not allowed
Music: possible

Wheelchair Access: yes
Insurance: not required

STERLING VINEYARDS

1111 Dunaweal Lane
Calistoga, CA 94515
(707) 942-5151
Reserve: 3 weeks in advance

Reached by an aerial tram ride up a steep 300-foot knoll, Sterling Vineyards, appears from the distance like a white castle on a mountaintop. Constructed in 1969 as a state-of-the-art winery, Sterling has architecture reminiscent of an old Mediterranean monastery, with white walls, clean straight lines and rounded belfries. Unique to Sterling is the self-guided tour—passageways and overlooks that allow guests to view the entire winemaking process without a guide. Guests park below and take the tram up for group functions. The Club Room, Main Tasting Room and Atrium all have panoramic views of the vineyards below and the Napa hills beyond. The winery holds many business events here, including tours, tastings, plus cooking and wine demonstrations.

CAPACITY: The Club Room can seat 80; the Main Tasting Room and Atrium, 200. The facility can hold 280 guests inside and with outdoor spaces, 350 maximum.

FEES & DEPOSITS: Half the total estimated winery cost is due approximately 1 month prior to the event. Winery costs include use of space, wine, guided tours, tables, chairs and glasses for up to 175 guests. Fees for use of space: receptions $7/person, luncheons $9/person, dinners $14/person (1–100 guests) and $12/person (over 100 guests). Rental minimums are $300 for lunch and $400 for dinner. The final balance is invoiced, payable 30 days following the event. Luncheon event fees include the tram ride. However, the tram fee for guests arriving 5–6:15pm is $200/group; 6:15pm onwards $400/group.

CANCELLATION POLICY: With 2 weeks' notice you will receive a full refund.

AVAILABILITY: Year-round, closed major holidays. Event hours are 10am–11:30pm.

SERVICES/AMENITIES:

Restaurant Services: no
Catering: preferred list or BYO, licensed
Kitchen Facilities: ample
Tables & Chairs: up to 175
Linens, Silver, etc.: caterer
Restrooms: wca
Dance Floor: Atrium

Parking: large lots
Overnight Accommodations: no
Telephone: pay phone
Outdoor Night Lighting: yes
Outdoor Cooking Facilities: CBA
Cleanup: Sterling and caterer
Special: wine tours, tram ride, wine information

RESTRICTIONS:

Alcohol: provided, no BYO
Smoking: outside only
Music: amplified inside only

Wheelchair Access: yes
Insurance: not required
Other: no fireworks, weddings, birthday parties

Geyserville

ISIS OASIS RETREAT CENTER

20889 Geyserville Avenue
Geyserville, CA 95441
(707) 857-3524
Reserve: 6 months in advance

This is a New Age retreat for those who wish to relax, rejuvenate or expand the mind. Isis Oasis provides a supportive environment for private celebrations or groups coming for workshops and seminars. Occupying 10 acres of fertile wine country, the Center has 4 main buildings (some historical), yurts, a wine barrel room and an Egyptian-style meditation temple. There's also a theater, a redwood structure enhanced by stained glass with stage, balcony, and sound system. A separate dining pavilion serves as the main eating area and meeting room. The outdoor areas are a wonderful mix of the rustic and not-so-rustic. A pool, spa and sauna are available for those who want to unwind. For nature lovers, there's an expansive garden, the adjacent vineyard, a pond for waterfowl and a mini-zoo, featuring a variety of common and exotic animals. Pheasant, peacock, doves and emu are here, along with ocelots, serval cats, a llama, black sheep, pygmy goats and dwarf rabbits. Your Isis Oasis hosts are Lora Vigne, an artist, non-denominational minister and tarot reader and her partner, Paul, a Gestalt therapist, past-life guide and counselor who presides over men's con-sciousness-raising groups. At Isis Oasis, you'll be able to have an out-of-the-ordinary business meeting or a personal experience connecting you with both ancient wisdoms and the evolving New Age.

CAPACITY: Groups from 9 to 100 people. There is a wide range of facilities, with various capacities. Call for details.

MEETING ROOMS: 1 large, carpeted room that accommodates 50 seated participants; the Theater for 100 participants and the Dining Pavilion for 100.

FEES & DEPOSITS: 15% of the total lodging cost is due when reservations are confirmed. To rent the entire facility, the fee is $1500/night. The remaining 85% is payable on arrival. Rates for individual parts of Isis Oasis run about $20–25/person per night. Meals are served buffet style, with breakfasts at $5, luncheons at $7 and dinners at $12/person. An all-day meal rate is $24/day including tax. No gratuity is required. The payment for meals is due upon departure.

CANCELLATION POLICY: A 1–2 month notice is required, depending on which space(s) is reserved.

AVAILABILITY: Year–round, every day.

SERVICES/AMENITIES:

Restaurant Services: no
Catering: provided or BYO
Kitchen Facilities: ample, $75/day if BYO
Tables & Chairs: provided

Linens, Silver, etc.: provided
Restrooms: some wca
Dance Floor: pavilion
Parking: large lots

Overnight Accommodations: 22 guestrooms
Telephone: guest phone
Outdoor Night Lighting: yes
Outdoor Cooking Facilities: BBQ

RESTRICTIONS:
Alcohol: WB provided or BYO, no hard liquor
Smoking: outside only
Music: amplified w/in limits

Cleanup: provided or renter
Special: pool available, zoo tour, massage therapist, meditation temple

Wheelchair Access: limited
Insurance: sometimes required
Other: children need supervision

Guerneville

THE ESTATE

13555 Highway 116
Guerneville, CA 95446
(707) 869-9093
Reserve: 1–6 months in advance

For a small corporate retreat or personal party, The Estate cannot be surpassed. Originally the oversized home of Guerneville's bank president in the early 1900s, it is a quiet and sophisticated oasis in the heart of Sonoma's Russian River area. Make plans to stay overnight in this nicely detailed and elegantly furnished bed and breakfast. Each room is comfortable yet distinguished, with potted palms, stone fireplaces and windows overlooking the lush greenery outdoors. A beautifully designed pool area can be used for outdoor parties or meetings. The owners delight in catering to the needs of every guest, creating an environment conducive to good friendships and working relationships. A perfect setting in which to relax and unwind, The Estate is a handsome home away from home.

CAPACITY: The Estate can hold 10–20 guests; overnight stays are required.

FEES & DEPOSITS: A deposit in the amount of 1 night's stay will secure your reservation. The rate for the entire house on Friday, Saturday or Sunday is $1210 plus tax. Monday–Thursday rates are discounted by 20%. All stays include breakfast and coffee service throughout the day. Catering is provided. Luncheons range from $10–15/person, dinners $20–30/person and hors d'oeuvres start at $10/person. The Estate's cordial and accommodating owners will customize any menu for your private party. The balance is due upon departure.

CANCELLATION POLICY: With 30 days' notice, a full refund will be given. With less than 30, a full or partial refund is possible only if the rooms can be rebooked.

AVAILABILITY: Year-round, every day.

SERVICES/AMENITIES:
Restaurant Services: no

Catering: provided, no BYO

Kitchen Facilities: n/a
Tables & Chairs: provided
Linens, Silver, etc.: provided
Restrooms: wca
Dance Floor: no
Parking: large lot
Overnight Accommodations: 10 guestrooms

Telephone: guest phone
Outdoor Night Lighting: yes
Outdoor Cooking Facilities: BBQ
Cleanup: provided
Other: event coordination
Special: pool available

RESTRICTIONS:
Alcohol: WB provided,
BYO $5/bottle corkage at meals
Smoking: outside only
Music: no amplified

Wheelchair Access: yes
Insurance: not required
Other: no children, no pets

Healdsburg

ALDERBROOK WINERY

2306 Magnolia Drive
Healdsburg, CA 95448
(707) 433-9154 Kathy Mooney
Reserve: 1–3 months in advance

The drive to Alderbrook takes you through some very pretty country filled with vineyards. The 63-acre ranch was purchased in 1981 and transformed into Alderbrook Winery. Surrounded by 55 acres of estate vineyards, the Winery now features a new but old-fashioned looking gray structure with broad verandas and railings painted in contrasting white. Inside, there's one large, open room with a light hardwood floor, white brick fireplace and walls of bleached pine. This is a spacious and airy space with tropical plants and lots of French doors and glass. The wide porches have great views of the surrounding vineyards and hillsides, and one side faces a magnificent line of Lombardy Poplar trees that change color in the fall. Dressed up for a formal party or dressed down for a relaxed country-style picnic, the Alderbrook Winery succeeds because it's well designed and offers a refreshing, simple elegance to a company or private party.

CAPACITY: Alderbrook can hold up to 200 guests, depending on the season.

FEES & DEPOSITS: A $200 cleaning/security deposit is required, $50 of which is nonrefundable. The rental fee and deposit are required to reserve a date. The deposit is usually returned within 5 working days of the event. The rental fee is $250. For groups of 60 or more, a $60 staff fee is required. For any cleanup time beyond 11:30pm, a charge of $50 is applied. A minimum wine purchase of 2 cases, at a 10% discount, is required.

CANCELLATION POLICY: Written notice is needed 30 days prior to your function for a full refund of the rental fee.

AVAILABILITY: For events, the winery is available daily from 6pm-10:30pm except for major holidays.

SERVICES/AMENITIES:

Restaurant Services: no

Catering: select from list

Kitchen Facilities: ample

Tables & Chairs: BYO

Linens, Silver, etc.: BYO

Restrooms: wca

Dance Floor: yes

Parking: large lot

Overnight Accommodations: no

Telephone: restricted

Outdoor Night Lighting: yes

Outdoor Cooking Facilities: BYO BBQ

Cleanup: caterer

Other: special box lunches CBA

RESTRICTIONS:

Alcohol: provided, WC only

Smoking: outside only

Music: amplified ok

Wheelchair Access: ramp

Insurance: indemnification clause and extra liability required

Other: minimum wine purchase required

MADRONA MANOR ★★

1001 Westside Road

Healdsburg, CA 95448

(707) 433-4231

Reserve: 2–12 months in advance

Madrona Manor is an exceptionally lovely Victorian house set high over the Dry Creek Valley of Sonoma County, surrounded by eight acres of wooded and landscaped grounds. Built in 1881 by John Paxton, a wealthy San Francisco businessman, the three-story stately Manor and adjacent buildings originally served as his summer home and weekend retreat. Now a large bed and breakfast inn, the Manor complex provides its guests with an elegant country ambiance. The Manor's interior rooms come complete with antique furniture, Persian carpets and hand-carved rosewood detailing. Outside a sizable deck overlooks a meticulously manicured lawn and flower beds. A Carriage House providing additional guestrooms, an herb, vegetable and citrus garden, plus pool create a wonderful environment for corporate events, reunions and parties. Madrona Manor offers an extensive wine list and beautifully prepared meals containing ingredients that are always fresh. The Manor is so pleasant, pretty and tranquil, we guarantee you'll want to come back for more after the party's over.

CAPACITY: The Manor can accommodate up to 100 guests, 135 in good weather.

MEETING ROOMS: The Manor has a meeting room for up to 35 participants.

FEES & DEPOSITS: The rental fee for meeting rooms is $50/day. Food service is provided and ranges from $5/person (coffee service only) to $45/person. Other fees will vary according to the needs of the group. A 6.25% sales tax and 15% gratuity are applied to the total bill.

CANCELLATION POLICY: If you cancel 30 days prior to the event, your deposit will be refunded in full.

AVAILABILITY: Meetings from Monday–Saturday, 8am–5pm. Special events and parties, any time.

SERVICES/AMENITIES:

Restaurant Services: yes
Catering: provided, no BYO
Kitchen Facilities: n/a
Tables & Chairs: provided
Linens, Silver, etc.: provided
Restrooms: wca
Dance Floor: yes

Parking: large lot
Overnight Accommodations: 21 guestrooms
Telephone: pay phone
Outdoor Night Lighting: yes
Outdoor Cooking Facilities: no
Cleanup: provided
Other: made-to-order special event desserts

RESTRICTIONS:

Alcohol: provided, WBC only
Smoking: allowed
Music: no amplified

Wheelchair Access: yes
Insurance: not required
Other: decorating restrictions

Kenwood

KENWOOD DEPOT

314 Warm Springs Road
Kenwood, CA 95452
(707) 833-5190
Reserve: 2–3 months in advance

In the heart of Sonoma's Valley of the Moon you'll find the Kenwood Depot—a most unusual party spot. The building was a train depot, established in 1888 for passenger and freight traffic through the Valley. It's a charming and rustic structure, built of large hand-chiseled stone and wood. The tracks are gone now and the trains no longer operate, but the picturesque Depot remains. Although appropriate only for smaller business functions or celebrations, the Depot makes up for this limitation by having a cozy, intimate ambiance. For a winter party, there's a blazing fire in the fireplace and in the heat of the summer, the stone walls make the interior a cool oasis for guests. If you want a small country gathering in an historic building, the Depot is worth a look.

CAPACITY: The Depot can accommodate up to 125 standing guests, 80 seated.

FEES & DEPOSITS: A $100 refundable security/cleaning deposit is required to secure your date. These fees are due 30 days prior to your event.

Day	Time	Fee
Saturday & Sunday	6am–2am	$250
Saturday & Sunday	6am–5pm	150
Friday Evenings	5pm–2am	150
Monday-Friday	6am–5pm	$20/hour or $100/day

CANCELLATION POLICY: If you cancel 30 or more days prior to the event, your deposit will be refunded in full. If less than 30 days, 50% will be refunded.

AVAILABILITY: Any day; times are noted above.

SERVICES/AMENITIES:

Restaurant Services: no
Catering: BYO or CBA
Kitchen Facilities: moderate
Tables & Chairs: provided
Linens, Silver, etc.: BYO
Restrooms: no wca
Dance Floor: yes

Parking: ample
Overnight Accommodations: no
Telephone: local calls only
Outdoor Night Lighting: no
Outdoor Cooking Facilities: no
Cleanup: caterer or CBA extra fee
Other: horse & carriage CBA

RESTRICTIONS:

Alcohol: BYO
Smoking: allowed
Music: amplified until midnight

Wheelchair Access: yes
Insurance: certificate required
Other: no tacks or staples

ORESTE'S GOLDEN BEAR

1717 Adobe Canyon Road
Kenwood, CA 95452
(707) 833-2327 Mark Barrett
Reserve: 2–3 months in advance

Oreste's Golden Bear Restaurant is located just off Highway 12, a few miles from the Sonoma wine country town of Kenwood. It's nestled on the slope of Hood Mountain and is approached from a lovely sun-dappled country road. This is where mineral springs, pond and cascading Sonoma Creek made the original 'Golden Bear' rustic lodge a popular place in the 1920s for hunters and fishermen. The legendary lodge was converted into a restaurant some time ago and is now owned by the sons of San Francisco's well-known chef, Oreste Orsi. Oreste's brings authentic Northern Italian cuisine to a stunning creekside setting within 35 acres of park-like grounds. Featuring a huge 40-foot stone BBQ, ideal for outdoor events, the restaurant also has umbrella-shaded terraces outdoors which hug the edge of rocky Sonoma Creek. During summer months, the creek is dammed to form pools next to which guests can relax and enjoy the celebration. If you want to get away from the crowds, this facility provides an exceptional outdoor setting from late spring to early autumn.

CAPACITY: The Restaurant can hold up to 150 seated guests and the outdoor terraces 200 seated guests.

FEES & DEPOSITS: A $250 refundable deposit is required when you reserve your event date. No rental fee is required. Food service is provided. Special menus can be arranged for parties of less than 50, however for buffets and large BBQ parties, you need a minimum of 50 guests. Oreste's is well known for its full course, seated BBQ meals, $18-$25/person. Buffets start at $16/person. A 6.25% sales tax and 18% gratuity are applied to the final bill.

CANCELLATION POLICY: With 60 days' notice, your deposit is refunded.

AVAILABILITY: Year-round, Saturdays 7am–5pm and Monday–Friday until 5pm. Monday–Friday you can have an exclusive rental of the Restaurant with a guaranteed 150 guests. Sundays are not available for private parties.

SERVICES/AMENITIES:

Restaurant Services: yes

Catering: provided, no BYO

Kitchen Facilities: n/a

Tables & Chairs: provided

Linens, Silver, etc.: provided

Restrooms: wca

Dance Floor: yes

Parking: large lot

Overnight Accommodations: no

Telephone: pay phone

Outdoor Night Lighting: yes

Outdoor Cooking Facilities: 40-foot BBQ

Cleanup: provided

RESTRICTIONS:

Alcohol: provided,
BYO corkage $5/bottle, WBC only

Smoking: allowed

Music: amplified ok

Wheelchair Access: yes

Insurance: not required

Napa

CHIMNEY ROCK WINERY

5350 Silverado Trail
Napa, CA 94558
(707) 257-2641 Kathy Higgins
Reserve: 1–2 months in advance

Chimney Rock is located on the Silverado Trail near Yountville. It's a relatively new winery, set among 75 acres of vineyards in the famed Stags Leap District, known for its superlative wine growing conditions. Bordered by a stand of tall Lombardy poplars, the Hospitality Center was built for both wine tasting and special events. Designed in a Cape Dutch style, the building is tastefully appointed, with huge fireplace, beamed cathedral ceiling and hardwood floors. French doors lead to a large outdoor patio. The garden here is enclosed, sheltered on all sides by the walls of the buildings. On the upper portion of the winery building, facing guests as they enter the garden, is an impressive relief of Ganymede, cupbearer to the Gods. Sun plays with the relief's shadows during the day and at night when lit, the relief is stunning. The interior garden has a lush lawn, divided in half by a falling cascade. Pretty and private, Chimney Rock is well suited for entertaining.

CAPACITY: Indoors, the facility can hold up to 60 seated guests; outdoors up to 150 seated. The winery barrel room can hold up to 100 seated guests. The winery maximum is 150 guests.

FEES & DEPOSITS: A deposit of 50% of the total estimated rental is required to secure your date. The balance is due the day of the event. The rental fee is $30/person which includes all wine, wine service, glassware, flowers, tables, chairs and cleanup.

CANCELLATION POLICY: If you cancel, 25% of the deposit will be forfeited.

AVAILABILITY: Year-round, except for Christmas and Thanksgiving. Events outside, any time from 10am–11pm. Indoor functions from 5pm–11pm only.

SERVICES/AMENITIES:

Restaurant Services: no
Catering: preferred list
Kitchen Facilities: fully equipped
Tables & Chairs: provided
Linens, Silver, etc.: BYO
Restrooms: wca
Dance Floor: CBA

Parking: large lot
Overnight Accommodations: no
Telephone: business phone
Outdoor Night Lighting: yes
Outdoor Cooking Facilities: CBA
Cleanup: provided
Other: winery tours, barrel sampling

RESTRICTIONS:

Alcohol: W provided,
BYO champagne $5/bottle corkage
Smoking: outside only
Music: amplified ok

Wheelchair Access: yes
Insurance: not required
Other: no hard alcohol

CHURCHILL MANOR

485 Brown Street
Napa, CA 94559
(707) 253-7733 Joanna
Reserve: 1–12 months in advance

Set back from the street by an expansive green lawn dotted with annuals and a formal fountain, Churchill Manor is very impressive at first glance. Built in 1889 in the heart of historic residential Napa, the Manor is now a Victorian bed and breakfast inn featuring an antique-appointed interior, wide verandas and lovely landscaped grounds. The main entry doors with their detailed leaded glass inset panels, lead into several parlors, each with separate stone fireplaces, period furnishings, fine woodwork, original lighting fixtures and ornate ceilings. The spacious white-painted solarium adjacent to the main buffet room is very inviting, with large leaded glass windows, mosaic marble tile floor and white furniture. Churchill Manor's interior spaces all combine to make you feel like you've stepped back in time to a slower, more gracious period. This is a terrific spot for a peaceful and quiet corporate retreat or seminar. The Manor's staff take great pains to provide helpful service, assisting with every detail. You can even reserve all 10 guestrooms and have the entire Manor exclusively for your business group or party guests.

CAPACITY: In winter, the Manor accommodates a maximum of 80 guests inside. In spring and fall, including veranda, 175 guests. In summer, including garden and veranda, 215 guests.

MEETING ROOMS: 2 rooms, 60–75 max.

FEES & DEPOSITS: A nonrefundable $250 is required and will be credited against your bill if no damages are incurred. For a full-service event on Saturday, the fee is $1200. For Sunday-Friday events the fees vary: under 35 guests, $600; 35-60 guests, $900; and over 60 guests, $1200. If you wish to seat over 125 guests, there's an extra setup charge. The total balance, with a final guest count, is due 10 days prior to the event date.

If you reserve all 10 guestrooms, the total room rental fee is $1090/night plus tax. Note that if the event occurs on a Saturday between May and October, guestrooms must be booked for a minimum of 2 nights. Except for business meetings, a 6-hour maximum rental block is allowed and a $200/hour charge is levied for any time over 6 hours. Food service is provided and any menu can be customized. A buffet reception costs approximately $17.50–22.50/person including an hors d'oeuvres table. A 6.25% sales tax and 15% gratuity are added to the final food bill.

AVAILABILITY: If you reserve all 10 guestrooms, your party can extend, in a 6-hour block, from 1pm to 10pm. If you don't reserve the entire Manor, you are restricted to the hours of 1pm–5:30pm.

SERVICES/AMENITIES:

Restaurant Services: no
Catering: provided, no BYO
Kitchen Facilities: n/a
Tables & Chairs: most provided
Linens, Silver, etc.: provided
Restrooms: wca, plus guestrooms
Dance Floor: yes

Parking: 20 car lot, on street
Overnight Accommodations: 10 guestrooms
Telephone: house phone if local
Outdoor Night Lighting: yes
Outdoor Cooking Facilities: CBA
Cleanup: provided
Other: baby grand piano

RESTRICTIONS:

Alcohol: BYO, WCB only
Smoking: outside only
Music: amplified outside until 6:30, inside until 10pm

Wheelchair Access: limited
Insurance: not required
Other: children must be supervised

EMBASSY SUITES HOTEL

1075 California Blvd.
Napa, CA 94559
(707) 253-9161 Catering
Reserve: 1–6 months in advance

The Embassy Suites Hotel, located near downtown Napa, offers spacious and varied accommodations for any size party or business function. This Mediterranean-style hotel, with pastel walls, red tile roof, and stone arches, greets entering guests with fountains and a circular palm-tree-lined driveway. Moving through one of the outdoor courtyards, with a working wood mill and mill pond with waterfowl, lush plantings and small waterfalls, you step into an interior restaurant atrium resplendent in Mexican tile pavers, potted trees and high ceilings. The Embassy Suite facilities for special events adjoin the atrium. These spaces offer high ceilings, large tropical plants, terra cotta tile floors, skylight and indoor fountain. The surrounding rooms can be combined to expand in any way to meet your guest requirements. If you wish to stay overnight, the Embassy has saunas, spas and both indoor and outdoor pools in addition to distinctive suites with fireplaces and wet bars.

CAPACITY: The Embassy has a variety of spaces available and can accommodate a range of 25 to 250 seated guests.

FEES & DEPOSITS: A refundable $200–500 deposit is required when you reserve your date; the amount varies depending on the number of guests and the complexity of the event. Per person rates: luncheons are approximately $14, seated dinners $19, and buffet service $22. A 6.25% sales tax and 17% gratuity will be applied to the final bill. The total balance is due 72 hours prior to your event and any remaining balance is payable at the event's conclusion.

CANCELLATION POLICY: With less than 30 days' notice, the deposit is forfeited.

AVAILABILITY: 6am to 2am every day

SERVICES/AMENITIES:

Restaurant Services: yes
Catering: provided, no BYO
Kitchen Facilities: n/a
Tables & Chairs: provided
Linens, Silver, etc.: provided
Restrooms: wca
Dance Floor: yes

Parking: large lots
Overnight Accommodations: 205 suites
Telephone: pay phones
Outdoor Night Lighting: limited
Outdoor Cooking Facilities: no
Cleanup: provided
Other: grand piano

RESTRICTIONS:

Alcohol: provided, CW only,
BYO corkage $6/bottle
Smoking: allowed

Music: amplified ok
Wheelchair Access: yes
Insurance: not required

NAPA RIVER BOAT

Napa Valley Marina
1200 Milton Road
Napa, CA 94559
(707) 226-2628 Judy
Reserve: 3–6 months in advance

Plan your next event aboard the authentic sternwheeler, 'City of Napa' and return to a slower-paced, gentler period. Your unique event cruise can be as formal as an antebellum plantation ball or as casual as a relaxed weekend picnic. Antique lighting, oak bar and rich mahogany paneling grace the interior. Enjoy your meals, served on crisp linens and beautifully presented on settings of gleaming crystal and china. You can relax here. Your business meeting or event will be uninterrupted except for the sounds of splashing water from the Napa River Boat's paddlewheel.

CAPACITY: The entire vessel holds up to 100 standing and 80 seated guests.

MEETING ROOM: Upper deck; 48 seated. Lower deck; 36 seated.

FEES & DEPOSITS: A deposit of 25% of the estimated total fee is required when your contract is returned. For boat rental only, the fee is $250/hr for a 2-hour minimum cruising time. Rental plus food service runs $24–40/person, depending on whether it is a brunch or a 4-course gourmet seated meal. The rental fee is for a 3-hour rental. A tax of 6.25% and gratuity of 15% are added to the final bill which is due 3 working days prior to the event.

CANCELLATION POLICY: With 30 days' notice your deposit is fully refundable; less than 30 days' 80% is refundable if the date can be rebooked.

AVAILABILITY: Any day, any time.

SERVICES/AMENITIES:

Restaurant Services: no
Catering: provided, or BYO if rented by hour
Kitchen Facilities: full galley
Tables & Chairs: provided
Linens, Silver, etc.: provided or BYO if hourly rental
Restrooms: no wca
Dance Floor: yes

Parking: marina lots
Overnight Accommodations: no
Telephone: radio
Outdoor Night Lighting: yes
Outdoor Cooking Facilities: no
Cleanup: whoever caters event
Other: event services

RESTRICTIONS:

Alcohol: provided, BYO corkage $5/bottle
Smoking: outside decks only
Music: amplified ok, space limited

Wheelchair Access: lower deck only
Insurance: not required

NAPA VALLEY COUNTRY CLUB

3385 Hagen Road
Napa, CA 94558
(707) 252-1111
Reserve: 4–6 months in advance

Set amid a particularly beautiful golf course, the Clubhouse is well situated on a rise overlooking manicured fairways. The drive up to the Club is very scenic, through pretty country roads bordered by old farm houses and vineyards. The Clubhouse is a relatively small structure with a low roof profile, dark brown wood siding and a rustic appearance. It features one large dining room available for private parties which has a big river rock stone fireplace, full bar and wall-to-wall picture windows overlooking emerald green lawns. For a small gathering, the Napa Valley Country Club is a comfortable and pleasant place.

CAPACITY: The main dining room can accommodate 150 guests.

FEES & DEPOSITS: A $125 refundable security deposit and $50 nonrefundable cleaning deposit are required to secure your event date. For 80 guests, the fee is $100; for more than 80, the fee is $150. All fees are due within 30 days after the event. Food service is provided. Hors d'oeuvres receptions cost approximately $12-14/person, and seated meals between $12-18/person. Sales tax of 6.25% and a 15% gratuity are applied toward the total food and beverage cost.

AVAILABILITY: Tuesday-Sunday after 6:30pm.

SERVICES/AMENITIES:

Restaurant Services: yes
Catering: provided, no BYO
Kitchen Facilities: ample
Tables & Chairs: most provided
Linens, Silver, etc.: most provided
Restrooms: no wca
Dance Floor: yes

Parking: large lot
Overnight Accommodations: no
Telephone: pay phone
Outdoor Night Lighting: yes
Outdoor Cooking Facilities: BBQ
Cleanup: provided

RESTRICTIONS:

Alcohol: provided, BYO corkage $5/bottle
Smoking: allowed
Music: amplified ok

Wheelchair Access: no
Insurance: not required
Other: no staples

NAPA VALLEY WINE TRAIN

1275 McKinstry Street
Napa, CA 94559
(707) 253-0920 Gail Sepanek
Reserve: 1–4 months in advance

All aboard! You and your private party can return to the gracious era of elegant rail travel while gliding gently past the famous vineyards of Napa Valley. Embark at the Wine Train's station in the historic town of Napa. You are whisked away in luxury Pullman lounge and dining cars, painstakingly restored and resplendent in polished mahogany, brass and etched glass. Savor a gourmet brunch, lunch or an exquisitely prepared four-course dinner served in style: white damask linens, bone china, silver flatware and crystal. And, of course, the wine selection is superb, with over 28 Napa Valley varietals available by the glass for your own wine tasting. So hop aboard these turn-of-the-century cars. Every brunch, lunch and dinner round-trip excursion is a 36-mile, 3-hour nonstop adventure.

CAPACITY: The Wine Train can accommodate 10 to 240 guests.

FEES & DEPOSITS: A 50% refundable deposit is required to hold a group reservation. For private lunch or brunch groups, the group train fare is $26.10/person and food service is an additional $22/person. For group dinner parties, the fare is $12/person and dinners are $45/person. A final guest count guarantee plus the remaining fees are due 30 days in advance of your scheduled train party. A 6.25% sales tax and 15% service charge will be applied.

CANCELLATION POLICY: The deposit is refundable with 1 month's notice prior to your function.

AVAILABILITY: The trains operate year-round on a daily basis.

SERVICES/AMENITIES:

Restaurant Services: yes

Catering: no BYO

Kitchen Facilities: aboard train

Tables & Chairs: provided

Linens, Silver, etc.: provided

Restrooms: lounge car, no wca

Dance Floor: no

Parking: large lot

Overnight Accommodations: no

Telephone: pay phone

Outdoor Night Lighting: no

Outdoor Cooking Facilities: no

Cleanup: provided

RESTRICTIONS:

Alcohol: provided, BYO corkage $10/bottle

Smoking: not allowed

Music: no bands, pa system on train

Wheelchair Access: limited

Insurance: not required

Other: decorations restricted

SILVERADO COUNTRY CLUB AND RESORT

1600 Atlas Peak Road
Napa, CA 94558
(707) 257-5450 Catering
Reserve: 1–3 months in advance

Although primarily a first class golf course country club and a convention facility, the Silverado does allow private parties. The stately white mansion is the hub of the facility, and is approached by a formal, circular driveway lined with palms. The Patio Terrace located at the back of the mansion overlooks one of the fairway tees and is a lovely outdoor spot for small receptions complete with tables and colorful umbrellas. The convention facility next door houses the Ballroom. This enormous room can be partitioned into smaller segments. The room's appointments are in muted rose colors and huge chandeliers grace the ceiling. At one end of the Ballroom are French doors leading to the Fairway Deck, also with great views of the golf course. Other party spots include the Arbor, a brick patio with colonnades perfect for small gatherings with a backdrop of vines on a brick wall and the main Pool Area Patio adjacent to the Club's pool. The Picnic Grove in the center of the golf course has huge trees, a sea of green lawns and a quiet and peaceful outdoor environment. It's quite a hike from the mansion, so tell your guests to wear low-heeled shoes.

CAPACITY:

Space	Seated Capacity	Space	Seated Capacity
Ballroom	400 max.	Arbor	200 max.
Patio Terrace	100 max.	Picnic Grove	1000 max.
Pool Area Patio	250 max.		

FEES & DEPOSITS: Depends on the total number of guests and the season. Roughly, fees are $200/100 guests (minimum) and $2/person for over 100 guests. Food service is provided. A buffet reception costs approximately $30/person and seated meals cost $35-85/person. Alcoholic beverages are additional and sales tax at 6.25% and gratuity at 17% are applied to final food and beverage bill. Full payment is due 48 hours prior to your party. A 5-hour rental minimum is required.

CANCELLATION POLICY: With 30 days' notice, your deposit is refunded.

AVAILABILITY: March–November are busy months for conventions. For parties and events, it's easier to book a reservation between November and February. Spaces can be reserved for any day of the week, any time.

SERVICES/AMENITIES:

Restaurant Services: yes
Catering: no BYO
Kitchen Facilities: n/a
Tables & Chairs: provided
Linens, Silver, etc.: provided
Restrooms: wca
Dance Floor: CBA

Parking: adjacent lots, valet CBA
Overnight Accommodations: 278 condos
Telephone: pay phones
Outdoor Night Lighting: yes
Outdoor Cooking Facilities: BBQs
Cleanup: provided
Other: in-house audio-visual services

RESTRICTIONS:

Alcohol: provided, no BYO
Smoking: allowed
Music: amplified ok

Wheelchair Access: yes
Insurance: not required

Petaluma

GARDEN VALLEY RANCH

498 Pepper Road
Petaluma, CA 94952
(707) 795-0919   Robert Galyean
Reserve: 6–12 months in advance

If you are a rose lover, gardening or horticulture buff, Garden Valley Ranch, located 3 miles north of Petaluma, is the perfect location for your next outdoor event. Corporate BBQs, picnics, garden tour luncheons and wine tastings can be held amidst the roses. This 7-acre ranch contains some 4000 rosebushes cultivated for the sale of their blooms and a 1-acre garden where fragrant plants are grown for potpourri blends. Several Victorian-style structures, large lawn and adjacent gardens are available for events. Tents, canopies, tables with umbrellas and dance floor can be set up on the lawns, creating a comfortable environment for the ultimate garden party.

CAPACITY: The facility can accommodate up to 200 guests for outdoor functions.

FEES & DEPOSITS: A nonrefundable security deposit totaling 50% of the rental fee is payable when reservations are confirmed. A refundable security deposit of $300, the remaining 50% of the rental fee and equipment fees are due 2 weeks prior to the function. Rental rates for a 4-hour block: up to 50 guests $500, 51–100 guests $650, 101–150 guests $800, 151–200 guests $950. Extra time is available for an extra fee. Flowers can be purchased from May–October.

CANCELLATION POLICY: The security deposit will be refunded within 15 days after the event, depending on the condition of the property.

AVAILABILITY: May–October, Wednesday–Sunday 10am–8pm, one event per day. Because of weather conditions, the best times for events are 10am–2pm and 4pm–8pm.

SERVICES/AMENITIES:

Restaurant Services: no

Catering: BYO

Kitchen Facilities: moderate

Tables & Chairs: provided extra charge

Linens, Silver, etc.: BYO

Restrooms: wca

Dance Floor: at Belvedere

Parking: large lots

Overnight Accommodations: no

Telephone: office phone

Outdoor Night Lighting: no

Outdoor Cooking Facilities: BBQ with approval

Cleanup: caterer or CBA extra fee

Other: tents CBA extra fee

RESTRICTIONS:

Alcohol: BYO

Smoking: allowed

Music: amplified ok

Wheelchair Access: yes

Insurance: suggested

Other: children must be supervised, decorations restricted

Rutherford

AUBERGE DU SOLEIL

180 Rutherford Hill Road
Rutherford, CA 94573
(707) 963-1211 Karen Rowland
Reserve: 6–12 months in advance

On a Napa hillside, near the Silverado Trail, rests the lovely Mediterranean-style Auberge du Soleil. This is an outstanding facility for an elegant party. The entrance is upstairs, through an exquisite garden courtyard complete with a tastefully designed fountain and shaded canopy of gray olive trees. The beautifully appointed, yet understated lobby is all in light pastels. A curved staircase leads down to the private banquet rooms. The smaller room is circular and is appropriately named The Black Room because it really is painted black. But don't worry. The black walls highlight the many French doors and windows overlooking the valley below and the upholstered chairs and couches in black, green and pink floral patterns contrast well with the dark walls. Wood ceilings and floors and a large stone fireplace make this a very comfortable room. The Black Room serves as a cocktail area, expanded dinner seating room or as a place for band and dancing. It's also ideal for small group gatherings and dinners. The adjacent banquet room, the White Room, is large and airy with white walls and furniture plus excellent views. The gravel Terrace, just outside these two rooms, has unparalleled views and, on warm days or evenings, can be set up for outdoor dining with tables and white umbrellas. Also on the Terrace level, with a panoramic vista of Napa Valley, is a lavishly appointed board room with leather director's chairs and state-of-the-art meeting facilities.

MEETING ROOMS: Board room, 20 people conference style and 50 theater style.

CAPACITY: The Black Room holds up to 50 standing, and 30 seated guests. The White Room holds up to 76 guests and the Terrace, 50.

FEES & DEPOSITS: Up to 50 guests; $700 and between 50–120; $1200. The quoted deposit is due 2 weeks from the booking date, with 50% of the estimated total cost due 30 days prior to the event, balance due upon departure. For over 20 guests, there is no room rental charge. If under 20, the fee will vary depending on the guest count. Per person approximate rates: luncheons $33, for dinners $52. A 6.25% sales tax and 17% gratuity are applied to the final bill. The final balance is due at the conclusion of your event.

CANCELLATION POLICY: If the space(s) can be rebooked, the deposit will be refunded.

AVAILABILITY: Every day, from 11am–4pm and 6pm–1am.

SERVICES/AMENITIES:

Restaurant Services: yes

Catering: no BYO

Kitchen Facilities: n/a

Tables & Chairs: provided

Linens, Silver, etc.: provided

Restrooms: wca

Dance Floor: yes

Parking: large lot, valet

Overnight Accommodations: 48 guestrooms/suites

Telephone: pay phone

Outdoor Night Lighting: yes

Outdoor Cooking Facilities: no

Cleanup: provided

RESTRICTIONS:

Alcohol: provided, BYO corkage $15/bottle

Smoking: allowed

Music: no amplified

Wheelchair Access: ramp & elevator

Insurance: not required

RANCHO CAYMUS INN

1140 Rutherford Road (Hwy 128)
Rutherford, CA 94573
(707) 963–1777
Reserve: 6–9 months in advance

The Rancho Caymus Inn is a Spanish Mission–style facility, complete with big cacti, mosaics, red tile roof, stucco walls, arched windows, interior patios and abundant landscaping. The interior brick-paved patios, surrounded by wisteria-laden arbors, carry the calming sound of a trickling fountain. There are small tables with umbrellas and a large river rock fireplace, too. All of these amenities set the tone for a comfortable, outdoor party. For indoor meetings or private luncheons or dinners, the Mont. St. John Room, adjacent to the patio, has a large wood bar, hardwood floors, handsome stone fireplace, piano and stained glass windows. And if you'd like to stay here, the Inn has a variety of lovely suites from which to choose.

CAPACITY: The garden patio can accommodate 60 guests and the Mont. St. John Room can hold up to 50.

FEES & DEPOSITS: The $500 rental fee is used as a deposit and is due when the date is reserved. Per person rates for food service: modest hors d'oeuvres reception $8, a full buffet $22-25 and a full dinner $18-32. A 6.25% sales tax and 15% gratuity are added.

CANCELLATION POLICY: With 4 weeks' notice, the deposit is refundable.

AVAILABILITY: Every day, from 10am to 10pm.

SERVICES/AMENITIES:

Restaurant Services: yes
Catering: provided, no BYO
Kitchen Facilities: n/a
Tables & Chairs: provided
Linens, Silver, etc.: provided
Restrooms: wca
Dance Floor: yes

Parking: large lot
Overnight Accommodations: 26 suites
Telephone: house phone, local only
Outdoor Night Lighting: yes
Outdoor Cooking Facilities: no
Cleanup: provided
Other: event coordination services

RESTRICTIONS:

Alcohol: provided, BYO corkage
$5-7.50/bottle, BWC only
Smoking: allowed

Music: amplified until 8pm
Wheelchair Access: yes
Insurance: not required

Santa Rosa

CHATEAU DEBAUN WINERY

5007 Fulton Road
Santa Rosa, CA 95403
(707) 571-7500 John C. Burton
Reserve: 1 month in advance

Imagine a spectacular French chateau-style winery, surrounded by vineyards and walnut trees. The Chateau's elegant banquet room features brass chandeliers, a fireplace and a vaulted skylight in the 35-foot high ceiling. The spacious courtyard terrace is framed by fragrant roses and features a gazebo. The vineyard and distinctive architecture make Chateau DeBaun an unusual setting in the Wine Country for business functions as well as private parties.

CAPACITY:	*Area*	*Seated*
	Harmony Hall (Banquet Room)	140
	Concerto Courtyard	300
	Meadow	800
	Symphony Hall (Tasting Room)	50

FEES & DEPOSITS : A nonrefundable fee in the amount of 25% of the estimated total is required to secure your date. The remaining 75% is due 1 week prior to your function. Midweek rentals, Mon–Thurs run $10–18/person. For events on Friday, Saturday and Sunday, the rental fee starts at $18/person. A minimum guest count of 50 is required. The Chateau also holds group wine tastings which run $3–9/person depending on wine or champagne selection and time of day.

AVAILABILITY: Every day, except for major holidays. Individual areas (except Tasting Room) are available for events from 10am–1am. The entire facility is available for rental after 5pm.

SERVICES/AMENITIES:

Restaurant Services: no
Catering: BYO, preferred list
Kitchen Facilities: ample
Tables & Chairs: provided
Linens, Silver, etc.: provided
Restrooms: wca
Dance Floor: yes

Parking: ample lot, private road
Overnight Accommodations: no
Telephone: guest phone
Outdoor Night Lighting: yes
Outdoor Cooking Facilities: BBQ
Cleanup: caterer and staff
Other: limo, carriage and tents CBA

RESTRICTIONS:

Alcohol: provided, WC only
Smoking: outside only
Music: amplified ok

Wheelchair Access: yes
Insurance: required

Sonoma

BUENA VISTA WINERY

18000 Old Winery Road
Sonoma, CA 95476
(800) 926-1266 Bob Mosher
Reserve: 3 months in advance

The Buena Vista Winery, founded in 1857 by Count Agoston Haraszthy, is generally acknowledged as the birthplace of premium wines in California. The Old Winery is a striking two-story stone building in a grotto of eucalyptus, redwoods and lush greenery. The main tasting room has exposed stone, very high ceilings and a second story gallery displaying local artwork. The extended bank of wine racks, the long bar and the historic displays give the room a friendly and convivial atmosphere. Outside is a large paved courtyard, dotted with huge, old wooden wine kegs. The dappled sunlight from the tall canopy of trees provides a comfortable and relaxing atmosphere for outdoor dining and events. A second vine-covered, stone building (temporarily closed for restoration) houses a smaller tasting room. Adjacent is one of the winery's oldest cellars with antique wooden kegs that are currently in use. This tasting room has a curved bar along two of its sides and a wood burning stove for warming chilly evenings.

CAPACITY: The winery requires a minimum of 50 guests. Indoor facilities can seat 130 guests. Outdoor spaces can accommodate up to 200 guests for a seated dinner and 400 for a standing reception.

FEES & DEPOSITS: A refundable security deposit of 25% of the estimated total rental fee is required to reserve a date. The deposit is usually returned within 2 weeks after the event. The rental fee is $15–30/person and is due one week prior to your business or special event. The fee includes setup and cleanup, 2/3 bottle of wine/person, tables, chairs and staff. The fee varies depending on the type of event.

CANCELLATION POLICY: With 90 days' notice, the deposit will be refunded less 20%.

AVAILABILITY: Saturday only, 6:30pm–10:30pm.

SERVICES/AMENITIES:

Restaurant Services: no
Catering: BYO, approved list
Kitchen Facilities: n/a
Tables & Chairs: most provided
Linens, Silver, etc.: provided, extra charge
Restrooms: no wca
Dance Floor: yes, outdoor floor CBA

Parking: large lot
Overnight Accommodations: no
Telephone: pay phone
Outdoor Night Lighting: yes
Outdoor Cooking Facilities: BBQ
Cleanup: provided

RESTRICTIONS:

Alcohol: provided, WC only, no BYO
Smoking: outside only
Music: no amplified, acoustical until 10pm

Wheelchair Access: yes
Insurance: not required

DEPOT HOTEL 1870

241 First Street, West
Sonoma, CA 95476
(707) 938-2980 Gia Ghilarducci
Reserve: 1–6 months in advance

Originally a private home, the Depot Hotel has played an active role in Sonoma's past as a bar, restaurant and hotel. It is currently housed in an historic stone building near the Plaza in downtown Sonoma. Enter through the fireplace parlor comfortably furnished with overstuffed chairs and couches. The crisp white walls, luxurious blue upholstery and simple bar make the room cheerful and homey. Glass doors lead out onto a covered terrace encircling the formal garden. The garden is serene and secluded, landscaped with flowers, hedges and a large reflecting pool. The elegant and comfortable dining area adjacent to the bar is enlarged by a glass-enclosed garden room. Here you have the benefits of indoor dining while feeling that you're outdoors. The Depot offers the services of Chef Ghilarducci, who received the prestigious national award, Grand Master Chef of America.

CAPACITY: The Depot can accommodate up to 125 guests.

FEES & DEPOSITS: A refundable $200 deposit is required at the time you make your reservation and is applied towards the food and beverage cost. There is no rental fee. Food service is provided and prices range from an hors d'oeuvres reception at $12–17/person to seated meals at $10–30/person. All event costs are payable by the day of your party.

CANCELLATION POLICY: Your deposit will be refunded if your date can be rebooked.

AVAILABILITY: Smaller functions, Wed–Sun; larger parties on weekends from 11am to 4pm.

SERVICES/AMENITIES:
Restaurant Services: yes
Catering: provided, no BYO
Kitchen Facilities: n/a
Tables & Chairs: provided
Linens, Silver, etc.: provided
Restrooms: wca
Dance Floor: outside

Parking: large lots
Overnight Accommodations: no
Telephone: emergency only
Outdoor Night Lighting: yes
Outdoor Cooking Facilities: BBQ
Cleanup: provided

RESTRICTIONS:
Alcohol: provided, BYO corkage $8/bottle
Smoking: allowed
Music: amplified ok

Wheelchair Access: yes
Insurance: not required

SONOMA HOTEL

110 W. Spain Street
Sonoma, CA 95476
(707) 996-2996
Reserve: 3–6 months in advance

The Sonoma Hotel is a beautiful, Victorian structure located on a tree-lined plaza among other historic landmarks. The foyer of this vintage hotel captures California's early romantic history. A classic Saloon with an enormous wooden bar, mirrored back wall, and friendly bartender makes this a relaxed and convivial setting. The dining room is divided into three sections, furnished with antiques, delicately patterned wall paper and stained glass. The garden patio, available April through October, can be a very pleasant, shaded respite from your busy day. There are also 17 hotel rooms decorated with antiques to accommodate your out-of-town guests.

CAPACITY: 50 guests can be seated either in the dining room or the outdoor patio.

FEES & DEPOSITS: A $100 refundable deposit is required when you reserve your date. No rental fees are required. Food service is provided. The approximate costs are $10/person for hors d'oeuvres and $13.95–17.50/person for sit-down dinners. A 6.25% tax and 15% gratuity are added to the final bill which is due the day of the event.

CANCELLATION POLICY: With 2 weeks' notice, the deposit will be refunded.

AVAILABILITY: Year-round. No dinners on Wednesday evenings.

SERVICES/AMENITIES:

Restaurant Services: yes
Catering: provided, no BYO
Kitchen Facilities: n/a
Tables & Chairs: provided
Linens, Silver, etc.: provided
Restrooms: wca
Dance Floor: no

Parking: limited, on street
Overnight Accommodations: 17 guestrooms
Telephone: pay telephone
Outdoor Night Lighting: on patio
Outdoor Cooking Facilities: no
Cleanup: provided

RESTRICTIONS:

Alcohol: provided, BYO corkage $7/bottle
Smoking: allowed
Music: no amplified

Wheelchair Access: limited
Insurance: not required

SONOMA MISSION INN ★
AND SPA

Highway 12 and Boyes Boulevard
Sonoma, CA 95476
(707) 938-9000
Reserve: 2–6 months in advance

Set within 8 acres of eucalyptus trees, manicured lawns and colorful gardens, the Sonoma Mission Inn & Spa is an ideal setting for business retreats or special celebrations. The Inn offers state-of-the-art conference facilities, most with high ceilings, muted colors and natural sunlight. The largest conference room, the Sonoma Valley Room, and two conference suites offer fireplaces and French doors that open onto spacious terraces. Banquet menus range from simple coffee service to elegant, seated dinners and theme buffets. To help with your event, the Inn provides a professional, efficient and courteous staff. And if that weren't enough, the Inn also offers a world-class Spa with over 30 body and beauty treatments from which to choose, exercise facilities, aerobics, two pools, jacuzzis and tennis courts.

CAPACITY, FEES & DEPOSITS: The rental fee is used as a refundable deposit to reserve a date. Another nonrefundable deposit of 50% of the estimated event total is payable 90 days prior to your function. Fees vary:

Room	Standing	Seated	Fees
Sonoma Valley Room	275	135–150	From $500
Harvest/Carneros Suites	50	24	From $525
(with guest room)	25	10	—
Kenwood Room	—	32	From $200

Food service is provided. Meals start at $30/person with bar service and bartender additional. A 6.25% sales tax and 20% gratuity are applied to the final bill due the day of the event.

CANCELLATION POLICY: With 180 days' notice, your deposit will be refunded in full.

AVAILABILITY: Any day, any time.

SERVICES/AMENITIES:
Restaurant Services: yes
Catering: provided, no BYO
Kitchen Facilities: n/a
Tables & Chairs: provided
Linens, Silver, etc.: provided
Restrooms: wca
Dance Floor: yes

Parking: large lot, complimentary valet
Overnight Accommodations: 170 guestrooms
Telephone: pay phone
Outdoor Night Lighting: yes
Outdoor Cooking Facilities: yes
Cleanup: provided
Other: full event services

RESTRICTIONS:
Alcohol: provided, BYO corkage $8.50/bottle
Smoking: restricted
Music: amplified until 11pm

Wheelchair Access: yes
Insurance: not required

St. Helena

CAIN CELLARS ★

3800 Langtry Road
St. Helena, CA 94574
(707) 963-1616   Anne Pentland
Reserve: 2 weeks in advance

Cain Cellars is impressive. It is a small winery, but impeccably designed and built with high quality materials. The main dining area has orientals on the floor, a marble fireplace and a large deck. Light oak floors and wood ceiling give the room a comfortable warmth and two walls of glass, overlooking vineyards and the hills beyond, add light. Outside, there's a large patio with umbrella-shaded tables and lovely views. Cain Cellars even has its own chef, operating out of a gorgeous state-of-the-art kitchen. From the stone exterior to the sophisticated understated elegance of the interior, this spot offers first rate facilities for private parties and business functions.

CAPACITY: The inside can accommodate up to 50 guests, in combination with the outdoor spaces, up to 80 total.

FEES & DEPOSITS: A deposit of 50% of the estimated food and beverage total or $500 is required to secure your date. The balance is due the day of the event. The site rental fee is $20/person which includes tables, chairs, linens, wine, flowers, service staff and cleanup. The fee is for 4 hours maximum, $200/hour for any additional time. There is a $1000 minimum for special events. Food service is provided. Luncheons run $30/ person and dinners $50–70/person. Any menu can be customized for your group.

CANCELLATION POLICY: With 2 weeks' notice, a full refund can be arranged.

AVAILABILITY: Year-round, every day except major holidays and Mondays.

SERVICES/AMENITIES:

Restaurant Services: no
Catering: provided, no BYO
Kitchen Facilities: n/a
Tables & Chairs: provided up to 50
Linens, Silver, etc.: provided
Restrooms: no wca
Dance Floor: no

Parking: large lots
Overnight Accommodations: no
Telephone: house phone
Outdoor Night Lighting: CBA
Outdoor Cooking Facilities: no
Cleanup: provided
Other: winery tours, cooking classes/demonstrations

RESTRICTIONS:

Alcohol: provided, no B or hard liquor, no BYO
Smoking: outside only
Music: amplified ok

Wheelchair Access: yes
Insurance: not required

MEADOWOOD ★ RESORT HOTEL

900 Meadowood Lane
St. Helena, CA 94574
(707) 963-3646 or (800) 458-8080
Reserve: 3–12 months in advance

Driving into the Meadowood Resort is really a pleasure. You follow a narrow tree-shaded lane, flanked by immaculately tended vineyards and forested hillsides to the sophisticated resort complex, complete with wine school, executive conference center and first rate recreational facilities. The superbly designed buildings are reminiscent of New England during the early 1900s with white balconies, gabled roofs and gray clapboard siding. All is secluded on 250 acres of densely wooded Napa Valley landscape. The sprawling, multi-tiered Conference Center is set high, overlooking lush, green fairways and manicured lawns. The Vintner Room is fabulous with high ceilings and stone fireplace, decks with umbrella-shaded tables and outstanding views. The nearby lawn slopes down to steps leading to a dry creek bed planted with willows, with footbridge crossing over to golf fairways. For outdoor celebrations, Meadowood arranges tables and tents on the lawns next to the Vintner Room. There is something very special about this facility. It provides top flight cuisine prepared by highly trained chefs, first class accommodations and an environment to match. It ranks high on our list for special parties and executive conferences.

CAPACITY:	*Room*	*Standing*	*Seated*	*w/Outdoors*	*Classroom-Style*
	Vintner Room	175	110	250	80
	Madrone Room	35	24	40	32
	Wine Library	—	20	—	20
	Board Room	—	18	—	—
	Courthouse	—	—	—	30
	Woodside Theater	—	60	—	—

FEES & DEPOSITS: A $100–500 rental fee serves as your deposit and is due when the contract is signed. If your function includes an overnight stay, some or all of the rental fee may be waived. Half of the estimated event total is due 30 days prior to your event date, and the balance is due the day of the function. Per person rates: continental breakfasts and brunches range from $9–26.50, business mid-morning service starts at $7.50, luncheons start at $22 and dinners at $32. A 6.25% sales tax and a 17% service charge are additional.

CANCELLATION POLICY: If you cancel with less than 60 days' notice, you will lose your deposit. With less than 30 days' notice, the deposit plus 50% of the estimated total event cost will be forfeited.

AVAILABILITY: Year-round, every day.

SERVICES/AMENITIES:

Restaurant Services: yes
Catering: no BYO
Kitchen Facilities: n/a
Tables & Chairs: provided

Linens, Silver, etc.: provided
Restrooms: wca
Dance Floor: yes
Parking: multiple lots

Overnight Accommodations:
70 guestrooms and suites
Telephone: pay phones
Outdoor Night Lighting: yes

RESTRICTIONS:
Alcohol: provided, BYO corkage $10-22/bottle
Smoking: allowed
Music: amplified indoors only

Outdoor Cooking Facilities: CBA
Cleanup: provided
Other: recreation facilities,
golf, masseuse, wine school

Wheelchair Access: yes
Insurance: not required

MERRYVALE VINEYARDS

1000 Main Street
St. Helena, CA 94574
(800) 326-6069   Director of Special Events
Reserve: 1–12 months in advance

For an experience that's really memorable, have your special event or business dinner in Merryvale's (also known as Sunny St. Helena Winery) aging cellar. The cellar is lined with antique casks made in San Francisco in the late 1800s. The historic casks lining the walls hold up to 2,000 gallons, and the ones framing the steps as you enter hold an astonishing 16,000 gallons. These remarkable redwood wine barrels must be at least 16 feet in diameter! Banquets can be set up here for candelabra-lighted dinners. Behind the winery is the renovated "schoolhouse," a perfect setting for informal tastings and receptions, with a wide wisteria-framed veranda painted in crisp white. For receptions and tastings, the Veranda is an appealing space with an old world aura.

CAPACITY: Indoor and outdoor areas hold up to 160 guests maximum.

FEES & DEPOSITS: A nonrefundable deposit of 20% of the estimated total winery fees and signed contract are due within 1 month of making a reservation. Winery fees include rental, 30-minute winery tour, 30-minute wine tasting, 1/2 bottle wine/person for dinner, tables, chairs, glassware, wine service staff and candelabras. Catering can be provided. Luncheons start at $25/person and dinners start at $50/person. A 6.25% tax and 15%–18% gratuity are additional. The balance is due the day of the event or billing can be arranged in advance.

AVAILABILITY: Year-round. Every day until midnight, except for Christmas and Thanksgiving.

SERVICES/AMENITIES:
Restaurant Services: no
Catering: CBA or BYO with approval
Kitchen Facilities: ample
Tables & Chairs: provided
Linens, Silver, etc.: some provided
Restrooms: wca
Dance Floor: yes

Parking: large lot
Overnight Accommodations: no
Telephone: business phone
Outdoor Night Lighting: no
Outdoor Cooking Facilities: no
Cleanup: Merryvale and caterer

RESTRICTIONS:

Alcohol: provided, no BYO, no hard alcohol
Smoking: outside only
Music: amplified ok

Wheelchair Access: yes
Insurance: not required

ROBERT KEENAN WINERY ★★

3660 Spring Mountain Road
St. Helena, CA 94574
(707) 869-1268 Robert Green
Reserve: 6 months in advance

The stone-arched Robert Keenan Winery is reached after heading a few miles up Spring Mountain Road and then turning off onto a private unpaved road which winds its way uphill. When you get to the top, you'll love the panoramic and breathtaking views from the winery. You look out over the tapestry of vineyards, the Napa Valley and the mountains which enclose it. The winery's surroundings, although simple, are surprisingly striking. Railroad tie steps curve down through the lawns, flanked by multicolored impatiens into the gravel drive below. Outdoor parties take place on grass-covered stone terraces, with tables shaded by large umbrellas. On cool evenings heaters are brought outdoors. The indoor banquet room is very small, but it's furnished with unusual antiques and its walls are lined with oak wine barrels. It's constructed like a balcony so you can look down into the cellar at all of the wine-making paraphernalia. Needless to say, the aromas are quite wonderful. A dance floor can be set up on the crush platform outside the cellar for spectacular views while dancing. It's all uphill getting to the Robert Keenan Winery, but it's well worth the effort because this is one of the most special and beautiful sites we've encountered.

CAPACITY: The outdoor terraces can seat 150 guests and the private dining room can seat 50 guests for sit-down buffets.

FEES & DEPOSITS: 30% of the estimated total is required as a nonrefundable deposit when the date is booked. For use of the space, $10/person. There is an additional charge of $10/person for providing wine. Another 30% of total estimated costs is due 60 days prior to the event and the final 30% balance is due the day before the party. Per person rates: buffets approximately $55 for 50 guests, $45 for 100 guests and $40 for 150 guests or more. Seated dinners cost $75, minimum. A 6.25% sales tax and 15% gratuity are applied to the final bill.

AVAILABILITY: Every day, any time.

SERVICES/AMENITIES:

Restaurant Services: no
Catering: provided, no BYO
Kitchen Facilities: n/a
Tables & Chairs: some provided
Linens, Silver, etc.: provided
Restrooms: no wca
Dance Floor: yes

Parking: large lot
Overnight Accommodations: no
Telephone: house phone
Outdoor Night Lighting: CBA, extra charge
Outdoor Cooking Facilities: no
Cleanup: provided
Other: full event services

RESTRICTIONS:

Alcohol: Keenan Wines only, champagne CBA
Smoking: outside only
Music: no amplified

Wheelchair Access: yes
Insurance: not required

SPRING MOUNTAIN VINEYARDS

2805 Spring Mountain Road
St. Helena, CA 94574
(707) 963-5233 Kathy Hamberis
Reserve: 3 weeks–2 months in advance

Originally called the Mira Valle Estate, Spring Mountain is an idyllic winery set on a knoll overlooking Napa's vineyards. Built in 1884 by Tiburcio Parrot, an early California vintner, the pale green and white Victorian mansion has become well known since the filming of the TV show Falcon Crest. Highly detailed and framed by century-old palms, the mansion is an impressive example of Victorian architecture. At the front of the mansion, there's a terrace with pool that's got to be one of the most beautiful poolside settings we've seen. Private parties are not permitted. However, for a 3-hour afternoon business function, this is a fabulous site.

CAPACITY: Outdoor functions only, up to 80 guests, minimum 20.

FEES & DEPOSITS: A $100 nonrefundable deposit is required to secure your date. Half of the rental fee is due within 2 weeks prior to your function. The rental fee is $18/person which includes tables and umbrellas, chairs, glassware, wine and linens. The balance is due by the day of the event.

CANCELLATION POLICY: A 48-hour notice is required for any refund of the rental fee.

AVAILABILITY: April 15–October 15 only, Monday–Friday, between 11:30am and 4pm.

SERVICES/AMENITIES:

Restaurant Services: no
Catering: preferred list
Kitchen Facilities: no
Tables & Chairs: provided
Linens, Silver, etc.: provided
Restrooms: wca limited
Dance Floor: no

Parking: limited, car pooling encouraged
Overnight Accommodations: no
Telephone: business phone
Outdoor Night Lighting: no
Outdoor Cooking Facilities: BYO
Cleanup: caterer
Other: winery tours

RESTRICTIONS:

Alcohol: W provided
Smoking: allowed
Music: no amplified

Wheelchair Access: yes
Insurance: sometimes required

V. SATTUI WINERY

White Lane at Highway 29
St. Helena, CA 94574
(707) 963-7774
Reserve: 1–4 months in advance

V. Sattui Winery, located in the heart of Napa Valley, is a small, family winery founded in 1885. It occupies a massive stone building reminiscent of California's early wineries and is surrounded by 2 acres of tree-shaded picnic grounds, lush lawns, giant oak trees and 35 acres of vineyards. Guests can dine in a castle-like cellar lined with oak barrels and filled with the pungent aromas of aging wines. Through a stone archway are four caves where wines are aged behind heavy wrought iron gates. A second cellar provides a more intimate setting for smaller gatherings. Hand-hewn stone walls, heavy ceiling timbers and wine barrels create an old-world atmosphere suitable for elaborate formal dinners, informal luncheons or conferences. Outside luncheons and group picnics can also be arranged.

CAPACITY: The large cellar can hold 200 seated guests, the small cellar, 50 guests; 250 total. The outside lawn and terraces can accommodate more than 300.

FEES & DEPOSITS: A $200 deposit is required to secure your date. Food costs range anywhere from $15-50/person, depending on the style and complexity of your menu. A 6.25% sales tax will be added to the final bill.

CANCELLATION POLICY: With 60 days' notice, the deposit is fully refundable.

AVAILABILITY: Every day, from 9am–midnight.

SERVICES/AMENITIES:

Restaurant Services: no
Catering: BYO, select from list
Kitchen Facilities: minimal
Tables & Chairs: provided
Linens, Silver, etc.: caterer
Restrooms: wca
Dance Floor: yes

Parking: large lot
Overnight Accommodations: no
Telephone: pay phone
Outdoor Night Lighting: yes
Outdoor Cooking Facilities: BBQ
Cleanup: provided
Other: V. Sattui provides bar staff

RESTRICTIONS:

Alcohol: V. Sattui wine only, BYO champagne
Smoking: outside only
Music: amplified ok

Wheelchair Access: ramp
Insurance: extra liability required

WHITE SULPHUR SPRINGS

3100 White Sulphur Springs Road
St. Helena, CA 94574
(707) 963-8588 Betty or Buzz Foote
Reserve: 1–2 months in advance

California's first resort, established in 1852, is set in a canyon with nine white cottages, an inn, small hotel and lodge. It's reached by a road that starts from Spring Street in downtown St. Helena, and quickly narrows, winding into the foothills. White Sulphur Springs Creek meanders through the resort site and there are actually warm sulphur pools available to guests. From April-November, corporate picnics, informal workshops, family reunions and other events are held in the large Redwood Grove, a shaded glen adjacent to a trickling creek. There are rustic wood picnic tables and chairs, wrought-iron benches and BBQs plus a log foot-bridge to the Indian Meadow campground and fire circle. The Resort has a variety of outdoor activities including volleyball, basketball, horseshoes, badminton, croquet and hiking to year-round waterfalls. Indoor meetings, parties, and dances take place in the newly renovated Lodge, large dining room or smaller lounges. You're out in the country here and it's very quiet. The natural grounds, historic buildings and the attentive care of the owners make this place an ideal personal or business getaway.

CAPACITY:

Area	Standing	Seated
Redwood Grove	250 total	—
Lodge	200	150
Dining Room	150	100

FEES & DEPOSITS: A $300–500 nonrefundable deposit secures your space and when all fees are paid, it becomes the refundable security/cleaning deposit. 50% of the total estimated cost is due 4 months in advance and is nonrefundable. The remaining half is due one month in advance. Rental fees range from $6–85/person (meals are extra) depending on group size, duration of stay, weekend or weekday amenities required. The entire resort can be rented for $2000–4000/day.

CANCELLATION POLICY: If the facilities can be rebooked, the deposits may be refunded.

AVAILABILITY: Year-round

SERVICES/AMENITIES:

Restaurant Services: CBA
Catering: CBA or BYO
Kitchen Facilities: ample
Tables & Chairs: provided
Linens, Silver, etc.: BYO
Restrooms: no wca
Dance Floor: in Lodge

Parking: large lot
Overnight Accommodations: 8 cottages, 25 guestrooms
Telephone: pay phone
Outdoor Night Lighting: yes
Outdoor Cooking Facilities: 6 BBQs
Cleanup: whoever caters event
Other: museum & massage

RESTRICTIONS:

Alcohol: BYO, no hard alcohol
Smoking: outside only
Music: amplified ok

Wheelchair Access: limited
Insurance: sometimes required

Yountville

DRUMS RESTAURANT

6525 Washington Street
Yountville, CA 94599
(707) 944-2788
Reserve: 1–6 months in advance

Drums is located in the Vintage 1870 complex and is an attractive event space as well as a restaurant. For business functions or large receptions, Drums is an excellent location. The main dining room has French doors and multiple windows overlooking a garden area, making it light and airy. Soft pink and rose colors predominate. By opening several doors, a large L can be formed with an adjacent dining area. It has a large skylight and more doors leading into a garden. The smaller dining room is appealing, with a terra cotta colored brick wall and softwood floors. Overall, the decor is clean and fresh, expressing sophistication and a touch of elegance.

CAPACITY: Drums can accommodate 175 seated, 250 standing inside; with outdoor spaces 400 seated total.

FEES & DEPOSITS: There is no rental charge for use of space. Meal service is provided. Per person rates: luncheons from $11.50–15, dinners $16.50–27.50, buffets $17.75–23, BBQ service $14.50–24 and hors d'oeuvres $2.50–5. A refundable $500 deposit is required when reservations are confirmed; half of the estimated food and beverage is required with the returned contract. The balance is payable at the end of the event.

CANCELLATION POLICY: If the event space can be rebooked, the deposit will be refunded.

AVAILABILITY: Year-round, closed Christmas and New Year's. Every day 8am–1am.

SERVICES/AMENITIES:

Restaurant Services: yes
Catering: no BYO
Kitchen Facilities: n/a
Tables & Chairs: provided
Linens, Silver, etc.: provided
Restrooms: wca
Dance Floor: yes

Parking: multiple lots
Overnight Accommodations: no
Telephone: pay phones
Outdoor Night Lighting: yes
Outdoor Cooking Facilities: BBQ
Cleanup: provided

RESTRICTIONS:
Alcohol: provided, BYO corkage $8/bottle
Smoking: allowed
Music: amplified ok

Wheelchair Access: yes
Insurance: sometimes required

DURING LONG MEETINGS,
RALPH'S MIND WOULD TEND TO WANDER

Aptos

MANGELS HOUSE ★

570 Aptos Creek Road
Aptos, CA 95003
(408) 688-7982 Jacqueline Fisher
Reserve: 2–4 months in advance

You can sense something special, even before you see the house. Driving up the winding road and through the gates, you look up and are greeted by the sight of an impressive Victorian home set on higher ground. Built in the 1880s, the Mangels House was the country home of Claus Mangels, who, together with his brother-in-law, Claus Spreckels, founded the sugar beet industry in California. The house remained in the same family until 1979, when the current owners purchased the home and converted it into a bed and breakfast. Situated in 4 acres of lawn, orchard and woodland and bounded by the Forest of Nisene Marks, the house and surrounding garden are some of the loveliest and most peaceful we've encountered. A gracious and wide veranda beckons you to the front door. Inside, the interior is mostly period, and has been tastefully and carefully appointed to complement the house. The parlor, dining room, kitchen, rear porch and the outdoor spaces can all be used by guests for functions as well. Stay overnight just to savor the house, the grounds and the sensation of stepping back in time.

CAPACITY: The Mangels House can hold up to 16 guests inside and 25 maximum outdoors.

FEES & DEPOSITS: For day use, the rental fee is $660. To reserve the entire house with an overnight stay, the rental is $1000. A $200 cleaning deposit is required to hold your reservation. Fees for use of the garden vary and are dependent on guest count, day of week and hours rented. All fees and deposits are payable when reservations are confirmed.

CANCELLATION POLICY: With 60 days' notice, all fees and deposits are refunded.

AVAILABILITY: Year-round, every day except Christmas.

SERVICES/AMENITIES:

Restaurant Services: no
Catering: preferred list
Kitchen Facilities: setup only
Tables & Chairs: BYO
Linens, Silver, etc.: BYO
Restrooms: no wca
Dance Floor: no

Parking: small lot plus shuttle avail.
Overnight Accommodations: 6 guestrooms
Telephone: house phone
Outdoor Night Lighting: no
Outdoor Cooking Facilities: no
Cleanup: renter or caterer

RESTRICTIONS:

Alcohol: BYO
Smoking: outside only
Music: no amplified

Wheelchair Access: yes
Insurance: sometimes required

THE VERANDA

8041 Soquel Drive
Aptos, CA 95003
(408) 685-1881
Reserve: 1 week–3 months in advance

The Veranda is a restaurant occupying the main floor of the vintage 1878 Victorian Bayview Hotel in historic Aptos Village. All has been restored with attention to detail. The interior boasts several glass-walled verandas as well as a main dining room and outstanding bar. Muted colors in roses, off-whites and pinks blend to create a visually appealing space. The bar is in a separate room, accessible by double doors. There's a newly designed and constructed patio for outdoor events with brick pavers, roses and white lattice. The food here is distinctive and very good. For business parties or special celebrations, The Veranda creates an environment conducive to having a very good time.

CAPACITY: The Veranda indoors can accommodate 70 seated guests: main dining room 36, side veranda 28, front veranda 20, anteroom 10. The garden patio can hold up to 50 seated guests and 125 standing. The entire facility can hold up to 150–175 guests.

FEES & DEPOSITS: A refundable $300 deposit is required when reservations are confirmed. No rental fees are charged if meal service is provided. For groups, luncheons start at $12/person, dinners at $22/person and hors d'oeuvres start at $10/person.

CANCELLATION POLICY: Your deposit will be refunded with 30 days' notice or if the space can be rebooked.

AVAILABILITY: Year-round, every day by arrangement.

SERVICES/AMENITIES:

Restaurant Services: yes
Catering: no BYO
Kitchen Facilities: n/a
Tables & Chairs: provided
Linens, Silver, etc.: provided
Restrooms: wca
Dance Floor: CBA

Parking: large lot
Overnight Accommodations: 12 guestrooms
Telephone: pay phone
Outdoor Night Lighting: yes
Outdoor Cooking Facilities: yes
Cleanup: provided

RESTRICTIONS:

Alcohol: provided, no BYO
Smoking: only in bar or outside
Music: amplified, DJs ok

Wheelchair Access: yes
Insurance: not required

Ben Lomond

HIGHLANDS HOUSE AND PARK

8500 Highway 9
Ben Lomond, CA 95005
(408) 425-2696 Parks Department
Reserve: 2–12 months in advance

The Highlands House is a former private residence built in the 1940s. Set in a public park, surrounded by large redwoods and situated directly off Highway 9, the 2-story white wood house is available for private parties and business functions. The house is set below the main road, ensuring quiet and a sense of privacy. The setting is lovely with expansive lawns, huge magnolia and pine trees, well-maintained landscaping and nearby pool. Framed by several tall palms, the Highland House is an attractive and pleasant spot for gatherings.

CAPACITY: The facility can accommodate 200.

FEES & DEPOSITS: Fees and deposits are required when reservations are made. Bookings made less than 45 days in advance have a surcharge of $50 added. The rental fee for county residents is $504, non-county applicants, $655. The cleaning deposit is $200 with alcohol use, $100 without. These fees are for an 8-hour block. Weekday business functions run $63/hour for the entire house and outdoor lawn areas.

CANCELLATION POLICY: With 30 days' notice, all fees will be returned less a $100 cancellation charge. With less than 30 days, only the cleaning deposit will be returned.

AVAILABILITY: Year-round, from 10am–midnight. Weekday functions, 10am–10pm.

SERVICES/AMENITIES:

Restaurant Services: no
Catering: BYO
Kitchen Facilities: ample
Tables & Chairs: some provided
Linens, Silver, etc.: BYO
Restrooms: wca
Dance Floor: yes

Parking: large lot, fee on summer weekends
Overnight Accommodations: no
Telephone: pay phone
Outdoor Night Lighting: no
Outdoor Cooking Facilities: BYO BBQ
Cleanup: renter's responsibility
Other: spinet available

RESTRICTIONS:

Alcohol: BYO, WBC only
Smoking: outside only
Music: no live amplified, DJ ok

Wheelchair Access: yes
Insurance: not required

Capitola

THE INN AT DEPOT HILL

250 Monterey Avenue
Capitola, CA 95010
(408) 462-3376
Reserve: 1–3 months in advance

Located in the beachside resort of Capitola, this new bed and breakfast has been designed with considerable attention to detail. Once a grand railroad depot in 1901, the Inn retains the large exterior columns, and inside, the original 16-foot ceilings and round lobby (now dining room) with the old ticket windows. The owners have had lots of fun creating an unusual interior environment for their guests. The dining room has a trompe l'oeil scene that creates the illusion of a train dining car, complete with a vista of the Big Sur coast out the window. Continuing in the 'journey' mode, all of the 8 suites have been designed with different geographical themes: English countryside garden, urbane Paris, the white-washed Mediterranean, to name a few. Light pastels and clean lines make the interior spaces very appealing. Outdoors, in the back, there's a lovely garden courtyard, with lush planting, gazebo and fishpond. The garden has been nicely put together—a great place to mingle or sit under umbrella-shaded tables and chat with guests. For receptions, small business gatherings or events, this is a surprise destination.

CAPACITY: The Depot can accommodate 16 guests indoors and 40 outdoors; 60 in total.

FEES & DEPOSITS: For business functions, the entire Inn can be reserved. The rental fee is $1680/day including an overnight stay, a catered lunch for 16 guests, breakfast and coffee service during the day. For social events, a garden party can be arranged from noon–4pm, starting at $200 per 4-hour period. All fees are due when reservations are confirmed.

CANCELLATION POLICY: For business functions, a minimum 30 days' notice is required for a refund. If rooms can be rebooked, part or all will be returned. For social gatherings, 1 week's notice is required.

AVAILABILITY: Year-round, every day.

SERVICES/AMENITIES:

Restaurant Services: no
Catering: provided or BYO
Kitchen Facilities: setup only
Tables & Chairs: CBA or BYO
Linens, Silver, etc.: CBA or BYO
Restrooms: wca
Dance Floor: no

Parking: large lot across street, on street
Overnight Accommodations: 8 guestrooms
Telephone: house phone
Outdoor Night Lighting: yes
Outdoor Cooking Facilities: no
Cleanup: CBA or renter

RESTRICTIONS:
Alcohol: CBA or BYO
Smoking: outside only
Music: no amplified

Wheelchair Access: yes
Insurance: not required

SHADOWBROOK

1750 Wharf Road
Capitola, California 95010
(408) 475-1511
Reserve: 1 week–2 months in advance

Overlooking Soquel Creek and sitting beneath a steep hillside with gardens so lush they keep 2 full-time gardeners busy, Shadowbrook is place with a lot of character. The descent from the street, whether by quaint cable car or the winding narrow foot path offers panoramic vistas of Capitola and the ocean. The gardens present visitors with the delightful option of a journey down the hill, complete with ferns, technicolor flowers and trickling waterfall. The restaurant was originally a log cabin, built as a summer home in the 1920s. Left in ruins, by 1944 the only approach was by boat. It took 3 years of back-breaking work to restore the house and create a path down the steep, overgrown slope. Over the years it has been expanded to include multiple dining areas on different levels, each with a view of Soquel Creek. For celebrations and business functions, it's clearly a popular spot. Shadowbrook is more than just a local institution.

CAPACITY:	*Day*	*Hours*	*Seated Capacity*	*Availability*
	Saturday	daytime	30–90	year–round
	Sunday	daytime	45	year–round
	Sunday	evening	45	Sept 15–May 15
	Mon–Thurs	evening	90	Sept 15–May 15
	Mon–Thurs	daytime	200 (min 30)*	year–round

* call to make special group arrangements

FEES & DEPOSITS: A $100 deposit is required to secure your date and is due when reservations are made. There are no rental fees, however, for extended social or business events over 3 hours, a fee may be required. Meal service is provided. Luncheons start at $12/person, dinners start at $16/person. Breakfasts and custom menus can be arranged.

CANCELLATION POLICY: With 30 days' notice or if the dining area can be rebooked, the deposit is refunded.

AVAILABILITY: Year-round, every day from 8:30am to 11:30pm.

SERVICES/AMENITIES:

Restaurant Services: yes

Catering: no BYO

Kitchen Facilities: n/a

Tables & Chairs: provided

Linens, Silver, etc.: provided

Restrooms: wca limited

Dance Floor: in lounge

Parking: large lots above restaurant

Overnight Accommodations: no

Telephone: pay phone

Outdoor Night Lighting: no

Outdoor Cooking Facilities: no

Cleanup: provided

Other: celebration photos

Special: nightly music in lounge

RESTRICTIONS:

Alcohol: provided, no BYO

Smoking: allowed

Music: amplified restricted

Wheelchair Access: elevator provided

Insurance: not required

Felton

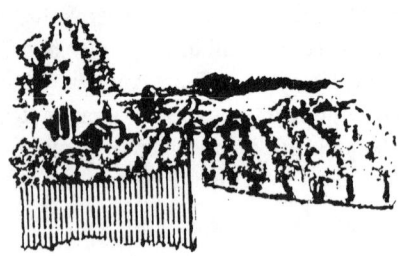

HALLCREST VINEYARDS

379 Felton Empire Road
Felton, CA 95018
(408) 335-4441 Lorraine
Reserve: 4–6 months in advance

Tucked in a residential area not far from the center of Felton is Hallcrest Vineyards. You must park in a lot off Felton Empire Road and walk along the edge of the vineyard down to the winery. This is a working winery and there is a tasting room for wine lovers and the aroma of crushed grapes in the air. (Business luncheons include a tour by the winemaker and winetasting). To one side of the winery's main building is a grassy knoll, with scattered picnic tables, terraced plantings and lovely oaks. At the bottom of the slope is a raised, redwood deck with lattice backdrop, a perfect spot for musicians and dancing. From the vantage point of the knoll and platform deck, the views of the surrounding Santa Cruz mountains and adjacent vineyard are sensational. This is a very pleasant site for a rustic and informal outdoor party.

CAPACITY: Outdoors, 100 guests total. The Upper Wine Cellar can accommodate up to 75 guests indoors.

FEES & DEPOSITS: A nonrefundable deposit of 50% of the total estimated cost is required and due when your reservation is made. A refundable cleaning and security deposit of $150 is due 30 days prior to your event. For use of the outdoor and indoor facilities, the fee is $500–600. The remaining 50% balance is due 30 days prior to your event. Fees for business functions vary, so call for specifics.

CANCELLATION POLICY: The cleaning and security deposit is usually refunded if you cancel.

AVAILABILITY: Every day, 9:30–6pm. From September 1–October 31 the winery will not take bookings.

SERVICES/AMENITIES:

Restaurant Services: no

Catering: preferred list

Kitchen Facilities: minimal

Tables & Chairs: BYO

Linens, Silver, etc.: BYO

Restrooms: wca

Dance Floor: yes

Parking: 40 spaces

Overnight Accommodations: no

Telephone: house phone, local only

Outdoor Night Lighting: no

Outdoor Cooking Facilities: BYO

Cleanup: caterer

RESTRICTIONS:

Alcohol: WC provided, BYO beer

Smoking: outside only

Music: no amplified

Wheelchair Access: yes

Insurance: liability required

ROARING CAMP

Graham Hill Road & Roaring Camp Road
Felton, CA 95018
(408) 335-4484
Reserve: 2 weeks–6 months in advance

Deep in the heart of the Santa Cruz Mountains is one of America's last steam-powered, daily-operated passenger railroads. The Roaring Camp and Big Trees Railroad still operates this narrow gauge steam train through forests of giant redwoods and over very steep grades and switchbacks to Bear Mountain. Your party group can board with other passengers or you can arrange an exclusive rental for your special event. The depot is located in the self-contained tiny crossroads "town" of Roaring Camp which is approached by foot from the main parking lot. The walk into "town" features the world's shortest covered bridge and a large, lovely pond. The train ride into the mountains is great fun for party-goers of all ages. Chuckwagon Bar-B-Qs can be arranged for your party, too. Unusual celebrations could be planned to coincide with Roaring Camp's famous moonlight steam train parties which include train excursion, chuckwagon BBQ and square dancing. Moonlight parties are scheduled on moonlit Saturday nights between 7–11pm, June–October. This is a terrific getaway for company picnics and business-related entertainment.

CAPACITY: For BBQs, the outdoor facilities can hold up to 2000 guests; for indoor parties, the General Store Annex can hold 125 standing and 85 seated guests.

FEES & DEPOSITS: A deposit of 25% of the total estimated cost is due when reservations are made; the remaining 75% is due in installments of 25% each, up to 2 weeks prior to the event. For a group rate you need 25 guests minimum, and that includes a combination of BBQ and train ride. The total cost runs up to $22/ person. A guaranteed headcount is due 7 days prior to your party.

CANCELLATION POLICY: The policy varies depending on the size of group and type of function—call for details.

AVAILABILITY: Open every day of the year, from dawn to dusk. In the summer, there are moonlight excursions, so call to get the details.

SERVICES/AMENITIES:

Restaurant Services: no
Catering: no BYO
Kitchen Facilities: n/a
Tables & Chairs: provided
Linens, Silver, etc.: provided
Restrooms: wca
Dance Floor: yes

Parking: large lots
Overnight Accommodations: no
Telephone: pay phones
Outdoor Night Lighting: yes
Outdoor Cooking Facilities: BBQs
Cleanup: provided
Other: square dancing w/caller, full event services

RESTRICTIONS:

Alcohol: BYO
Smoking: allowed
Music: amplified with restrictions

Wheelchair Access: CBA
Insurance: not required

Santa Cruz

CHAMINADE ★★

1 Chaminade Lane
Santa Cruz, CA 95065
(408) 475-5676 or 475-5600   Gary Heath
Reserve: 1–6 months in advance

Chaminade is primarily an exclusive conference center retreat set high on a mountain bluff overlooking Monterey Bay. Winding your way up from Highway 1, the final approach to the center is private and woodsy. The original Mission-style buildings, constructed in the 1930s as a boys' school, have been expanded and transformed into a well-designed complex that includes complete recreation facilities as well as meeting rooms and overnight guestrooms. The new structures at Chaminade maintain the red tile roofs, delicate arches and stucco exteriors that reflect the original architectural character of the old school buildings. Luckily, the center is available for more than just conference retreats. For your special event, there are decks, balconies, patios and expansive lawn areas that take advantage of views and warm weather. Many of Chaminade's interior rooms, including a prefunction area, are also available for parties so please ask to see them when you visit this facility. Chaminade, with its careful attention to service, culinary excellence and comfort, is a luxurious and private setting for a sophisticated business event or celebration.

CAPACITY: Chaminade can accommodate up to 200 guests; Sports Lawn up to 400.

FEES & DEPOSITS: A nonrefundable deposit of 50% of the estimated total is due when you make your reservations. Rental fees are $1/person with no dance floor and $3/person with a dance floor. Rates for business meetings and seminars vary, so call for specifics. Food service is provided. Breakfasts and luncheons run $15–25/person and dinners $23–45/person. These figures are approximate and include tax and gratuity. The remaining 50% balance is payable by the day of your event.

AVAILABILITY: Any day, morning through evening.

SERVICES/AMENITIES:

Restaurant Services: yes

Catering: no BYO

Kitchen Facilities: n/a

Tables & Chairs: provided

Linens, Silver, etc.: provided

Restrooms: wca

Dance Floor: charge for setup

Parking: several lots

Overnight Accommodations: 152 guestrooms

Telephone: pay phone

Outdoor Night Lighting: yes

Outdoor Cooking Facilities: BBQ

Cleanup: provided

RESTRICTIONS:

Alcohol: provided, no BYO

Smoking: allowed

Music: amplified restricted

Wheelchair Access: yes

Insurance: not required

COCOANUT GROVE

400 Beach Street
Santa Cruz, CA 95060
(408) 423-5590
Reserve: 12 months in advance

As unlikely as it may seem, this historic site is available for private functions. Built in 1907 as one of the first amusement parks and casino complexes, Cocoanut Grove still remains, located at the water's edge next to the famous Santa Cruz Beach Boardwalk. Inside there are several party spaces worth considering. The Bay View Room is ample-sized with dance floor and bay windows overlooking the ocean, beach and Boardwalk. It's adjacent to the expansive Ballroom, which has black ceilings, decorative lights, suspended and rotating mirrored ball, and hardwood dance floors. Both of these rooms are terrific dining and dance party spaces! The Bay View Bar and Lounge is connected to the Ballroom and Bay View Room and comes with oak curved bar, red carpets and great ocean views. The Sun Room is like a solarium with a retractable glass ceiling which rolls back to beckon in the ocean breezes. With a garden atmosphere and pastel colors, the Sun Room offers guests a really pleasant indoor/outdoor dining environment. Some rooms can be rented separately or in combination, so make sure you get the full tour in order to choose the most appropriate ones for your event.

CAPACITY: For large gatherings, the Ballroom and Balcony hold up to 425 guests, the Bay View Room, 180. The combined capacity is 600 guests. Note that the Bay View Room Lounge adjoins both of these rooms and is included as part of the rental. The Sun Room can accommodate up to 275 seated guests and up to 300 by using the adjoining Sun Room Terrace.

MEETING ROOMS: The Sun Room can hold up to 600 for meetings. Ballroom and Bay View Lounge, up to 700.

FEES & DEPOSITS: A nonrefundable deposit of $750 is required for the Ballroom or Bay View Room, $500 for the Sun Room. The deposit is payable when you sign your rental agreement. A security deposit is sometimes required depending on the size and complexity of your event. This fee will be negotiated when the agreement is signed. No rental fees are required when a guaranteed minimum number of meals is served. Per person food service rates: luncheon buffets $11.95–$13.75 and dinner buffets $15.50–$21.25. There's also a special bar and beverage package for private parties, so ask for rates. A 6.75% sales tax and 15% gratuity will be added to the final bill.

AVAILABILITY: Daily, 8am–4pm and 6pm–1am. On Sundays, the Bay View Room and Ballroom are available from 2pm–10pm for dinners and dinner dances.

SERVICES/AMENITIES:

Restaurant Services: yes
Catering: no BYO
Kitchen Facilities: n/a
Tables & Chairs: provided
Linens, Silver, etc.: provided
Restrooms: wca
Dance Floor: yes

Parking: discount at Boardwalk parking lot
Overnight Accommodations: no
Telephone: pay phone
Outdoor Night Lighting: no
Outdoor Cooking Facilities: no
Cleanup: provided
Other: 2 pianos

RESTRICTIONS:

Alcohol: provided, BYO corkage $4.50/bottle
Smoking: allowed, no cigars, clove cigarettes
Music: amplified ok

Wheelchair Access: yes
Insurance: sometimes required
Other: decorating restrictions

DARLING HOUSE

314 West Cliff Drive at Gharkey
Santa Cruz, CA 95060
(408) 458-1958 Darrell or Karen Darling
Reserve: 2–6 months in advance

The Darling House, with gracious veranda, lawn and stately palm trees, is a 1910 ocean-side architectural gem designed by William Weeks. Located right on West Cliff Drive which follows the ocean's edge, the Inn is a classic Spanish Revival-style home with unusual Arts and Crafts influences. Complete with Tiffany lamps, stairway and doors with delicate wood inlays, stenciled borders, terra cotta roof tiles, antique furniture, and leaded glass windows, this home has been maintained in pristine condition. The Darling House offers its entry and front parlor for parties, retreats and small conferences. Both are full of terrific details, including oak window seats set in alcoves, oriental carpets, tile-clad fireplace and leaded glass bookshelves. This historically significant house is now a bed and breakfast inn, with 8 guestrooms. All rooms are filled with antiques and those facing the ocean have glorious views of the Pacific and the distant Santa Cruz Wharf and Boardwalk. Horse-drawn carriages, sailing yachts, ocean fishing excursions and beach events can also be arranged. For small gatherings, the Darling House is a wonderful place for a personalized party, business meeting or seminar.

CAPACITY: The house parlor and entry can fit up to 50 guests for a standing buffet or meeting and approximately 25 for seated meals. If the garden is used, more guests can be accommodated.

FEES & DEPOSITS: 50% of the total estimated fee is due when you reserve your event or meeting date. Rental fees range depending on guest count: for 12 guests or less, $100; between 12 and 49 guests, $200; for over 50 guests, the fee is $300. The fee normally covers a 4-hour block and is waived when the entire house is reserved overnight on weekdays.

Rooms ($75–$175) are available if the event occurs on a weeknight. For a Saturday evening event, you must reserve the entire house for at least two nights (F&S or S&S) which runs $2150 minimum in addition to the rental fees. The fee balance is due in full 2 months prior to the event date.

CANCELLATION POLICY: With 2 weeks' notice, the deposit is refundable.

AVAILABILITY: Normally, noon to 4pm during the week. If all guest rooms are reserved for your special event, then your party can extend from 2pm to 11am the following day, with some advance notice.

SERVICES/AMENITIES:

Restaurant Services: no

Catering: BYO, CBA

Kitchen Facilities: no prep allowed

Tables & Chairs: CBA

Linens, Silver, etc.: CBA

Restrooms: no wca

Dance Floor: CBA

Parking: house lot

Overnight Accommodations: 8 guestrooms

Telephone: guest phones

Outdoor Night Lighting: minimal

Outdoor Cooking Facilities: BBQ

Cleanup: caterer

Other: event services provided

RESTRICTIONS:

Alcohol: BYO

Smoking: outside only

Music acoustical only

Wheelchair Access: no

Insurance: not required

Other: must book guestroom(s)

JERRY GRAHAM
Author and host of Bay Area Backroads

A friend who turned 40 decided that she wanted a 'Prom Night' birthday party. It was considered unfashionable to show up at a prom during her high school days in the mid-60s counter culture era. 'Hip' people were not seen at prom night. We rented Bimbo's 365 Club in San Francisco for the event. There were lots of crinoline and tuxes and corsages from the 60s time period. Music was 50s-style. Coincidentally enough, my friend was elected as Queen of the Prom, and the event was a nostalgic night for all! However, I would not ever repeat this kind of party theme—I'm all prommed out!

HOLLINS HOUSE

20 Clubhouse Road
Santa Cruz, California 95060
(408) 425-1244 Margy Seifert
Reserve: 6–12 months in advance

The Hollins House, built in 1929 by championship golfer Marion Hollins, is located in the Pasatiempo Golf Course Complex in the Santa Cruz Mountains, not far from Highway 17. Approached through acres of green fairways, the house is situated atop a knoll and has impressive views of the distant Monterey Bay. You can reserve either the entire facility or just the Hollins Room and patio. The main dining room is very long, with high ceilings, big mirrors and picture windows with views of the garden and ocean beyond. There's also a fireplace and hardwood parquet dance floor. The Tap Room is a more informal space, with a long wood bar, fireplace and windows overlooking garden and ocean. The adjacent garden is narrow with a lawn bordered by profusely blooming impatiens. A medium-sized patio surrounded by wisteria and situated next to the Hollins Room is a picturesque place for an outdoor party. The Hollins Room is small, with a big mirror over the fireplace, chandelier, rounded bay windows with bench seat and a vista of the Pacific Ocean framed by nearby oak trees. The house staff aim to please and will assist you with all of your event arrangements, from flowers to specialized menus. And for business functions, play golf nearby and then have dinner or a BBQ after the 18th hole.

CAPACITY: The entire facility can accommodate up to 250 guests maximum in the summer and fall, 175 guests during cooler months. The Hollins Room and patio combined can accommodate 45 guests.

FEES & DEPOSITS: When reservations are made, a nonrefundable deposit of $5 per person, based on an anticipated number of guests, is required. The rental fee for the entire Hollins House is $4 per person. For the Hollins Room and patio it's only $1.50 per person. Per person rates: hors d'oeuvres/buffets are approximately $20 and seated meals vary from $12–20. These fees do not include a 6.75% sales tax and 15% gratuity. You may customize your menu with help from the chef and/or event coordinator. The total balance is due in full by the end of your event.

AVAILABILITY: For the entire Hollins House; Saturdays 11am to 4pm and Sundays 4pm to 9pm. For the Hollins Room and patio; Wed–Fri 9am to 3:30pm for business breakfasts or luncheons, 6pm to midnight for dinners.

SERVICES/AMENITIES:

Restaurant Services: yes
Catering: no BYO
Kitchen Facilities: n/a
Tables & Chairs: provided
Linens, Silver, etc.: provided
Restrooms: wca
Dance Floor: yes

Parking: large lots
Overnight Accommodations: no
Telephone: pay phone
Outdoor Night Lighting: yes
Outdoor Cooking Facilities: BBQ CBA
Cleanup: provided

RESTRICTIONS:

Alcohol: provided, BYO corkage fee $70/case

Smoking: allowed

Music: amplified ok if entire facility rented

Wheelchair Access: ramp

Insurance: not required

Big Sur

NEPENTHE

Highway 1
Big Sur, CA 93920
(408) 667-2345
Reserve: 2 weeks in advance

Nepenthe is a Big Sur legend. Perched on a cliff overhanging the surging Pacific, it's decks and restaurant windows have an unsurpassed and unobstructed view of the ocean mists and orange-red sunsets. The original log cabin was purchased by Orson Wells and Rita Hayworth in the mid 1940s, and after their divorce, was bought by the family that still owns and operates Nepenthe. In the 1940s and 50s, the restaurant was infamous as the bohemian social center of Big Sur, with patrons such as Henry Miller, Anais Nin, Man Ray and Salvador Dali. This is where many films have been made, including The Sandpiper with Elizabeth Taylor and Richard Burton. It's a mecca of sorts because of its views, hearty food and convivial atmosphere. You can celebrate your special event below at the Cafe Amphora and relocate to Nepenthe for post-event cocktails. Considered extraordinary in 1949, Nepenthe is still unique.

CAPACITY: The dining room can hold up to 30–40 guests and, combined with the outdoor decks, 100–200 guests.

FEES & DEPOSITS: Nepenthe's deposit is negotiable and is due when you book your event date. Cafe Amphora requires a $100 nonrefundable deposit to reserve a date, with 30% of the estimated total due 2 weeks prior to the event. No rental fee is required. Food service is provided from Nepenthe's menu which ranges from $8–21.50/person, however, they will customize it for private parties. A 6.75% sales tax and 15% gratuity are applied to the final bill.

AVAILABILITY: Luncheons are from 11:30am–4:30pm and dinners from 5pm every day.

SERVICES/AMENITIES:
Restaurant Services: yes
Catering: no BYO
Kitchen Facilities: n/a
Tables & Chairs: provided
Linens, Silver, etc.: some provided
Restrooms: wca
Dance Floor: yes

Parking: large lot
Overnight Accommodations: no
Telephone: pay phone
Outdoor Night Lighting: yes
Outdoor Cooking Facilities: no
Cleanup: provided

RESTRICTIONS:
Alcohol: provided, BYO corkage $10/bottle
Smoking: allowed
Music: no amplified

Wheelchair Access: yes
Insurance: not required

Carmel

THE CARMEL BEACH HOUSE

Address withheld to maintain privacy
Carmel, CA
(408) 446-9619   Jim Hill
Reserve: 3 months in advance

Listen to the waves breaking on the sand—this private residence is right at the ocean's edge. For corporate events or special occasions, this beachfront setting offers guests unparalleled ocean views and a chance to enjoy the outdoors close at hand. Thrill-seeking guests who wish to sample the icy ocean can take the private stairway leading from the house down to the beach. For those more inclined to watch the water from afar, there is a glass-enclosed patio. It provides shelter for guests who linger outside to savor breathtaking sunsets. Inside, a house-long wall of windows offers views from Point Lobos to Pebble Beach. With woodburning fireplaces in the living room, dining room and master bedroom, fully equipped kitchen, gas barbecue and 5 bedrooms, this understated yet sophisticated facility has considerable appeal. If you're looking for exclusivity and privacy, this is the place.

CAPACITY: The house can hold up to 40 guests.

FEES & DEPOSITS: The rental fee is $530/day including an overnight stay. Half is due when the contract is submitted; the balance payable 30 days prior to the function. A $3000 refundable security deposit is also required. Discounts are available for multiple nights.

CANCELLATION POLICY: With 60 days' notice, half of the rental is forfeited. With less than 60, all fees are forfeited except for the security deposit which is returned.

AVAILABILITY: Year-round, every day.

SERVICES/AMENITIES:

Restaurant Services: no
Catering: BYO
Kitchen Facilities: ample
Tables & Chairs: BYO
Linens, Silver, etc.: BYO
Restrooms: limited wca
Dance Floor: no

Parking: driveway and street
Overnight Accommodations: 5 guestrooms
Telephone: house phone
Outdoor Night Lighting: no
Outdoor Cooking Facilities: BBQ
Cleanup: renter or CBA
Other: event coordination

RESTRICTIONS:

Alcohol: BYO
Smoking: outside only
Music: amplified ok

Wheelchair Access: limited
Insurance: sometimes required
Other: children require supervision

LA PLAYA HOTEL ★★

Camino Real and 8th Street
Carmel, CA 93921
(408) 624-6476
Reserve: 2–9 months in advance

Occupying several acres in the heart of residential Carmel, just two blocks from the beach, La Playa is one of the loveliest and most inviting places we've seen. Originally built in 1904 as a private residence, La Playa was converted and expanded into a hotel in 1916. Boasting an exceptionally beautiful Mediterranean style, with terra cotta tile roofs, soft pastel walls and formal gardens, this full-service resort hotel offers a contemporary freshness as well as romantic old-world appeal. For outdoor celebrations, the wrought-iron gazebo is the spot, set amid brick patios, fountain, technicolor annuals, manicured lawns and climbing bougainvillea. The entire setting is lush and private. Our favorite space is the outdoor Terrace, dotted with tables, red umbrellas, overflowing planters and views of the garden and beyond. Outdoor dining here is informal and relaxed. Inside are rooms of various size for private functions, with wood paneling, antiques, lithographs and memorabilia of early Carmel. Tasteful furnishings, French doors, big windows and magnificent views are standard amenities. This is a wonderful site for a party and an equally great location for an overnight stay or company retreat.

CAPACITY, FEES & DEPOSITS:

Room	Deposit	Capacity Standing	Capacity Seated
Garden Room	$200	50	36
Fireside Room	75	25	20
Poseiden Room	500	200	100
The Terrace	—	—	50 (cannot be reserved)
Carmel Conference Room	300	120	100

Deposits must be submitted within 10 days of making your reservation. All deposits are applied to the total food and beverage bill. There are no rental fees when functions include food and beverage service. 70% of the estimated total balance is due the week of the function and the remaining amount within 30 days after the event. There may be rental fees for weekday meetings not involving food service. Call for rates. Per person rates: reception buffets about $25, seated luncheons start at $12.50 and dinners at $25. A 6.75% sales tax and 16% gratuity are applied to the final bill.

CANCELLATION POLICY: Any functions including meal service require cancellation 45 days prior to the event for a refund.

AVAILABILITY: Every day, any time.

SERVICES/AMENITIES:

Restaurant Services: yes
Catering: no BYO
Kitchen Facilities: n/a

Restrooms: wca
Dance Floor: portable
Parking: on street

Tables & Chairs: provided
Linens, Silver, etc.: provided
Overnight Accommodations: 75 guestrooms
and 5 cottages

RESTRICTIONS:
Alcohol: provided, BYO corkage $12/bottle
Smoking: allowed
Music: booked thru La Playa, over by 10pm

Telephone: pay phones, guest phones
Outdoor Night Lighting: limited
Outdoor Cooking Facilities: no
Cleanup: provided

Wheelchair Access: yes
Insurance: not required

MISSION RANCH ★

26270 Dolores
Carmel, CA 93923
(408) 625-0373 Steve and Marilyn
Reserve: 3–12 months in advance

Mission Ranch, once a working dairy, has been a resort for almost 50 years. With white-painted cottages, farm house, bunk house and old cow barn, the Ranch is delightfully rustic and unpolished. This is the charm of Mission Ranch. Set in a large 20-acre parcel with 100-year-old cypress, overlooking the edge of rugged Point Lobos and Carmel River "lagoon", these historic buildings offer the kind of quiet and old-fashioned ambiance not found in nearby bustling downtown Carmel. Parties and celebrations are often held under the huge cypress trees on the lawns within the Ranch complex. The 'Party Barn' is known for its large dance floor and friendly bar. It *really is* a barn, with a no-frills interior boasting a large bar, upright piano, stage for band, dance floor and high open truss ceiling. The structure, also the home of the Monterey Peninsula Jazz Orchestra, appearing every Monday night, is appropriately painted barn red with white trim. The Farm House is a century-old white house, with intimate parlor which could be used for small meetings. The Ranch caterers are ready and willing to fulfill any creative request, from square dancing to theme parties. If you're looking for a place to hold a fun BBQ or upscale dinner in Carmel, this is it.

CAPACITY: The Party Barn holds up to 200 standing and 100 seated guests; there's a required minimum of 40 guests. The Farm House parlor seats 25 and the outdoor areas at Mission Ranch can accommodate over 150 guests.

FEES & DEPOSITS: A 50% deposit on all services is due 60 days prior to the event with the remaining 50% due 10 days prior. The Party Barn rental fee is $100/hour with a 3-hour minimum and a 6-hour maximum rental.

Mission Ranch caterers will customize any menu to suit your needs and offer a multitude of theme party services. Buffet and dinner prices vary: 40–59 guests, $20/person; 60–99 guests, $18.50/person and 100 guests start at 16.50/person. A 6.75% sales tax and 16% gratuity are applied to the final bill.

AVAILABILITY: Tuesday-Sunday until 12am.

SERVICES/AMENITIES:
Restaurant Services: yes
Catering: provided, no BYO

Kitchen Facilities: n/a
Tables & Chairs: provided for 100 guests

Linens, Silver, etc.: provided
Restrooms: wca
Dance Floor: in Barn
Parking: large lot
Overnight Accommodations: 25 guestrooms

Telephone: pay phones
Outdoor Night Lighting: CBA
Outdoor Cooking Facilities: CBA
Cleanup: provided
Other: full event planning services

RESTRICTIONS:
Alcohol: provided, no BYO
Smoking: allowed
Music: amplified with restrictions

Wheelchair Access: yes
Insurance: not required

HIGHLANDS INN ★★

Highway 1
Carmel, CA 93921
(408) 624-3801
Reserve: 1 week or more in advance

Built in the Carmel Highlands in 1916, just south of Carmel, the Highlands Inn is one of the most sought-after event locations in California. Noted for its breathtaking views and extraordinary cliffside setting, the Inn provides an idyllic environment for parties, special celebrations and business functions. After its multi-million dollar, award-winning renovation, Highlands Inn is more stunning than ever. Commanding one of the world's most spectacular vistas, with exploding waves crashing two hundred feet below, the Inn offers a variety of first class facilities for special affairs. For outdoor receptions, a redwood deck complete with contemporary gazebo is perched just above the rocky cliffs overlooking the Pacific. Indoors, six individual rooms, all with uninterrupted glass-walled views of the rugged coastline, provide ideal settings for events or executive conference retreats. The Inn's chefs are renowned for culinary excellence and the wine and champagne list is extensive. The staff can organize a traditional affair or a more creative event for the adventuresome. If you are looking for a very special place, the incomparable Highlands Inn should be high on your list.

CAPACITY:

Area	Standing	Seated	Area	Standing	Seated
Yankee Point room	—	50	Gazebo & Deck	20	80
Monarch Room	—	14	Wine Room	—	40
Surf Room	—	110	Groves North & South	80	60
Fireside Room	180	—			

FEES & DEPOSITS: The space rental fee is the deposit and is payable when the event date is reserved. The rental fees are: Gazebo & Deck, $350; Monarch Room $150; Yankee Point Room $400; Grove Room $250 and Surf Room $550. A dance floor is an extra $85. Approximate per person rates for food service: luncheons $19, dinners $25 and buffet brunches with champagne $24. A 6.75% sales tax and 17% gratuity are additional. Half the estimated total bill is due 4 weeks before and the balance is due 7 working days prior to the event. A final confirmed guest count is required 3 working days in advance of the function.

CANCELLATION POLICY: The deposit will be fully refunded if the date can be rebooked with an equal number of guests. A partial refund may be negotiated. With less than 6 weeks' notice, the deposit is forfeited.

AVAILABILITY: Any day, any time.

SERVICES/AMENITIES:

Restaurant Services: yes

Catering: provided, no BYO

Kitchen Facilities: n/a

Tables & Chairs: provided

Linens, Silver, etc.: provided

Restrooms: wca

Dance Floor: extra charge

Parking: complementary valet

Overnight Accommodations: 142 guestrooms

Telephone: pay phone

Outdoor Night Lighting: yes

Outdoor Cooking Facilities: BBQs

Cleanup: provided

Other: special event services

RESTRICTIONS:

Alcohol: provided, BYO corkage $12.50/bottle

Smoking: allowed

Music: amplified restricted

Wheelchair Access: yes

Insurance: not required

Carmel Valley

CARMEL VALLEY RANCH RESORT

1 Old Ranch Road
Carmel Valley, CA 93923
(408) 625-9500
Reserve: 2–6 months in advance

Opened in June of 1987, this stylish resort complex is set on a hillside overlooking sunlit Carmel Valley, amid 1700 acres of lush green fairways, spreading oaks, recreation facilities and ranch-style vacation homes. The drive up to the lodge is beautifully landscaped. Privacy is paramount, so you'll first have to be checked in through a gatehouse before proceeding to the Lodge. The hub of resort activities, this building mixes modern architecture, antiques, original artwork and early California furnishings with a tasteful contemporary flair. A variety of meeting spaces is available, so get the full tour of the facility. The Grand Ballroom divides into 8 sections and accommodates small to very large parties. This room has high ceilings and tall, vertical windows with shutters. Doors from the Ballroom lead outside to a large tiled courtyard with raised planters, majestic oaks, colorful annuals and recessed heat lamps that take the chill off after sunset. Tables with umbrellas, outdoor BBQs and removable awnings create versatile outdoor event spaces that can accommodate both formal and informal setups.

CAPACITY: The Ballroom has a maximum seated capacity of 180 guests and the Courtyard 150 guests. Combined, the two can hold up to 250–300 people.

MEETING ROOMS: 9 rooms, capacity 10–200 people.

FEES & DEPOSITS: For events, a nonrefundable rental deposit is required to secure your reservation; the amount varies depending on the room(s) selected. The event's total estimated cost is due 1 month prior to the event. Per person rates: luncheons start at $20, dinners start at $30 and buffets range $24–45. The Ballroom rental is $3000–$6500, depending on season, day of the week and guest count. The rental fee may be waived if you guarantee a prearranged amount for food and beverage service. Tax of 6.75% and gratuity of 18% will be applied to the final bill. For business meetings with food service, the rental will vary depending on the room(s) selected and the number of guests.

AVAILABILITY: Any day, any time up to 1am.

SERVICES/AMENITIES:

Restaurant Services: yes

Catering: provided, no BYO

Kitchen Facilities: n/a

Tables & Chairs: provided

Linens, Silver, etc.: provided

Restrooms: wca

Dance Floor: yes, extra charge

Parking: several lots

Overnight Accommodations: 100 suites

Telephone: pay phones

Outdoor Night Lighting: yes

Outdoor Cooking Facilities: BBQ

Cleanup: provided

Special: full event planning

RESTRICTIONS:

Alcohol: provided, no BYO

Smoking: allowed

Music: amplified within reason

Wheelchair Access: yes

Insurance: not required

THE RIDGE RESTAURANT
at Robles Del Rio Lodge

200 Punta Del Monte
Carmel Valley, CA 93924
(408) 659-0170
Reserve: 2 weeks–3 months in advance

Getting to the Ridge is half the fun. It's located up a beautiful, winding road leading to a hilltop where the restaurant overlooks Carmel Valley. Charming and rustic in appearance, The Ridge is actually part of an old lodge. The interior has two main dining areas, one with a glassed-in terrace with terrific views of the valley. Seated meals are generally the rule inside, receptions can be arranged for the garden areas outdoors. The

Lodge has a meeting space, and the patio, pool area and lawns can accommodate larger parties. The Ridge has the best ambiance and views at night when the sun sets and the lights come up in the Valley.

CAPACITY: The main dining room can hold up to 60 seated guests; the deck, 50 and the outside patio and garden 250 maximum.

MEETING ROOM: 1 meeting room, 40 seated.

FEES & DEPOSITS: A nonrefundable $150 deposit secures your date and is due when reservations are made. For small groups staying overnight, the deposit is sometimes waived. Half of the estimated food and beverage cost is due 30 days prior to the function and the balance is due on the day of the event. Per person rates: luncheons start at $7.50, dinners start at $16, buffets range from $10–30 and Sunday brunch from $14.75. Tax of 6.75% and 15% gratuity will be added to the final bill.

CANCELLATION POLICY: You must cancel more than 72 hours prior to your event to receive a refund of the food and beverage deposit.

AVAILABILITY: Year-round, closed Mondays. For groups of over 50 guests, Mondays can be made available.

SERVICES/AMENITIES:

Restaurant Services: yes
Catering: no BYO
Kitchen Facilities: n/a
Tables & Chairs: mostly provided
Linens, Silver, etc.: mostly provided
Restrooms: wca
Dance Floor: several areas
Parking: large lots

Overnight Accommodations: 31 guestrooms
Telephone: pay phone
Outdoor Night Lighting: yes
Outdoor Cooking Facilities: BBQ
Cleanup: provided
Other: full event coordination
Special: pool

RESTRICTIONS:

Alcohol: provided, BYO corkage $7.50/bottle
Smoking: allowed
Music: amplified, DJs ok

Wheelchair Access: yes
Insurance: not required

STONEPINE ★

150 E. Carmel Valley Road
Carmel Valley, CA 93924
(408) 659-2245
Reserve: 6–12 months in advance

Built by Henry Russell for his wife, a member of the Crocker banking family, Stonepine is now an exclusive resort, which has been restored to its former grandeur. Located off of the Carmel Valley Road, the one-mile long drive gets you in an expectant mood as you preview the estate's phenomenal 330 acres of rolling hills, dotted with oaks and other vegetation. Russell was one of the founders of thoroughbred racing on the West Coast, and magnificent horses were once stabled here. The estate is now used for executive conferences, overnight guests and private parties. The mansion is designed in an elegant Mediterranean style with light stucco walls and red tile roofs. The stately home with formal gardens creates an atmosphere that is both relaxed and comfortable. Since Stonepine offers numerous areas for functions, set up an appointment and ask for the grand tour of the facilities (which include one of the loveliest settings for a pool party that we've seen). Carriage rides around the estate are a fun diversion for guests during the course of an event. Note that you can reserve the entire estate for the exclusive use of your group and that it's a terrific spot for a retreat.

CAPACITY: Stonepine can hold up to 250 guests.

FEES & DEPOSITS: The site rental fees are the refundable deposit required to secure a date and are due when you reserve a specific spot for your event. Other deposits apply depending on the party location, so ask for specifics. Rental fees vary depending on the area chosen, from $1000–5200. Should you wish exclusive use of Stonepine for your event, the fee is $5200. Stonepine offers their private dining facilities to guests only. Per person rates: an hors d'oeuvres party starts at $25, buffets at $35 and full dinners at $45. A 6.75% sales tax and 15% gratuity will be applied to the final bill.

CANCELLATION POLICY: With 90 days' notice, the deposit will be refunded.

AVAILABILITY: Any day, any time.

SERVICES/AMENITIES:

Restaurant Services: private dining facilities

Catering: no BYO

Kitchen Facilities: n/a

Tables & Chairs: provided

Linens, Silver, etc.: provided

Restrooms: wca limited

Dance Floor: CBA, extra charge

Parking: valet, extra charge

Overnight Accommodations: 12 suites

Telephone: guest phone

Outdoor Night Lighting: CBA

Outdoor Cooking Facilities: CBA

Cleanup: provided

Other: carriage rides

RESTRICTIONS:

Alcohol: provided, BYO corkage $10/bottle

Smoking: allowed

Music: amplified until 10pm

Wheelchair Access: limited

Insurance: not required

Other: children restricted from some areas

Monterey

LA MIRADA

The Castro Adobe, Frank Work Estate
720 Via Mirada
Monterey, CA 93940
(408) 372-3689
Reserve: 2–4 months in advance

La Mirada is an historic home, situated on a 3-acre knoll overlooking Laguinta Mirada and Lake El Estero. Originally built as the residence of Jose Castro, one of the most prominent men in California during the Mexican period, the old adobe portion of the house reflects the early days of Monterey. It has been restored and a 2-story wing plus drawing room were added early in this century. Although the house is now a part of the Monterey Peninsula Museum of Art, it still has the warmth and ambiance of a comfortable, lived-in home with fine antique furnishings and gallery pieces. The outdoor courtyards feature a richly planted garden, old rock walls and mature rhododendrons. This is a terrific spot for business or nonprofit organizations to have gatherings. Note that private social events are not allowed.

CAPACITY: The maximum capacity indoors is 60 seated guests; the formal dining room can seat 22. The outdoor courtyards accommodate up to 350 seated.

FEES & DEPOSITS: A refundable $150–250 booking fee is required to hold your date. Half of the rental donation is due 3 weeks prior to the event, and the balance is due the day of the event. If tour docents are desired, the charge is $25/docent. All rental fees include security and basic insurance and may be adjusted somewhat for nonprofit groups. Rental fees are:

Group Size	Breakfasts	Luncheons	Dinners
under 25	$100	$350	$450
25–60	150	500	750

For meetings (no meals) the rental for under 35 guests is $250 (half day); over 35 guests $350 (half day); and for a full day, the charge is $350–450, depending on the guest count. The rental charge for the drawing room, perfect for formal gatherings in the evenings, ranges from $500 to $1500.

CANCELLATION POLICY: With 4 weeks' notice, you'll receive a full refund.

AVAILABILITY: Year-round, every day from 7am–11pm.

SERVICES/AMENITIES:

Restaurant Services: no
Catering: BYO or CBA
Kitchen Facilities: ample
Tables & Chairs: provided, extra charge
Linens, Silver, etc.: provided, extra charge

Restrooms: no wca
Dance Floor: CBA
Parking: lot nearby, carpooling encouraged
Overnight Accommodations: no
Telephone: house phones

Outdoor Night Lighting: yes
Outdoor Cooking Facilities: CBA
Cleanup: whoever caters event

Other: event coordination, tents CBA, extra charge
Special: grand piano

RESTRICTIONS:
Alcohol: BYO, no red wine in drawing room
Smoking: outside only
Music: no amplified

Wheelchair Access: yes
Insurance: not required

MONTEREY BAY AQUARIUM ★★

886 Cannery Row
Monterey, CA 93940
(408) 648-4800
Reserve: 12–18 months in advance

If you've already been to the sensational Monterey Bay Aquarium you'll be delighted to learn that it's available for private events. If you haven't been here yet, then this is a great opportunity to see one of the most beautifully designed buildings in the United States. Constructed on the site of the old Hovden Cannery on the bay's edge in the heart of Monterey's historic Cannery Row, this facility is unsurpassed in its range of Monterey Bay displays and exhibits. One extraordinary feature is a 3-story tank complete with kelp forest swaying in rhythm with tidal undulations. Some of the touch-and-learn exhibits, where you can pet swimming bat rays or multi-colored sea stars, are open at night and there are countless other exotic-looking sea creatures to see. The aquarium is perfect for a variety of evening events and has facilities for meetings and other programs during the day. The nicely appointed Portola Cafe and the private Ocean View Conference Room are also available. As an added dimension to an already exceptional setting, aquarium guides will be available during your exclusive evening event. Reserve early—this is a much sought-after place.

CAPACITY:	*Area*	*Standing*	*Seated*
	Kelp Forest	200	80
	Marine Mammals Gallery	500	275-300
	Portola Cafe	75	75
	Ocean View Conference Room	100	14–100
	Auditorium	—	273
	Entire Aquarium	2000	—

FEES & DEPOSITS: An initial deposit is required 6 months in advance of the event and complete payment is required one month prior to the event. Admission fees will be quoted at the time of your inquiry. Per person food service rates: an hors d'oeuvres reception $10–15, a sit-down dinner or buffet $24–60. Breakfast, lunch and coffee-break menus are also available. A sales tax of 6.75% and gratuity of 16% are applied to the final bill.

CANCELLATION POLICY: With 6 months' notice, your deposit will be fully refunded; 3–6 months, 50% will be refunded; less than 3 months, no refund.

AVAILABILITY: Days and evenings, depending upon the event. Closed Christmas.

SERVICES/AMENITIES:

Restaurant Services: yes

Catering: provided, no BYO

Kitchen Facilities: n/a

Tables & Chairs: provided

Linens, Silver, etc.: provided

Restrooms: wca

Dance Floor: yes

Parking: City lots, employee lots

Overnight Accommodations: no

Telephone: pay phones

Outdoor Night Lighting: yes

Outdoor Cooking Facilities: no

Cleanup: provided

Other: full range of event services

RESTRICTIONS:

Alcohol: provided, BYO corkage $8/bottle

Smoking: outside only

Music: amplified ok

Wheelchair Access: yes

Insurance: extra liability required plus indemnification clause

Other: decoration restrictions

MONTEREY PLAZA

400 Cannery Row
Monterey, CA 93940
(408) 646-1700 Catering Department
Reserve: 2–6 months in advance

Built right on the water's edge, just a heartbeat away from the Monterey Bay Aquarium and Cannery Row, the Monterey Plaza is an oceanfront resort offering both indoor and outdoor facilities for meetings, theme parties, conventions and retreats. From the Grand Entry and Lobby to the outdoor Terrace perched above the water, the Plaza provides all the luxuries and conveniences of a large, professionally staffed hotel. Broad eaves, bold timberwork, trusses and trellises typify the exterior. The interior has walls paneled in natural redwood and adorned with painted panels depicting the Monterey Coast landscape. The Plaza has a blend of 18th Century Chinese and formal Italian Empire period furnishings with rattan, fruitwood and teak furniture plus exotic marble finishes, porcelain objets d'art and murals. With an emphasis on hospitality and top-drawer treatment, the Plaza is sure to competently manage all the details if you're considering a large social or business event.

CAPACITY: The Ballroom can accommodate 600 standing and 500 seated guests; the Ohloni Room can hold up to 75 standing and 50 seated guests.

MEETING ROOMS: 13 rooms holding from 10–500 people. The Plaza has full conference capabilities with fax, typing services, 24-hour message service, telex and conference coordinator.

FEES & DEPOSITS: A refundable deposit of 50% of the total estimated food and beverage cost is due when you make your reservation. Rental fee for the Ballroom is $1000. If food and beverage services exceed $2000, the rental fee is waived. Other smaller rooms at the Plaza range from $100-400. Per person food service rates:

continental breakfast/full breakfast is $7.50–16, luncheons $14–26, dinners $28–46 and hor d'oeuvres $15–30. A 6.75% sales tax and 16% gratuity are applied to the final bill.

CANCELLATION POLICY: If you cancel with less than 60 days' notice, 50% is returned; 30 days' notice, 25% is returned; less than 7 days, no refund.

AVAILABILITY: Any day, any time.

SERVICES/AMENITIES:

Restaurant Services: yes

Catering: provided, no BYO

Kitchen Facilities: n/a

Tables & Chairs: provided

Linens, Silver, etc.: provided

Restrooms: wca

Dance Floor: CBA

Parking: valet CBA, $9/car

Overnight Accommodations: 290 guestrooms

Telephone: pay phone

Outdoor Night Lighting: yes

Outdoor Cooking Facilities: yes

Cleanup: provided

Other: conference coordinator, recreation activities CBA

RESTRICTIONS:

Alcohol: provided

Smoking: allowed

Music: amplified ok in all lower level rooms

Wheelchair Access: yes

Insurance: not required

OLD MONTEREY INN

500 Martin Street
Monterey, CA 93940
(408) 375-8284
Reserve: 4–6 months in advance

Identified as "The Perfect Inn" by Country Inns of California, the Old Monterey Inn, a 1929 Tudor country house, is located in a quiet residential section of town. Monterey's first elected mayor built this 3-story mansion, which has been thoughtfully restored and improved over the years. Surrounded by more than an acre of English-style gardens, you can breakfast or enjoy afternoon tea amongst hydrangeas, begonias, rhododendrons, fuchsias and roses. A canopy of redwoods, oaks and pines frames all the vistas from the garden. Inside, there are lovely handcrafted details such as the ceiling panels in the dining room, fireplace hood and Gothic archways. Each of the 10 guestrooms is well appointed and comfortable. Although limited to the off-season, for business conferences it is a unique and desirable executive retreat.

CAPACITY: The Inn can accommodate 20 guests, only with an overnight stay.

FEES & DEPOSITS: Payment is due in full when reservations are confirmed. The Inn will book small conferences November–April. The entire house rental is $1883/night, Sunday–Thursday, which includes a full breakfast and evening wine and cheese.

CANCELLATION POLICY: With 3 months' advance notice, you'll receive a full refund. With 2 months', a 50% refund or more, depending on what has been rebooked.

AVAILABILITY: November–April, Sunday–Thursday. Check–in is between 2:30pm–8pm, departure by noon.

SERVICES/AMENITIES:

Restaurant Services: no
Catering: provided, breakfast and lunch only
Kitchen Facilities: n/a
Tables & Chairs: provided
Linens, Silver, etc.: provided
Restrooms: no wca
Dance Floor: no

Parking: limited to 12 cars
Overnight Accommodations: 10 guestrooms
Telephone: pay phone, private lines
Outdoor Night Lighting: no
Outdoor Cooking Facilities: no
Cleanup: provided

RESTRICTIONS:

Alcohol: white wine provided, no red, BYO with approval
Smoking: in garden only

Music: no amplified
Wheelchair Access: no
Insurance: not required

OLD WHALING STATION

391 Decatur St.
Monterey, CA 93940
(408) 375-5356
Reserve: 2 weeks–3 months in advance

This historic adobe structure reflects the character and history of early Monterey. Most sources indicate that the Old Whaling Station was built in 1847 by a Scottish adventurer as a home for his wife and daughter. In 1855, The Old Monterey Whaling Company began using the building for on-shore whaling operations, hence the unusual name. Local legend has it that whalers kept their lookout from the upstairs windows which have an unimpeded view of the Bay. When the whaling business waned at the turn of the century, the building fell into disrepair. Now leased by the Junior League of Monterey County, Inc., the property has undergone an extensive restoration. The result is an appealing facility and technicolor garden available for small, private events.

CAPACITY: The Station can hold up to 50 inside; the garden up to 100 seated guests. The facility's total capacity is 150 guests.

FEES & DEPOSITS: The contract must be returned within 10 days of making a tentative reservation along with a nonrefundable $50 booking deposit. A nonrefundable $175 is required 6 weeks prior to the event, and a final $175 plus a $200 refundable security deposit are due when keys are transferred to the renter. These fees total $400 for an all-day rental. For nonprofit organizations, the rental fee is $200. If you'd like an additional half-day rental for setup or cleanup, the fee is $100.

CANCELLATION POLICY: With 6 weeks' notice, the final $175 rental fee and security deposit are refundable.

AVAILABILITY: Year-round, every day from 8am to midnight.

SERVICES/AMENITIES:

Restaurant Services: no
Catering: BYO
Kitchen Facilities: full kitchen
Tables & Chairs: some provided
Linens, Silver, etc.: some provided
Restrooms: wca limited
Dance Floor: CBA

Parking: Heritage Harbor lots
Overnight Accommodations: no
Telephone: house phone
Outdoor Night Lighting: yes
Outdoor Cooking Facilities: CBA
Cleanup: whoever caters event

RESTRICTIONS:

Alcohol: BYO
Smoking: outside only
Music: amplified restricted

Wheelchair Access: no
Insurance: not required
Other: no pets

VICTORIAN CARRIAGE HOUSE AND GARDEN

201 A Van Buren
Monterey, CA 93940
(408) 625-2404   Flowers Ltd.
Reserve: 3 months in advance

The Victorian Carriage House is tucked away behind the Perry House, a lovely, century-old home in the older part of town. Overlooking Monterey Bay and situated amongst other historic buildings in a quiet, residential neighborhood, the Carriage House has the feel of a garden pavilion, with Tiffany-style skylight and detailed wood doors that open onto an English garden with gazebo. Flowers and mature trees make this a sheltered and cozy spot for a garden party. (An interesting historic aside is that the garden still retains the first drinking water well in Monterey). For business luncheons or private parties, the Carriage House and gardens are a pleasant and distinctive location.

CAPACITY: The Carriage House can hold up to 90 standing and 35 seated guests. Combined with the garden, the facility can accommodate a total of 250 guests.

FEES & DEPOSITS: A refundable $100 cleaning deposit plus the $400 rental fee are due when reservations are made.

CANCELLATION POLICY: If you give 60 days' notice, or the facility can be rebooked, the deposit is refunded. With less than 60 days' notice, 50% of the deposit will be forfeited.

AVAILABILITY: Year-round, every day from 8:30am to 10:30pm.

SERVICES/AMENITIES:

Restaurant Services: no

Catering: BYO

Kitchen Facilities: minimal

Tables & Chairs: BYO

Linens, Silver, etc.: BYO

Restrooms: wca

Dance Floor: patio

Parking: garage nearby

Overnight Accommodations: no

Telephone: no

Outdoor Night Lighting: yes

Outdoor Cooking Facilities: BYO

Cleanup: whoever caters event

Other: special flowers, linens CBA

RESTRICTIONS:

Alcohol: BYO

Smoking: allowed

Music: amplified w/in limits

Wheelchair Access: yes

Insurance: not required

Other: no pets

Pacific Grove

ASILOMAR CONFERENCE CENTER ★★

800 Asilomar Blvd.
Pacific Grove, CA 93950
(408) 372-8016
Reserve: 12–24 months in advance

Although Asilomar is not a secret, most people don't know it's available for special events.Widely recognized as one of California's most extraordinary conference facilities, Asilomar (literally 'Refuge-by-the-Sea') was established as a YMCA retreat in 1913. As part of the California State Park System, it now offers the public an unparalleled environment for any kind of gathering. Architecturally, Asilomar is outstanding. Many of the buildings are historic landmarks, designed in craftsman style by Julia Morgan in the early 1900s. Even the newer structures harmonize with the surrounding beach and forest. After the meeting or festivities, guests can enjoy white sand beaches, dune boardwalks and tidepools nearby. Swimming, bicycling, oceanfront strolling and picnicking are favorite activities. Asilomar's character is unique. It combines an unbeatable 105-acre location next to the ocean with reasonably priced accommodations and distinctive meeting spaces.

CAPACITY: 1200 guests, minimum group must be 10 guests

MEETING ROOMS: 48 rooms, ranging from a boardroom or informal living room for 10 to a large conference space for 850 participants.

FEES & DEPOSITS: To reserve a date, contact the conference office to request an application. A deposit of $10/person is required when a contract is submitted, usually 8–12 months in advance of the event. An estimated guest count is required both 90 and 60 days prior to the function with a final count due in writing 30 days in advance. Conference rates for 2 or more nights are $41–52/person. For 1 night, $43–61/person. There are reduced rates for children. Rates include accommodations, meals, tax, meeting spaces, grounds and recreation facilities. The charge for off–grounds participants is $6/person per day. The event balance is due upon departure.

CANCELLATION POLICY: With 120 days' notice, the deposit will be fully refunded minus a $25 administration fee.

AVAILABILITY: Year-round, every day. Arrival time 3pm, departure time 12 noon.

SERVICES/AMENITIES:

Restaurant Services: yes
Catering: provided, no BYO
Kitchen Facilities: n/a
Tables & Chairs: provided
Linens, Silver, etc.: provided
Restrooms: mostly wca
Dance Floor: yes

Parking: many large lots
Overnight Accommodations: 313 guestrooms
Telephone: guest phone, pay phone
Outdoor Night Lighting: yes
Outdoor Cooking Facilities: BBQ
Cleanup: provided

RESTRICTIONS:

Alcohol: BYO
Smoking: restricted in public use areas
Music: amplified, DJs ok,
hours & volume w/approval

Wheelchair Access: yes, except in historic bldg.
Insurance: sometimes required

THE GREEN GABLES INN

104 Fifth Street
Pacific Grove, CA 93950
(408) 375-2095 Claudia Long
Reserve: 3–9 months in advance

The Inn is a detailed Queen Anne-style mansion on the edge of Monterey Bay. This half-timbered, step-gabled residence, built in 1888, is an exquisite gem among Pacific Grove's many Victorian homes. The panoramic views from the garden and Inn, plus its proximity to the water's edge create a peaceful and special setting for small meetings and parties. Indoors, the living room features large bay window alcoves facing the seascape, a lovely collection of antique furnishings and a unique fireplace framed by stained-glass panels. During functions, you can catch glimpses of waves breaking on the rocks, migrating whales, sea lions basking in the sun and otters frolicking in the surf. The Inn is also a wonderful overnight destination.

CAPACITY: The Inn can accommodate 30 people in the Parlor and 10–15 in the Dining Room.

FEES & DEPOSITS: As a refundable deposit, one full night's room rate is required to secure your reservation and is payable when you set your date. Business functions are excepted. For groups, a $500–1500 refundable security deposit may be required. To reserve the entire Inn, the cost is $1600. The rental fee is the price of each guestroom for one night plus a 10% room tax. Smaller parties or meetings can be arranged without guestroom rental.

CANCELLATION POLICY: For business functions or events, if you give more than 1 month's notice, your deposit will be refunded in full.

AVAILABILITY: For parties and special events, by arrangement only. Business functions from 1pm to 4pm.

SERVICES/AMENITIES:

Restaurant Services: no
Catering: CBA or BYO
Kitchen Facilities: ample
Tables & Chairs: BYO
Linens, Silver, etc.: BYO
Restrooms: no wca
Dance Floor: no

Parking: on street
Overnight Accommodations: 11 guestrooms
Telephone: guest phone
Outdoor Night Lighting: CBA
Outdoor Cooking Facilities: CBA
Cleanup: whoever caters event

RESTRICTIONS:

Alcohol: WC provided
Smoking: outside only
Music: amplified within limits

Wheelchair Access: no
Insurance: not required

MARTINE INN

255 Oceanview Blvd.
Pacific Grove, CA 93950
(408) 373-3388 Marion
Reserve: 2–6 months in advance

The Martine Inn is set high, right on the edge of Monterey Bay, overlooking the rocky coastline of Pacific Grove. Originally designed as an oceanfront Victorian mansion in 1898, it was remodeled as a Mediterranean Villa by James and Laura Park (of the Park Davis pharmaceutical company) when Victoriana went out of style in the early 1900s. Although the exterior is Mediterranean, the Inn's decor is strictly Victorian, in rose and pink hues. There are elegantly furnished rooms complete with museum-quality American antiques and from interior windows, guests have wonderful views of waves crashing against the cliffs. The Martines can help you design your event and/or conference to meet your specific requirements and will even provide a staff consultant to plan for food, music, decorations or entertainment.

CAPACITY: The Parlor can hold 30 guests and the courtyard up to 120. The conference room holds up to 20 guests, the dining room is perfect for 12, the library holds 20, and there's a game room with pool table and spa. If you rent the entire Inn for your party, it can accommodate 120 guests indoors.

FEES & DEPOSITS: For under 10 guests, there's a $100 event fee; between 10–35 guests, a $150 fee is required. If there are more than 35 guests, you must reserve the entire Inn for which there is a $500 event fee. In addition, the group must reserve the entire house, which costs approximately $3100/night. All fees are due upon making your reservation. For business meetings and conferences of less than 10 guests, there's a $150 conference room fee. For over 10, special rates are available depending on the type of meal service desired.

CANCELLATION POLICY: Event fees will be forfeited with less than 30 days' notice; 50% of the fees will be refunded with over 30 days' notice. The guestroom rental fees are refundable, less $10/room, with 72 hours' advance notice. With less than 72 hours' notice, your room fees are refundable only if they can be rebooked.

AVAILABILITY: If you book the entire Inn, the event hours are negotiable. If you reserve only a portion of the Inn, the hours are usually 1pm–4pm.

SERVICES/AMENITIES:

Restaurant Services: no
Catering: provided, no BYO
Kitchen Facilities: n/a
Tables & Chairs: provided
Linens, Silver, etc.: provided
Restrooms: wca
Dance Floor: yes

Parking: on street, medium lot
Overnight Accommodations: 20 guestrooms
Telephone: guest phone
Outdoor Night Lighting: minimal
Outdoor Cooking Facilities: no
Cleanup: provided
Other: full event services, audio-visual equipment

RESTRICTIONS:

Alcohol: provided, no BYO, WBC only
Smoking: restricted
Music: amplified with volume limit

Wheelchair Access: yes
Insurance: not required

Pebble Beach

BEACH AND TENNIS CLUB ★★

Pebble Beach, CA 93953
(408) 625-8507
Reserve: 1–12 months in advance

Just two quick minutes from the Lodge at Pebble Beach is the resort's private Beach and Tennis Club which has tennis courts, pool, spa, and fitness center. Although this is a private club, you don't have to be a member to reserve the banquet facilities! And that's a good thing because the Surf Room is one of the most wonderful places for a party or corporate event we've run across. The location and ambiance rivals—no, surpasses— The Lodge at Pebble Beach in providing outstanding views in an intimate setting. The main dining room juts out almost to the ocean's edge. And since three of the four dining room walls are glass, the vistas over Carmel Bay, nearby fairways and cliffs are unparalleled. With muted pastel colors, white linens and brass and mirror details, the Surf Room is sophisticated yet comfortable. The adjacent poolside patio can be tented for outdoor dancing, bar service or buffet meals. Another room that's available is the Terrace Room, which has a working black marble-faced fireplace and is decorated in whites and cream colors. This room is primarily for small, seated functions or it can be used for buffet table service when guests are seated in the Surf Room.

CAPACITY: The Surf Room holds 200–250 for a seated party (depending on use of the dance floor), the Terrace Room holds up to 50 seated guests and the Patio can hold up to 90 seated guests.

FEES & DEPOSITS: A refundable $1000-1500 deposit is due within 2 weeks after you make your reservation. The rental fee is $1000, which reserves the entire club. Food service is provided. Buffets start at $44/ person and dinners range from $45–50/person. A 6.75% sales tax and 17% gratuity are applied to the final bill. The total is due 14 days in advance of your party.

CANCELLATION POLICY: With 6 months' notice, the deposit will be refunded.

AVAILABILITY: Monday-Sunday, from 6pm until midnight. This is a private club, consequently availability is limited.

SERVICES/AMENITIES:

Restaurant Services: yes
Catering: no BYO
Kitchen Facilities: n/a
Tables & Chairs: provided
Linens, Silver, etc.: provided
Restrooms: wca
Dance Floor: yes

Parking: large lot
Overnight Accommodations: at Lodge
Telephone: pay phone
Outdoor Night Lighting: yes
Outdoor Cooking Facilities: CBA
Cleanup: provided
Other: tents for patio CBA, extra charge

RESTRICTIONS:

Alcohol: provided, BYO corkage $10/bottle
Smoking: allowed
Music: amplified ok

Wheelchair Access: yes
Insurance: not required

THE INN AT SPANISH BAY

17 Mile Drive
Pebble Beach, CA 93953
(408) 647-7500
Reserve: 1–6 months in advance

Right off of the famous 17 Mile Drive, this new resort stands at the edge of the Del Monte Forest, barely 300 yards from the ocean's edge. The Inn is designed in the Old Monterey and Spanish California style, with sloping roofs, arched windows and light stucco walls. The Inn is surrounded by lush golf fairways and windswept dunes sloping down to the ocean. Inside, the Inn offers guests fireplaces, tasteful appointments in soft colors and various special amenities. This is a large complex featuring 270 guestrooms, restaurants, retail shops, recreation facilities as well as banquet accommodations. A wide range of rooms is available for private parties including the sizable Ballroom and the Bay Club Restaurant. There are quite a few smaller rooms and special boardroom facilities for your business functions.

CAPACITY: The Bay Club Restaurant, available on Saturdays for lunch only, seats 60 guests. The Ballroom seats 300 guests comfortably and the Fairway Patio can hold 250 guests for a cocktail party.

MEETING ROOMS: 15 rooms, capacity varies so call for details.

FEES & DEPOSITS: A nonrefundable $500–1000 deposit, depending on the size of the room, is due when you book your reservations. Room rentals for business functions vary depending on room selection. For events, per person rates: luncheons $22–30, buffets start at $35, and dinners at $38. A sales tax of 6.75% and a gratuity of 17% are additional.

CANCELLATION POLICY: If you cancel less than 2 months prior to your event, your deposit will be forfeited unless the Inn can rebook the date.

AVAILABILITY: Any day, 6am until 2am.

SERVICES/AMENITIES:

Restaurant Services: yes
Catering: no BYO
Kitchen Facilities: n/a
Tables & Chairs: provided
Linens, Silver, etc.: provided
Restrooms: wca
Dance Floor: yes

Parking: large lots
Overnight Accommodations: 270 rooms
Telephone: pay phones
Outdoor Night Lighting: CBA
Outdoor Cooking Facilities: BBQs
Cleanup: provided
Other: business amenities & equipment

RESTRICTIONS:

Alcohol: provided, no BYO
Smoking: allowed
Music: amplified ok

Wheelchair Access: yes
Insurance: not required

THE LODGE AT PEBBLE BEACH

17 Mile Drive
Pebble Beach, CA 93953
(408) 624-3811
Reserve: 1–12 months in advance

Since opening in 1919, the Lodge has served as the hub of one of the world's premier and most challenging golf courses. The emerald green, meticulously manicured fairways follow the serpentine edge of Carmel Bay and lie directly below the Lodge. With its sweeping ocean panoramas, setting and relaxed elegance, the Lodge is one of Northern California's favorite spots for special celebrations, corporate events and meetings. Inside are a variety of rooms suitable for private parties. Most have great views and are well appointed.

A conference center large enough to hold up to 330 seated guests comes complete with fax, private phones and audio-visual equipment. For those with limited time to coordinate an event, The Lodge's professional and courteous staff can assist you with every detail of your function.

CAPACITY, FEES & DEPOSITS:

Room	Seated Capacity	Meeting Rental
Garden Room	30 max.	—
Pebble Beach Room	120–150	$500/day
Library Room	60	$500/day
Card Room	30	$250/day
Conference Center	330	$1000/day

The exterior lawn can be rented for croquet games and lawn parties. Call for individual quotes. A refundable deposit of approximately $1000 is due within 2 weeks after making your reservation. Per person rates for food: hors d'oeuvres start at $25, luncheons start at $22–27 and dinners at $40–50. A sales tax of 6.75% and 17% gratuity are additional.

MEETING ROOMS: The lodge has 4 (capacity varies) plus the conference center.

CANCELLATION POLICY: With 6 months' notice, the deposit will be refunded.

AVAILABILITY: Any day, any time until midnight.

SERVICES/AMENITIES:

Restaurant Services: yes
Catering: no BYO
Kitchen Facilities: n/a
Tables & Chairs: provided
Linens, Silver, etc.: provided
Restrooms: wca
Dance Floor: yes
Parking: large lots

Overnight Accommodations: 161 guestrooms
Telephone: pay phone
Outdoor Night Lighting: limited
Outdoor Cooking Facilities: CBA
Cleanup: provided
Other: tents for outdoor lawn parties CBA

RESTRICTIONS:

Alcohol: provided, BYO corkage $10/bottle
Smoking: allowed
Music: amplified outside until 11pm

Wheelchair Access: yes
Insurance: not required

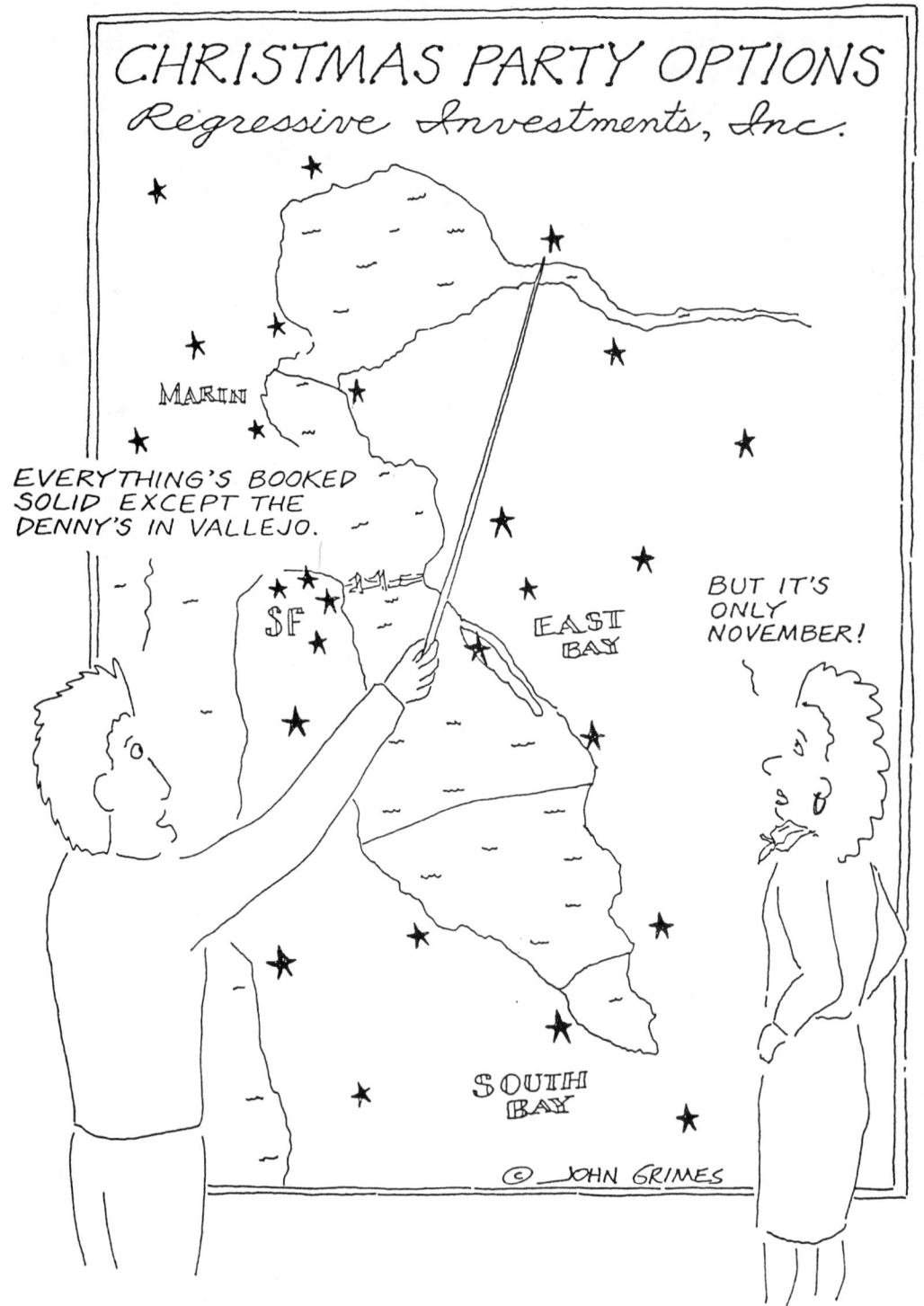

Amador City

IMPERIAL HOTEL

14202 Highway 49
Amador City, CA 95601
(209) 267-9172
Reserve: 2 weeks in advance

Built originally as a mercantile store, this building was developed into a hotel in 1879 because the town had insufficient lodging. In 1988, after a 51-year hiatus, the Imperial Hotel was restored by its present innkeepers. It has a restaurant and bar in addition to overnight accommodations. The dining room is simple yet stylish with high ceilings, white walls and contemporary art which gives the interior an art-gallery ambiance. The bar is also appealing, with features reminiscent of an Egyptian oasis. With outstanding food and an environment to match, the Imperial is a splendid destination for a creative celebration, private party or unique business retreat.

CAPACITY: The dining room can hold up to 55 seated guests for dinner and up to 60 for lunch.

FEES & DEPOSITS: For weekday meetings, the rental fee is $100. If meal service is provided, the charge is waived. Food service starts at $10/person for lunch and dinners start at $14/person. A deposit of 50% of the estimated event cost is due 7 days in advance of the function. The balance is due an the end of the event.

CANCELLATION POLICY: With 7 days' notice, the deposit is fully refundable.

AVAILABILITY: Year-round, every day except for the first 2 weeks in February. Most Friday and Saturday group events are scheduled between 5pm–7pm.

SERVICES/AMENITIES:
Restaurant Services: yes
Catering: provided, no BYO
Kitchen Facilities: n/a
Tables & Chairs: provided
Linens, Silver, etc.: provided
Restrooms: wca
Dance Floor: no

Parking: on street, parking lot
Overnight Accommodations: 6 guestrooms
Telephone: house phone
Outdoor Night Lighting: no
Outdoor Cooking Facilities: no
Cleanup: provided

RESTRICTIONS:
Alcohol: provided, no BYO
Smoking: allowed
Music: amplified restricted

Wheelchair Access: yes
Insurance: sometimes required

Auburn

AUBURN VALLEY ★ COUNTRY CLUB

8800 Auburn Valley Road
Auburn CA 95603
(916) 269-2775
Reserve: 6 months in advance

The Auburn Valley Country Club is one of those unexpected gems. You drive down a curvy scenic road for miles, wondering if the destination at the end will be worth the drive. Well, this one is. Set atop a knoll, the Club overlooks a gorgeous golf club studded with lakes, rolling hills and deep green trees. The view is breathtaking, and the surroundings so peaceful that all you hear are the birds and the breeze. The dining room faces this picture-book valley through floor-to-ceiling windows, providing a light and airy space for any event. A large, nicely landscaped patio is also a great place for outdoor functions.

CAPACITY:

Area	Seated	Standing
Patio	250	400
Lounge	50	—
Dining Room	125	175

FEES & DEPOSITS: The facility rental fee is $350 for 6 hours. A $300 deposit is due at the time of booking. 90% of all costs and a guaranteed guest count are due 1 week prior to the event. The balance is payable on departure. Catering fees run about $14-23 for a sit-down meal and $14–20 for a buffet.

CANCELLATION POLICY: A refund is only given with 30 days' notice.

AVAILABILITY: Every day, 4pm-midnight in the winter, 5pm-midnight during the rest of the year.

SERVICES/AMENITIES:

Restaurant Services: yes
Catering: provided
Kitchen Facilities: n/a
Tables & Chairs: provided
Linens, Silver, etc.: provided
Restrooms: wca
Dance Floor: yes

Parking: lot
Overnight Accommodations: no
Telephone: pay phone
Outdoor Night Lighting: yes
Outdoor Cooking Facilities: BBQ
Cleanup: provided

RESTRICTIONS:

Alcohol: provided or BYO CW, corkage $2/bottle
Smoking: allowed
Music: amplified ok

Wheelchair Access: yes
Insurance: not required

POWER'S MANSION INN

164 Cleveland Ave.
Auburn, CA 95603
(916) 885-1166
Reserve: 3–6 months in advance

One of Auburn's landmarks, this century-old Victorian is a bed and breakfast inn with a business side. The large dining room and adjoining parlor and library are often used for meetings and conferences, and the concierge service is a plus that businesses will appreciate. The Inn has been nicely restored with custom wallpaper, antiques, period fixtures and beautiful colors. The elegant interior, terraced garden patio, and wrap-around porches and decks make this a lovely spot for private parties as well.

CAPACITY: Dining room 35, library 20, parlor 20; the entire facility 75 guests total.

FEES & DEPOSITS: One third of the estimated charges are due at the time of booking. The balance is due the day of the event. The facility rents for $400/day if no lodging is reserved, and there is a $20 credit for each room reserved. Catering is handled by the Inn and runs $9-15/person for lunch and $14-25/person for dinner.

CANCELLATION POLICY: With partial rental, you will receive a full refund with 2 weeks' notice. If you have reserved the entire Inn, 1 month's notice is required.

AVAILABILITY: Year-round, every day.

SERVICES/AMENITIES:

Restaurant Services: no
Catering: provided, no BYO
Kitchen Facilities: n/a
Tables & Chairs: provided
Linens, Silver, etc.: provided
Restrooms: wca
Dance Floor: CBA for fee

Parking: on and off street
Overnight Accommodations: 15 guestrooms
Telephone: guest phones
Outdoor Night Lighting: yes
Outdoor Cooking Facilities: no
Cleanup: provided
Special Services: concierge & valet service

RESTRICTIONS:

Alcohol: BYO, corkage $5/bottle
Smoking: outside only
Music: no restrictions if you rent entire Inn

Wheelchair Access: 1st floor only
Insurance: not required
Other: children by arrangement

VICTORIAN HILL HOUSE

195 Park Street
Auburn, CA 95604
(916) 885-5879
Reserve: 2 months in advance

The road to the Victorian Hill House winds briefly through overhanging trees and ends at the top of a hill overlooking Old Town Auburn. As you walk through the gate down the stoney path to the inn, you notice the old well and bucket on your right. Totally surrounded by trees, the house and grounds feel secluded and private. Inside, the Dining Room is very Victorian, with floral carpet from Scotland made specially for this house. The Living Room has a bay window covered with Austrian sway drapes and comfortable eclectic furnishings. When the weather permits, a large lawn area makes a lovely setting for outdoor events. Bordered by flowers, magnolias and other foliage, the yard enjoys an excellent view of the Auburn Courthouse. Whether you're inside the house or out, you're bound to appreciate the quiet charm of this Victorian retreat.

CAPACITY:

Area	Capacity	Area	Capacity
Dining Room	12	Indoor Total	50
Parlor	25	Outdoor Total	300
Garden	200 seated, 300 standing		

FEES & DEPOSITS: A deposit of $100 is required to reserve your space. Fees are negotiable.

CANCELLATION POLICY: With 30 days' notice, the deposit is refunded. With less, the refund depends on the space being rebooked.

AVAILABILITY: Year-round, every day.

SERVICES/AMENITIES:

Restaurant Services: no
Catering: provided, BYO
Kitchen Facilities: minimal
Tables & Chairs: some provided, extra for fee
Linens, Silver, etc.: some provided, extra for fee
Restrooms: wca
Dance Floor: carport, patio

Parking: off street
Overnight Accommodations: 4 guestrooms
Telephone: guest phones on request
Outdoor Night Lighting: yes
Outdoor Cooking Facilities: BBQ
Cleanup: caterer or renter

RESTRICTIONS:

Alcohol: BYO
Smoking: outside only
Music: no restrictions if you rent entire house

Wheelchair Access: 1st floor only
Insurance: not required

Columbia

ANGELO'S HALL

State Street
Columbia, CA 95310
(209) 532-4301 Donna or Sharon
Reserve: 2–6 months in advance

A Mother Lode dance hall, this has also been used as Columbia's town hall and for community gatherings over the last century. Historic Angelo's Hall is a pleasant yet unassuming wood structure with one large room. Because of its hardwood floors and spacious interior, it has been (and still is) one of the most popular dance halls around. The Hall is a very flexible space and can support any type of function from election campaign meetings, to receptions or square dancing.

CAPACITY: The Hall can handle 199 people standing, 150 seated.

FEES & DEPOSITS: A $100 refundable cleaning deposit secures your reservation and is due when reservations are booked. Up to 50 guests, the fee is $50/day, between 51–100 guests $100/day, 101–200 guests $200/day. Rental fees are payable the day of the event.

CANCELLATION POLICY: If the Hall is left clean, the cleaning deposit will be returned. You must pick up your deposit at the Museum.

AVAILABILITY: Year-round, any day until midnight.

SERVICES/AMENITIES:

Restaurant Services: no
Catering: BYO or CBA
Kitchen Facilities: no
Tables & Chairs: provided
Linens, Silver, etc.: BYO
Restrooms: wca
Dance Floor: yes

Parking: rear lot
Overnight Accommodations: no
Telephone: no
Outdoor Night Lighting: no
Outdoor Cooking Facilities: no
Cleanup: whoever caters event

RESTRICTIONS:

Alcohol: BYO, some restrictions
Smoking: outside only
Music: no amplified

Wheelchair Access: limited
Insurance: sometimes required

AVERY RANCH

Forest Service Road 3N03
Columbia, CA 95310
(209) 533-2851 or (415) 752-6434
Reserve: 1–6 months in advance

Getting here is part of the fun. Avery Ranch, a full-service wilderness resort, is set in a remote and beautiful meadowland overlooking the Stanislaus River Canyon, forty minutes from historic Angel's Camp. You can elect to arrive by car, air-conditioned van, helicopter or by boat! Avery Ranch is at an elevation of 2700 feet, encircled by thousands of acres of Stanislaus National Forest. Once an old homestead, the site still has the original Avery cabin, complete with stone fireplace. The spacious Main Lodge serves as the center for dining and entertaining, and there are private cottages and log cabins for overnight guests. Here you'll find the perfect blend of rustic comfort and really good food. Everything is homemade yet prepared with attention to variety and creativity. Versatility, a commitment to good fun and good friends makes this place a rare treat. The Ranch can handle everything from spectacular theme parties, private events, stage shows, dances, group retreats to secluded 'hide-outs' for famous entertainers. This is a superb and tranquil setting for conferences, seminars and human development gatherings. Recreation activities abound; river rafting, hiking, bicycling, horseback riding, swimming and fishing. This is an extraordinary, peaceful and relaxed environment.

CAPACITY: The Avery Cabin can hold 20-30 seated guests, the Lodge dining room 75. A maximum of 250 guests can be accommodated in conjunction with the outdoor spaces.

MEETING ROOMS: Avery Cabin for meetings, 20 seated. Main Lodge, lecture seating for 100.

FEES & DEPOSITS: A $100 refundable deposit secures your reservation and is due when the reservation is booked. 25% of the estimated total is due 1 week prior to the event and the final 75% is due at the end of the event. Each function is unique, so charges vary. The normal range is $25–75/person per day. Call to make specific arrangements.

CANCELLATION POLICY: With 4 weeks' notice, you'll receive a full refund.

AVAILABILITY: Year-round, every day.

SERVICES/AMENITIES:

Restaurant Services: no
Catering: provided, can BYO extra charge
Kitchen Facilities: full industrial
Tables & Chairs: provided
Linens, Silver, etc.: provided
Restrooms: limited wca, CBA
Dance Floor: yes

Parking: lots
Overnight Accommodations: 15 guestrooms
Telephone: radio phone
Outdoor Night Lighting: CBA
Outdoor Cooking Facilities: BBQ
Cleanup: whoever caters event
Other: outdoor stage, full event consulting

RESTRICTIONS:
Alcohol: provided, BYO corkage $2/bottle
Smoking: outside only
Music: amplified ok

Wheelchair Access: limited, CBA
Insurance: sometimes required
Other: no pets

CITY HOTEL

Main Street
Columbia, CA 95310
(209) 532-1479
Reserve: 1–3 months in advance

Built in 1856 and located in Columbia State Historic Park, four miles north of Sonora, the City Hotel still provides hospitality on a daily basis. Small and intimate, the hotel appears to have been left intact as a remnant of California's gold mining past when Columbia had 5,000 residents, 150 saloons and shops. The parlor rooms upstairs, which can be used for small meetings, are furnished with antiques and open directly onto the main sitting parlor. Dining here is a memorable event; the food is terrific and the wine list extensive. For special events, the Main Dining Room and adjacent Morgan Room are perfectly suited for group luncheons and/or business dinners. If you want to stay overnight there are 9 guestrooms upstairs or the City Hotel can arrange for other Columbia lodgings.

CAPACITY: The Main Dining Room can seat 60 guests; 100 standing. The Morgan Room can hold a maximum of 25 seated.

MEETING ROOMS: Morgan Room 25 max. plus screen and blackboard.

FEES & DEPOSITS:	Deposit Day	Deposit Eves	Meeting Fees 3 hours max.
Morgan Room	$ 50	$200	$25 (no meal service)
Main Dining Room	$100	$200	—
Upstairs Parlor	—	—	$25 (no meal service)

A refundable deposit is required, due within 2 weeks of making the reservation. The rental charge for meetings is waived if you're staying overnight or you have your meals here. For luncheon or dinner events, food service is provided. Lunch starts at $11/person, dinners at $20/person. Tax at 6.25% and a 15% gratuity are added to the total bill which is due at the end of the event.

CANCELLATION POLICY: With more than 2 weeks' notice, you will receive a full refund.

AVAILABILITY: Every day; from 8am to 11pm, depending on the type of function arranged.

SERVICES/AMENITIES:
Restaurant Services: yes
Catering: provided, no BYO
Kitchen Facilities: n/a
Tables & Chairs: provided

Linens, Silver, etc.: provided
Restrooms: limited wca
Dance Floor: no
Parking: lot behind Hotel

Overnight Accommodations: 9 guestrooms
Telephone: pay phone
Outdoor Night Lighting: limited

RESTRICTIONS:
Alcohol: provided, BYO corkage $5/bottle
Smoking: restricted
Music: restricted

Outdoor Cooking Facilities: no
Cleanup: provided
Other: historical tours, stagecoach, gold panning

Wheelchair Access: limited
Insurance: not required
Other: no pets

FALLON HOUSE THEATRE

Broadway
Columbia, CA 95310
(209) 532-4644
Reserve: 2–12 months in advance

It seems that Gold Rush audiences couldn't get enough theater. Within 2 years of its founding, Columbia boasted 3 playhouses, including one Chinese. Traveling entertainers played the Mother Lode circuit, drawing wildly enthusiastic crowds from long distances. An historic playhouse, the Fallon House Theatre has been restored to its original splendor. The interior has burgundy upholstered seating, stage, balcony and professional sound and lighting systems and is used during some of the year for local theatrical productions. Decorative wallpaper, wood wainscoting and period detailing make this a very unique setting for a business meeting, seminar, training session or private musical event. You can rent the Theatre or Ice Cream Parlor for your private party or business function in between theater productions, or the outdoor rose garden for receptions.

CAPACITY: The Theater space can hold up to 250 seated; an additional 35 with the balcony. The adjacent Ice Cream Parlor can accommodate 75–100 standing and the outdoor rose garden another 100 standing.

FEES & DEPOSITS: The Theatre rental fee is $100/event, due 2 weeks in advance of the event. Technical support may be required. The costs will vary depending on the number of technicians desired and the work involved. A refundable $100 cleaning deposit is also required, to be returned 30 days after the event if the Theatre is left in clean condition. Ice Cream Parlor and rose garden rental is $50/event, which can be credited toward ice cream purchase.

CANCELLATION POLICY: With 1 week's notice, the deposit will be refunded.

AVAILABILITY: Year-round. The Theatre and Ice Cream Parlor spaces are subject to the theater production schedule; the rose garden is available any time.

SERVICES/AMENITIES:
Restaurant Services: no
Catering: BYO or CBA, no food in Theatre
Kitchen Facilities: no
Dance Floor: on stage

Tables & Chairs: parlor or rose garden BYO
Linens, Silver, etc.: BYO
Restrooms: wca

Parking: large lot
Overnight Accommodations: Fallon Hotel
Telephone: business phone

RESTRICTIONS:
Alcohol: BYO or CBA through City Hotel
Smoking: outside only
Music: amplified until 11pm

Outdoor Night Lighting: CBA
Outdoor Cooking Facilities: nearby BBQ
Cleanup: renter's responsibility

Wheelchair Access: yes
Insurance: sometimes required

Ione

THE HEIRLOOM

214 Shakeley Lane
Ione, CA 95640
(209) 274-4468
Reserve: 1–6 months in advance

A twenty minute ride from Sutter Creek, Ione is one of those little foothill towns that sprang up with the advent of the Gold Rush. Although a bit hard to find, the town has The Heirloom, the home of one of the earliest settlers in the Ione Valley. It has since been turned into a jewel of a bed and breakfast by Melisande and Patricia, the two gracious and accommodating innkeepers. The house is primarily brick with decks and railings all in white trim, giving it a colonial appearance. The Heirloom's interior is in pristine condition thanks to the loving care of the last 6 owners over the past 125 years. Outside, there's a lovely, pastoral garden setting with gazebo and during events, umbrella-shaded tables dot the lawns. If you're seeking a relaxing, country setting for a special party or business event, The Heirloom is worth the drive.

CAPACITY: For outdoor events; 150 guests. The indoor capacity is 30.

FEES & DEPOSITS:

	Deposits	Fees	Timeframe
Weekday Meetings	$100	$100/half day, $150/full day	9am–5pm
Weekday Special Events	$200	$100/hour w/4 hr. min.	8am–10pm
Weekend Meetings	$200	$600/day or $125/hour	to be arranged
Weekend Special Events	$200	$1000 or $125/hour	to be arranged

(rooms are included in all weekend fees)

Deposits are required when reservations are made. The rental fee for business meetings is due 1 week in advance and fees for special events are due 3 weeks in advance.

CANCELLATION POLICY: Weekday events require a 72-hour notice for a full refund. For weekend special events, with less than 3 weeks' notice, you will forfeit both your deposit and rental fee unless the facility can be rebooked. For any return of fees or deposits, there will be a small service charge.

AVAILABILITY: Year-round, every day except for Thanksgiving and Christmas.

SERVICES/AMENITIES:

Restaurant Services: no
Catering: BYO, approval required
Kitchen Facilities: minimal
Tables & Chairs: some provided
Linens, Silver, etc.: some provided
Restrooms: no wca
Dance Floor: no, outside only
Parking: large lot

Overnight Accommodations: 6 guestrooms
Telephone: guest phone
Outdoor Night Lighting: yes
Outdoor Cooking Facilities: BBQ
Cleanup: provided
Other: square grand piano
Special: event consulting, baby sitting CBA

RESTRICTIONS:

Alcohol: WB CBA, BYO service
Smoking: outside only
Music: amplified ok w/ approval
Wheelchair Access: limited

Insurance: not required
Other: no pets, kids need supervision, decorations w/approval

Jackson

WINDROSE INN ★

1407 Jackson Gate Road
Jackson, CA 95642
(209) 223-3650 Sharon & Marv Hampton
Reserve: 1–2 months in advance

The Windrose Inn lies just outside of downtown Jackson. This is a beautiful, restored Victorian which sits on a magnificent piece of property. There's a trickling stream and bridge you cross as you make your way up to the front door. Well manicured lawns, a restful gazebo with white lawn furniture, colorful flowers, fish pond, large shade trees and personal attention by the owners complete the picture of this idyllic country house. For a quiet and peaceful business retreat or for a party of friends and family, the Windrose is a must if you plan to celebrate in the Gold Country.

CAPACITY: For outdoor events; 150 guests. The indoor capacity is 15–20. The solarium and parlor/living room can handle up to 20 for meetings.

FEES & DEPOSITS: Half of the estimated total is due when you book your event. The balance is due 30 days prior to you function. Rental fees for a 2-hour minimum: 1–25 people $100/hour; 26–100 guests $125/ hour; 101–150 $150/hour. For weekday business functions, rates and times vary. Call for details.

CANCELLATION POLICY: With 30 days' notice, you'll receive a full refund; 15–29 days a 50% refund; less than 14 days, no refund.

AVAILABILITY: Every day; hours are negotiable.

SERVICES/AMENITIES:

Restaurant Services: no

Catering: CBA or BYO from list

Kitchen Facilities: moderate

Tables & Chairs: BYO or CBA

Linens, Silver, etc.: BYO or CBA

Restrooms: no wca

Dance Floor: CBA

Parking: lot, on street

Overnight Accommodations: 4 guestrooms

Telephone: house phone

Outdoor Night Lighting: yes

Outdoor Cooking Facilities: BBQ

Cleanup: caterer, CBA for extra fee

Other: event consulting

RESTRICTIONS:

Alcohol: WBC only, server needs license

Smoking: outside only

Music: amplified ok before 9:30pm

Wheelchair Access: yes

Insurance: some required

Other: no pets

Jamestown

JAMESTOWN HOTEL

18153 Main Street
Jamestown, CA 95327
(209) 984-3902
Reserve: 2 weeks–4 months in advance

The restored Jamestown Hotel rests in the center of this historic Gold Rush town. With brick exterior and flower boxes, it feels homey and old fashioned. For those that want to relax before the festivities, the comfortable lounge has period furniture, an inviting fireplace and nicely detailed oak bar with large mirror. The main dining room has light floral wall paper and is an attractive room with both bench seating and individual tables. Right outside there's a garden patio—a wood deck which is enclosed by overhead lattice and side screens. On a warm day this is a pleasant place for receptions or business functions. And, if you're from out of town, your group can stay overnight in cozy rooms upstairs, all nicely furnished with Gold Rush-era antiques.

CAPACITY: The dining room holds 64 seated, the lounge 36 seated and the garden patio 84 seated. The total capacity for a standing reception is 140 guests.

FEES & DEPOSITS: A $100 deposit is required when reservations are made which is applied to the final bill. No rental fees are required if food service is provided. Per person rates: luncheons range $9–11, buffet lunches start at $10, seated dinners at $20 and dinner buffets at $15. These prices generally include tax and gratuity.

CANCELLATION POLICY: With 1 week's notice, you'll receive a full refund.

AVAILABILITY: Year-round, every day.

SERVICES/AMENITIES:

Restaurant Services: yes
Catering: provided, no BYO
Kitchen Facilities: n/a
Tables & Chairs: provided
Linens, Silver, etc.: provided
Restrooms: wca
Dance Floor: no

Parking: lot nearby, on street
Overnight Accommodations: 8 guestrooms
Telephone: pay phone
Outdoor Night Lighting: yes
Outdoor Cooking Facilities: BBQ
Cleanup: provided
Other: event coordination

RESTRICTIONS:

Alcohol: provided, BYO corkage $3–5/bottle
Smoking: dining room is non-smoking
Music: amplified ok

Wheelchair Access: yes
Insurance: not required

THE NATIONAL HOTEL

Main Street
Jamestown, CA 95327
(209) 984-3446
Reserve: 2 weeks–6 months in advance

One of the oldest continuously operating hotels in California, The National is a good example of 1860s Mother Lode architecture. Its rooms have been authentically restored to convey a feeling of the past. Of special note is the saloon which has the Hotel's original bar, dating back to 1859! Here you'll find wainscoting, period furnishings, oak stools and a convivial ambiance popular with the locals. The Hotel's dining room can be set up for any type of gathering and outside is the garden courtyard, festive with white furniture and blue Campari umbrellas. Overhead is an arbor with lush vines and lattice work detailing. Although the National has added some new amenities, it has successfully retained its 19th century charm.

CAPACITY: The total seated capacity is 60; the standing capacity is 120 maximum.

FEES & DEPOSITS: A nonrefundable deposit in the amount of 20% of the total estimated bill is due when reservations are made. Food service is provided. Luncheons range from $9–11/person and dinners from $15–18/person. Tax and service charge are included. The event balance is due the day of the party.

AVAILABILITY: Every day, any time.

SERVICES/AMENITIES:

Restaurant Services: yes
Catering: provided, no BYO
Kitchen Facilities: n/a
Tables & Chairs: provided
Linens, Silver, etc.: provided

Restrooms: no wca
Dance Floor: no
Parking: on street
Overnight Accommodations: 11 guestrooms
Telephone: pay phone

Outdoor Night Lighting: yes

Outdoor Cooking Facilities: no

Cleanup: provided

RESTRICTIONS:

Alcohol: provided, BYO corkage $4/bottle

Smoking: allowed

Music: amplified ok

Wheelchair Access: downstairs only

Insurance: not required

RAILTOWN 1897

Sierra Railway Depot
Fifth Avenue
Jamestown, CA 95327
(209) 984-3953 Fred Helmbold
Reserve: 2 weeks in advance

Rent a steam train and relive the past! Railtown provides an authentic glimpse of the era when America steamed innocently into the 20th Century. This is a living museum, with vintage steam locomotives which have served the Sierra Railway since its inception in 1897. Railtown, a working facility that maintains and dispatches it's historic equipment for excursion rides and filming operations, has contributed to nearly 200 feature movies, television shows and commercials. Steam engine #3, Hollywood's favorite, has become the most photographed locomotive in the world. Your group can charter one car or an entire train, depending on the nature of your celebration. Special events have included a mystery train tour, pumpkin tours at Halloween and train dance parties. Now a 26-acre State Historic Park, including a large picnic area, Railtown remains much the same as it was at the turn of the century.

CAPACITY, FEES & DEPOSITS:

Option	Capacity	Timeframe	Cost	Includes
Train Excursion	450	1 hour on Saturdays (10:30–3pm)	$8/Adults $4/Kids (3–12)	Train ride only
Evening Train Excursion	450	5–7:30pm Saturday Eves	$16/Adults $10/Kids	Train ride, snacks, no host bar and hors d'hoeuvres
Train Excursion	325	July 1–Labor Day 5–7:30pm	$32.50/Adults $18.50/Kids	Train ride, western BBQ-style dinner buffet & country-western band entertainment
Private Charter	450	Mon–Thurs possible Friday any time	Fees vary, call for rates	Any kind of event, 46-mile route, special menu can be arranged
Picnic Area	325	Any time except when reserved for BBQ train dinners Sunday 4pm–1am	Rental only $125/ 1–100 guests $1/person for over 100 guests	For company picnics, or any type of party

CANCELLATION POLICY: With 48 hours' advance notice, you'll receive a full refund.

AVAILABILITY: Every day, year-round, depending on the type of event planned.

SERVICES/AMENITIES:

Restaurant Services: no
Catering: provided or BYO
Kitchen Facilities: no
Tables & Chairs: some provided, BYO
Linens, Silver, etc.: BYO
Restrooms: wca
Dance Floor: dance train car

Parking: large lot
Overnight Accommodations: no
Telephone: pay phone
Outdoor Night Lighting: yes
Outdoor Cooking Facilities: BBQs
Cleanup: whoever caters event
Other: full event coordination

RESTRICTIONS:

Alcohol: provided, BWC only, no BYO
Smoking: outside only
Music: amplified restricted

Wheelchair Access: yes
Insurance: sometimes required

Sutter Creek

GOLD QUARTZ INN

15 Bryson Drive
Sutter Creek, CA 95685
(800) 752-8738
Reserve: 1–3 months in advance

The Inn is actually a new building, but it's designed with a 19th century ambiance and attention to historic detailing. The style is Queen Anne, with gables, peaked gray roofs and wrap-around porch. Abundant lattice work and many balconies give the Inn an overall feeling of a home, rather than a hotel. The interior boasts a Victorian style with historic fixtures, antiques and floral wallpaper. For small gatherings, the cozy parlor with its overstuffed furniture, lace curtains and fireplace is very comfortable. For business functions, the banquet room is designed for group meetings. Nice touches include a baker on staff who cooks at night, ensuring that there are goodies during the day, and a croquet set for use on the lawn.

CAPACITY: The parlor can seat 49 guests, the 2 dining rooms can hold up to 44, and the maximum capacity for all public areas is 80 people.

MEETING ROOMS: The banquet room can hold up to 49 people.

FEES & DEPOSITS: A refundable deposit of 15% of the total estimated event cost is due when reservations are made. For meetings in the banquet room a $100/day fee is required. Weekday business luncheons start at $15/person. Friday–Sunday business retreats start at $2500 (rooms are included); special group weekday rates are available. For special events on weekends, there is no rental fee. Food service is provided, with luncheons starting at $15/person and dinners at $25/person, 15 guests minimum.

CANCELLATION POLICY: Business functions require a 60-day notice for a refund. Non-business events require a 30-day advance notice. There is a small service charge for cancellations.

AVAILABILITY: Year-round, every day.

SERVICES/AMENITIES:

Restaurant Services: no

Catering: provided, no BYO

Kitchen Facilities: no

Tables & Chairs: provided

Linens, Silver, etc.: provided

Restrooms: wca

Dance Floor: CBA for extra fee

Parking: large lot

Overnight Accommodations: 24 guestrooms

Telephone: pay phone

Outdoor Night Lighting: yes

Outdoor Cooking Facilities: BBQ CBA

Cleanup: provided

Other: event coordination

RESTRICTIONS:

Alcohol: WBC provided, BYO corkage $2/bottle

Smoking: outside only

Music: no amplified

Wheelchair Access: yes

Insurance: required for hard alcohol

Other: BYO hard alcohol, no pets

Tuolumne

OAK HILL RANCH ★

18550 Connally Lane
Tuolumne, CA 95379
(209) 928-4717
Reserve: 1–3 months in advance

This bed and breakfast inn, situated one mile south of the old lumber town of Tuolumne, is one of the few places in the area that can accommodate special events. Oak Hill Ranch is an appealing, yellow with white trim Victorian-style home, sitting on a knoll amidst 56 acres of oaks and pines. Lacy Japanese maples and yellow roses frame the front entry, and white wicker furniture dots the wide veranda. Built by the present owners, it sits in a very pretty setting of flower gardens, lawns and gazebo. Inside, historic artifacts collected over the past 25 years are displayed. The foothills beyond can be viewed from the patio and deck, which have tables with yellow umbrellas for outdoor events. A private cottage, set away from the main house, can be rented separately. This is a well-maintained, inviting and beautiful garden party setting.

CAPACITY: Main parlor can hold 25 seated guests, the dining room 18 seated; total 25 indoors. With the garden included, the facility can hold up to 100 guests.

FEES & DEPOSITS: If you plan to stay overnight, your first night's lodging is the deposit. If more than one night's stay is planned, 50% of the total estimated rental is due within 1 week after making the reservation. No deposit or rental fee is required for weekday business functions. For special events without lodging, the fee is $150/day.

CANCELLATION POLICY: With 7 days' notice, you'll receive your deposit minus a $10/room cancellation fee. If the rooms cannot be rebooked, the deposit will be forfeited.

AVAILABILITY: Year-round, every day.

SERVICES/AMENITIES:

Restaurant Services: no

Catering: BYO

Kitchen Facilities: $35 fee for use

Tables & Chairs: BYO or CBA extra charge

Linens, Silver, etc.: BYO

Restrooms: wca

Dance Floor: patio outdoors

Parking: large lot, valet CBA

Overnight Accommodations: 5 guestrooms

Telephone: house phone

Outdoor Night Lighting: yes

Outdoor Cooking Facilities: BBQ

Cleanup: caterer, CBA for extra fee

Other: event coordination

RESTRICTIONS:

Alcohol: BYO, must be served

Smoking: outside only

Music: no amplified, no DJs

Wheelchair Access: limited

Insurance: not required

MIKE DAYTON
Guiness World Record Holder, Strength; Claim to Fame San Francisco, 1986

My most memorable party goes back to one night in 1977, at Cobb's Pub in San Francisco. A press conference was held concerning the planning of a stunt with Jack LaLanne involving our jumping off the Golden Gate Bridge. Members of the SF Chronical were there including reporter Bernie Jarvis. Other guests included Carol Doda and Lyle Tuttle, the infamous SF tattoo artist. A guy at the bar recognized me and come over to challenge me to an arm-wrestling match. I declined at first and tried to ignore the guy, but he began to get more and more obnoxious. He bet $10,000 that he could beat me at arm-wrestling. I finally went along with it and offered to wrestle him using only my little finger against his fist. Much to his surprise, I beat him. He nonchalantly whipped out his checkbook and wrote a check for $10,000. He wrote another check to cover a round of drinks for everybody in the house. As it turned out, however, both checks bounced!

Groveland

THE IRON DOOR SALOON

18761 Main Street
Groveland, CA 95321
(209) 962-5947
Reserve: 1 month in advance

On your way to Yosemite, you probably passed the oldest operating saloon in California without knowing it. Built in 1852, The Iron Door Saloon was initially called the 'Granite Store' most likely because the front and back walls are made of solid granite. The sidewalls are of rock and mortar, and the roof consists of three-foot-thick sod, covered with tin. Inside are reminders of the region's colorful past: bullet holes, historic pictures of the pre-dam Hetch Hetchy Valley and paraphernalia of the Old West. Although moose heads and deer antlers adorn the walls, the interior feels more like a natural history museum; the owners are ecology-minded and provide information about the status of these animals. Outside, don't miss the outstanding mural on the building's front—a collage of western scenes depicting miners, mountain men, Indians, wild horses and stampeding buffalo along with a portrait of John Muir. Peter and Bettike Barsotti refurbished The Iron Door in 1985, after falling in love with the historic lore of the building. The staff is efficient and friendly, and since both owners are producers for Bill Graham Presents, events are handled very professionally. This is a fun spot to have a party.

CAPACITY: The indoor capacity is 150 for a reception, 75 guests seated.

DEPOSITS & FEES: A nonrefundable $500 deposit for Friday–Saturday night or $250 for Sunday–Thursday is due when reservations are confirmed. The rental fee varies depending on the time of year and ranges from $250-500/event. It may be waived depending on the total amount of services requested. Per person rates: dinners start at $20, luncheons at $10, hors d'oeuvres at $10 and buffets at $15. Gourmet picnics-to-go are available and costs vary depending on the menu selected. The balance is due the day of event; tax of 6.25% and a 15% gratuity are additional.

AVAILABILITY: Year-round, every day, any time.

SERVICES/AMENITIES:

Restaurant Services: yes
Catering: no BYO
Kitchen Facilities: n/a
Tables & Chairs: provided
Linens, Silver, etc.: provided
Restrooms: no wca
Dance Floor: yes

Parking: medium lot
Overnight Accommodations: no
Telephone: pay phone
Outdoor Night Lighting: no
Outdoor Cooking Facilities: no
Cleanup: provided
Other: full event coordination, theme parties

RESTRICTIONS:
Alcohol: provided, no BYO
Smoking: allowed
Music: amplified ok

Wheelchair Access: yes
Insurance: sometimes required

Yosemite

YOSEMITE FACILITIES ★★

Yosemite Park and Curry Company
Yosemite National Park, CA 95389
(209) 372-1122
Reserve: 12–24 months in advance

Have your special event in the most beautiful place on earth—Yosemite. It never fails to leave its visitors with a sense of awe and wonder. The park's unparalleled beauty is an inspiring backdrop for any function, whether it's a private party or business gathering. Here you'll find the classically elegant and sophisticated Ahwahnee, the versatile Yosemite Lodge and the well-equipped Curry Village. After the festivities or business programs, enjoy a multitude of summer and winter activities. Savor Yosemite. It transforms any event into a special celebration.

CAPACITY:

THE AHWAHNEE

Room	Dining Capacity	Meeting Capacity	Room	Dining Capacity	Meeting Capacity
Main Dining Room	(by reservation only)		Tresidder Room	—	10–50
Winter Club Room	10–45	25–50	Colonial Room	—	25–50
Mural Room	10–45	25–50	Tudor Lounge	—	25–100
Solarium	40–125	—			

YOSEMITE LODGE

Room	Dining Capacity	Meeting Capacity	Room	Dining Capacity	Meeting Capacity
Mt. Room Broiler	40–90	40–100	Redwood Room	10–40	15–40
Four Seasons	50–130	—	Cliff Room	75	40–120
Cliff & Falls Rooms	150	250	Falls Room	75	40–120
Mt.Broiler & Redwd	140	—			

CURRY VILLAGE
(Available November–March)

Room	Dining Capacity	Meeting Capacity	Room	Dining Capacity	Meeting Capacity
Entire Facility	700	550	Pine Cone Room	10–40	20–40
Poolside Room	10–40	20–40	Glacier Pt. Room	75–100	50–100
Main Body	150–250	150–250			

FEES &DEPOSITS: Meeting room rentals vary: Ahwahnee $95-125/day, Yosemite Lodge $95-200/day and Curry Village $95-595/day, depending on room selection. A nonrefundable deposit is required and is due 2 weeks after booking the event. Overnight rooms vary considerably, call for rates. There are no rental fees for special events if meal service is provided. Menu selection for groups is to be submitted at least 6 weeks in advance and a final guest count must be submitted 72 hours prior to your function. The estimated total is due 4 weeks prior to the event and the final balance is payable prior to departure. Sales tax of 6% and a 20% service charge are added to the final total.

CANCELLATION POLICY: With less than 90 days' notice, 25% of the estimated event total is the cancellation fee.

AVAILABILITY: Special events, year-round. Meetings and seminars, Oct 1–Apr 30 only.

SERVICES/AMENITIES:

Restaurant Services: various choices
Catering: no BYO
Kitchen Facilities: n/a
Tables & Chairs: provided
Linens, Silver, etc.: provided
Restrooms: wca
Dance Floor: several locations

Parking: large lots
Overnight Accommodations: wide range
Telephone: pay phones
Outdoor Night Lighting: no
Outdoor Cooking Facilities: BBQ
Cleanup: provided
Other: full event coordination

RESTRICTIONS:

Alcohol: all alcohol thru Yosemite Park & Curry Co.
Smoking: restricted areas
Music: subject to approval, no amplified outdoors

Wheelchair Access: yes
Insurance: not required

Marysville

MARYSVILLE ART CLUB

420 10th Street
Marysville, CA 95901
(916) 673-3199
Reserve: 1–2 months in advance

This colonial style building, with white pillars, porch, and brick entryway sits on a well tended lawn next to Lincoln Park. The interior, consisting of one large salmon pink and white room, has a down-home atmosphere. Low lighting enhances audio-visual presentations, and a stage with piano give the club more versatility. A small lawn in the back, protected by trees, can be set up for al fresco dining. The Art Club isn't fancy, but it's a functional and easy-to-use space.

CAPACITY: The Art Club can accommodate 111 seated guests and 248 for a reception.

FEES & DEPOSITS: A $50 refundable deposit is due when the rental agreement is submitted. The rental fee for Saturday is $135/day. Sunday from 2pm the rental is $135/day, without food service $35–50 for 2 hours. Weekday functions without food service is $35 for 2 hours, with food $50 for 2 hours. The rental balance is due the day prior to the function.

CANCELLATION POLICY: With 45 days' notice, the deposit will be refunded.

AVAILABILITY: Every day. Social functions are planned around the Club's scheduled events.

SERVICES/AMENITIES:

Restaurant Services: no
Catering: BYO
Kitchen Facilities: minimal
Tables & Chairs: provided
Linens, Silver, etc.: BYO
Restrooms: no wca
Dance Floor: no

Parking: street
Overnight Accommodations: no
Telephone: pay phone
Outdoor Night Lighting: no
Outdoor Cooking Facilities: no
Cleanup: renter or caterer
Other: coffee urn

RESTRICTIONS:

Alcohol: BYO, WBC only
Smoking: outside only
Music: no amplified

Wheelchair Access: limited
Insurance: certificate required
Other: decorations restricted, no food/drink on stage

Oroville

JEAN PRATT'S RIVERSIDE BED & BREAKFAST

1124 Middlehoff Lane
Oroville, CA 95965
(916) 533-1413   Jean Pratt
Reserve: 2–6 months in advance

This is one of those places that is off the beaten path and well worth the trip. The Inn consists of three buildings set just above the Feather River, surrounded by pine, cedar and toyon trees. The river meanders by at a lazy pace, and the warm fragrance of dry grasses permeates the air. Furnishings are comfy and casual—you can put your feet up and really unwind. The rear patio outside the main Inn overlooks a lawn that slopes down to the river, while a bench swing and umbrella-shaded table invite you to enjoy the view. This is a wonderful setting for a retreat—secluded and quiet, it allows you to sever all ties with civilization. Jean Pratt, owner and Innkeeper, has created a refuge that is "conducive to complete relaxation and appreciation of nature. It's like going back to Aunt Tillie's place for summer vacation." The Inn is for business functions only, no private parties are permitted.

CAPACITY:

Room	Capacity	Room	Capacity
Lodge*	34	Upstairs Room	12
Living Room	15–30	Cottage	10

Use of the Lodge also includes reservation of 4 guestrooms in the same building.

FEES & DEPOSITS: Fees depend on the number of rooms and nights reserved. Rooms rent for $48.50–80 per night, double occupancy. 50% of the fees are due at the time of booking and the balance is due 1 month prior to the function. There is a 10% discount in fees if 3 or more nights are reserved.

CANCELLATION POLICY: A full refund will be given with 1 month's notice. With less than a month's notice, a refund minus a $25 handling charge is given only if the space is rebooked.

AVAILABILITY: Every day

SERVICES/AMENITIES:

Restaurant Services: no
Catering: select from list or BYO
Kitchen Facilities: adequate
Tables & Chairs: most provided
Linens, Silver, etc.: most provided
Restrooms: wca
Dance Floor: no

Parking: off street
Overnight Accommodations: 15 guestrooms
Telephone: house phone
Outdoor Night Lighting: yes
Outdoor Cooking Facilities: BBQ
Cleanup: provided for a fee
Special Services: custom meals CBA

RESTRICTIONS:

Alcohol: BYO
Smoking: outside only
Music: approval required

Wheelchair Access: limited
Insurance: not required

Rocklin

FINNISH TEMPERANCE HALL

4090 Rocklin Road
Rocklin, CA 95677
(916) 624-3391 Diana
Reserve: 3–12 months in advance

This recently remodeled 1905 hall is a surprisingly fresh and inviting space. Light pouring through tall windows with stained glass panels makes the room bright and cheerful. Painted off-white and light olive green with clean, straight lines, the hall succeeds in creating a warm, eye-pleasing environment. A raised stage, beautiful maple flooring, and overhead spot lighting add to the room's ambiance.

CAPACITY: The Hall can accommodate 144 seated guests and 300 for a reception.

FEES & DEPOSITS: A $250 refundable deposit is due when the contract is submitted and the rental fee is due 15 days prior to the function. A $15 service fee is included in the rental totals below. Any hours over 12 will be billed at the hourly rate. The extra hours shown are free, courtesy of the Hall.

Hourly Rate	*3 Hour min.*	*6 Hours*	*7 Hours*	*8 Hours*
$26	$93	$171+1 hour	$197+1 hour	$223 + 4 hours

CANCELLATION POLICY: With up to 31 days' notice, 25% of the rental fee will be forfeited. With less than 30 days, 50% will be retained; less than 10 days, 100%.

AVAILABILITY: Year-round, every day, any time.

SERVICES/AMENITIES:

Restaurant Services: no
Catering: BYO
Kitchen Facilities: fully equipped
Tables & Chairs: provided
Linens, Silver, etc.: BYO
Restrooms: wca
Dance Floor: yes

Parking: adjacent lot
Overnight Accommodations: no
Telephone: pay phone
Outdoor Night Lighting: no
Outdoor Cooking Facilities: no
Cleanup: renter or caterer
Special Services: stage

RESTRICTIONS:

Alcohol: BYO, some restrictions apply
Smoking: allowed
Music: amplified with approval

Wheelchair Access: yes
Insurance: not required
Other: decorations restricted

SUNSET WHITNEY COUNTRY CLUB

4201 Midas Ave.
Rocklin, CA 95677
(916) 624-2402 Catering Dept.
Reserve: 1 week–12 months in advance

While its main claim to fame may be its golf course, the Sunset Whitney Country Club is also a popular place for parties and business functions. Both the Sunset and Whitney Rooms have vaulted wood-beamed ceilings, and stone, wood and glass construction. They are spacious, airy, and a nice refuge from the heat in summer. The Whitney Room has a unique 4-sided fireplace that creates a warmth and intimacy in all corners of the room during cooler weather. It also opens out onto a large tree-shaded patio with pool—a delightful area to set up tables outdoors. Out of the main metropolitan area, the Sunset Whitney Club is a relaxed and versatile facility.

CAPACITY, FEES & DEPOSITS:

Room	Maximum Guests	Service Fee
Sunset Room	225	$250
Whitney Room	130	200
Patio	300	200

A refundable $100 deposit is due when reservations are confirmed. An additional $400 nonrefundable deposit, applied toward the event total, is payable 2 months prior to the event; the balance payable at the end of the function. The room service fee includes setup, cleanup, tables, chairs, linens, etc. Food service on a per person basis: Sunday brunch $13, breakfasts $5, buffets start at $9, luncheons at $6, dinners at $8 and hors d'oeuvres at $7. Tax of 6.25% and a 15% gratuity are additional.

CANCELLATION POLICY: If the space can be rebooked or with 3 months' notice, the deposit is refundable.

AVAILABILITY: Year-round, every day from 7am–midnight. Closed Christmas and Thanksgiving days.

SERVICES/AMENITIES:

Restaurant Services: yes
Catering: provided, no BYO
Kitchen Facilities: n/a
Tables & Chairs: provided
Linens, Silver, etc.: provided
Restrooms: wca
Dance Floor: yes

Parking: large lots
Overnight Accommodations: no
Telephone: pay phones
Outdoor Night Lighting: yes
Outdoor Cooking Facilities: yes
Cleanup: provided
Special Services: piano

RESTRICTIONS:

Alcohol: provided , no BYO
Smoking: allowed
Music: amplified ok
Wheelchair Access: yes

Insurance: not required
Other: decorations restricted,
no confetti or open flames

Roseville

HAMAN HOUSE RESTAURANT

424 Oak Street
Roseville, CA 95678
(916) 791-2545 Business Office
Reserve: 2 weeks–6 months in advance

This old redwood-shaded Victorian has been transformed into a restaurant and art gallery, combined..The restaurant is on the ground floor and is a wonderful place for receptions and parties. The front parlor has a bay window, chintz curtains, dark rose ceilings and white walls. Tables are covered with pink and white cloths, and art livens up the walls. Two more rooms have similar appeal, and all three flow into each other, creating a feeling of intimacy. A wide veranda winds around the house, providing outdoor seating. The art gallery upstairs is accessible during all events. The word "charming" is often overused, but for the Haman House it's perfectly appropriate.

CAPACITY:

Area	Seated	Reception
Restaurant	50	65–70
Veranda	30–35	30–35
Garden	200	300

MEETING ROOMS: The Victorian Room can accommodate 20–22 people.

FEES & DEPOSITS: A refundable $150 rental deposit and $250 damage deposit are required when the date is confirmed. The rental deposit is applied to the rental balance. On Friday, Saturday and Sunday the house rents for $200/day, the house and grounds together $350/day. Monday–Thursday the house and grounds rent for $65–115/day. The rental fee for meetings is $115/day with no food service. The balance is due 2 weeks prior to the event. Per person rates: brunch $5, hors d'oeuvres $8–12, seated luncheons $6, buffet luncheons $8.50–10, seated dinners $10–18, dinner buffets $8.50–12. Business breakfast can be arranged. Tax 6.25% and 15% gratuity are additional.

CANCELLATION POLICY: With 90 days' notice, the deposits are refunded.

AVAILABILITY: Year-round, every day 8am–midnight. Closed Christmas and New Years days.

SERVICES/AMENITIES:

Restaurant Services: yes
Catering: provided, no BYO
Kitchen Facilities: n/a
Tables & Chairs: provided or BYO
Linens, Silver, etc.: provided or BYO
Restrooms: no wca
Dance Floor: no

Parking: adjacent City lot
Overnight Accommodations: no
Telephone: office phone
Outdoor Night Lighting: yes
Outdoor Cooking Facilities: yes
Cleanup: provided
Other: event coordination, piano

RESTRICTIONS:

Alcohol: WBC provided, BYO ok
Smoking: mostly outside only
Music: amplified ok

Wheelchair Access: yes
Insurance: certificate required
Other: decorations restricted

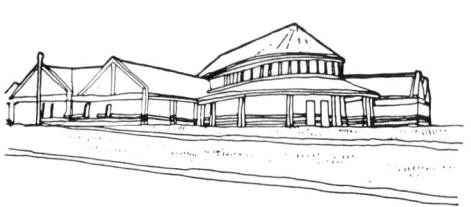

MAIDU COMMUNITY CENTER

1550 Maidu drive
Roseville, CA 95661
(916) 781-0690
Reserve: 1–6 months in advance

This large, ultra-modern facility is the City of Roseville's brand new community center. Built to serve every segment of the community, it houses space for meetings, dance classes, parties and senior citizen activities. The interior is fresh, airy and well designed. The lobby is impressive with a high vaulted ceiling and windows around the top letting in lots of sunlight. A spacious patio with a gazebo in back are enclosed by a high brick fence that provides privacy and quiet. Surrounded by undeveloped park land, the center also enjoys a peaceful, natural environment.

CAPACITY, FEES & DEPOSITS:

Room	Seated	Reception	Cleaning Deposit	Security Deposit	Rental Fees/Hour
Reception Hall	280	450	$200	$200	$22–88
Meeting Room 1	70	100	50	50	6–24
Meeting Room 2	40	50	50	50	4–15
Meeting Room 1 & 2 Combined	130	150	100	100	12–39
Senior Activity Room	50	70	50	50	5–19
Senior Meeting Room	50	85	50	50	4–14

Rental fees vary depending on residential, nonprofit, and business status plus a few other factors. A refundable security deposit is required when reservations are confirmed. The cleaning deposit and rental balance are due 2 weeks prior to the event. The cleaning deposit is usually returned after the event if the facility is left in clean condition.

CANCELLATION POLICY: The security deposit is only refunded if the space(s) can be rebooked.

AVAILABILITY: Year-round, Sunday–Thursday 6pm–11pm, Friday–Saturday 6am–1am. Closed major holidays.

SERVICES/AMENITIES:

Restaurant Services: no
Catering: BYO
Kitchen Facilities: setup only
Tables & Chairs: provided
Linens, Silver, etc.: BYO
Restrooms: wca
Dance Floor: yes
Parking: large lot

Overnight Accommodations: no
Telephone: pay phone
Outdoor Night Lighting: yes
Outdoor Cooking Facilities: BYO
Cleanup: caterer or renter
Other: PA system, podium,
portable bar ext. fee, tot lot

RESTRICTIONS:

Alcohol: BYO
Smoking: outside only
Music: amplified ok

Wheelchair Access: yes
Insurance: sometimes required
Other: decorations restricted, no open flames

ROSEVILLE OPERA HOUSE

Lincoln and Main
Roseville, CA 95678
(916) 773-0768 Kim Delgado
Reserve: 2 months in advance

From the street, you would never know that this facility exists. You enter through an unmarked door on the side of an old Roseville building, and walk upstairs to a large ballroom. Recently redecorated, the room is painted light pink with a cream colored ceiling and deep green trim. Drapes are artfully hung over the windows, adding softness to an otherwise unadorned space. Hardwood floors and a stage make the room adaptable to both private parties and presentations.

CAPACITY: The Opera House can accommodate 250 seated guests and 400 for a reception.

FEES & DEPOSITS: A refundable $200 cleaning deposit is required when the date is confirmed. The rental fee for Saturday and Sunday is $350/hour for a 24-hour period. Hourly rates can be specified for Monday–Thursday. The rental balance is due 1 month prior to the event.

CANCELLATION POLICY: With 30 days' notice, the deposit is refunded.

AVAILABILITY: Year-round, every day, any time.

SERVICES/AMENITIES:

Restaurant Services: no
Catering: BYO
Kitchen Facilities: minimal

Tables & Chairs: some provided
Linens, Silver, etc.: BYO
Restrooms: no wca

Dance Floor: yes
Parking: adjacent lot
Overnight Accommodations: no
Telephone: no

RESTRICTIONS:
Alcohol: BYO, any sale requires license
Smoking: allowed
Music: amplified ok

Outdoor Night Lighting: no
Outdoor Cooking Facilities: no
Cleanup: renter or caterer
Other: event coordination

Wheelchair Access: no
Insurance: certificate required
Other: no red wine or punch, no candles

Sacramento

AMBER HOUSE

1315 22nd Street
Sacramento, CA 95816
(916) 444-8085
Reserve: 1 week–2 months in advance

Shaded by towering elm trees, Amber House is an elegant yet comfortable Craftsman-style inn. The warmth of wood in the beamed ceilings, staircase, wainscotting and floors blends well with the serenity of the interior. Antiques, oriental carpets and a brick fireplace make you feel right at home. The Inn is convenient for business functions, affording a quiet place for meetings or small receptions only a few blocks from the Capitol. This is an especially good place for executive retreats when small business groups need to stay overnight just minutes from downtown Sacramento.

CAPACITY: The facility accommodates 50 people.

MEETING ROOMS: There are 3 meeting rooms that accommodate 5–25 people.

FEES & DEPOSITS: A refundable deposit of 50% the rental fee, which starts at $100, is based on the amount of time reserved and guest count. For meetings, beverage service is offered throughout the day. Overnight stays are possible, call for rates.

CANCELLATION POLICY: For special events, a full refund is given with 30 days' notice. Otherwise, a refund is given only if the space is rebooked. For meetings, 7 days' notice is required.

AVAILABILITY: Every day, any time.

SERVICES/AMENITIES:
Restaurant Services: no
Catering: BYO, licensed
Kitchen Facilities: adequate
Tables & Chairs: provided

Linens, Silver, etc.: caterer
Restrooms: no wca
Dance Floor: no
Parking: on street, lot

Overnight Accommodations: 7 guestrooms, 2 suites
Telephone: guest phones
Outdoor Night Lighting: no
RESTRICTIONS:
Alcohol: BYO
Smoking: outside only
Music: no amplified

Outdoor Cooking Facilities: no
Cleanup: caterer
Other: full event coordination

Wheelchair Access: no
Insurance: not required

AUNT ABIGAIL'S BED & BREAKFAST

2120 G Street
Sacramento, CA 95816
(916) 441-5007
Reserve: 2–3 months in advance

The regulars who frequent Aunt Abigail's refer to it as their "home away from home." Built in 1912, this cube-style Colonial Revival structure retains many of the characteristics of the period. The Dining Room and Living Room, used for both business meetings and special events, have hardwood floors, oriental carpets and antique pieces throughout. The large fireplace, cheery light cream walls, and lace curtains add warmth and charm. The garden patio area is a quiet retreat for small gatherings. Situated on a tree-lined residential street, Aunt Abigail's provides a comfortable and restful getaway.

CAPACITY: The facility can accommodate 35 guests.

MEETING ROOMS: The Dining Room can hold up to 20 people.

FEES & DEPOSITS: For meetings, the fee is $70 for the first hour and $25 for each additional hour with a 2-hour minimum. The maximum cost is $170 for a 7-hour day. Special event rental of the facility for 4 hours (11 am–3 pm) is $400; for 7 hours (1pm–8pm) including overnight booking the fee is $1000. 50% of the fee is due when reservations are confirmed, and the balance is due 1 month prior to the event.

CANCELLATION POLICY: For special events, 1 month's notice is required for a full refund. With less than 30 days' notice, refunds apply only if the space is rebooked.

AVAILABILITY: Every day.

SERVICES/AMENITIES:
Restaurant Services: no
Catering: BYO licensed
Kitchen Facilities: ample
Tables & Chairs: some provided
Linens, Silver, etc.: caterer
Restrooms: no wca
Dance Floor: no

Parking: on and off street
Overnight Accommodations: 5 guestrooms
Telephone: guest phones
Outdoor Night Lighting: no
Outdoor Cooking Facilities: no
Cleanup: caterer

RESTRICTIONS:

Alcohol: BYO, no red wine
Smoking: outside only
Music: no amplified

Wheelchair Access: no
Insurance: not required

BEAR FLAG INN

2814 I Street
Sacramento, CA 95816
(916) 448-5417
Reserve: 1 month in advance

The Bear Flag Inn, tucked away in downtown Sacramento, reflects an era when politicians first traveled to the state capitol and desired the comfortable surroundings of a home-like atmosphere after a long journey. In contrast to its Victorian predecessors, this California craftsman bungalow showcases its simpler style in rich natural woods, nine-foot ceilings, and functional space throughout. An arc-shaped fireplace, constructed of rose quartz, provides an inviting atmosphere for socializing, reading or relaxing. The comfortable sitting room and dining room are also available for small meetings. For business functions, the Inn is a really nice spot.

MEETING ROOMS: The Dining Room and Living Room can accommodate 10.

FEES & DEPOSITS: The meeting area rents for $25/hr with a 3-hr minimum. 50% of the fees are due when reservations are confirmed, and the balance is payable the day of the meeting. If all overnight accommodations at the Inn are booked, there is no fee for the use of meeting rooms. Catering fees (if catering is arranged through the Inn) are generally prepaid 1 week prior to day of the meeting.

CANCELLATION POLICY: The cancellation policy varies depending on the type of meeting arrangements made.

AVAILABILITY: Every day.

SERVICES/AMENITIES:

Restaurant Services: no
Catering: preferred list or BYO licensed
Kitchen Facilities: ample
Tables & Chairs: some provided
Linens, Silver, etc.: provided
Restrooms: no wca
Dance Floor: no

Parking: on and off street
Overnight Accommodations: 5 guestrooms
Telephone: guest phones
Outdoor Night Lighting: no
Outdoor Cooking Facilities: no
Cleanup: caterer

RESTRICTIONS:

Alcohol: not allowed
Smoking: outside only
Music: n/a

Wheelchair Access: no
Insurance: not required

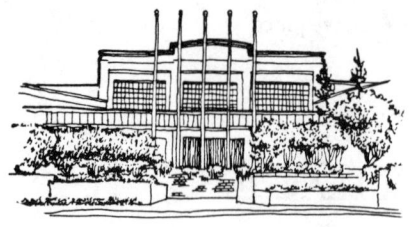

BLUE DIAMOND VISITORS CENTER

1701 C Street
Sacramento, CA 95814
(916) 446-8409
Reserve: 2–3 months in advance

For nonprofit organizations only, this facility is a real find. You not only get a spacious lobby for your festivities, but also the use of a large theater with projection room for presentations. The lobby is modern with a high ceiling, skylights, and greenery cascading down from planters near the ceiling. An enormous stuffed almond known affectionately as "Mr. Blue Diamond," presides over the room attired in top hat and tuxedo, or any outfit suitable for your function. All this, and for such a nominal fee!

CAPACITY: The Lobby holds 150 seated, up to 230 for a reception; the Theater up to 233 seated guests.

FEES & DEPOSITS: The facility rents for $75, payable when the contract is signed.

CANCELLATION POLICY: With 1 week's notice, the deposit is refunded.

AVAILABILITY: Monday–Friday 5:30–10pm.

SERVICES/AMENITIES:

Restaurant Services: no
Catering: BYO
Kitchen Facilities: minimal
Tables & Chairs: some provided, fee for extra
Linens, Silver, etc.: caterer
Restrooms: wca
Dance Floor: no

Parking: on street
Overnight Accommodations: no
Telephone: pay phone
Outdoor Night Lighting: no
Outdoor Cooking Facilities: no
Cleanup: caterer

RESTRICTIONS:

Alcohol: BYO, license required for sales
Smoking: outside only
Music: no amplified

Wheelchair Access: yes
Insurance: liability required

CALIFORNIA STATE RAILROAD MUSEUM

111 I Street
Old Sacramento, CA 95814
(916) 445-7373
Reserve: 2–6 months in advance

For those of you who harbor a secret passion for trains, the Railroad Museum is nirvana. Home to 23 locomotives and cars, it is the finest train museum in North America. Lighting throughout is subdued, imbuing these historical gems with a certain mystery. The largest locomotive here weighs over a million pounds while the oldest dates back to 1862. Many of the trains are displayed in the Roundhouse, a stark, vaulted structure that serves as a train "hangar". Events take place here, guests mingling among these monuments to railroad ingenuity. This is definitely one of the more unusual event locations we have seen.

CAPACITY: The Museum accommodates 600 standing, 400 seated guests.

FEES & DEPOSITS: A refundable $250 cleaning deposit is due at the time of booking. The basic rental fee is $1250. If engines need to be moved, however, there is an added charge of $750 for the first one and $250 for the second. All fees are payable 30 days prior to the event.

CANCELLATION POLICY: With two weeks' notice, the deposit is refunded.

AVAILABILITY: Every day, 5pm–11pm except Thanksgiving and Christmas week.

SERVICES/AMENITIES:

Restaurant Services: no

Catering: BYO

Kitchen Facilities: no

Tables & Chairs: BYO

Linens, Silver, etc.: BYO

Restrooms: wca

Dance Floor: in Roundhouse

Parking: on street, lot

Overnight Accommodations: no

Telephone: pay phone

Outdoor Night Lighting: no

Outdoor Cooking Facilities: no

Cleanup: renter or caterer

RESTRICTIONS:

Alcohol: BYO, license required for sales

Smoking: outside only

Music: amplified ok

Wheelchair Access: yes

Insurance: liability required

Other: food restricted to Roundhouse

CAPITOL PLAZA HALLS

1025 Ninth Street, Suite 201
Sacramento, CA 95814
(916) 443-4483
Reserve: 1 week–12 months in advance

When walking through this facility's undistinguished entrance, you wonder what it could possibly have to offer. A quick trip up the elevator, however, reveals an extraordinary pair of rooms. Over 100 years old, both halls have 25-foot hand-painted ceilings restored by a local artist. The colors—teal green, pink, mauve, blue and gold leaf—are exquisite. Tall draped windows and chandeliers complete the feeling of elegance. Downstairs is another hall used for large events. It's more contemporary, with wood paneled walls and subdued lighting. Several smaller rooms used primarily for business meetings, are also available. These halls are worth seeing even if you don't have your event here!

CAPACITY:	*Room*	*Seated*	*Standing*
	Fraternity Hall	220	450
	Temple Hall	220	450
	Silver Room	250	500

For meetings of up to 100 guests, the halls can be set up to accommodate business activities in one half of the room and dining or social activities in the other.

FEES & DEPOSITS: Weekend rates run $750–850. Weekday rates starting at $250, are negotiable. For special events, a $250 deposit is due at the time of booking and the balance is due 1 week prior to the event. Fees for meetings are payable on the day of the meeting.

CANCELLATION POLICY: The policy is flexible.

AVAILABILITY: Every day.

SERVICES/AMENITIES:

Restaurant Services: no
Catering: provided or BYO
Kitchen Facilities: minimal
Tables & Chairs: provided
Linens, Silver, etc.: provided for fee
Restrooms: wca
Dance Floor: yes

Parking: on street, lot
Overnight Accommodations: no
Telephone: pay phone
Outdoor Night Lighting: no
Outdoor Cooking Facilities: no
Cleanup: provided
Special Services: event planning

RESTRICTIONS:

Alcohol: provided or BYO
Smoking: foyers or outside only
Music: amplified ok

Wheelchair Access: yes
Insurance: liability required if BYO alcohol
Other: decoration restrictions

DRIVER MANSION INN

2019 21st Street
Sacramento, CA 95818
(916) 455-5243 Sandi & Richard Kann
Reserve: 3–12 months in advance

Built in 1899, this colonial revival mansion is one of Sacramento's most significant Victorian residences. Set back on a grassy slope, the Inn appears regal and imposing as you walk up the steps to the entrance. Once inside, however, the warmth and airiness make you feel at home. The Garden Suite, used frequently for business functions, is spacious and lovely with hardwood floors, tall windows and lots of natural light. Oriental carpets, a working fireplace and antique fixtures add to the feeling of relaxed elegance. The Dining Room, with its dark peach walls, lace curtains and high ceilings is also a comfortable space for small get-togethers. For outdoor events, the Inn has a large garden patio shaded by an enormous picture-perfect oak tree. Located in a residential neighborhood, the Driver Mansion Inn provides its guests with quiet and privacy as well as all the attractions of downtown Sacramento, only minutes away.

CAPACITY: The facility can accommodate 100 guests.

MEETING ROOMS: There are 2 meeting rooms with a total capacity of 25 people.

FEES & DEPOSITS: A nonrefundable deposit of $250–800, depending on the type of event, is required. Rental fees range from $250–2000 depending on guest count, day of week, time of day and space(s) reserved.

AVAILABILITY: Year-round, every day.

SERVICES/AMENITIES:

Restaurant Services: no
Catering: provided
Kitchen Facilities: n/a
Tables & Chairs: provided
Linens, Silver, etc.: provided
Restrooms: no wca
Dance Floor: yes

Parking: on street
Overnight Accommodations: 9 guestrooms
Telephone: guest phones
Outdoor Night Lighting: no
Outdoor Cooking Facilities: BBQ
Cleanup: provided

RESTRICTIONS:

Alcohol: provided by caterer
Smoking: outside only
Music: amplified indoors only

Wheelchair Access: no
Insurance: not required

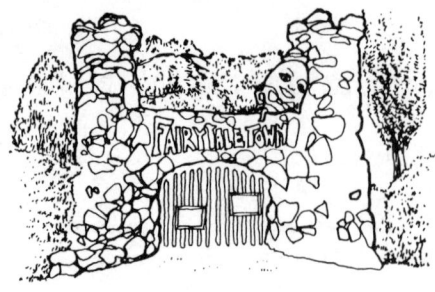

FAIRYTALE TOWN

1501 Sutterville Road
Sacramento, CA 95822
(916) 449-8563
Reserve: 2–3 months in advance

King Arthur's Castle is a source of intrigue for most of the kids who wend their way through a maze to the mysterious castle core. What awaits them? A very special room where the birthday boy or girl can preside as King Arthur or Queen Guinevere for a day. A bona fide throne occupies the place of honor at the round table, and multicolored benches provide seating for the loyal subjects. And if the Castle leaves your child unenthralled, there's also Sherwood Forest where, as Robin Hood or Maid Marion, he or she can run wild with their band of merry girls and boys. Fairytale Town provides everything you need to insure that your party will be a success: cake, ice cream, magic, juggling, storytelling, and much more. The "town" is also inhabited by live sheep, geese, ducks, chicken and pigs. Not just for kids, this charming little park is also available to adults after closing. If you've still got a youthful imagination, it's a terrific place to play.

CAPACITY: For children's birthday parties during regular business hours, King Arthur's Castle and Sherwood Forest can accommodate 15 kids, 7 adults, max. After 6pm, the Town can hold up to 3500 guests for a group function until dusk.

FEES & DEPOSITS: A refundable cleaning/security deposit of $100 is required when the application is submitted. The rental fee is $100/hour for a 2-hour minimum with the rental balance due 10 days prior to the event.

CANCELLATION POLICY: With 30 days' notice, the deposits are refunded.

AVAILABILITY: Year-round, every day. Closed when raining and on Christmas day. Birthday parties can be held M–F 10am–5pm or Sat 10am–6pm. The entire facility can be rented 6pm–dusk for events.

SERVICES/AMENITIES:

Restaurant Services: no
Catering: some provided or BYO
Kitchen Facilities: no
Tables & Chairs: BYO
Linens, Silver, etc.: BYO
Restrooms: wca
Dance Floor: no

Parking: large lot
Overnight Accommodations: no
Telephone: pay phone across street
Outdoor Night Lighting: n/a
Outdoor Cooking Facilities: no
Cleanup: renter or caterer

RESTRICTIONS:

Alcohol: BYO, permit required
Smoking: outside only
Music: amplified within limits, permit required

Wheelchair Access: yes
Insurance: not required
Other: no balloons, plastic straws, lids

HYATT REGENCY ★ SACRAMENTO
At Capitol Park

1209 L Street
Sacramento, CA 95814
(916) 443-1234
Reserve: 1 week–6 months

The Hyatt may be the busiest hotel in Sacramento. It has every kind of event space you can think of, including a terrace on the 12th floor and access to the lovely park across the street. The lobby sets the tone—light, airy and soothing to the eye. Soft shades of grey, dusky pink, teal and mauve, touches of marble and an abundance of glass create a tasteful and distinctive environment. The Ballroom has an intricately patterned, 16-foot ceiling, special lighting and mirrors which add sparkle. All of the meeting rooms are fully equipped for conferences and presentations. And for outdoor events, the hotel can arrange your affair among the trees on the Capitol grounds. For variety, elegance and all the amenities a cosmopolitan hotel can offer, the Hyatt is an excellent choice.

CAPACITY, FEES & DEPOSITS:

Room	Seated	Theater-style	Reception
Golden State	1200	1500	1000–1500
Big Sur & Carmel	80–100	80–100	80–100
Trinity, Ventura, Santa Barbara & Tahoe	40–50	40–50	40–50
Capitol Boardroom	12	—	—
Sequoia Boardroom	12	—	—
Busby Berkeley Lounge	60	—	200
Poolside Area	200	—	200
Dawson Restaurant	available for private parties, call for details		

A nonrefundable deposit ranging from $200–$1000 is required, the rate dependent on room(s) reserved. The deposit is due when the contract is submitted. With no food service, meeting rooms rent for $200–2000/day depending on the group size and room(s) reserved. Per person rates: full breakfasts $10, buffet brunches $15, luncheons $12, buffet luncheons $15, dinners $22, buffet dinners $27 and hors d'oeuvres start at $12/person. The estimated balance plus a final guest count are required 48 hours prior to the function. Tax 6.25% and 17% gratuity are additional. If food and beverage service is provided, all or a portion of any room rental may be waived.

CANCELLATION POLICY: With 90 days' notice, the deposit will be refunded.

AVAILABILITY: Year-round, every day, any time.

SERVICES/AMENITIES:

Restaurant Services: yes
Catering: provided, no BYO
Kitchen Facilities: n/a
Tables & Chairs: provided
Linens, Silver, etc.: provided
Restrooms: wca
Dance Floor: yes
Parking: adjacent lots

Overnight Accommodations: 503 guestrooms
Telephone: pay phones
Outdoor Night Lighting: yes
Outdoor Cooking Facilities: yes
Cleanup: provided
Special Services: full event planning
& business services

RESTRICTIONS:

Alcohol: provided, no BYO
Smoking: allowed
Music: amplified w/in limits

Wheelchair Access: yes
Insurance: sometimes required

MASONIC TEMPLE

1123 J Street
Sacramento, CA 95814
(916) 443-5058   Don Pierce
Reserve: 1 week–2 months in advance

An enormous ballroom, the Masonic Temple has provided a distinctive space for public dancing and other events for many years. The dimensions are impressive—6500 square feet under a domed, elaborate 30-foot ceiling. The entire space is painted dusky pink and cream, and has a beautiful hardwood floor, recently refinished. Tall windows on three sides admit daylight, but the atmosphere inside is still a little sultry. An anteroom can be used alone for smaller events, or in conjunction with the ballroom. Spacious and unique, the Masonic Temple takes you on a nostalgic trip to a bygone era.

CAPACITY: This facility can accommodate between 25–500 guests.

MEETING ROOMS: Three meeting areas have a capacity of 60–225 people.

FEES & DEPOSITS: The larger event spaces require a $150 refundable deposit plus a $200 security/cleaning deposit, due when reservations are confirmed. For smaller groups under 100 people, fees and deposits will vary. The rental balance is due 14 days prior to the function. Large groups over 350 guests require security guards.

CANCELLATION POLICY: With 30 days' notice, the deposit is refunded. The security/cleaning deposit is only refunded if the building is left in satisfactory condition after the event.

AVAILABILITY: Year-round, every day up to midnight. Closed most major holidays.

SERVICES/AMENITIES:
Restaurant Services: no
Catering: BYO
Kitchen Facilities: minimal
Tables & Chairs: provided
Linens, Silver, etc.: BYO
Restrooms: no wca
Dance Floor: yes

RESTRICTIONS:
Alcohol: BYO
Smoking: designated areas
Music: amplified ok

Parking: adjacent lots
Overnight Accommodations: no
Telephone: pay phone
Outdoor Night Lighting: no
Outdoor Cooking Facilities: no
Cleanup: caterer or renter
Other: setup/takedown CBA

Wheelchair Access: yes
Insurance: certificate required

THE PENTHOUSE

2901 K Street
Sacramento, CA 95816
(916) 448-8520
Reserve: 2–6 months in advance

The Penthouse, located on the top floor of the Sutter Square Galleria, is a striking, super-modern structure housing a collection of trendy shops. Only two years old, the Penthouse has already become a popular spot for events. It's a large multi-function room that has been custom-designed down to the tables and chairs to provide maximum comfort and flexibilty. Eye-soothing tones of mauve and teal green, and an immaculate and fresh appearance make this space very inviting. There is also an excellent setup for caterers, and the management specializes in providing impeccable service.

CAPACITY: Suite A holds 125 seated, 150 standing; Suite B holds 60 seated, 80 standing. These rooms can be combined for a total 185 seated, 245 standing guests.

FEES & DEPOSITS:

	Meetings Half-Day	Meetings Full-Day	Events Half-Day	Events Full-Day*	
Suite A	$150	$300	$600 Fri–Sun	$300/5 hrs	$500 Mon–Thurs
Suite B	$ 75	$150	$350 Fri–Sun	$200/5 hrs	$300 Mon–Thurs
Suites A&B	$225	$450	$950 Fri–Sun	$500/5 hrs	$750 Mon–Thurs
				*$100 for 6th hour	

A holding deposit of $100–250 is required at the time of booking and will be subtracted from the room rental fee. A $150 refundable security deposit is due with the balance of fees 2 weeks prior to the event.

CANCELLATION POLICY: With 90 days' notice, the deposit will be refunded.

AVAILABILITY: Every day except Christmas, Thanksgiving and Easter.

SERVICES/AMENITIES:

Restaurant Services: 6 located in Galleria
Catering: provided or BYO
Kitchen Facilities: adequate
Tables & Chairs: provided
Linens, Silver, etc.: caterer, linens CBA extra fee
Restrooms: wca
Dance Floor: CBA extra fee

Parking: garage
Overnight Accommodations: no
Telephone: pay phone
Outdoor Night Lighting: no
Outdoor Cooking Facilities: no
Cleanup: caterer
Special Services: event planning

RESTRICTIONS:

Alcohol: BYO, license required for sales
Smoking: interior balcony only
Music: amplified ok

Wheelchair Access: yes
Insurance: liability required

RANCHO ARROYO

9880 Jackson Road
Sacramento, CA 95827
(916) 364-7980
Reserve: 1–12 months in advance

Rancho Arroyo literally has something for everyone. The Bar and Lounge area has a dance floor, suspended video screen, and sound system. The Restaurant down the hall is spacious, and has a glass wall overlooking the lagoon at the entrance of the facility. Several meeting rooms are available, the most noteworthy featuring a floor-to-ceiling bay window that offers a view of the tennis courts, lagoon, and gazebo below. Rancho Arroyo may seem modest in size at first glance, but when you explore the place you are in for a surprise. In addition to all the "regular" event spaces, there are indoor tennis courts and an olympic-size swimming pool where Olympic Gold Medalist Mark Spitz trained. When the courts are removed, this indoor area can accommodate 4,000 people! The only complex in the area with so much to offer, Rancho Arroyo is quite a unique facility.

MEETING ROOMS: 3 rooms with a seated capacity of 65 guests each, all combined they can hold up to 200.

CAPACITY, FEES & DEPOSITS:

Room	Seated	Reception	Fee/5 hours
VIP Room	25	—	$ 125
Restaurant	250	500	950
Poolside	500	1000	1500
Bar & Lounge	200	300	1250
Meeting Rooms	65/each, 200 combined	—	200 each
Indoor Tennis Courts	2400 all 8 courts	6000 all 8 courts	500/court
	300 each	750 each	500/court

A refundable security deposit of $75–250, depending on which space(s) is reserved, is required when reservations are confirmed. With food service, rental fees or a portion thereof may be waived. The estimated total food and beverage balance is payable 48 hours prior to the event. Per person rates: seated luncheons $8–15, dinners $10–20, brunches $12–15, full breakfasts $5–10, hors d'oeuvres $7–17, and buffets $13–20. Tax of 6.25% and a 17% gratuity are additional. Sometimes an additional security fee is required.

CANCELLATION POLICY: With 30 days' notice, the deposit will be refunded.

AVAILABILITY: Year-round, every day until 2am except some major holidays.

SERVICES/AMENITIES:

Restaurant Services: yes
Catering: provided, no BYO
Kitchen Facilities: n/a
Tables & Chairs: provided
Linens, Silver, etc.: provided
Restrooms: wca
Dance Floor: yes
Parking: large lot

Overnight Accommodations: no
Telephone: pay phone
Outdoor Night Lighting: yes
Outdoor Cooking Facilities: yes
Cleanup: provided
Special Services: event coordination, piano, bartenders, light & sound

RESTRICTIONS:

Alcohol: provided, BYO corkage $5/bottle
Smoking: designated areas
Music: amplified ok

Wheelchair Access: yes, elevators
Insurance: sometimes required
Other: decorations restricted

RIVERBOAT DELTA KING

1000 Front Street
Old Sacramento, CA 95814
(800) 248-4354, (916) 444-5464
Reserve: 2–6 months in advance

The last of the true California paddlewheelers, the Delta King is the impressive result of 5 years of painstaking restoration at a cost of 9 million dollars. During her heyday in the 20s and 30s, the Delta King and her twin, the Delta Queen, made their famous nightly passages between San Francisco and Sacramento to the music of jazz bands and the gentle swish of the paddlewheel. When this era ended, the boat went into gradual decline and finally sank in 1981. Looking at her now, it's hard to believe she was ever anything but graceful, elegant and luxurious. With 5 decks, meeting rooms, a theater, lounge, restaurant and hotel, the Delta King can accommodate almost any kind of function. Teak, mahogany, brass appointments, antique lanterns, and nautical touches preserve the ship's original ambiance. Add to this an extended view of the river, balmy breezes and royal treatment by staff and you have an exceptional event location!

CAPACITY:

Area	Capacity	Area	Capacity
Theater	115 seated	Pilot House Restaurant	150 seated
Captain's Quarters	30 standing	Paddlewheel Saloon	100 seated

MEETING ROOMS: There are 5 meeting rooms with capacities from 8–150.

FEES & DEPOSITS: For meetings, the rate is $150-350 per day depending on the size of the room rented. Half-day rates are also available, and all meeting fees are due on the day of the meeting. A discount is offered if meals are included. For special events, a deposit of $300-500 is due within 30 days of the booking. Room rental fees run $150-350, and catering about $12–18/person for lunch or buffet, and $17-25/person for dinner. The balance, including all food costs, is due on the day of the event.

CANCELLATION POLICY: For special events, a full refund is given with 30 days' notice. Otherwise, a refund is given only if the space is rebooked. For meetings there is a variable fee for cancellation on short notice.

AVAILABILITY: Meeting rooms any time; Paddlewheel Saloon Sunday evenings, Monday & Tuesday any time; Wednesday–Friday days only; Theater available only if not scheduled for Delta King events.

SERVICES/AMENITIES:

Restaurant Services: yes
Catering: provided
Kitchen Facilities: n/a
Tables & Chairs: provided
Linens, Silver, etc.: provided
Restrooms: wca
Dance Floor: yes

Parking: on street, lot, valet
Overnight Accommodations: 44 staterooms
Telephone: guest phones
Outdoor Night Lighting: yes
Outdoor Cooking Facilities: no
Cleanup: provided

RESTRICTIONS:

Alcohol: provided, no BYO
Smoking: ok
Music: amplified w/restrictions

Wheelchair Access: yes except 2 upper decks
Insurance: not required

RIVER ROSE INN

8201 Freeport Blvd.
Sacramento, CA 95832
(800) 695-1998, (916) 665-1998
Reserve: 2–6 months in advance

Thirty years ago Alice Thomas decided she'd like to have her own inn. Now, at the tender age of 70, she has realized her dream. The River Rose Inn is the first entirely new building in Freeport in a century. Although the construction is thoroughly modern, the decor is old-fashioned American country—unpretentious and relaxed. Portraits of family ancestors, comfortable furniture and a couple of fireplaces make the Inn feel like a home. Outside, a large redwood deck, well-tended lawn and custom-designed cement patio provide the perfect environment for all types of events. But perhaps the most appealing aspect of the Inn is the Innkeeper herself. Entrepreneur, manager and chef, she still finds time to welcome everyone and attend to their needs in a very personal way.

CAPACITY: Inside, the Inn holds 60 seated or 100 standing guests; outside capacity is 200 guests. The maximum capacity of the Inn is 200.

MEETING ROOMS: 3 meeting rooms can accommodate 30–40 people.

FEES & DEPOSITS: Meeting rooms rent for $50/day each. Beverage service is provided for a small additional fee. For meeting space only, the entire rental fee is due at the time of booking. If 3 or more overnight accommodations are included, a discount will be given for use of the meeting room(s), and 1 night's lodging and fees are due at the time of booking. The balance is due on arrival. Rental for special events is $100/hour on weekends, and $50/room/day on weekdays. There is no additional charge for use of the grounds. A deposit of $200-300 is due when the date is booked, and the balance of the fees is payable on or before arrival. Catering costs run $10-12 for lunch and $15–18 for dinner, and are due 3 weeks prior to your meeting or event.

CANCELLATION POLICY: With 30 or more days' notice a full refund is given. Otherwise a refund is given only if the space is rebooked.

AVAILABILITY: Every day.

SERVICES/AMENITIES:

Restaurant Services: yes
Catering: provided, no BYO
Kitchen Facilities: n/a
Tables & Chairs: provided
Linens, Silver, etc.: provided
Restrooms: wca
Dance Floor: yes

Parking: lot, off street
Overnight Accommodations: 10 guestrooms
Telephone: house phones
Outdoor Night Lighting: yes
Outdoor Cooking Facilities: no
Cleanup: provided

RESTRICTIONS:

Alcohol: provided, no BYO
Smoking: outside only
Music: amplified w/volume limits

Wheelchair Access: yes
Insurance: not required

SACRAMENTO HISTORY CENTER

101 I Street
Old Sacramento, CA 9584
(916) 449-2057
Reserve: 1 month in advance

The old fashioned brick facade of this museum belies its totally modern interior. Only 5 years old, it houses displays and information about much of Sacramento's local history. The lobby is intriguing with its high reflective metal ceiling, slate floor and huge mural peopled by anonymous folks from the region's past. The museum has an open design—various galleries flow together and are visible to each other from different levels. All exhibits are accessible during your event. The museum's pride and joy is its 1928 kitchen, complete with stove, pantry, table and chairs, apron and dozens of period details. And if you want to combine a few history lessons with your function, docents are available. The History Center is a fascinating place, certain to enhance any event.

CAPACITY: The facility accommodates 700 people.

MEETING ROOMS: The Conference Room holds 15–20 people.

FEES & DEPOSITS : Call for information regarding fees.

AVAILABILITY: Meetings every day except Monday; special events Tues–Sun, 5pm to a negotiable hour.

SERVICES/AMENITIES:

Restaurant Services: no
Catering: preferred list or BYO w/approval
Kitchen Facilities: minimal
Tables & Chairs: BYO
Linens, Silver, etc.: BYO
Restrooms: wca
Dance Floor: no

Parking: on street, lot
Overnight Accommodations: no
Telephone: pay phone
Outdoor Night Lighting: limited
Outdoor Cooking Facilities: no
Cleanup: caterer

RESTRICTIONS:

Alcohol: BYO
Smoking: outside only
Music: amplified ok

Wheelchair Access: yes
Insurance: liability required

STERLING HOTEL ★

1300 H Street
Sacramento, CA 95814
(800) 365-7660, (916) 448-1300
Reserve: 3 months in advance

The Sterling Hotel is one of the most charming hotels in Sacramento. Close to downtown, but on a tree-lined residential street, this white Victorian accommodates a wide variety of functions. The elegant tone is set by dusky pink and cream walls, marble floors, high ceilings and striking light fixtures. You can have your event in the intimate living room or in the completely private all-glass garden conservatory. For small business meetings, several spacious hotel suites are also available. Chanterelle, the hotel's 4-star restaurant, caters all events and can also provide a contemporary space for small private get-togethers.

CAPACITY: The Living Room can hold 48 seated, 110 standing; the Glass Garden 110 seated, 200 standing and the four Suites 15 seated guests each.

FEES & DEPOSITS: A nonrefundable deposit of 75% of the rental cost is due when reservations are confirmed, with the balance due the day of the function. Catering is done through the Chanterelle Restaurant, and the entire catering fee is due the day of the event. Daytime rental fees for the Living Room are $775 for 5 hours, evening fees are $1900 for 5 hours including 7 guestrooms (other packages are negotiable). The Glass Garden daytime rental is $925 for 5 hours and evening fees are $995 for 5 hours. For small receptions there is an additional charge of $275 for the first hour and $150 for each additional hour.

AVAILABILITY: Every day.

SERVICES/AMENITIES:

Restaurant Services: yes
Catering: provided
Kitchen Facilities: n/a
Tables & Chairs: provided
Linens, Silver, etc.: provided
Restrooms: wca
Parking: on and off street, lot

Dance Floor: portable
Overnight Accommodations: 12 suites
Telephone: guest phones
Outdoor Night Lighting: no
Outdoor Cooking Facilities: no
Cleanup: provided
Special Services: business services

RESTRICTIONS:

Alcohol: provided, BYO corkage $5/bottle
Smoking: outside only
Music: some restrictions

Wheelchair Access: yes
Insurance: not required
Other: decorations restricted

TOWE FORD MUSEUM

2200 Front Street
Sacramento, CA 95818
(916) 442-6802   Kristin
Reserve: 1–2 months in advance

This is not an ordinary place to hold an event. Essentially a car museum, this warehouse (located 1 mile south of Old Sacramento) is an automobile lover's paradise. While antique Fords are the car of choice here, many other vintage varieties are also on display. The building itself is spare—cement floor, bare-bulb lighting, and a domed roof overhead are the only amenities. However, a special events area complete with stage is planned for fall, 1990. And anyway, when you have hundreds of gorgeous vehicles surrounding you, how much more do you need? For those of you who want to indulge in automotive memorabilia, the museum's gift shop is always open for guests during an event.

CAPACITY: The Museum can accommodate 300 seated guests and 500 standing guests for a reception.

FEES & DEPOSITS: A refundable $100 cleaning deposit is required 1 month prior to the event. The rental fee is $500 for 6pm–midnight use of the building, payable in advance of the function.

CANCELLATION POLICY: If the Museum is left in clean condition, the deposit is refunded.

AVAILABILITY: Year-round, every day from 6pm–midnight. Closed Christmas, Thanksgiving and New Years holidays.

SERVICES/AMENITIES:

Restaurant Services: no
Catering: BYO
Kitchen Facilities: no
Tables & Chairs: provided
Linens, Silver, etc.: BYO
Restrooms: wca
Parking: large lot

Dance Floor: CBA, ext. fee
Overnight Accommodations: no
Telephone: office phone
Outdoor Night Lighting: yes
Outdoor Cooking Facilities: no
Cleanup: renter or caterer

RESTRICTIONS:

Alcohol: BYO, any sales need permit
Smoking: outside only
Music: amplified ok

Wheelchair Access: yes
Insurance: certificate required

THE TRAVELER CENTRE

428 J Street
Sacramento, CA 95814
(916) 736-1000
Reserve: 2 weeks–6 months in advance

This large lobby is a throw-back to the 1920s. A crystal chandelier sparkles overhead in the main entryway. The floor is reminiscent of Grandma's house with miniature white and grey hexagonal tiles throughout. In the center of the lobby is a fountain, and as you glance up at the high ceiling, you notice the elaborate molding with gold leaf and white fixtures from the period. The mezzanine floor railing is wrought iron filligree covered with gold. Lighting here is very subdued, and is best suited to evening affairs.

CAPACITY: The Lobby can accommodate 300 guests, total.

FEES & DEPOSITS: A refundable $250 deposit is required when the contract is submitted. The rental fee is $500–700 per day, depending on guest count. A payment schedule is developed with several payments required prior to the function; the balance is due 3 weeks prior to the event.

CANCELLATION POLICY: With 2 months' notice, the deposit is refunded.

AVAILABILITY: Year-round, Monday–Friday 5:30pm–2am, weekends any time until 2am.

SERVICES/AMENITIES:

Restaurant Services: no
Catering: BYO
Kitchen Facilities: no
Tables & Chairs: BYO
Linens, Silver, etc.: BYO
Restrooms: wca
Parking: adjacent lots

Dance Floor: Lobby floor
Overnight Accommodations: no
Telephone: office phones
Outdoor Night Lighting: no
Outdoor Cooking Facilities: no
Cleanup: renter, caterer & janitorial staff
Special: 24-hour security guard provided

RESTRICTIONS:

Alcohol: BYO, any sales need permit
Smoking: allowed
Music: amplified ok

Insurance: certificate required
Other: decorations restricted
Wheelchair Access: yes

Yuba City

HARKEY HOUSE

212 C Street
Yuba City, CA 95991
(916) 674-1942   Lee Limonnoff & Bob Jones
Reserve: 2–4 months in advance

Harkey House is not only a bed and breakfast inn, but a delightful spot for business and private functions. The house is a creamy yellow, classical Italian Victorian over 100 years old. In back, there is a wonderful brick patio with willow tree furniture and a covered trellis providing shade. A spa, pool, and cement patio are added options. The Dining Room, often used for meetings, has a black and white tile floor and high windows, providing light and privacy. The Living Room has a marble fireplace, comfortable seating and a unique piano that traveled all the way around the Cape. Each guestroom has a different theme, and the entire house is fresh and inviting.

CAPACITY: The facility can accommodate 60 guests inside and 100 outdoors (total 160).

MEETING ROOMS: There are 4 meeting rooms that can accommodate 6-36 people.

FEES & DEPOSITS: A refundable security deposit of $125 and the rental fee are due 4 weeks prior to the event. The rental fee for use of either the inside or outdoor space is $175; rental of the entire facility costs $350.

CANCELLATION POLICY: A full refund will be given with 1 month's notice. With less than a month's notice the deposit will be refunded only if rebooked.

AVAILABILITY: Every day except Christmas.

SERVICES/AMENITIES:

Restaurant Services: no
Catering: BYO
Kitchen Facilities: adequate
Tables & Chairs: some provided
Linens, Silver, etc.: caterer
Restrooms: no wca
Dance Floor: outside patio

Parking: on street
Overnight Accommodations: 4 guestrooms
Telephone: guest phones
Outdoor Night Lighting: yes
Outdoor Cooking Facilities: BBQ
Cleanup: caterer

RESTRICTIONS:
Alcohol: BYO
Smoking: outside only
Music: amplified ok

Wheelchair Access: no
Insurance: not required

THE REFUGE
RESTAURANT & LOUNGE

1501 Butte House Road
Yuba City, CA 95991
(916) 673-7620
Reserve: 3–6 months in advance

So popular is The Refuge Restaurant that some companies have booked their Christmas parties here several years in advance. With a Banquet Room, Dining Room and Lounge, the facility handles all types of events with ease. The decor is eclectic: the Dining Room has tables with umbrellas, black ceiling and walls, decorative fans, and waterfowl prints. The other two rooms also have black as the predominant color, and lighting throughout is subtle. Two small sections of the Dining Room are often used for business meetings and private parties. The Lounge has a long, fully stocked bar, a fireplace and a dance floor. Add to all this the fact that the restaurant does its own catering (of course!) and you have a facility that can satisfy just about all of your needs.

CAPACITY: This facility can accommodate 250 seated and 400 standing guests for a reception.

MEETING ROOMS: There are 4 rooms that can accommodate 15–250 people.

FEES & DEPOSITS: A refundable deposit of $100 is required 10 days from making tentative reservations. The rental fee ranges from $100–$350 if food service is not provided. With service, the rental charges are usually waived. The balance is due at the end of the event. Per person rates: champagne brunch $11, luncheons $6–10, seated dinners $13–19, hors d'oeuvres $8–20, and buffets $13. For all meal service, tax 6.25% and a 15% gratuity are additional.

CANCELLATION POLICY: With 30 days' notice, the deposit will be refunded.

AVAILABILITY: Year-round, every day, any time except Mondays.

SERVICES/AMENITIES:
Restaurant Services: yes
Catering: provided, no BYO
Kitchen Facilities: n/a
Tables & Chairs: provided
Linens, Silver, etc.: provided
Restrooms: wca
Dance Floor: yes
Parking: large lot

Overnight Accommodations: no
Telephone: pay phone
Outdoor Night Lighting: no
Outdoor Cooking Facilities: no
Cleanup: provided
Special: event coordination, theme parties, live entertainment weekends

RESTRICTIONS:

Alcohol: provided, BYO corkage $3/bottle
Smoking: designated areas
Music: amplified ok

Wheelchair Access: yes
Insurance: not required

THE WICKS

560 Cooper Avenue
Yuba City, CA 95991
(916) 674-7951
Reserve: 1 week–6 months in advance

Built in the early 1920s, this craftsman-style bungalow was originally a hunting lodge in the middle of an orchard. Today it is a distinctive bed and breakfast on a quiet residential street. The front rooms on the main floor are adaptable for small business functions, as well as private parties. The Parlor is an airy, pleasant room with a fireplace, oak paneled walls and comfortable furniture. The Library is perfect for small conferences and can accommodate presentations. The most charming room, however, is the Dining Room. It has its own large fireplace, and a wall hutch full of glassware and china. The decor here changes with the seasons—in late summer a grapevine with fruit and leaves is suspended artfully over the fireplace. The walls are a soft pink, and a colorful border has been painted just below the ceiling. In addition to the inn's obvious comforts, the innkeeper happens to be an award-winning chef. Centrally located between Chico and Sacramento. The Wicks offers convenience, comfort, and hospitality.

CAPACITY: The facility can accommodate 60 seated and 75 standing guests for a reception.

MEETING ROOMS: The Library or Living Room can accommodate 20–50 people.

FEES & DEPOSITS: A nonrefundable deposit of 1/3 of the estimated event total is required when reservations are confirmed. The rental fee ranges from $35–$350, depending on the room(s) rented and the guest count, and may be waived with a guaranteed guest count or food service. The balance is due 1 week prior to the event along with a final guest count. Wicks packages include a continental breakfast, lunch and afternoon snack for $15–20/person. Also available is a "How To Host a Murder Mystery Dinner" that runs $85–170/couple. All menus are customized for patrons. Per person rates: luncheons start at $10.50, dinners at $20, brunches $10.50 and hors d'oeuvres start at $7.50. Teas are offered the first and third Saturdays of each month and include linens, gold flatware, china, flowers, classical music, personalized cards, and a light 4-course meal. For all meal service, tax 6.25% and a 15% gratuity are additional.

AVAILABILITY: Year-round, every day 8am–10:30pm.

SERVICES/AMENITIES:

Restaurant Services: no
Catering: provided, no BYO
Kitchen Facilities: n/a
Tables & Chairs: provided
Linens, Silver, etc.: provided

Restrooms: no wca
Dance Floor: library
Parking: on street & offstreet
Overnight Accommodations: 2 guestrooms
Telephone: house phone

Outdoor Night Lighting: no
Outdoor Cooking Facilities: no

RESTRICTIONS:
Alcohol: BWC provided, BYO corkage $3/bottle
Smoking: outside only
Music: no amplified

Cleanup: provided
Special: tea service

Wheelchair Access: no
Insurance: not required
Other: no hard alcohol

Ryde

GRAND ISLAND INN

14340 Highway 160
Ryde, CA 95680
(916) 776-1318
Reserve: 2 weeks–6 months in advance

Now the Grand Island Inn, the historic Ryde Hotel was once owned by film star Lon Chaney's family. It was built as a classy gambling house that would cater to the riverboat crowd coming from San Francisco and was a famous speakeasy and casino during prohibition. The 4-story hotel, with pink stucco and navy blue canvas awnings, is designed in a classic California 1930s style. Inside it's all Art Deco with potted palms, small Egyptian statues, black lacquered ceiling fans and large Erte 30s-style posters. Available for business functions and private parties, the Inn provides distinctive spaces for any type of gathering.

CAPACITY: The inside capacity, main level, is 100 seated guests, 150 for a reception; lower level (Cabaret) 250 seated, 350 for a reception. Combined with outdoor areas, the capacity is 700 guests, depending on the season.

MEETING ROOMS: Meeting space for 10–250 seated guests.

FEES & DEPOSITS: A $200 deposit is required to hold your date; 90 days prior to the function, the deposit increases another $800. For meetings, the deposit stays at $200; the room rental fee is $100/day. For business functions on weekdays, there's a retreat package including rooms, meeting space, continental breakfast and coffee service. Fees range $42.50–62.50/person with a 10-room minimum rental.

Event rental fees: $50/hour for a 4-hour block; each additional hour is $100. Rental fees may be waived for mid-week luncheons, maximum 2 hours. Luncheons range $8–15/person, dinners $11–20/person. A 6.75% tax and 15% gratuity are added to the final total.

CANCELLATION POLICY: With 90 days' notice, the deposit is fully refundable.

AVAILABILITY: Year-round, every day from 7am–1am.

SERVICES/AMENITIES:

Restaurant Services: yes
Catering: provided, no BYO
Kitchen Facilities: n/a
Tables & Chairs: provided
Linens, Silver, etc.: provided
Restrooms: limited wca
Dance Floor: yes

Parking: large lot
Overnight Accommodations: 50 guestrooms
Telephone: pay phone
Outdoor Night Lighting: limited
Outdoor Cooking Facilities: CBA
Cleanup: provided
Other: swimming pool, recreation & docking facilities

RESTRICTIONS:

Alcohol: provided, BYO corkage $5/bottle
Smoking: allowed
Music: amplified ok, DJ ok

Wheelchair Access: yes
Insurance: not required

Walnut Grove

GRAND ISLAND MANSION

13415 Grand Island Road
Walnut Grove, CA 95690
(916) 775-1705
Reserve: 2 weeks–6 months in advance

On Grand Island, in the heart of California's lush Delta, lies an impressive, 58-room mansion. Surrounded by miles of orchards, the Grand Island Mansion has 4 stories, a terra cotta roof, spacious balconies with intricate iron railings and an entrance highlighted by enormous Corinthian columns. A cypress-lined circular driveway adds to the extraordinary setting. The estate faces a waterway and has its own yacht facility. Inside, the expertise of imported European craftsmen is seen everywhere: the white marble entrance hall, featuring a sweeping circular stairway, the ballroom with hardwood floors, beveled mirrored walls, sculptured fireplace, gold-gilded columns and crystal chandeliers. French doors lead to a brick courtyard surrounding a tiled swimming pool and spa. This place has it all: an 18-seat cinema, billiards room, a regulation bowling lane with new AMF automatic pinsetter and a charming old fashioned soda fountain.

CAPACITY: The inside capacity is 200 seated, buffet setup 500 guests, and combined with outdoor areas, 1000 guests, depending on the season. There is a 100-guest minimum for an event.

FEES & DEPOSITS: A $200 deposit is required to secure your date; 90 days prior to the function, the deposit amount increases another $800. There are no rental fees if meal service is provided. Per person rates: luncheons range $19–25, dinners $22–26, buffets $21–23 and hors d'oeuvres start at $19.50. A 6.75% tax and 15% gratuity are added to the final total. Functions are usually allowed a 5-hour block with $200 for each extra hour.

CANCELLATION POLICY: With 90 days' notice, the deposit is fully refundable.

AVAILABILITY: Year-round, every day. Events usually take place between 11am–4pm or 6pm–11pm.

SERVICES/AMENITIES:
Restaurant Services: no

Catering: provided, no BYO

Kitchen Facilities: n/a

Tables & Chairs: provided

Linens, Silver, etc.: provided

Restrooms: no wca

Dance Floor: yes

Parking: driveway, large lot

Overnight Accommodations: no

Telephone: house phone

Outdoor Night Lighting: yes

Outdoor Cooking Facilities: CBA

Cleanup: provided

RESTRICTIONS:
Alcohol: provided, WBC only, BYO corkage $5/bottle

Smoking: outside only

Music: amplified ok, DJ ok

Wheelchair Access: limited

Insurance: not required

Lodi

JAPANESE PAVILION AND GARDENS
Micke Grove Park

11793 Micke Grove Road
Lodi, CA 95240
(209) 953-8800 or (209) 331-7400
Reserve: 6–12 months in advance

Sheltered by large pines, bamboo, azaleas and camellias, the Japanese Pavilion is an unexpected sight in Micke Grove Park. It's located in a separate, fenced area within the park, and is evocative of the Far East. The Pavilion resembles a tastefully designed pagoda, with wood floors, simple wood detailing and decks plus a distinctive high pitched roof that slopes upward at the edges. Adjacent to the structure is a small pool with fountain and red footbridge. In the front, a generous expanse of lawn leads to several wide steps up to the Pavilion; in the back, a gentle ramp leads back into the garden. A popular location for receptions and business meetings, the Pavilion has a special ambiance.

CAPACITY: The Pavilion and garden can be rented for 175 guests; inside seating is 50 guests and the garden alone, can hold up to 175.

FEES & DEPOSITS: There is a $50-200 cleaning deposit for indoor use, $50-600 for outdoor use. The amount is based on guest count. The Pavilion and garden rental fee is $125 per 4-hour block and the garden alone rents for $65 per 2-hour block. Vehicle entry into the park is $2/car weekdays and $3/car on weekends; group passes can be purchased in advance. Fees and deposits are due within 2 weeks of making a reservation. The cleaning deposit is returned 20 days after the event. Note that there may be some restrictions regarding setup areas for food and alcohol.

CANCELLATION POLICY: With 21 days' notice, rental fees and cleaning deposit will be refunded. There's a cancellation fee of $25.

AVAILABILITY: Year-round, any time except for Christmas day.

SERVICES/AMENITIES:

Restaurant Services: no
Catering: BYO or CBA
Kitchen Facilities: no
Tables & Chairs: BYO
Linens, Silver, etc.: BYO
Restrooms: wca nearby
Dance Floor: no dancing

Parking: large lots
Overnight Accommodations: no
Telephone: pay phones
Outdoor Night Lighting: no
Outdoor Cooking Facilities: no
Cleanup: whoever caters event
Other: decorating CBA

RESTRICTIONS:
Alcohol: BYO, sales require permit
Smoking: outside only
Music: amplified ok, DJ ok

Wheelchair Access: yes
Insurance: not required

WINE AND ROSES ★ COUNTRY INN

2505 West Turner Road
Lodi, CA 95242
(209) 334-6988
Reserve: 2 weeks–3 months in advance

Secluded on a magnificent 5-acre setting with towering trees, the Wine and Roses Country Inn is an outstanding destination for business functions, retreats or special celebrations. Lush lawns and old fashioned flower gardens surround the lovely, 88-year-old home that has been converted into a 10-room country inn. The Inn's courtyards and terrace are great for outdoor events and the inside is tastefully decorated in soft rose, rich burgundy with cream trim and windows with lace curtains. All meals are prepared with the finest and freshest of ingredients by the chef, who is a graduate of the San Francisco Culinary Academy. The inn is family owned and operated and the staff has expertise in coordinating all types of events. This is a very special place.

CAPACITY: The dining room can hold up to 65 seated and 90 standing guests. The sitting room holds up to 35 standing and the outside garden up to 200 guests.

FEES & DEPOSITS: A nonrefundable deposit of 50% of the rental fee is required to secure your date. For weekday business meetings, the fee for half-day functions is $100 and for a full day, $200. For dinner meetings, Sunday-Thursday the rental fee is $50/hour. The rental fee for Saturday and Sunday is $750–1375, depending on guest count. The remainder of the rental fee is due 6 weeks prior to the event along with 50% of the estimated catering total; the balance is due the day of the function. Per person rates: business luncheons $9–18, dinners $16–22, and buffets start at $15. Tax and service charges are additional.

CANCELLATION POLICY: If the Inn can be rebooked for a similar event, your deposit will be refunded less a $50 cancellation fee.

AVAILABILITY: Every day, any time.

SERVICES/AMENITIES:
Restaurant Services: no
Catering: provided, no BYO
Kitchen Facilities: n/a
Tables & Chairs: provided
Linens, Silver, etc.: provided

Restrooms: wca
Dance Floor: courtyard or CBA extra fee
Parking: large lot
Overnight Accommodations: 10 guestrooms
Telephone: house phone

Outdoor Night Lighting: yes
Outdoor Cooking Facilities: no
Cleanup: provided

RESTRICTIONS:
Alcohol: WBC provided, BYO corkage $5/bottle
Smoking: outside only
Music: amplified restricted

Other: baby grand piano,
business presentation equipment
Special: event coordination

Wheelchair Access: yes
Insurance: sometimes required
Other: balloons discouraged

Stockton

BOAT HOUSE

Oak Grove Regional Park
4520 West Eight Mile Road
Stockton, CA 95209
(209) 953-8800 or (209) 331-7400
Reserve: 6–12 months in advance

This popular park, located between Interstate 5 and Highway 99, is an oasis on a hot summer's day. Lush green lawns, a meandering waterway, amphitheater, plus huge oaks and willows combine to create a wonderful destination for a company picnic or private party. Large, colorful inflatables looking like tricycles on the water are available for rental. Of note is the Boat House, a simple wood structure with deck situated at the water's edge. With the adjacent BBQ and picnic tables, the Boat House can be used as an informal indoor/outdoor facility. For a small gathering of friends, family or co-workers, this is an ideal spot for fun.

CAPACITY: The Boat House can accommodate 32 seated and 50 standing guests.

FEES & DEPOSITS: The cleaning deposit is $50. The Boat House rental fee is $50 per 6-hour block and $20 for each additional hour. Vehicle entry into the park is $2/car weekdays and $3/car on weekends; group passes can be purchased in advance. Fees and deposits are due within 2 weeks of making a reservation. The cleaning deposit is returned 20 days after the event. Note that there may be some restrictions regarding alcohol.

CANCELLATION POLICY: With 21 days' notice, rental fees and cleaning deposit will be refunded. There's a cancellation fee of $25.

AVAILABILITY: Year-round, any day.

SERVICES/AMENITIES:
Restaurant Services: no
Catering: BYO or CBA
Kitchen Facilities: minimal
Tables & Chairs: provided
Linens, Silver, etc.: BYO

Restrooms: wca
Dance Floor: no
Parking: large lots
Overnight Accommodations: no
Telephone: pay phones

Outdoor Night Lighting: yes
Outdoor Cooking Facilities: BBQs

RESTRICTIONS:
Alcohol: BYO, sales require permit
Smoking: outside only
Music: amplified ok, DJ ok

Cleanup: whoever caters event

Wheelchair Access: yes
Insurance: not required

Lynn Broadwell & Associates
Services and Products

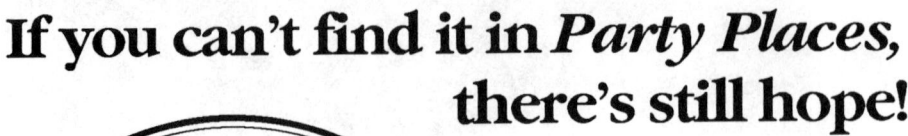

If you know the 4 best ways to grab attention, keep it and get results . . .

don't read the next page.

Party Places
Service Directory

If you need assistance with your party or special event, the professionals listed on the following pages can help. *We appreciate their support and thank them for choosing to advertise with us.*

Since we take *no money* from any of the facilities listed in *Party Places*, the advertising serves two purposes: it helps defray our printing and production costs and gives our readers information about services and products available in the event industry.

▼

A Note for Advertisers

Hopscotch Press will be reprinting this edition of *Party Places* in February/March 1991.

Our wedding location guidebook *Here Comes The Guide* has been so successful, we'll be introducing the second edition in winter 1990/1991.

Only The Best, our newsletter will take limited advertising. Quarterly editions will commence October 1990.

If you would like to inquire about advertising in any of our publications, please call us at
415-525-0448

Aleta Childs Catering

♦

(415) 863-8569

DISTINCTIVE MENUS
EXCITING TASTES

Catering For All Occasions

MAILING ADDRESS:
320 SANCHEZ STREET
SAN FRANCISCO
CALIFORNIA 94114

(415) 582-5147

**Fine
Catering**

*"Dedicated to
quality food
and
exceptional
service"*

**Providing Personalized
Full Service For
Every Occasion**

THE LOFT

**FULL CATERING &
EVENT PLANNING
SPECIALIST**

Serving the Entire Bay Area

FREE WEDDING CONSULTING

- Unique Hors D'oeuvres
- Elegant Buffets & Brunches
- Gourmet Menus
- Decorated Party Trays To Go
- Show Pieces
- Ice Sculptures
- European Wedding Cakes
- Floral Arrangements
- Music & Photography

- Invitations
- Economy Package
- Kosher Catering
- Theme Parties
- Food To Go
- Free Consultation
- Four Exclusive Halls
  —50-500
- Wedding Packages

Elegant or Casual Service

**LIST OF OVER 200 HALLS, MANSIONS &
YACHTS
EXCLUSIVE INDOOR & OUTDOOR
FACILITIES**

TEL: (408) 866-2203 • FAX: (408) 866-2366 • CORP: (400) 866-2200
2081 S. Winchester Blvd., Campbell 95008

EVENT Planners

Make Northern California's prestigious Wine Country the setting for your next corporate function, party or wedding and reception.

At Event Planners we find the perfect location, customize all arrangements and offer the finest resources available in:
- gourmet food & wine
- entertainment & music
- photography
- floral design
- audio visual equipment
- conference materials
- transportation

All services and special requests are arranged to enhance your style and special occasion.

Envision your business meeting or celebration at a winery or vineyard, on a private estate, at a charming bed & breakfast, or a western ranch. Make your event simply the best— make it a planned one!

PO BOX 5537 NAPA, CA 94581 707 224-7937

AMERICAN HOSPITALITY

EVENT DESIGN, PRODUCTION & CELEBRATED CORPORATE CATERING

Our Professionalism Paves The Way For You To Enjoy Your Events Success

415/ 653-6699
FAX: 415/653-3363

408/945-8581
FAX: 408/945-1685

MIKE TSE

PEN & INK ILLUSTRATION

415/ 638-5131 or 763-2128
5020 Crystal Ridge Court, Oakland CA 94605

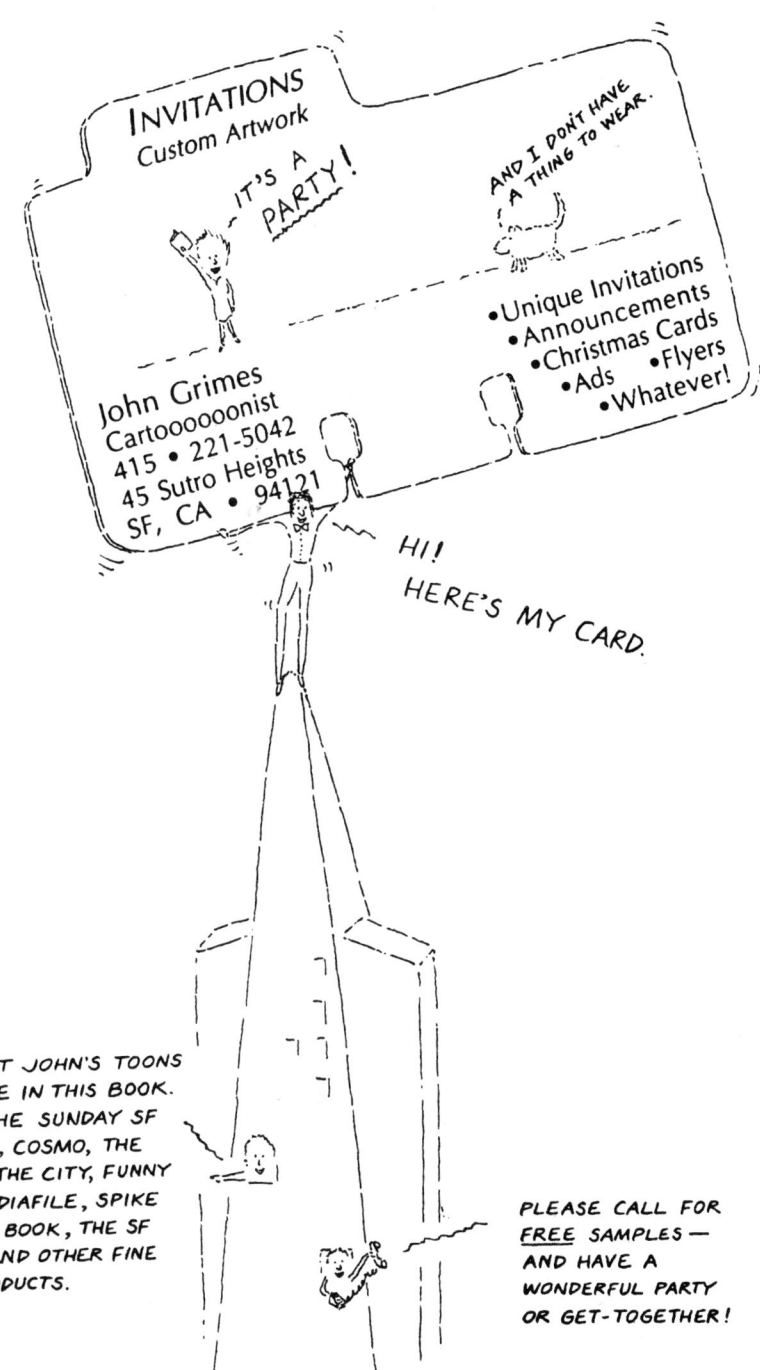

Musicians

Pastries

Photography

Flowers

Wedding Services

Index

About the Cover Illustrator

Sarah Waldron is originally from Seattle, Washington. She moved to San Francisco in 1979, to work as a staff designer for internationally known Primo Angeli, and in 1984, received her MFA in Advertising Illustration from the Academy of Art in San Francisco. Sarah is a nationally known illustrator, with a studio in Petaluma, California. She also teaches at the Academy of Art in San Francisco. Some of her clients include: A&W Brands, Cosmopolitan Magazine and Ballentine Books.

About the Facility Illustrator

Michael Tse is a bespectacled Bay Area freelance illustrator whose life depends on rapidograph art and baseball scores. He is currently working on a bachelor's degree at the California College of Arts and Crafts in Oakland. Michael speaks fluently in English, Cantonese and malapropisms.

About the Production Person

Chris Molé is a freelance graphic designer who works out of her home in Lafayette. She was converted to the Macintosh back in 1986 and has been happily designing and producing logos, newsletters, brochures, books and ads with it ever since. Her clients include Apple Computer, PG&E, Pacific Bell, Arthur D. Little, Golden Gate University and the Institute of Chinese Herbology.

About the Author

Lynn Broadwell is a marketing professional
whose consulting services, publications and products
are designed to meet the needs of
both the novice and the event professional.
She has been featured in articles, on radio and TV
throughout Northern California.

Hopscotch Press is one 'arm' of Lynn Broadwell & Associates,
which publishes *Party Places*, *Here Comes The Guide*,
Party Papers and *Only The Best!*

Lynn is a graduate of U. C. Berkeley,
with an undergraduate degree in landscape architecture
and a masters degree in business.
She lives in the Berkeley Hills
with her husband and
two-year-old son.